Praise for
Get Capone

"In *Get Capone*, Jonathan Eig gives us a fresh portrait of the most wanted of most wanteds, laced with newly unearthed details—including hitherto secret IRS files and federal wiretaps—that Eig deploys to build a taut and compelling narrative of the gangster's life and the federal drive to end his reign."

—Erik Larson, author of *The Devil in the White City*

"*Get Capone* is a masterful biography, a scrupulously researched history of a pivotal time in America, and a page-turning crime story that thunders ahead like the very best of novels. Using never-before-published research, Eig conjures to life not only America's most famous gangster but the streets of Chicago. You can see and hear Capone walking through the windblown pages of history, straight at you. *Get Capone* is for anyone who wants to be enthralled, entertained, and enlightened."

—Doug Stanton, author of *Horse Soldiers* and *In Harm's Way*

"*Get Capone* is narrative history at its finest. It is deeply reported, fun and fast to read, and thrillingly evokes gangland Chicago and its most infamous gangster while shattering myths all along the way."

—David Maraniss, author of *Clemente* and *Rome 1960*

"I thought I knew the Capone story, but Eig's riveting telling of this iconic American story is both fresh and utterly dazzling. An extraordinarily rich panorama of America in the 1920s, *Get Capone* brings our most notorious antihero vividly to life, masterfully interweaving the epic tale of his rise and fall with the equally fascinating stories of the politicians, lawmen, gangsters, and reporters who inhabited his world."

—Ken Burns

"Panoramic yet sharply focused, *Get Capone* is as much a dark history of urban America between the world wars as it is another mobster's life story."

—James McManus, *The New York Times Book Review*

"Riveting . . . Eig's book is full of fascinating details about the Windy City, as well as the rest of America in the 1920s."

—Elizabeth Bennett, *The Dallas Morning News*

"Journalist Jonathan Eig has carved out quite a career taking on figures like Capone—familiar faces from history that everyone knows about or at least thinks they do—and breathing fresh life into them. . . . Eig's book excels for its scrupulous reporting and—believe it or not—fresh research that adds depth to the Capone story. . . . A rollicking read."

—Steve Warmbir, *Chicago Sun-Times*

"A fascinating, fast-paced hybrid: a biography and an intensely reported look at the cat-and-mouse chase between Capone and the federal investigators trying to bust him."

—Noah Isackson, *Chicago Tribune*

"A masterly portrait of America's all-time favorite crime boss . . . Eig's account is rich in detail and historical context, and as a writer he can turn a phrase with the best of them."

—David Holahan, *The Christian Science Monitor*

"Fascinating . . . Eig's book is a sweeping account of Capone's life set against the backdrop of a city where corruption was the norm and a country dealing with the hypocrisy of Prohibition and the devastation of the Great Depression."

—George Anastasia, *The Philadelphia Inquirer*

"As Jon Stewart said when he had Jonathan Eig on *The Daily Show*, the author's new book, *Get Capone: The Secret Plot That Captured America's Most Wanted Gangster*, should be subtitled *Everything You Thought You Knew About Capone Is Wrong*. . . . [A] rip-roaring chronicle."

—John Hood, *The Miami Herald*

"The man who, in the end, brought [Capone] down was district attorney and tax sleuth George E. Q. Johnson. . . . [Eig] had the good fortune to gain access to a large cache of Johnson's papers, neglected for years. Among other revelatory things, they contained transcripts of phone calls tapped by Eliot Ness, another publicity hound, though, as it emerges in this wonderful book, utterly useless in the matter of bringing gangsters to justice."

—Katherine A. Powers, *The Boston Globe*

"A remarkable and satisfying read."

—Mike Vaccaro, *New York Post*

"Scrupulously researched account of the men who made the 1920s roar, and the straight-arrows who stopped them . . . vibrant historical storytelling and a nuanced, enigmatic portrait of Capone and his Chicago milieu . . . Eig constructs a plausible, often surprising narrative of criminality, but he also fleshes it out into a colorful urban social history. . . . An impressive, accessible history of a troubled time."

—Kirkus Reviews

"Eig has brought new life to the story of Al 'Scarface' Capone, reporting on the life, crimes, and fall of America's most notorious gangster. . . . Eig is a fascinating storyteller who throws in the occasional bon mot that readers will enjoy. . . . This book should be very popular with true crime and Prohibition history buffs; highly recommended."

—Library Journal

"In a page-turning account, Eig details the chase for the elusive Capone, dissecting both the man and his myth. . . . Using previously unreleased IRS files, Johnson's papers, even notes he discovered for a ghostwritten Capone autobiography, Eig presents a multifaceted portrait of a shrewd man who built a criminal empire worth millions."

—Publishers Weekly (starred review)

Get Capone

The Secret Plot That Captured
America's Most Wanted Gangster

JONATHAN EIG

Simon & Schuster Paperbacks
New York   London   Toronto   Sydney

Simon & Schuster Paperbacks
A Division of Simon & Schuster, Inc.
1230 Avenue of the Americas
New York, NY 10020

First Simon & Schuster trade paperback edition April 2011

SIMON & SCHUSTER PAPERBACKS and colophon are registered
trademarks of Simon & Schuster, Inc.

For information about special discounts for bulk purchases,
please contact Simon & Schuster Special Sales at
1-866-506-1949 or business@simonandschuster.com.

The Simon & Schuster Speakers Bureau can bring authors
to your live event. For more information or to book an event,
contact the Simon & Schuster Speakers Bureau at
1-866-248-3049 or visit our website at www.simonspeakers.com.

Designed by Jill Putorti
Map design by Paul J. Pugliesi

Manufactured in the United States of America

10 9

Library of Congress Control Number: 2009033949

ISBN 978-1-4165-8059-1
ISBN 978-1-4165-8060-7 (pbk)
ISBN 978-1-4391-9989-3 (ebook)

For Lillian

CONTENTS

PART TWO—KING CAPONE

PART THREE—CAPONE FALLING

Contents

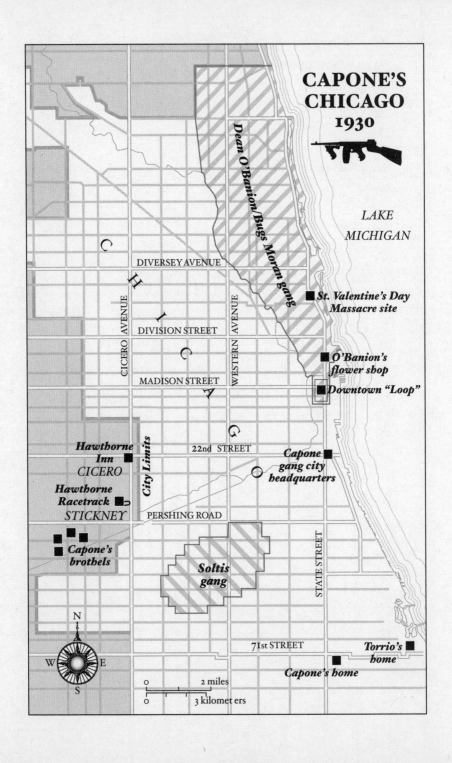

CAPONE'S CHICAGO 1930

LAKE MICHIGAN

Dean O'Banion/Bugs Moran gang

DIVERSEY AVENUE

CICERO AVENUE

WESTERN AVENUE

DIVISION STREET

MADISON STREET

■ St. Valentine's Day Massacre site

■ O'Banion's flower shop

■ Downtown "Loop"

Hawthorne Inn ■
CICERO

City Limits

22nd STREET

■ Capone gang city headquarters

Hawthorne Racetrack ■
STICKNEY

PERSHING ROAD

■ ■ ■
■ Capone's brothels

Soltis gang

STATE STREET

N
W E
S

71st STREET

■ Torrio's home

■ Capone's home

0   2 miles
0   3 kilomet ers

PART ONE

CAPONE RISING

1

THE GETTING OF IT

Al Capone stood on the sidewalk in front of a run-down saloon called the Four Deuces, the wind whipping at his face. He shoved his hands in his pockets and pulled his jacket collar high to protect against the cold, or maybe to cover the scars on his left cheek.

"Got some nice-looking girls inside," he said.

Capone was twenty-one years old and new in town. He worked in Chicago's Levee District, south of downtown, a neighborhood of sleazy bars and bordellos, where a man, if he cared about his health, tried not to stay long and tried not to touch anything. Automobiles with bug-eyed headlamps rumbled up and down the block. It was January 1920, the dawn of a rip-roaring decade, not that you'd know it from looking around this neighborhood.

The Great War was over. Men were back home, maybe a little shell-shocked, maybe a little bored, certainly thirsty. They put on jackets and ties and snap-brimmed hats and went to places such as the Four Deuces, which was named not for the winning poker hand but for its address: 2222 South Wabash. It was a four-story, brick, turn-of-the-century building with a massive arched door that looked like the mouth of a cave. Inside, cigarette and cigar smoke clung to the ceiling. Some customers came for the drinks. Others climbed the stairwell at the back and went upstairs, where the smoke faded slightly but the aromas became more complex. There, on the second floor, high-heeled women paraded in varying states of undress, their movements lit by a bare bulb on the ceiling. A madam urged the customers to hurry up and choose.

When the place got busy, Capone would head inside to warm himself and to make sure the customers behaved. He was a dark-haired fellow, not quite big enough or ugly enough to scare anybody at first glance. He stood five feet ten and a half and weighed about two hundred pounds, with a powerful chest and hands as big as a grizzly's. His hairline was already beginning to recede. His eyebrows were thick and wide, and the two horizontal scars on his cheek were light purple and still raw-looking. His eyes were a changeable greenish gray. He charmed people with his broad smile.

Capone cared deeply about his image. He asked photographers to capture his portrait from the right, avoiding his scarred cheek. He wore the finest clothes and, despite his girth, looked comfortable in them. It is nearly impossible to find a photograph in which he is not the best-dressed man in the room, even when he was young and poor. He had style, but he walked a fine line. He would wear suits in bright colors such as purple and lime that other hoodlums would never dare, and pinkie rings with fat, glittering stones that would put to shame many of Chicago's wealthiest society women. But he would never be seen in an ascot.

At the Four Deuces, he slid his body through the crowd with grace. He was a good host: vivacious, quick with a joke, flashing that smile. The men in the bar enjoyed his company. When he finished his shift, he would walk back to the dumpy little apartment he shared with his wife, Mae, and their one-year-old son, Albert Francis. The place wasn't much, but it was better than anything he'd ever had growing up.

Capone was born and raised in Brooklyn, part of a big Italian family. His parents were immigrants. Capone grew up poor, one of nine children, and dropped out of school in sixth grade. He ran with street gangs as a boy and young man, and worked a series of menial jobs as a teenager that made good use of his size, strength, and bravado. He found his true calling as a bouncer at a dive bar on Coney Island, where he mixed with some of New York's toughest thugs.

He had come to Chicago to work for Johnny Torrio, once one of the legends on the Brooklyn gang scene and now a rising force in the Chicago underworld. Some accounts suggest that Torrio recruited Capone to join his organization because he spotted talent in the young man. Others suggest that Capone fled Brooklyn after a bar fight in which he nearly killed a man with his fists.

Capone took to Chicago, which the poet Carl Sandburg described this way:

Hog Butcher for the World
Tool Maker, Stacker of Wheat,
Player with Railroads and the Nation's Freight Handler;
Stormy, husky, brawling,
City of the Big Shoulders:
They tell me you are wicked and I believe them,
* for I have seen your painted women under the gas lamps luring farm boys.*
And they tell me you are crooked and I answer:
* Yes, it is true I have seen the gunman kill and go free to kill again.*

Chicago hugged the lower edge of Lake Michigan, spreading in every direction that it could. In 1850, the city had been home to only thirty thousand hardy souls. By 1870 the population had shot up to three hundred thousand. Without the watery boundaries of New York, people felt no need to jam themselves into cramped, unforgiving spaces. Neighborhoods lined up one after another along the crescent-shaped coast, wooden shanties and muddy streets stretching on into the prairie. The city grew quickly and uncontrollably. Immigrants came in search of work: building, forging steel, slaughtering cattle, loading boxcars. Criminals came, too: pimps and prostitutes, pickpockets and safecrackers, con men, dope dealers, burglars and racket men. The police department—a mere afterthought in the city's earliest days of development—could never catch up.

The city burned to the ground in 1871. The Great Fire burned for days and left seventy-three miles of streets a wreck of embers and soot. Nearly a third of the city's residents were rendered homeless. But Chicago rose again, with even more speed and vigor. This time, buildings of iron, granite, and steel filled the landscape. And of course, the vice world came back stronger than ever, too. In the first eight months of 1872, the city issued an astonishing 2,218 licenses for saloons.

If anything, the fire proved a great boost to the economy, setting off a kind of Gold Rush. The opportunities were limitless, and men of energy and ambition sought to take advantage. Great architects, great salesmen, great lawyers, great artists, and great criminals would forge the city's new identity.

In 1893, the World's Columbian Exposition brought another spurt of population growth, and with it, more vice. By 1910, a special commission reported that five thousand full-time prostitutes and ten thousand

part-timers worked the city, and that, combined, they were responsible for
more than 27 million sex acts a year. Clean up Chicago? If anyone even
mentioned it, they were either dreaming or joking.

———————

By the time of Al Capone's arrival in 1920, the population had climbed
to 2.7 million, making it the second-largest city in the nation, after New
York. And still it felt uncrowded and untamed. As more immigrants arrived from Italy, Ireland, Poland, Germany, China, Russia, and Greece,
everyone shoved aside and made room. New neighborhoods attached
themselves to old. The city just kept stretching: twenty-six miles long and
fourteen miles wide, more jigsaw puzzle than melting pot. The sprawling
geography allowed ethnic groups to cling to their old languages and customs to a greater extent than they ever could in New York.

The wealthy lived mostly on the city's near West and near North
sides. The working class lived mostly on the South and the far West sides.
New arrivals could tell in an instant from the odors if they were in one
of the city's poorer sections. Small steel mills coughed soot, and tanneries
leached chemicals. But the strongest and foulest stench came from the
Union Stockyard: five hundred acres of livestock, living and dead. The
smell buckled legs. The work was worse. Millions of cattle, sheep, and
hogs moved through the stockyards, their throats slashed, their carcasses
split and sliced, their entrails washed into the Chicago River. An army of
seventy-five thousand men and women did the work. This was the work
of Chicago.

At the hub of the city sat the Loop, the city's central business district,
where elevated trains screeched on metal tracks, and trolleys and trucks
jammed the streets. Here, the city felt like a city: noisy, crowded, and
dangerous. Chicago was the nation's first city of skyscrapers. Buildings
rose higher here than anywhere else, stabbing at the clouds in handsome
shades of green, gray, brown, and blue.

Yet it wasn't everyone's idea of paradise.

"Having seen it," Rudyard Kipling wrote of Chicago, "I urgently desire never to see it again. It is inhabited by savages. Its . . . air is dirt."

Chicago welcomed the strong and spat out the weak. If you couldn't
hack it, there was always a train leaving for Des Moines. That's why
it attracted men such as the scorching jazz trumpeter Louis Armstrong;

the crusading lawyer Clarence Darrow; and the meatpacking titan Philip Armour, who treated his workers shabbily but gave generously to charity and once said, "I do not love the money, what I love is the getting of it."

The getting of it: That's what this city was all about.

———

When he wasn't working the door or tending bar at the Four Deuces, Capone decorated. In an empty storefront adjoining the saloon, he arranged some bookshelves, a broken-down piano, and some old tables and chairs to make the place look like an antiques store. It was Johnny Torrio's idea. Torrio wanted Capone to learn to carry himself with the air of a legitimate businessman. Capone printed cards that read:

ALPHONSE CAPONE
Second Hand Furniture Dealer
2220 South Wabash Avenue

The Levee District had always been home to entrepreneurs. Though it was only two miles from the elegant hotels and skyscrapers of the Loop, the district operated within its own special universe, with its own special rules.

Movie stars and titans of industry had visited the parlors of the neighborhood's elegant whorehouses, including the famous Everleigh Club, where they spent great fortunes on wine, food, and women. Politicians had not only put up with the debauchery, they also had participated in it. But things began to turn during the years of World War I. A wave of temperance swept the country. Americans were expected to sober up and sacrifice for their nation. Even Chicago cleaned itself up a little. Saloons were raided. Licenses were revoked. The high-end whores and drug dealers, fearing arrest, quit working in bordellos and dance halls and moved to hotel lobbies, where they could be more discreet. In time, the Levee District became the exclusive domain of ripened prostitutes, customers who couldn't afford better, and the low-level pickpockets and jackrollers who preyed on anyone dumb enough to wander the streets alone and unarmed. This was where Capone got his start. His timing was perfect.

In 1917, Congress asked every state in the union to vote on the Eighteenth Amendment to the Constitution, banning the sale, manufacture,

and transportation of intoxicating liquor nationwide. The measure passed
with no great opposition, and most people believed the law would be
quickly and easily implemented, that Americans on a massive scale would
voluntarily give up drinking. The evangelist Billy Sunday bade good-bye
to demon alcohol with flourish, saying, "You were God's worst enemy.
You were hell's best friend. I hate you with a perfect hatred." He went on
to predict a new age of prosperity and clean living, saying "slums will soon
be a memory. We will turn our prisons into factories and our jails into
storehouses and corncribs. Men will walk upright now, women will smile,
and children will laugh. Hell will be forever for rent."

Torrio and Capone had other ideas.

The Prohibition law took effect at midnight on January 16, 1920, a day
before Capone's twenty-first birthday. But by then the war was over and the
mood of the country had already shifted. Sacrifice? That was for saps.

"Like an overworked businessman beginning his vacation," wrote the
journalist and historian Frederick Lewis Allen, "the country was finally
learning how to relax and amuse itself once more." Americans wanted to
dance and drive fast and spend money. They wanted to shock their parents with their sharp clothes and impress their neighbors with handy new
gadgets such as electric irons and vacuum cleaners. And they wanted to
drink. By making booze illegal, the government unwittingly glamorized it.
The bubbles in a glass of champagne seemed more scintillating, the foam
on a mug of beer more refreshing. Homemade alcohol had a tendency to
taste like battery acid, which led to the invention of cocktails; the addition
of sweet flavors and herbs made the drinks even more alluring, especially
to women. Irving Berlin summed up the state of affairs and put it to a
snappy tune when he wrote, "You Can Not Make Your Shimmy Shake
on Tea."

Congress passed the Volstead Act to provide for enforcement of the
Eighteenth Amendment, and at least in the early years under the new
set of laws, alcohol consumption in America dropped dramatically. But
the Volstead Act failed to anticipate the massive criminal operations that
would go to work creating an underground network for the manufacture
and sale of alcohol.

A man didn't have to be a genius to recognize this once-in-a-lifetime
opportunity. Overnight, general miscreants such as Capone became bootleggers (the phrase has roots in America's colonial days, probably deriv-

ing from "boot-leg," the upper part of a tall boot where bottles could be hidden). Their experience running bars, brothels, and gambling joints suddenly came in handy. They already knew how to move money, how to sell booze, how to subdue competition, and how to service multiple businesses across the city. The trick now was learning to think big. A massive legitimate business had just been declared illicit. If they moved quickly, they could take over operations. Just for starters, bootleggers needed trucks and confederates in other cities to help them with supplies. In New York, there was Meyer Lansky; in Philadelphia, Boo Boo Hoff; in Detroit, the Purple Gang; in Cleveland, Moe Dalitz. They patched together a network that would eventually become a loosely organized national crime syndicate.

As bootleggers, their position in society actually improved. Small-time reprobates no longer had time for safecracking, pickpocketing, and mugging. Those lines of work were too dangerous, too risky, and didn't pay well enough.

Bootlegging also offered a certain kind of dignity. As bootleggers, they provided a useful service and catered to a respectable class of customer. Flush with cash, they dressed with panache and consorted with a higher class of friends. They became romantic figures, celebrated by journalists who liked their style, their slang, and their nicknames—not to mention their booze.

Every city had its share of bootlegging, but Chicago seemed to have more. Alcohol soaked the city through, which is why the 1922 song "Chicago" called it "that toddlin' town." No one believed for a moment that the city would sober up under Prohibition. Lake Michigan would dry up first.

Once it became clear that Chicagoans, and in fact much of the rest of the American population, had no intention of giving up drinking, the government would face a decision: How much money and effort would it invest in fighting this new wave of crime? The answer turned out to be, not much. Torrio and Capone, among others, stood ready to take advantage.

GOOD-BYE, DIAMOND JIM

The Levee District had made Chicago one of the nation's premier environments for vice long before Prohibition. Now, though, the high-end brothels were not so high-end anymore. The only ritzy establishment that remained from the glory days was Colosimo's Restaurant, which sat a block north of the Four Deuces, at 2128 South Wabash. Like a prizefighter past his prime, Colosimo's was clinging tenuously to its power and glory. It still attracted the big-name politicians and stars of stage and screen, but it was working harder all the time to do it.

The owner of the place was Jim Colosimo, a figure so monumental that he had two nicknames: Big Jim and Diamond Jim. Colosimo was square-jawed and stocky, with heavily lidded eyes and a dark mustache that hid almost his entire mouth. He wore the sheerest of white linen suits. Diamonds sparkled from his fingers, his shirtfront, his watch chain, his cuffs, his suspender clasps, and his garters. He kept a pouch full of diamonds in his pocket, too, and in idle moments he would pour them out on a white tablecloth and tease them with a fingertip, rearranging their radiance, admiring their glow, and savoring his own wealth. Though he had begun his professional life as a pickpocket and small-time con man, Colosimo had married well, to Victoria Moresco, the madam of a profitable brothel.

In the brothels, Big Jim found his life's calling. The women trusted him, and the men liked his company. He knew how to bribe, how to flatter, how to threaten, and how to make a good plate of pasta. He was the first gangster to go high-class, which included keeping his hands clean when there was violent work to be done. As a result, Colosimo reigned as king of the city's underworld, and his establishment enjoyed a long run as one of the city's most popular nightspots. The restaurant's signature dish was spaghetti à la Colosimo.

It was Colosimo who'd brought Johnny Torrio from Brooklyn—by some accounts the men were related by marriage—and helped him establish his loosely knit chain of saloons and brothels. Colosimo and Torrio were business partners. But by 1920 Big Jim was losing the passion for his work. While Torrio sought to explore new opportunities connected to the advent of Prohibition, Colosimo seemed uninterested. He had recently divorced his wife, married a young singer, and had taken her on a long, luxurious honeymoon.

Shortly after his return, on the afternoon of May 11, 1920, Big Jim strapped on a pair of diamond-studded suspenders, slid on his suit jacket, and went down to his restaurant. As he walked into his office, Colosimo found his secretary and his chef discussing the evening's menu. The three men chatted for ten or fifteen minutes until Colosimo excused himself, saying he was supposed to meet someone in the lobby. A moment later, the secretary and chef heard gunshots. They emerged from the office to find their boss stretched on the floor, blood oozing from a mealy bullet wound behind his right ear and spreading across the porcelain tiles. He was dead by the time they reached him.

Police ruled out robbery as a motive, noting that the gunman hadn't taken Colosimo's wallet or his diamonds. They ruled out passion, saying that Colosimo's ex-wife had an airtight alibi. Eventually they concluded that the assassination had probably been the work of Torrio. As the second in command of Colosimo's criminal organization, Torrio had the most to gain from Big Jim's death. They suspected that Torrio had brought Frankie Yale from Brooklyn for the job. Yale was seen in Chicago at the time of Colosimo's murder.

Torrio and his lieutenant Capone were well acquainted with Yale. In 1916 or 1917, when Capone had been working as a $9-a-week cloth cutter at the United Paper Box Company in Brooklyn, Yale had hired him as a dishwasher on Coney Island at the Harvard Inn, one of the toughest saloons in New York City. It was Yale's idea of a joke to name the place Harvard. Yale would sit at a table near the door of the Harvard Inn, where he sipped whiskey and chatted with friends and customers. He was a good-humored fellow, a bit plump, with ink-black hair worn shiny and close to the head. He had made his money organizing Brooklyn's small-time icemen into a vicious racket, but his specialty was violence. Some came to Yale's table to shoot the breeze. Others came to purchase his service as a killer. He had a reputation for doing good, clean work, without emotion or witnesses. He was a useful fellow to know.

If Torrio wanted to get rid of Colosimo, Yale would have been the perfect man for the job, and Capone would have been his likely accomplice. He was spotted in Chicago at the time of the murder. Later, when police in New York caught up with Yale, they questioned him about the killing. Briefly, it looked as if Chicago might solve a murder for a change. But somehow Yale talked or bribed his way out of it. Capone was never even questioned. Eventually, the investigation fizzled. No one was ever charged with the murder of Big Jim Colosimo.

———

With Colosimo out of the way, Torrio became the city's top crime boss, and Capone became one of his top lieutenants. Capone's move to Chicago looked like a shrewd one. Just five months into his new career and he was finished playing the bouncer at the Four Deuces. He was in management now.

Torrio and Capone were like explorers, sailing off in uncharted directions; taking wrong turns; and, when necessary, slaughtering the natives who got in their way. Beginning in the summer of 1920, they tested any route that looked promising. The men were experts in saloon life and criminal networking, which tended to revolve around saloons in the first place. They had spent their lives developing good instincts for which cops to bribe and which to dodge, which tough guys to kill and which to conscript, when to fight and when to flee. Very quickly they developed so many angles, tapped so many supply lines for booze, took a piece of so many brothels, and found so many ways to make money that it would become nearly impossible to stop them. They soon controlled whorehouses and gambling parlors all over Chicago, as well as in the suburbs of Cicero, Chicago Heights, Stickney, Forest View, and Blue Island. Local affiliates in each of those towns would run the joints and supply the prostitutes, but it was usually up to the Torrio-Capone machine to stock the places with booze and to provide security.

Under the rules of Prohibition, brewers were still allowed to produce near beer, which contained only a minute concentration of alcohol. But those who tried to make a living selling the alcohol-free stuff discovered quickly that beer without alcohol was about as marketable as candy without sugar. Others tried making alcohol for medicinal purposes, but after 1921 federal legislation banned beer as a medicinal product, which cut dramatically into the market available to the nation's legitimate breweries.

With so many brewers facing ruin, Torrio and Capone recognized another opportunity. They hired a brewmaster and, with financial backing from several more gangsters, gradually took over some of Chicago's biggest beer-making operations, including the Manhattan, Stege, Pfeiffer, Standard, Gambrinus, and Hoffman breweries. Knowing the places would probably be raided, they made certain not to invest too heavily in any one brewery. They also installed flunkies in the front offices. When one flunky got arrested, they would hire another. Still, the gangsters could not possibly have manufactured and distributed such massive quantities of beer without the help of the legitimate businessmen who had been running the breweries before Prohibition. One of those brewers, unnamed in an article by the *Chicago Daily News,* was the purported key to the gang's success. "Torrio is absolute in the field of vice and fixers and profit-takers; the brewer is king of the beer racket," the newspaper noted. "And the brewer is so completely above the law, so thoroughly protected from prosecution, that it is unsafe to mention his name, though the police and prosecutors of crime know quite well who he is. . . . Natural attraction brought the pair together and their dovetailing abilities put crime on its new basis." The brewer's identity would be revealed later as Joseph Stenson, owner of the Stenson Brewing Company on the city's Northwest side.

"Torrio is unhampered, with the sky as his limit, in his vice and gambling districts down in the southern end of the county," the *Daily News* reported in 1924. "Torrio . . . and Capone absolutely control the wide-open gambling and vice in Cicero and other western suburbs. Working for them are the gangs and the gunmen. Feuds may and often do break out between the gangsters and gangs, without any word from higher up, but the real wars come when the kings of crime order an upstart put out of the way. They all dance when Torrio and his colleague pull the strings—gangsters, gangs leaders and politicians."

Beer sold for $50 a barrel or more, but even after the gangsters paid off the police, aldermen, precinct captains, prosecutors, and judges, they still made a profit of about $15 per barrel. Margins on pure alcohol were even better. Alcohol sold for about $0.60 a gallon at the warehouse. The middlemen who delivered it would charge bootleggers about $8 a gallon. After cutting the alcohol three or four times, the bootleggers would typically charge their customers about $12 a gallon. With markups like that, a single freight car full of alcohol could net a profit of $250,000.

No wonder bootleggers could afford to spread around the bribes so lavishly. Besides, it didn't take much to pay off a cop. Patrolmen in the city started at salaries of only $1,600 a year, which was less than most dogcatchers made. Federal Prohibition agents were just as easy to handle. For starters, the entire army of federal agents numbered only about fifteen hundred, and those agents were no better paid than the local cops, with salaries of $1,500 to $2,400 a year. "There were no Civil Service requirements," wrote Elmer Irey, the Treasury Department official who supervised the federal agents, "and, as a result, the most extraordinary collection of political hacks, hangers-on, and passing highwaymen got appointed as Prohibition agents." Irey told the story of a top agent who spent two years building a case against a bootlegger only to see it evaporate in fifteen minutes when a judge, calling for a fifteen-minute recess in a trial, retired to his chambers and found two hookers and some bootleg whiskey waiting for him. Case dismissed. Two days later, the same Prohibition agent was offered $10,000 in cash to turn his back so that a truck full of whiskey could depart a warehouse that had been under surveillance. "He turned his back," recalled Irey.

Still, the key to success for bootleggers boiled down to the public's thirst. From the first day of Prohibition, huge numbers of Americans resented the law. They felt their freedom had been stripped by religious fanatics. Even when violence in the bootlegging business erupted, the gangsters who controlled the booze were never entirely blamed. Most Americans seemed to understand that these criminals were like boils—irritating, yes, but also a symptom of a deeper and more persistent disease.

Torrio was a nonthreatening figure. He dressed conservatively and spoke politely. He was a handsome man with green gray eyes and graying auburn hair. Businessmen found him reasonable and reliable and not so different from themselves, while gangsters treated him with fear and respect.

In the first months and years of Prohibition, most of the city's big criminals cooperated with Torrio. In addition to Capone, Torrio's most important aide was Samuel J. "Nails" Morton. Morton was a Jew (real name: Samuel Markowitz), a hero of World War I, an accused cop killer, and a gambler capable of throwing away more than $10,000 on a single game of craps. Torrio and Capone liked Morton. He was tough, which explained the nickname. Morton grew up in a mostly Jewish enclave around Maxwell Street, just south and west of downtown, where he and his young pals would patrol the streets at night with baseball bats to protect the shops belonging to Jewish merchants. Morton entertained Torrio and Capone with terrific stories about his childhood in Chicago and his heroic adventures on the battlefields of Europe. Best of all, he seemed to know every bartender and crook in town.

As the only native Chicagoan in the triumvirate of power, it was most likely Morton who introduced Torrio and Capone to the city's key criminal players, among them Dean O'Banion, a soft-spoken florist, a brilliant arranger of bouquets and homicides; Earl "Hymie" Weiss, safecracker, assassin, ladies' man, and reputed coiner of the phrase "take him for a ride"; Vincent "Schemer" Drucci, a virulent hater of cops and daring wheelman who once jumped a car across a jackknifed bridge during a chase with the police, completing the jump quite nicely, only to get snagged in a traffic jam. Also, George "Bugs" Moran, a Minnesotan of French-Canadian descent who possessed little intellect but had a great knack for avoiding bullets; the Terrible Genna Brothers, of whom there were six, all involved in alcohol-cooking operations in Little Italy; Julian "Potatoes" Kaufman, son of a millionaire broker, who ran with the North Side gang; Hymie "Loud Mouth" Levin, a bootlegger and bookmaker; John "Dingbat" Oberta, a snappy dresser, fine teller of jokes, and an astute businessman; William "Three-Fingered Jack" White, a ruthless assassin who wore a glove to hide his mangled right hand; and Louis "Two Gun" Alterie, who dressed like a cowboy and may have been responsible for introducing the machine gun to the Chicago underworld. These men were not legendary criminals, not archvillains, not anarchists, not rebels, not psychopaths (with one or two possible exceptions). History would remember them as warriors battling for the fat profits of Prohibition and the press would make them objects of affection. But when they set out in the bootlegging trade in the early 1920s, they were simply hoodlums.

Given his local connections and natural leadership skills, Morton—and not Capone—might have emerged as Torrio's successor. Unfortunately, while riding on horseback one day at the corner of Clark Street and Wellington Avenue, on the city's North Side, he was thrown from his mount and kicked in the head on his way down. He died instantly. According to legend, Morton's criminal counterparts were so upset and so thoroughly programmed for revenge that they dragged the horse from its stable one night and executed it.

Torrio tried to teach Capone to keep a low profile and to present an image of calm, cool professionalism. Capone did the best he could. But he was young and impulsive and flush with cash and power. There were, on occasion, slips.

Early in the morning on August 30, 1922, for instance, Capone got fried-to-the-hat drunk and went for a drive. Seated by his side was a young woman. Behind him, on the backseat, were three associates. Tucked under Capone's left armpit was a gun, which he wasn't supposed to conceal. Hidden in one of his pockets was a Cook County sheriff's badge, which he wasn't supposed to have. Parked alongside North Avenue was a taxi, which happened to find itself in the way of the drunken gangster's careening vehicle. Capone crashed.

Automobiles were making Americans feel bolder. Roads were springing up everywhere, and cars were traveling them with speed heretofore impossible. It was a new sensation, one that thrilled and frightened. In Chicago there were no painted lines, no traffic lights, no one-way streets, no speed limits. Cars were big, crude things—an assortment of bolted-together blocks atop slender tires—and city drivers tended to be as arrogant and aggressive behind the wheel as they were in the rest of their lives.

After the crash, Capone became enraged. He leaped from his car, pulled out his weapon, and muscled his way toward the taxi driver, who was badly hurt. He shouted and flashed his badge at the injured man as a trolley rumbled by, its passengers staring wide-eyed. When the trolley's conductor shouted at Capone to put away his gun, Capone made it clear that the conductor would be wise to shut up and move on.

Police arrived. They didn't recognize Capone. But they could tell in an instant that he was drunk. It was a hot, humid night. Capone crowed at the cops, telling them they would be wasting their time making an arrest. "I'll fix this thing so easy you won't know how it's done," he said. He was nevertheless booked for assault with an automobile, driving while intoxicated, and carrying a concealed weapon. The allegations were serious enough that in another time or place they might have ended his career.

But Capone was fortunate to live in Chicago in the 1920s, where judges, lawyers, and politicians could be acquired at a discount, and he was right when he told the cops that night that he'd "fix this thing." The charges were dropped and he was back in business quickly, probably before his hangover wore off.

At about the time of this incident, when Capone was twenty-two years old, he noticed a lesion on his penis. Whether he recognized it at the time as the first symptom of syphilis, no one can say. The disease was certainly no mystery to young men in the early part of the twentieth century. One survey in 1920 reported that syphilis—usually passed along by direct contact with a sore during sexual intercourse—occurred in 10 to 15 percent of all Americans.

Even in the 1920s, there was a fairly reliable cure: an arsenic-based drug called Salvarsan. Introduced in 1910, it quickly became the most widely prescribed pharmaceutical in the world, the first true blockbuster drug. It wasn't perfect. It wasn't effective, for example, for patients with late-stage syphilis. For Capone, it probably would have worked. But he didn't take it.

Maybe he couldn't admit to himself—or to Mae—that he had contracted the disease. Maybe he decided to roll the dice, hoping it would disappear. If Capone's case was typical, the lesion went away within days, replaced by dark, reddish-brown rashes on his palms or the bottoms of his feet. There may have been other symptoms, including muscle aches, a sore throat, and fatigue. Those symptoms, too, probably disappeared within a few weeks.

But the syphilis didn't disappear. The disease merely entered its latent phase. Like a professional killer, it lay dormant, waiting.

A LITTLE HOUSE
ON SOUTH PRAIRIE

The bootleg business was new. Its operators were mostly gravy-stained losers—men in their twenties who still lived with their mothers. Like the young men who rose to sudden wealth and power in the oil fields of Texas, bootleggers possessed a combination of daring and naïveté. When everything clicked, they found themselves riding fantastic waves of entrepreneurial extravagance. When things didn't click, they lost not only their money but also their lives.

Some brewed beer. Some developed elaborate systems to cook up alcohol from raw ingredients. Others drove trucks. A few brave ones signed on for goon-squad work, breaking bones, firing guns, and throwing bombs. But they all had a single goal: keeping the city soaked in alcohol and reaping the profits that resulted. Violence was an unavoidable part of the life. It erupted when one bootlegger tried to steal from another, or when disputes arose with bar owners over pricing or, most commonly, when one gang tried to grab another's turf.

Clarence Darrow, the legendary Chicago lawyer who defended bootleggers in the 1920s, explained it clearly: "The business pays very well, but it is outside the law and they can't go to court, like shoe dealers or real-estate men or grocers when they think an injustice had been done them, or unfair competition has arisen in their territory.

"So . . . they shoot."

Torrio and Capone were smarter and had a bigger operation than most bootleggers. As a result, they managed to avoid getting personally involved in much of the dirty work. They hired smugglers and burglars to get the alcohol they needed for their brothels and casinos, and because they served as a clearinghouse, they maintained plenty of open channels. When one supplier was arrested or killed, there was always another one ready to take his place.

Still, their organization was young. In fact, at this stage in their careers, in 1923, a full three years into Prohibition, Capone found time to do a little work outside the booze business, dabbling as a promoter for a featherweight boxer named Mike Dundee of Rock Island, Illinois. "You see, I've always liked Mike both as a fighter and as a man," he told the *Davenport Democrat and Leader* in what may have been his first published interview, in December 1923. "The kid has had a lot of tough breaks in the last few years but I hope his financial troubles are over." Capone went on to say he was repping Dundee free of charge. "And by the way," he said, "you can tell the world that I'll lay $25,000 that he can beat Johnny Dundee [who was of no relation] for the featherweight title."

Mike Dundee eventually got his shot at the title. And lost. Capone—who always loved the sporting life but had terrible luck picking winners—went back to crime.

Except for his drunken car crash, Capone was never charged with a crime during his early bootlegging days, despite the fact that several people who knew him then claimed he earned the respect and trust of Torrio mostly by doing his dirty work.

"They snatch guys they want information from and take them to the cellar," one hoodlum told a Chicago judge name John H. Lyle. "They're tortured until they talk. Then they're rubbed out." The torturer was said to be Capone, his torture chamber a filthy back room at the Four Deuces. Corpses were dragged through a tunnel that opened to a trapdoor in the alley, then loaded in a car, and disposed of on a country road or in a rock quarry. Judge Lyle claimed to have seen the tunnel himself, but only years after the torture had supposedly occurred.

Capone put a softer spin on the early years of his bootlegging career. With Dean O'Banion's men infesting the North Side, the six Genna brothers controlling the South Side, Terry Druggan and Frankie Lake dominating the West Side, and countless other gangs muscling in at the margins, clashes were inevitable and gunfire erupted often. Still, Capone claimed that everyone got along pretty well, all things considered.

Torrio and Capone controlled the tap on much of the city's beer, which earned them respect and cooperation. It helped, too, that many of their saloons and brothels were in the suburbs, where fewer rivals and fewer cops operated. Capone, in one of his early interviews, said he and Torrio had tried to persuade the other bootleggers to maintain a cooperative and friendly business environment as their operations grew. There were profits enough for all, they said.

But the others didn't listen.

Just as Capone was getting established in his career, his personal life threatened to come undone. On the evening of November 14, 1920, back in Brooklyn, his father, Gabriele, made the short walk from his home on Garfield Place to a pool hall on the same block. While watching a game there, he collapsed and died, probably from a heart attack. He was fifty-four.

Gabriele Francesco Saverio Capone was born in 1865 in a small town called Angri in the Campania region of Italy, near Mount Vesuvius, according to civic and church records recently discovered there. Gabriele's parents made and sold their own pasta from a small shop in the center of town. He married a local girl—a farmer's daughter named Teresa Raiola—and brought her to America. In Italy, Gabriele had worked as a printer. In America, he became a barber. He and Teresa settled in the slums of Brooklyn and raised nine children: eight boys and one girl.

Alphonse Capone—born January 17, 1899—was the fourth-born. While his father had toiled with scissors and blades to keep men of modest means looking a bit cleaner, a bit more respectable, Al Capone would take an entirely different approach. He carved wealth and power with ferocious haste.

Given that he would become internationally famous before he was thirty, and hunted by newsmen, biographers, and Hollywood screenwriters, Capone revealed surprisingly little about his childhood. He would grow up to be a man who fished, hunted, boxed a little bit, and enjoyed watching almost every kind of sports event. He loved spending money but never bothered saving any. He seldom left the house unshaved, and prided himself on dressing well. He was a man's man if ever there were one. And yet he never mentioned whether he acquired any of his passions or quirks of personality from his father, never told a single story about

going to see the Superbas or the Robins (both later known as the Dodgers) at Washington Park or Ebbets Field or learning to fish in Brooklyn's
Gowanus Canal with his old man. If his father ever skimmed money from
the register at the barber shop, gambled a week's pay on a card game, or
took a second or third job to help feed and clothe his big family, his son
never mentioned any of it.

With Gabriele's death, the Capone family had no leader. Al's oldest
brother, Vincenzo (also known as James), had disappeared a few years earlier. The last anyone heard, he was traveling out West, perhaps with a circus. Of all the other Capone boys, Al's prospects seemed best. So Teresa
and her other six children—Raffalo (Ralph), Salvatore (known as Frank),
Ermino (John or Mimi), Umberto (Albert), Amado (Matthew), and Mafalda
(named in honor of Italy's young princess, Mafalda Maria Elisabetta Anna
Romana of Savoy)—were on their way to Chicago.

Almost immediately, Al became the head of the family. Two of his
older brothers, Frank and Ralph, went to work with him in the bootlegging business. Eventually he would help some of his other siblings buy
bars and restaurants to support their families.

Al and Mae went shopping for a house—the family's first. They settled
on a brick bungalow at 7244 South Prairie Avenue in Grand Crossing,
which was south and west of downtown by about ten miles. It was a
neighborhood of small groceries, fruit stands, and butcher shops where
the owners worked alone, slicing the meat, wrapping it, and ringing up
sales on the register. On Sunday nights in summertime, the neighbors
would sit on blankets and listen to concerts at the grandstand in the park,
the women in loose frocks that covered them from ankle to wrist, the men
in seersucker suits and straw hats, while children chased fireflies.

The Capones picked an unpretentious house, two stories tall, with
big, square windows facing east so that by early morning the rooms at the
front were as bright as the day. The house was an early version of the classic Chicago two-flat, built by an architect who cranked out dozens more
just like it. Plain little bungalows lined the avenue like humble workers on
a factory floor, not to impress but to do a job. Model Ts and Packards sat
by the curbs. Small yards offered room for kids to toss a ball and for men
to toss horseshoes.

As they had in Brooklyn, the Capones avoided an all-Italian enclave in
favor of a neighborhood of mixed ethnicity. But this time they were much

better off financially. In Brooklyn they'd had nothing but crowded tenement apartments. Now they had a whole house to themselves in a quiet neighborhood with little traffic, little noise, and no big industry. Most important, this time they weren't renting; they owned the place. The house was valued at about $15,000, according to Cook County property tax records, or roughly $180,000 in today's dollars. They covered part of the transaction with cash, but they also took a mortgage, agreeing to pay 6 percent interest on a $4,400 loan. The loan documents were signed by Al, his wife, and his mother, who had begun spelling Theresa with the "h."

Al and Mae were practically still newlyweds, yet Mae could not possibly have imagined how dramatically her life would have changed since her wedding. She was a painfully shy young woman with a pronounced overbite that she tried to hide in photographs. Otherwise she was lovely, with sparkling brown eyes, sculpted cheekbones, and a lissome figure. She and Al had met at a box company in Brooklyn where they both worked.

Their first and only child—Albert Francis "Sonny" Capone—had been born on December 4, 1918, in Brooklyn. Al and Mae married three weeks later. There's nothing unusual about a woman giving birth out of wedlock, but in Mae's case, it raised questions. One Capone relative—Deirdre Marie Capone, the granddaughter of Al's brother Ralph—claims that Sonny was Al's child but not Mae's. Capone impregnated a girl, according to this version of events. When the mother died during childbirth, Teresa Capone arranged a marriage. Apparently Teresa knew Mae Coughlin and her parents from church. Teresa proposed that Mae marry her son and become Sonny's mother. The Coughlins agreed to the match because Mae was twenty-one years old and so shy that her family thought she would never find a husband.

If true, the arrangement seemed to work well enough for all involved. Al and Mae grew to love each other. And Mae turned out to be a wonderful mother. She put Sonny at the center of her universe, educating him in Catholic schools, raising him with strong moral values, and keeping him far from her husband's circle of troublesome friends. But now Mae was taking on even more of the Capones. The house on South Prairie Avenue was mobbed. Even around her in-laws, Mae could not overcome her shyness. While the rest of the family prepared for dinner, she stayed in her room, taking care of the baby or reading a book. She would come downstairs to eat and help clean up. Then, while the rest of the men and women gossiped and played cards and drank anisette, she would excuse herself and return to her room. The Capones didn't hold it against her. She doted on her little boy, respected her mother-in-law, and stood by her husband despite his many crimes and sexual indiscretions. Capone would disappear for days at a time, sometimes to take care of business, sometimes to meet women, sometimes to go hunting or fishing with his pals. He lived for weeks at a time in hotels. But when he came home, he always did so with style, greeting Mae with hugs, kisses, and gifts that no ordinary girl could imagine.

Al Capone was Catholic. His wife and mother attended mass daily, making the short walk to St. Columbanus Church, two blocks away from their home, at Seventy-first Street and Calumet Avenue. Sonny was enrolled there in school. He was a sickly child, suffering from mastoiditis, an infection of the mastoid bone that can cause redness, swelling, and pain behind the ear. The condition rendered him partially deaf and led Mae to dote even more on the boy.

The church was an overwhelming presence, physically and spiritually, in the neighborhood and in the Capone family. It was a hulking building, twice as big as anything around, with a gothic tower visible from every corner of the parish. Nuns in robes and collared priests strolled the neighborhood's streets and sat next to parishioners at the local diners and coffee shops. Legend has it that Al Capone paid for the custom-built Kilgen pipe organ in the choir loft. But he seldom attended mass. He was much too busy.

"I'M SURE IT WAS CAPONE"

In 1923, at about the time Capone moved into his new house, the business environment in Chicago began to change. What initially seemed like a turn for the worse turned unexpectedly to the advantage of Torrio and Capone.

Since 1915, Chicago had been run by Mayor William Hale Thompson. Big Bill, as everyone called him, may have been the most crooked politician Chicago ever elected. He was also one of the cleverest. He resembled a six-foot pigeon—tall, fat, and gray, with a beak for a nose and a flaccid chin that drooped all the way to his chest. When political opponents took the high road, branding him a liar and a cheat in their newspaper ads, Big Bill took a different road and aimed his campaign at the poor and illiterate who didn't read the papers. In the Polish wards of the city, he was anti-German. In the German wards, he was anti-Polish. And at times, in an effort to appeal to the city's enormous Irish population, he promised that if he ever met King George V of England, he would punch him in the nose.

Thompson strutted, shouted, boasted, drank, gambled, and cheated. And he made no attempt to hide his duplicity, which is probably why Chicagoans warmed to him.

It came as no surprise when Big Bill made it clear to those in his administration that he was not going to exert a lot of energy clamping down on vice. Crime and politics in the Thompson era went together like barley and hops. The mayor's friends and political appointees set out to get rich doing business with the city. Breaking the law became the most efficient way to get things done. Bootleggers operated in the open and bribed their way out of trouble. Even violent criminals knew that the police department—one of the smallest per capita in the nation and one of the most corrupt—posed little threat.

Gangsters were killing each other at a rate of about fifty a year. Union organizers turned to violence, too. Even politicians made guns and bombs, the preferred tools for settling differences. In one long-running campaign battle pitting John "Johnny Da Pow" Powers versus Tony D'Andrea for the position of Nineteenth Ward alderman, thirty lives were lost. Bombs exploded on Powers's front porch. Campaign workers were gunned down in the street, outside pool rooms, and behind cigar-store counters until, finally, on the night of May 11, 1921, D'Andrea himself had his chest ripped open with two blasts of a shotgun while on the front steps of his home. He died the next day. Of the thirty murders connected to the campaign, only one resulted in a trial—which, of course, ended in an acquittal.

It wasn't entirely Thompson's fault that Chicago so dramatically failed to enforce the law. Prohibition made it hard on even the most vigilant elected officials. Technology also was a factor. Smoother roads, faster cars, and rapid-firing guns all helped criminals stay ahead of the police. The same things were happening nationwide. Morals were loosening. Getaway cars were getting faster. But everything criminal was more pronounced in Chicago. It seemed as though the forces of nature had conspired in this city by the lake to create fertile soil for the growth and development of criminal activity.

Before and during the Thompson years, the court system was a cesspool. Trials were routinely delayed for years. Crooked lawyers bribed crooked cops to testify the right way before crooked judges. Criminals went about their business like professionals—paying in advance to protect their interests.

The cops and judges and lawyers who managed to remain honest eventually became dispirited and, all too often, gave up hope. There were men in Thompson's administration who gave it a good effort, among them the state's attorney, Robert Crowe. With only forty police officers at his disposal and with an eye on becoming mayor himself, Crowe used his office to attract publicity. Systemic corruption made it difficult for him to do much else. He made a series of high-profile raids on gambling dens and brothels in and around the Levee District. With a gaggle of cigar-chomping newspapermen waiting behind the patrol wagons, Crowe's men would smash through the doors, rounding up prostitutes and seizing roulette wheels, racing sheets, slot machines, and dice tables. He got the big headlines he wanted, even if he did little in the long run to curtail crime.

By 1922, Big Bill Thompson was in trouble. The city was out of control, and the mayor's endless explanations were beginning to strike a lot of Chicagoans as just so much flapping of the gums. The school system was a disaster. The *Tribune* broke one story after another about the mayor's pals bilking the government for millions. And the crime went on and on. Gangsters such as Torrio and Capone were not openly allied with Big Bill, but everyone knew that the Thompson administration made life easy for them.

Finally, in 1923, Crowe and others led a reform movement. Business and religious leaders embraced it. They nominated a clean-cut Democrat named William Emmett Dever to run against the mayor. Thompson responded aggressively. He went on a building binge—giving the city wider streets and bold new bridges, and bragging about them as if they were his personal gifts to the people of Chicago. But with Crowe preparing a new round of indictments against some of Thompson's closest associates, Big Bill finally dropped out of the race. Dever took office promising sweeping change.

Dever was no Goody Two-shoes. He was a pragmatic, experienced lawyer who understood the dirty dealing involved in city politics. To win the support of the Democratic Party, he had made a deal of his own, letting the chairman of the Cook County Democratic Party control the hiring at City Hall. That compromise was enough to give the new mayor enough clout to get things done. He began his reform effort by ordering the police to step up their raids on gambling dens and brothels, and he made a special point of shutting down "black and tan" saloons, where the races mixed. Dever knew that by targeting the black and tans he would gain the support of many conservative white voters who loathed race mixing. Then and only then did he begin a widespread push against saloons. In the course of one hundred days, he padlocked some four thousand of them. For a short time the city appeared to be turning a corner. Dever became a national celebrity, known as "the mayor who cleaned up Chicago," even if the title was applied a bit prematurely.

Under Dever, bootleggers, gamblers, and speakeasy operators faced more raids. In the past, all they had needed to do was bribe their local alderman or their local police captain to stay in business. Now, as they found their approaches blocked by Dever's do-gooders, or goo-goos (short for good-government supporters), as they were known, many of the small-time criminals turned to Torrio and Capone for help.

In fact, Dever's reform era may have done more to empower Torrio and Capone than anything since the murder of Colosimo.

The outfit, as Capone referred to the organization, grew bigger, stronger, and much more profitable. It helped, too, that Torrio and Capone had plenty of businesses in the suburbs, away from Dever's goo-goos.

Modern organized crime may have been born in this moment.

In the fall of 1923, Capone transferred his headquarters from the Four Deuces in Chicago to the Hawthorne Inn in Cicero. Nestled at Chicago's western edge, Cicero was the state's fourth-largest city. It looked exactly like a working-class section of Chicago, with several big manufacturing plants—the biggest of them belonging to Bell Telephone's Western Electric company—where more than ten thousand men and women built and assembled telephones.

All around the factory sat the usual smattering of churches, schools, and small brick houses. The Hawthorne Inn was on Twenty-second Street, the city's main drag. It was a modest, two-story hotel. Like everything else on the block, it was redbrick, with white tile set in the top of the facade. Attached to the hotel was a restaurant, also called the Hawthorne, no wider than a railroad car. A gambling house called the Ship sat next door, open to the public, with a sign out front to make it simple to find. It was a place where roulette, faro, craps, blackjack, stud poker, and chuck-a-luck games ran around the clock, and supposedly on the square.

All over Cicero at the time of Capone's arrival, saloons and casinos were cropping up like weeds in an abandoned lot. Prohibition was flouted so routinely and so brazenly that the writer Fred Pasley called Cicero the first city in the nation to secede from "the United States of Volstead." As one of the saloonkeepers explained, "When the cops and the Prohibition agents come here all the time to get drunk with us, why, of course they go along with us. They always tip us off to the raids. An injunction means nothing. When the owner of a place is caught by one he opens up somewhere else under another name."

The town government was controlled completely by Torrio and Capone, who paid off the mayor and members of the city council. Once, to show his disdain for some recent bit of public policy, Capone slugged the town president, Joseph Z. Klenha, knocking him down on the steps of City Hall as police officers stood by and watched.

"The Free Kingdom of Torrio," the *Chicago Tribune* snidely labeled the town. "It has gambling and liquor and everything, including a police force."

––––––––

In the spring of 1924, when election day came around in Cicero, Klenha, a Republican, was concerned that the same reformers who had helped elect Dever in Chicago might try to bring reform to his fair town. He turned to Capone and Torrio for help. They assured the mayor he had no reason to worry.

On the eve of the election, the Democratic candidate for town clerk, a reformer named William K. Pflaum, received a visit from a group of so-called political activists who beat him with their revolver butts, sacked his office, and fired several shots into the ceiling before they fled. A Democratic campaign worker was shot through both legs and dumped in a basement where eight other would-be reformers had already been locked up. An election clerk was gagged, tied, and stashed in a saloon until after the voting was done. A policeman was blackjacked; two men—presumably Democrats—were shot dead on Twenty-second Street; and another man had his throat slashed. It was a tough campaign.

Election day—April 1, 1924—dawned cold and gray. Outside a polling station at Twenty-second Street and Cicero Avenue stood Frank Capone; his cousin, Charlie Fischetti; and a third man, who was probably Al Capone. The three men were handsomely dressed, with overcoats, jackets, silk ties, and snap-brimmed fedoras. Each brandished an automatic weapon. They meant for their presence to serve as a reminder to vote Republican.

By late afternoon, a judge in Cook County decided that the election was beginning to look like a riot, with fights breaking out and gunshots echoing across town. In an attempt to restore order, the judge sent more than one hundred police officers into Cicero. A cold rain started to fall. When the cops got to Cicero, they used their nightsticks and pistols to push back at the gangsters. The three men were still standing at Twenty-second and Cicero as hundreds of workers began pouring out of the Western Electric factory across the street. Just then, a police car pulled up at the polling station. Police cars in the 1920s were often indistinguishable from ordinary sedans, which might explain why the gangsters didn't move.

Three patrolmen stepped out, guns raised and ready. Fischetti froze. Frank Capone took off running to the north. The man whom police assumed to be Al Capone took off running, too, in another direction. The police later claimed that Frank Capone ducked into a clump of tall grass and began firing at them, but at least one witness said the gangster never raised his weapon. What happened next is beyond dispute: Sergeant William Cusack fired, bullets flew, and Frank Capone fell to the sidewalk, gulping air, choking, and dying there on the concrete.

The headline in the *Tribune* read "Gunman Slain in Vote Riots," and in smaller print, "G.O.P. Ticket Wins."

Al and Ralph Capone identified their brother's corpse at the morgue.

The next day, the Capone home on South Prairie Avenue was filled with hundreds of men and women paying their respects. So many flower arrangements were delivered that the Capones needed fifteen cars to carry the bouquets to the cemetery. Every gangster in Chicago, it seemed, came out to offer condolences to Theresa Capone. Neighborhood children lined up by the dozens across the sidewalk to watch the spectacular parade of expensive cars and men in dark suits. Even the police officer who fired the fatal shots made an appearance and expressed his sympathy.

With Cicero locked up at least until the next election and the booze business becoming more lucrative by the day, the Torrio-Capone empire steadily grew. Capone's take of the profits in 1924 came to more than $123,000, or about $1.5 million by modern standards, according to an estimate made several years later by the Bureau of Internal Revenue. But the bigger the business got, the more violence it engendered. And while Torrio was generally mature and mild-mannered enough to avoid becoming personally involved in the brutal work, his younger partner was not. Capone was learning from Torrio the ways of the booze business, but he had not mastered the emotional control that helped make his boss so successful for so long.

For a second in command, it was not such a serious character flaw to fly off the handle from time to time, and nothing in Capone's behavior in those early years suggests he aspired to run the Chicago outfit. There's certainly no indication that he had designs on removing Torrio.

A few weeks after the death of Frank Capone, a small-time hoodlum named Joe Howard showed up at Hymie Jacobs's saloon, just down the street from the Four Deuces. Howard was twenty-eight, still lived above his mother's South Side fruit store, and made his living by burglary and beer-running. It was six o'clock in the evening. He was sitting at the cigar counter, trying to choose a smoke, when the saloon's doors swung open with a flutter behind him.

"Hello, Al," Howard said, smiling, turning around, and putting out a hand in greeting.

Police would later concluded that Al was almost certainly Al Capone. Coming through the door with him was another man—bigger than Capone—also unidentified by witnesses at the scene.

The men said nothing as they entered and walked briskly toward the bar. The big man grabbed Howard by the coat and held him tight. Capone pulled a gun, put the muzzle to Howard's cheek, and pressed. He pulled the trigger. Blood, bones, and tooth particles exploded across Hymie Jacobs's bar, but Howard was still sitting on the stool, his body suspended in the hands of Capone's accomplice. Capone fired five more shots. The big man released his grip. The rest of Howard fell from his stool into a puddle of his own blood. Capone and the big man turned and walked out of the bar.

Thirty minutes later, police told reporters they had identified their suspect.

"I am sure it was Capone," announced Chief of Detectives Michael Hughes. But the detective went on to complain, in frustration, that the men in the bar sitting next to and across from Joe Howard were refusing to identify the killer. Each of them claimed he had been looking away when the man entered the bar and that the gunman was gone by the time the victim fell from his stool. Hymie Jacobs, who was standing opposite the victim, behind the cigar case, said he had seen the whole thing but didn't recognize the man Howard had greeted as "Al." Another eyewitness, who lived at 2220 South Wabash, next door to the Four Deuces, claimed he had never seen nor heard of anyone named Al Capone.

Chief Hughes knew the runaround when he was getting it.

"It's an old story already," he complained.

The next day, Capone's picture appeared in the *Chicago Tribune*. It was a mug shot soon to be familiar to Chicagoans.

The investigation dragged on for weeks. Chief Hughes said he knew exactly what had happened, "but for the life of me I can't tell the motive."

A story had begun to go around on the gangland grapevine. According to the gossip among hoodlums, Howard had recently hijacked a load of booze. After the heist, he'd gone to a speakeasy to celebrate. Drunk and trying to act big, he'd decided to pick on one of the smallest, chubbiest, and most harmless-looking men he could find. Unfortunately for Howard, the victim he selected was none other than Jack "Greasy Thumb" Guzik, chief bookkeeper for the Torrio and Capone syndicate. Howard didn't just beat Guzik, he also humiliated him, slapping him back and forth across the face a few times and then letting him have it with a fist to the head. After the beating, Howard had bragged to friends that he'd "made the little Jew whine."

Just before Capone had pulled the trigger, according to the story passed around among Chicago gangsters, Capone had muttered into Howard's ear, "Whine, you f—ing fink."

Amnesia and temporary blindness continued to afflict the witnesses in the days after Howard's murder. Capone made himself scarce. If the murder of Joe Howard didn't elevate Capone's reputation among Chicago's gangsters, demonstrating both his brutality and his loyalty, what happened next surely did.

A month later, on June 11, Capone walked in of his own accord to a police station and said he'd heard a rumor that the cops had been looking for him. He said he was "curious to know what it was for."

The police delivered Capone to the state's attorney's office in the criminal courts building, where he was told he was wanted for questioning in Howard's murder. The interrogation turned out to be brief.

"Well," Capone explained, "I don't know anything about the shooting because I was out of town at that time."

That was a good enough explanation for the young assistant state's attorney assigned to the case, William H. McSwiggin.

Capone walked.

FUNNY NOTIONS

On Sunday afternoons, all the Capones gathered for dinner at the house on South Prairie Avenue. Theresa cooked. Her daughter, Mafalda, helped. Mae stayed upstairs until dinner was ready. The rest of the women were allowed to carry dishes and set the table.

But the kitchen belonged to Theresa.

Everything about Theresa looked heavy, from her hips to her bust to the severe expression of her face. Blue eyes shone beneath thick brows. She wore her hair cut short and dyed black as ink. Though she understood English quite well, she spoke only in Italian in her home. The children treated her with affection, respect, and a healthy dose of fear. For Sunday dinners, the food came from Chicago's finest butchers and bakers, but also from Italy. Theresa's family in Angri occasionally sent packages of meats and cheeses she couldn't get in the United States. Once, the Capone children got a big laugh because the salami that had just arrived from Italy turned out to have been made a mile or so away, at the Armour meat factory. It had been shipped halfway around the world and back again.

While the men smoked and drank and laughed and the women smoked and gossiped and watched the children, Theresa commanded the kitchen. To make her bracciola, she would begin with a piece of steak pounded thin as the palm of an old baseball glove. Atop the meat she would sprinkle parsley, pine nuts, and garlic. No measuring cups, no tablespoons. She measured ingredients with her fingertips and palms. After seasoning, she would roll the steak, tie it with string, and sauté it. In an instant, the whole house filled with the fragrance of garlic and olive oil.

When the meat was brown, Theresa would add tomato paste and peeled tomatoes. While the bracciola cooked, she prepared her meatballs, which were composed of three kinds of ground meat—beef, pork, and veal—as well as garlic, eggs, salt, pepper, pine nuts, fresh parsley, and half a loaf of moist, shredded Italian bread. She fried them in lard and put them in the oven to keep warm.

The meal was served on mismatched plates, accompanied by copious amounts of red wine, which the Capones referred to as Dago Red. After dinner they would sip homemade anisette, nibble on fruit and Italian pastries, and play a few games of *sette-e-mezzo,* Italian for seven and a half, a form of blackjack popular in Italy. The Capone boys were ferociously competitive and loved to gamble. They'd bet on anything, from horse races to ball games to which bird on the telephone wire would shit first. But when it came to *sette-e-mezzo,* Theresa almost always won.

On January 11, 1925, a Sunday night, dinner ran a little later than usual. Perhaps the family was celebrating Al's twenty-sixth birthday, which was six days away. When the festivities wound down at about 3:00 A.M., Capone asked his chauffeur to drive two of the guests home.

It was a cold and wet morning, with two inches of fresh snow on the city's streets. Capone's big Packard was moving northbound through the slushy, puddled intersection of Fifty-fifth and State in a neighborhood of broken sidewalks, vacant lots, and greasy spoons with billboards boasting of chicken dinners for five cents. The streets were cast in a yellowish light. Nothing was moving. But suddenly Capone's Packard had company. It was a touring car with curtains over the rear windows—never a welcome sight.

Quickly the car pulled alongside the Packard and forced it to the curb. The Packard scraped against a lamppost and crunched to a stop. Then came the sound of a Thompson machine gun, *Brruupp!,* a flash of light, and drifting smoke from the touring car's window. Bullets pocked the door on the driver's side of the Packard.

The touring car roared off into the early-morning darkness.

Fortunately for the men in the Capone's sedan, machine guns were not easy to aim, especially when fired from a moving vehicle. Capone's chauffeur, identified by police as Sylvester Barton, wound up with holes in his overcoat, sport coat, and underwear, but most of the bullets only

skimmed his flesh. He would be fine. His two passengers—never named—
were completely unhurt.

After surveying the scene and getting the driver to the hospital, Captain James Allman of the Woodlawn police station phoned Capone at home. The police officer suspected that Capone had been in the car at the time of the attack and fled the scene, but he couldn't prove it.

"Well, we've got your Packard at the station, Al," he said.

Capone asked about his chauffeur.

"He's been shot. Were you there?" the captain asked.

Capone said no.

Several weeks earlier—on November 10, 1924—dapper Dean O'Banion, boss of the North Side, had been gunned down while arranging funeral bouquets in his flower shop. The murder was a huge blow to the North Side gang world, where O'Banion wielded as much power, if not more, than Capone wielded on his turf. Almost everyone assumed that Torrio and Capone had ordered the hit and that O'Banion's men had now tried to attack Capone in revenge. The police captain asked the gangster if he had any idea why someone would be trying to kill him.

"Well, some people have funny notions," Capone said without missing a beat.

Two weeks later, on January 24, Torrio and his wife went shopping on Michigan Avenue. They returned home late in the afternoon as the gray sky darkened to slate and the temperature slid. They were stepping out of their chauffeur-driven sedan when two men leaped from a big black Cadillac parked across the street. One of them opened fire. Five bullets struck Torrio in the face and chest. He spun, slumped, and buckled, but somehow stayed on his feet. Since he never carried a gun, he had no chance to return the fire. Dripping blood, he staggered into his home. The assassins jumped back in their Cadillac and drove off into the deepening dark.

Later, Torrio said he recognized his attackers. While he almost certainly told Capone, he honored the gangland code of *omerta* by refusing to supply names to the police. The cops assumed that the attack on Torrio was retaliation for the murder of O'Banion. But they had no better luck getting information from Capone, who sat down for a long interrogation yet said little. Capone identified himself in the interview as a furniture dealer and said he had met Torrio three years ago at a boxing match in Chicago. He claimed not to know Dean O'Banion or any of his cohorts. Asked what kind of work he had done back in Brooklyn, Capone said, "I was in the paper- and leather-cutting business," which happened to be true.

"Ever been arrested before?" they asked.

"Ever arrested before!" he shouted. "For everything that happens in this town!"

"Do you know who shot him?" the cops asked, referring to Torrio.

"I'm not saying."

"Would you tell us if you knew?"

"No. I value my life too much. I bought a home here and I want peace."

"Do you know Sylvester Barton?"

"Yes, he's my brother Ralph's chauffeur."

"Do you know why he was shot the other day in your car?"

"No."

"Where does Ralph live?"

"Sometimes in Cicero and sometimes with me."

"What does he do?"

"He runs the Ansonia [Hotel] in Cicero, but there's nothing doing there now."

"What does he deal in there? Booze, beer, and gambling?"

"Oh, no! Just soda pop."

"Are you going to try and find out who shot Torrio?"

"Say, I got enough troubles of my own."

"Will you sign this statement?"

"Sure. Why not? There's nothing in it."

That night, Capone stood watch at his boss's hospital bed, like a shopkeeper guarding his store after a fire, trying to prevent further damage. A young reporter told the story of spotting Capone in the hospital lobby and running to confront him. Capone, surprised and suspicious, stuck a hand in his coat pocket. Some of his men did the same. The reporter introduced himself. Capone said nothing. He stared straight into the reporter's eyes and froze him with a leer.

"Well, Mr. Capone," the reporter asked nervously, "how did you find Mr. Torrio today?"

Capone didn't answer. He continued to fix the reporter with his hardest stare.

"I understand he is getting along fine," the reporter stammered. "Did you find him looking better?"

Nothing. Not a word. Not a blink of an eyelash.

Beads of sweat began to surface on the reporter's forehead.

"Ah . . . er . . . Mr. Capone, do you think your friend will be able to leave the hospital soon?"

Still, nothing. The cub reporter looked like he would wet his pants at any moment.

Suddenly Capone threw his empty arm in the air and shouted "Boo!"

The reporter jumped back two feet. Capone chuckled, turned, and left.

Torrio was recovering nicely. But this soft-spoken, wealthy man, a pioneer of urban gangsterdom, had decided he'd had enough of Chicago. The profits at stake in the bootlegging game had grown too large, the men involved too unstable. And the murder of O'Banion had sparked a greater firestorm than anyone imagined. Torrio spent a little time in jail after pleading guilty to a violation of the Prohibition act that had resulted from a raid on one of his breweries. After completing his sentence, he went back to New York, and then to Europe for a long vacation.

He left Capone in charge.

Soon after, on April 6, 1925, Chicago cops caught a break that nearly put Capone out of business. In a raid on a doctor's office at 2146 South Michigan Avenue, a block and a half away from the Four Deuces, police arrested Frank Nitti and seized what appeared to be the complete financial records of the Torrio-Capone machine: financial ledgers, customer lists, purchase orders, even a roster of prostitutes with details on how much each of them earned. The cops found booze stacked neatly on shelves and a telephone bill showing phone calls to Miami, New York, and New Orleans. William McSwiggin—the same assistant state's attorney who had let Capone go after the Joe Howard murder—was placed in charge of the county's investigation. Federal Prohibition and tax agents informed McSwiggin that they were eager to see the records as well. In part, the feds were curious to learn if any of their men appeared on the Torrio-Capone payroll sheets, but they also were eager to determine if they could use any of the information to shut down this budding criminal syndicate. Three days later, to almost everyone's shock, Municipal Judge Howard Hayes ordered that the seized records be returned to Torrio and Capone.

Everyone assumed that Judge Hayes had been paid off by the mob. Was McSwiggin in on the deal, too? Had he seen the records? If he knew the details of the mob and couldn't be bought off, he would be a dangerous man to have working in the state's attorney's office. If he had seen the records and helped dispose of them, he would have been a very useful man to keep around.

The night that Hayes ordered the return of the records, Capone was arrested for speeding and carrying revolvers in his car. Once again, he was living on the edge, carrying on like the young and suddenly wealthy man he was. In the future, he would be more careful. But his incarceration following the speeding and gun-possession arrest turned out to be no great inconvenience. On his first night in jail, he treated his fellow prisoners to steak dinners, shelling out $25 to have the meals delivered. The next day he was released on bond, and eventually all the charges were dropped.

Capone was trying to remember Torrio's advice. He was trying to keep a low profile. But it wasn't easy for him.

A MAN OF DESTINY

With Torrio gone, Capone was the undisputed boss of the Chicago crime scene. While he made no overt attempt to replace O'Banion in the North Side, Capone's influence grew all across the city. Cicero, however, remained the center of his empire. He controlled everything that moved there, a fact that was well known to every bootlegger in a hundred-mile radius.

But on the evening of April 27, 1926, a couple of up-and-coming booze peddlers—the brothers Myles and "Klondike" Bill O'Donnell—decided to press their luck. The O'Donnells had recently been approaching the town's speakeasy owners and offering to sell them beer at the bargain rate of $50 a barrel—$10 less than Capone's price. They claimed that Capone's brew tasted like piss. As if that weren't brazen enough, they were promenading around Cicero as if they had a perfect right to be there.

This night the O'Donnells were out for a good time, driving past brick bungalows and shadowy oak trees, drinking and picking up friends along the way. They were unaware that at some point they also had picked up a tail. As their big blue Lincoln pulled up in front of the Pony Inn, the tailing car crept closer, headlights off. The O'Donnells and their chums stepped out of the Lincoln.

First came the roar of an engine and then a burst of fire from a Thompson submachine gun. The explosion lasted about five seconds, time enough for the Tommy to discharge more than one hundred rounds. Three men dove for cover. Three more dropped to the sidewalk, blood pouring like spilled paint from their bodies. Three fedoras and a set of horned-rim glasses tumbled to the sidewalk.

Gangsters got knocked off all the time in Chicago. Law enforcement personnel seldom seemed to take the trouble to figure out who did it or why. Lines got crossed, deals were welched on, cheaters were cheated, witnesses were eliminated—so much so that on any given day in any given part of town, any outlaw might have reason for killing any other. When the cops came around—*if* they came around—nobody talked.

The Pony Inn shooting would have been another piece of routine business in Chicago—no big news—except for one important detail. While two of the three dead men were in fact beer peddlers, the third was William McSwiggin, the well-known assistant state's attorney. McSwiggin was twenty-seven years old, an up-and-comer with a reputation for talking a good game but letting a lot of gangsters slip away. Why was he out drinking with a bunch of bootleggers, including two whom he had tried and failed to prosecute? No one said.

Had McSwiggin been on the take? Probably. But still, his killing violated one of the other rules of protocol for Chicago hit men: Public officials, no matter how crooked, were off-limits. As a result of this breach in etiquette, the McSwiggin murder made banner headlines nationwide and put pressure on police to take the unusual but not entirely unprecedented step of attempting to solve the crime.

They had a fair idea where to start.

Until that moment, Al Capone, twenty-seven years old, had been a minor character on the Chicago stage and unknown on the national stage. Even now, in covering the shooting, the city's newspapers variously identified him as Al Caponi, Al Caproni, or Al Brown, the latter being Capone's favorite alias. The only thing they reported with consistent accuracy was his nickname: Scarface.

McSwiggin's boss, State's Attorney Robert E. Crowe, deputized three hundred Chicago police officers, and gave them an order: Bring in Capone. The cops raided the gangster's haunts in Chicago and Cicero, snatching weapons, taking hatchets to beer barrels, boxing up accountants' ledgers found in casinos, and arresting dozens of men. They searched the house on South Prairie Avenue. They dropped by sporting goods shops and took down the names of those who had recently bought machine guns. But Capone was nowhere to be found.

Immediately after the shooting of McSwiggin, Capone had left town. He drove east into Michigan and holed up with a few of his men in a cabin at Round Lake, just outside Lansing. He stayed all summer. He swam, played cards, and served as master of ceremonies for a fantastic fireworks display on the Fourth of July. He also enjoyed the company of a blond woman who was not his wife.

Capone had been growing huskier of late. He carried himself as if he were bigger than five feet ten and a half. He stood straight on tree-trunk thighs and swaggered a little. He could be a menacing figure. But the vacationing families at Round Lake witnessed nothing but his gentler, more reasonable side. For three months, the only disturbances around came from buzzing mosquitoes.

Capone knew it couldn't last, though. One day late in July, he phoned a couple of newspaper reporters in Chicago and told them he was planning to return to the city. He said he had nothing to do with the murder of McSwiggin and intended to prove it. So much for keeping a low profile.

It was a counterintuitive move. Yet given the nature of the 1920s, when the spotlight of fame moved quickly and shone brightly—illuminating ballplayers, flagpole sitters, and daredevil pilots—it was fitting that Capone might give in to vanity.

Americans in the summer of 1926 were fascinated by the bestselling book *The Man Nobody Knows*, which portrayed Jesus Christ as a successful businessman and organizer, "a go-getter," and "the most popular dinner guest in Jerusalem." Its author, Bruce Barton, was an advertising executive who believed in the power of the individual to shape his own image, to promote his own brand, to forge his own destiny. The book fed a nationwide mania. Like Christ, Barton wrote, great businessmen had to possess personal magnetism and sincerity. Then they needed the wisdom to surround themselves with good men. Modesty was not part of the program.

Even if Capone didn't read *The Man Nobody Knows* that summer at Round Lake, he certainly liked to think of himself as a go-getter, a salesman, a skilled business executive, a man of destiny. He believed in creating wealth and moving his family up on the socioeconomic ladder. He was ready to get back to business, and he did not intend to be shy about it.

On a Wednesday morning, July 28, 1926, Capone's Packard passed from Michigan into Indiana, skirting the flat southern shore of Lake Michigan. He drove by steel mills and cement factories. It was not yet 10:00 A.M., but already the air was thick and heavy, as if it couldn't decide if it wanted to be wet or dry, stormy or calm.

The car coughed to a stop at the corner of Indianapolis Boulevard and 106th Street, where Indiana and Illinois meet. The fumes of swamp and industry greeted Capone as he stepped out and stood alongside the road. He wore a blue-serge suit, a crisp white shirt, and a checkered tie. A natty straw boater rested lightly atop his head. A federal agent named A. P. Madden met Capone at the border. Together, they made the sixteen-mile drive into downtown Chicago.

They arrived at the criminal courts building on Hubbard Street, the same place where Nathan Leopold and Richard Loeb, a couple of University of Chicago students, had been convicted two years earlier for the murder of a fourteen-year-old boy.

No rain had fallen. The sidewalks radiated heat. The city streets were cluttered with horses, wagons, cars, trucks, and trolleys. Office workers had opened their windows at the courthouse, hoping for a breeze but getting only the sounds of the city. Capone's hair was slicked black and shiny, sticking to the back of his thick, sweaty neck. Reporters crowded him and shouted questions as he stepped into the building. He smiled for photographers and tried to show reporters he was relaxed.

"Of course I didn't kill him, I liked the kid," he said, referring to McSwiggin. "When I learned of the killings I knew the police, looking for a goat, would naturally blame me. So rather than stay in a cell for a long time and be blamed for everything, I went away. . . . Any official who has a right to question me can find out all I know. If the police have anything but hot air, they can use it. I'll answer any question about the murder. I had nothing to do with the killing of McSwiggin, my friend. . . . Why, ten days before he was killed I talked with Bill. There were friends with me, too. If we had wanted to kill him we could have then, but we didn't. We never wanted to."

In fact, Capone went on, he had good reason for keeping the young prosecutor alive. "I paid McSwiggin," he said. "I paid him plenty and I got what I was paying for."

Just like that, McSwiggin's reputation was dead, too.

County officials had been vowing for months that they would pin this murder on Capone. They had questioned the survivors of the attack, including Klondike Bill O'Donnell. They had questioned Capone's gang-

ster brother Ralph, and relieved him of the huge cache of weapons found
in his home. They had even questioned Ralph's wife, the lovely Peggy
Capone, who had shown up at the police station swathed in far more fur
than the temperature had required. But none of Capone's friends and
allies had chirped. Investigators found only one witness who claimed to
have proof of the big man's guilt: A waitress at a restaurant in Cicero said
she saw Capone on the night of the murder get up from his table, pull a
machine gun from a hidden compartment in the wall, and leave in a hurry.
But when police checked the restaurant, they found no hidden compartment. Given the absence of evidence and the fact that the state's attorney
had failed to issue an indictment, Capone expected his court appearance
to be brief. But Judge Thomas J. Lynch had other ideas. He ordered the
suspect held overnight.

———————

At noon the next day, another hot one, Capone appeared again before
Judge Lynch. The courtroom was packed. It was clear from the size of
the crowd and the number of reporters milling about that Capone had
been transformed over the course of the summer from a thug of small
importance to a heavyweight. In addition to the dozens squeezed into the
courtroom, more than two hundred oglers waited on the street outside,
"necks craned and mouths agape to see . . . the 'great criminal,' " as one of
the city's daily newspapers, the *Chicago American,* put it. A few blocks away,
only a dozen Chicagoans showed up to greet the train carrying America's
biggest movie star, Rudolph Valentino, in town to promote his movie *Son
of the Sheik,* and to confront a Chicago reporter who had recently questioned his masculinity.

Capone came to court wearing the same suit he'd had on the day
before, with the same boater hat canted atop his head. But he didn't seem
bothered.

Clean-shaven and smiling, he removed his hat in the courtroom and
chatted with his lawyers. When Judge Lynch asked the lawyers to approach the bench, Capone accompanied them. This time the judge made
it quick. He asked if the prosecution had any evidence tying Capone to
the death of McSwiggin. The prosecutors admitted they did not, and
Lynch dismissed the case.

Capone, grinning, put on his boater and walked out of the courtroom.

The only challenge remaining in his otherwise perfectly executed return was getting out of the courthouse and back to Cicero. Worried that someone in the crowd would shoot or knife him, he whispered to one of his lawyers that he needed to move fast.

Out on Hubbard Street, one person posed a particular threat. Sergeant Anthony McSwiggin of the Chicago police department, father of the slain prosecutor, had been telling reporters for weeks that he held Capone responsible for his son's death. Now he was standing on the sidewalk, dressed in a wrinkled suit and a straw hat just like Capone's, telling the press that he was furious about the prosecution's failure to put the finger on his son's killer. "They pinned a medal on him and turned him loose," McSwiggin raged.

Capone looked out the courthouse door to Hubbard Street. Seven police officers on horseback worked the crowd. Reporters darted about with their notebooks open, hoping to record a few of the freed gangster's words. Photographers lugged their big, boxy Speed Graphic cameras, reloading their film sheets after every shot and trying to anticipate where Capone was headed. When a Marmon roadster pulled up in front of the courthouse, Capone ran from the building, past the gathered crowd, and hopped in the car. His friend Louis Cowen—a gambler, a former Yiddish-newspaper boy, and current owner and editor of the *Cicero Tribune*—sat behind the Marmon's wheel.

"Come on!" Capone shouted, beckoning for his lawyers to follow.

They chose not to.

The car door closed with a solid thud, and the Marmon lunged forward. Traffic in every direction slowed as motorists strained to see what the commotion was all about. The mounted cops scanned the crowd for guns and bombs. The camera jockeys tried for one last shot as the car drove off, but Capone ducked. As the car rumbled down the road, the only thing visible was the top of his hat.

In that moment as much as any, the legend of Al Capone was born.

"Who killed McSwiggin?" became a common piece of banter among Chicagoans, a running gag. A cartoon in the *Chicago Tribune* showed a gaggle of foolish detectives tiptoeing and crawling on their knees in search of clues while the regally dressed Capone swaggered out of jail.

The cops were the joke, not Capone.

A story, unverified, also began to circulate that Sergeant McSwiggin

drove out to Cicero later that day and, finding his nemesis at the Hawthorne Inn, backed him against a wall, intent on taking justice in his own
hands. Capone was said to have reached under his left armpit, pulled out
his automatic, and offered it to McSwiggin along with the following pronouncement: "If you think I did it, shoot me."

McSwiggin, the story goes, gave the gun back to Capone and walked
away.

7

HEAT WAVE

The waves of heat kept coming throughout the summer of 1926, one after another, with scarcely enough time in between for Chicagoans to gasp for breath. Thousands slept fitfully on park benches, beaches, and in backyards. The *Tribune* took up a collection to provide free ice to those who couldn't afford it and encouraged apartment dwellers to escape the heat at night by sleeping on flat roofs. Dozens died from heat prostration, and several drowned in the too-crowded lake.

But such sweltering heat didn't hurt the beer business. Nor did it quell the summer's violence. The sizzling weather gave rise to flaring tempers all over the city. It had dogs biting owners, shop owners squabbling with their customers, husbands snapping at their wives. And it had gangsters shooting at gangsters even more than usual.

Torrio's retirement, O'Banion's death, and Capone's summer vacation had turned Chicago's disorganized booze business into something approaching chaos. For a brief moment, a power vacuum existed. In response, alcohol producers with vats in their basements, truck drivers who supplemented their legitimate income by making booze runs to Canada, big-shot brewers trying to squeeze a few illicit bucks from factories that were supposed to be shuttered, and countless other finaglers surged forth to grab a piece of the action. They were part of a fast-growing economy. The work was obviously dangerous, but the rewards were too great to be easily dismissed.

After three months at Round Lake in Michigan, Capone needed time to adjust—not just to the oppressive weather but also to changes in the business environment. Journalists speculated that his operation had been permanently crippled as a result of his absence: His key men had scattered, his customers had found new suppliers, his choke hold on city officials had slipped. Capone was not heard from for several weeks after his court date, and it was possible to imagine that his moment had come and gone, like the movie actor with only one successful film. Newspapers named Ralph Sheldon, one of Capone's former satellite operators, as the most feared criminal in the city.

Like a lot of other men in the bootlegging business, John "Mitters" Foley kept his jacket on through much of the summer to conceal the revolver tucked under his sweaty armpit. Better hot than dead, the thinking went. Foley, twenty-eight years old, was big, strong, and handsome, with a neck nearly as wide around as his head. With his beefy frame, he could have been mistaken for a heavyweight fighter. His great bulk and his willingness to get rough qualified him for a job as a labor organizer in the ice-cream-wagon business. But Foley quickly realized that he also was qualified for beer work, so he branched out and did a little bootlegging for Ralph Sheldon, who did a little bootlegging for Capone.

Sheldon was such a stoic that earlier in 1926, when his brand-new Lincoln was blown to bits by a powerful bomb, he had told the police it was probably just a prank by neighborhood kids. "I haven't an enemy in the world," he'd said at the time.

Foley, too, had been the subject of an assassination attempt earlier in the year, when he and a pal were wounded in a shoot-out in a saloon on the South Side. Foley took the same approach as Sheldon in response to the attack, telling police he had no idea who had been shooting at him or why anyone would want to hurt a man whose only concern was the safe remittance of ice cream. Everyone knew, of course: These shootings—like most in Chicago—were over turf. Foley was trying to muscle his way into the business. The saloons he approached were already in the control of an ambitious bootlegger named Joe Soltis, a.k.a. "Polack Joe."

On the afternoon of August 6, 1926, with thermometers registering eighty-five, Foley paid a visit to his mother's house on the South Side. When the telephone rang, Foley answered, listened, then returned the receiver to its cradle and walked out of the house. Apparently warned that someone was coming after him, he got into his car and drove south, down Sacramento Avenue. Bungalows slid past his open windows. The neighbors were all out on their porches, fanning themselves, sipping cool drinks from sweating glasses.

Foley turned east onto Sixty-fourth Street, then hooked a right on Richmond. That's when he spotted a green Cadillac moving slowly toward him. The Caddy had been parked on the block, waiting, for more than an hour. Foley flew into a panic. Without stopping his car, he opened the door, jumped out, and took off running. His driverless automobile rolled on until it crashed into an iron signpost. The green Cadillac stopped. A man with a shotgun got out. Foley ran but didn't get far before he tripped. The man with the shotgun closed in on him. Foley was looking up at his pursuer when he felt the muzzle of the shotgun press against his sternum. The gun roared, and Foley's chest burst inside out wetly. All through the neighborhood, heads turned in the direction of the blast. Then came another blast, this one from a shot that cratered Foley's head and sent the contents splattering. Within seconds the Cadillac was gone.

John P. Stege, Chicago's acting chief of detectives, sped to the scene. The sight of another shredded body did not surprise him, but this did: A landscaper working at the nearby Marquette Elementary School swore that he could identify the men in the Cadillac if he were to see them again.

Stege was an honest cop. He already had a good idea who'd killed Foley and why, so he brought the landscaper downtown and showed him pictures of Joe Soltis (whose name was usually spelled "Saltis" in newspaper accounts) and three of his men, John "Bingo" Alberto, Edward "Big Herb" Herbert, and Frank "Lefty" Koncil. The landscaper said, yes, those were the men, he was sure of it. Another witness from the neighborhood confirmed the identifications. Stege told reporters that Soltis and Foley had been fighting for control of a few saloons and taking shots at each other for months. What's more, Stege found the green Cadillac used in the shooting, which had been abandoned, and took it to Soltis's mechanic, who confirmed that Soltis was its owner. Chicago's upscale department store Marshall Field & Company couldn't have gift-wrapped the case any better, and Stege knew it. "Jubilant" was the word the *Herald and Examiner* used to describe the lawman, who typically had more luck getting his picture in the paper—holding a captured machine gun or leading a crook to jail—than getting convictions. This time it looked like he had finally caught a break. So jubilant was Stege that he allowed himself some premature bragging, saying, "I believe we have figured out a scheme that will elimi-nate at least some of this promiscuous street shooting and some murders. Our plan may not be a cure-all, but we are going to get somewhere this time. This rough stuff has got to quit."

Four days later, Schemer Drucci, Hymie Weiss, and a couple of their associates strode through the intersection of South Michigan Avenue and Ninth Street. It was nearly noon, the sun crashing straight down on the crowns of their hats. The mighty Standard Oil Building towered over the men, windows open, shades drawn. Cars snaked up and down Michigan in both directions.

Drucci and Weiss had decided to unload some of the cash they'd been keeping in safe-deposit boxes. They called a few friends, including George Moran and Julian Kaufman, to escort them on their errand. The men stuffed their pockets full of green and headed downtown to an office building on Michigan Avenue, where they planned to make a cash deposit—$500,000, by one account—on a real estate deal.

On their way into the building, Drucci and Weiss bumped into John Sbarbaro. As much as any Chicagoan, Sbarbaro embodied the city's love-hate relationship with bootleggers. He held two jobs—one as an assistant state's attorney, the other as a funeral home director—so that when he wasn't putting gangsters in jail, he was putting them in coffins. But Sbarbaro was on the take, which meant that he didn't get around to convicting too many hoods. This had two benefits for Sbarbaro: It left the criminals out on the street, where they were more likely to get whacked, and it instilled in the men of the underworld a sense that Sbarbaro was a fellow they could do business with when the time came to bury one of their chums. His ceremony for O'Banion, featuring a $10,000 silver and bronze coffin and $50,000 in flowers, would be remembered for decades as the ultimate gangdom fare-well, the standard against which all others would be judged.

On this steamy late morning, though, his meeting with the gangsters appeared to be accidental. Weiss said hello, and Sbarbaro returned the greeting. Weiss asked if Sbarbaro could recommend a good place for lunch. Sbarbaro pointed out a greasy spoon just to the south and waved good-bye. Seconds later, a car rumbled up Michigan Avenue. From it came the ear-splitting machine gun blasts Chicago was beginning to make famous, *Brruupp! Brruupp!* Bullets drilled into cars, shop windows, and streetlamps, the noise like rocks hitting the empty bed of a dump truck. Weiss and most of the others took off running, but Drucci stayed behind. He ducked. Pedestrians ran for cover. A truck driver screamed as one shot ripped through the door of his cab and into his leg. Drucci drew his .38, looked around for a target, and started shooting until he ran out of ammunition.

He leaped to the running board of a parked car and waved his gun at the stranger behind the wheel.

"Drive on quick!" he shouted.

But before Drucci could get away, a policeman tackled him from behind. While Weiss disappeared completely, Drucci went quietly to the station. He knew the drill. He began by giving the cops a fake name, which was a joke, given how many times he'd led them on chases and how many times he'd been in and out of the clink. Then he said he had no idea why anyone would want to shoot him. Another joke. At last, after admitting his true identity, he was asked to explain why he had $13,200 in cash in his pocket. Was it booze money? Bribe money? Gambling money? Drucci—whose first published nickname was "Skimmer," not "Schemer"—would say only that he was carrying the money for a real estate deal.

The cops booked him for assault with intent to kill and disorderly conduct. Within hours, he was released on bond. Not long after that, the charges were dropped.

Though the attack on Drucci and Weiss wasn't fatal, it worried cops for several reasons: because it had taken place on a busy street in the middle of the day; because Drucci would no doubt go after the men who'd shot at him; and, finally, because the Michigan Avenue assault looked like the work of Capone's gang, which made a specialty of the shooting from passing cars. The word on the street was that Capone had heard about the Drucci-Weiss real estate detail and sent his men to relieve them of their cash.

Was Capone really after the money, or was he preparing to go to war with Weiss, Drucci, and Moran for a piece of O'Banion's North Side turf? Was he seeking revenge against the men who'd shot Torrio? Was he after Soltis, too? No one knew, and no one knew what to do. The cops tried what they always tried: They conducted a halfhearted effort to round up the men most likely to kill or be killed. When they succeeded in finding them, however, the men all sang the same song: *Who, me? Why would anyone want to hurt me?*

And then they were let go.

"HE WILL KNOCK YOU FLAT JUST FOR FUN"

The summer's scorching heat faded at last.

On September 20, 1926, a Monday, Capone was eating lunch at the Hawthorne Restaurant, attached to the Hawthorne Inn. The place smelled of hamburger grease, cigarettes, and coffee. If Capone followed his routine, he would be sitting at the last of fifteen tables in the long, narrow eatery, facing the front door so he could see everything, including the big clock behind the counter, which showed the time just shy of two.

Outside the restaurant, the sidewalks of Cicero were unusually crowded. Hundreds of horse owners and trainers were visiting for the second week of the fall season at the Hawthorne racetrack. In addition, thousands of Chicagoans, having quit work early, were streaming in by car and train for the event. This year, the Hawthorne had attracted some of the country's finest horses and jockeys. For a brief period, Cicero enjoyed an air of legitimacy and excitement. The streets around the track had been paved, and a fresh coat of white paint had been slapped on the racetrack's facade. There was a new clubhouse, an expensive new dining room, and even a new gymnasium at the track where jockeys could exercise. It was the jewel of Cicero.

The weather had been fine the past few days, the grandstands packed: a sea of straw hats and dark suits, everyone smoking cigars or cigarettes, scanning the racing forms, and quizzing friends for tips. It had been a week of upsets, which tended to make for an irritated, anxious crowd. A day earlier, a horse named Columbia II, owned by the gangster Terry Druggan, stormed to a huge lead and then all but quit running down the stretch, as if the animal had changed its mind about being a horse. A twenty-five-to-one shot named Pequot took the win. Also that afternoon, a sure thing named Stout finished out of the money, beaten badly by a worthless nag named The Runt.

The races at Hawthorne were one of life's great pleasures for Capone, who drank in moderation but gambled heavily, especially on the horses and dogs. He sat among the crowd. He chomped cigars. He shook hands and patted backs and cheered and stomped his feet when his horses won and cursed when they lost. They usually lost. Despite his love of gambling and his affection for horse racing, Capone was a rotten bettor. The writer Damon Runyon called Capone the worst gambler he'd ever met. But given that he did all his business in cash and neither saved nor invested his profits, and given that Capone almost certainly received a cut of the profits at the racetrack, it's no wonder he put big dough on the ponies and didn't blow a gasket when he lost. It was practically play money.

As post time approached for the day's first race, Capone was still at the restaurant. Then, from outside and down the block, came that familiar sound: the rolling thunder of a Thompson submachine gun. By now, everyone even loosely connected with the world of gangs in Chicago recognized it. When diners at the Hawthorne heard it, they dropped their utensils and dove for the floor. Waitresses and busboys scrambled for the kitchen. Capone crawled under his table.

The Thompson was named after General John Taliaferro Thompson, a West Point graduate who began working in 1915 to create a firearm strong enough to bring a swift end to World War I. He came up with an automatic weapon small enough and light enough to be employed by one man—"a trench broom," he called it, for sweeping out enemy fighters. He named it a submachine gun because it was smaller and lighter than traditional machine guns, which sat on tripods and usually required two men to operate.

Thompson brought his vision to reality in 1919, building a weapon that weighed only nine pounds. It had a finned barrel, twin pistol grips, a short butt, and could fire four hundred rounds per minute. Unfortunately for Thompson, the war ended before he could complete delivery of his first shipment. Though he tried after the war to sell his invention to police forces and military outfits, the response was not great, so he decided to advertise in search of an alternative market. Once the gun went on sale in hardware stores, sporting goods shops, and by mail order, he found his target market: Gangsters, who had plenty of disposable cash, made the gun an essential tool of the trade.

The Tommy changed the nature of bootlegging. It separated the big crooks from the little crooks. It spread fear—among rival gangsters and ordinary civilians—like nothing before it. And it was easy to acquire and easy to use. The only trick was aiming low, because the weapon had a ferocious kick, which tended to make bullets sail high. Chicago gunmen had already learned the advantages of drive-and-go shooting, but shooting on the move became much more effective and much more intimidating with the advent of the Tommy, which was also known as the Chicago Typewriter, the Chopper, the Chatterbox, the Gat, and the Ack-Ack.

As patrons inside the Hawthorne Restaurant ducked for cover, six or seven cars rumbled in a line down Twenty-second Street—"a veritable battalion of death," as one newspaper called it. Machine guns blasted from the open windows of the automobiles: glass flew, metal clanged, the screams of men, women, and children pierced the air. When the last car in the caravan reached the hotel, a man in khaki overalls stepped from the running board to the street. He knelt down, rested his Tommy on one knee, and like a gardener watering his flowers, sprayed the entrance of the hotel. Without pausing to admire his work, he got up and jumped back in his car, which followed the others back toward Chicago.

As smoke from the machine guns drifted over the street and the smell of gunpowder lingered, Capone peeled himself off the floor and stepped outside to survey the damage. Twenty cars had been parked in front of the Hawthorne, and every one of them was damaged. A Chrysler with Kentucky plates was "shot to pieces," according to the *Daily News*. One of Capone's men had intercepted a slug with his left shoulder. A Louisiana horse owner and his wife had been grazed by bullets and showered with glass. But given the sheer volume of metal flying through the air—police estimated a thousand bullets—the injuries were remarkably few. After the shooting, boys from the surrounding neighborhoods rode their bikes to the scene, their feet crunching glass on the sidewalk. They counted bullet holes. Capone was standing among the crowd, still full of swagger, when the *Daily News* caught up with him.

"Sure I saw it," he told a reporter. "It's a wonder no one was killed." He told another reporter that the gunmen had shot so erratically that he doubted they were aiming for anyone or anything in particular. With that, he quickly excused himself, saying he had a meeting with his lawyers.

Police named the following suspects, in no particular order: Schemer Drucci, Hymie Weiss, Frank Gusenberg, Peter Gusenberg, Vincent McErlane, Ernest Applequist, Ben Applequist, Danny Vallo, Puggy White, Frank Foster, Bugs Moran, Dominic "Libby" Nuccio, Morris Cohen, John Tuohy, Bingo Alberto, and a man identified only as Darrow. Considering the number of cars involved in the attack—not to mention the impressive number of men who by now had reason to wish Capone dead—it was possible that all of these men and a few more were involved. The cops arrested two prominent North Siders, Moran and Peter Gusenberg. That development—arrests!—would have been worthy of banner headlines if not for the fact that the cops booked the men only for vagrancy. The judge mocked the prosecution for bringing such trifling charges and dismissed the case.

These open hostilities, these O. K. Corral shoot-outs on busy city streets, were beginning to inspire not just fear but indignation as well. A cartoonist for the *Herald and Examiner,* one of the papers owned by William Randolph Hearst, captured the mood with a drawing of a gangster sitting atop a barrel of moonshine, smoking gun in hand, rivals dead at his feet. Says the sneering gangster, rhetorically, "An' what ya goin' to do about it?"

In the same newspaper, an editorial writer weighed in:

> This is war. . . .
>
> The state's attorney is "roused," and once again orders wholesale arrests; but what of it?
>
> This of it, at least: That from Australia to Nova Zembla the papers of the world again carry the gossip that the main streets of Chicago, second largest city in America, are not safe from battalion murder even in the daytime; that in the depths of the Tennessee Mountains, in London's Whitechapel, there was less utter contempt for law than in Cook County, Illinois.
>
> We might ask the state's attorney whether, if he is not moved by the responsibility of his office or by the murder of one of his assistants, he ought not at least to consider the effect of this sort of thing on real estate values. We might ask the

Association of Commerce, the Bar Association and similar in-
fluential bodies, whether the kill-or-let-kill policy as applied to
gangsters and gunmen is one calculated to increase this city's
reputation and develop its trade. We might ask the people of
Chicago whether we, all of us, can AFFORD to let this sort of
thing go on. . . .

There remains only the assertion that the methods of law
must change. . . . There is authority enough in the law, and
force enough behind the law, to clean them up, if that authority
and force are unrelentingly applied.

But who thinks they will be? Who killed McSwiggin, and
why?

Less than two weeks later, on October 1, 1926, a new combatant
publicly entered the war on crime in Chicago. The federal government
that day indicted Capone and seventy-eight other men on charges of
conspiracy to violate the Prohibition laws. The indictments were the
work of Art Madden, who went by his initials, A.P., a special investigator for the Bureau of Internal Revenue later to be known as the Internal
Revenue Service. Madden had come to Chicago at about the same time
as Capone, assigned by the Department of the Treasury to hunt down
tax cheats. He had spent time with the gangster. It was Madden who had
driven out to the state line to bring Capone back to Chicago after his vacation on Round Lake in Michigan. "Madden had made a professional
and amateur hobby of Al Capone" according to his boss in Washington,
Elmer Irey.

"Al is a fathead," Madden said in a report to Irey. "He is one mobster
who doesn't care about money. He wants to be the Big Guy, and if he can
take the bows he doesn't care much who gets the cash; just so long as he
can bet on horses, buy the horrible junk he calls clothes, and collect jewelry. He likes women, but they don't cost him a nickel. He just gives them
the night off. He is sensitive about that source of income. . . . Capone
doesn't kill anymore. He brings in thugs to do it for him. Frank Nitti, 'The
Enforcer,' handles the arrangements, and if the thugs fail, 'The Enforcer'
has them knocked off. Al is a cruel louse, especially when he is drunk.
He'll laugh a lot with anybody sober, but he will knock you flat just for
fun when he's drinking. He's the boss, make no mistake about that, but

he listens to advice; particularly from lawyers. He has many friends in the police force."

Madden knew that greedy men fell faster and harder than the rest, and it troubled him that Capone wasn't more money-grubbing. But the agent wasn't giving up. He began looking at the bankbooks and checks recovered by police in raids on brothels and speakeasies in Cicero. He found a large number of checks drawn on accounts from the Pinkert State Bank of Cicero, and he became convinced that those checks were connected to beer sales, gambling, and prostitution. From his review of those books and ledgers, he estimated that the bootleggers had earned at least $10 million in profit since 1922. The man controlling much of the cash flow, according to the government, was Fred Ries, described by one newspaper as a gambler and "beer operator." Madden found that Ries had written more than $95,000 in checks to Capone associates Louis LaCava and Jimmy Mondi. LaCava and Mondi were among Capone's many partners in gambling operations. And though the revenue agent had not yet found concrete evidence that any money from Pinkert State Bank went to Capone, he claimed that he had discovered proof that Capone and his brother Ralph had been responsible for several large shipments of alcohol.

"This is just the beginning," vowed one of the attorneys who filed the charges, noting that four hundred witnesses had been subpoenaed and the investigation was just getting started. "We are going to clean up Cicero—and then we are turning our attention to Chicago."

Added another prosecutor: "The whole power of the United States government will be used to smash the crime trust." The U.S. attorney for the Northern District of Illinois, Edwin A. Olson, vowed that he would bring the Cicero bootleggers to trial before his term expired at the end of the year.

In that moment, it seemed as if Chicago's era of lawlessness might soon come to an end. Newspapers reported that Capone was in secret meetings with the feds, trying to cut a deal, although his lawyer flatly denied it.

One newspaper cartoon showed an angry Uncle Sam towering over the town of Cicero and spraying insect powder on its tiny gangsters, the bad little men trying to scurry out of sight. "The modern gangster is remarkable for his hardihood," read the caption. "Even so, he probably can not face the active hostility of the United States secret service without a shudder." The newspaper warned that the government crackdown "may fill the bad men of the suburb with a sudden and mysterious urge to go to church on Sunday and eschew utterly the ways of evil."

But the full might of Uncle Sam was not yet employed in the battle against Capone. In fact, to that point, only the Chicago agents of the Justice Department were involved, and it was not clear whether they had enough muscle to get the job done. Capone was quickly freed on a $10,000 bond. He wasn't eschewing anything yet.

THE PEACEMAKER

If the cops didn't know who shot up the Hawthorne Inn with Al Capone in it, Capone had a pretty fair idea.

"Weiss will never kill me by any such silly stage play in broad daylight," he said, referring to Hymie Weiss. "He might as well come after me with a brass band."

Before the beer business enabled him to buy a fancier cut of suit and bed a higher class of woman, Hymie Weiss was known to Chicago police as a run-of-the-mill hood. As a teenager, he and Dean O'Banion had worked at Louis Greenberg's saloon on Market Street, collecting debts from welshing customers and rolling those who were too snozzled to fight. Greenberg was Jewish, a native of the White Russian city of Minsk, who had worked his way up from small-time thievery to loan-sharking, from bartending to saloon ownership, and who would eventually make his way into banking. Hanging around with Greenberg, who never liked to pay for any beer or whiskey he could steal, Weiss and O'Banion learned many lessons that would come in handy during Prohibition, the most important lesson being that a buck or two a week bought a great deal of goodwill from cops. They also put in time working as safecrackers, or "yeggs" in the parlance of the day.

But yegg work was going out of style by the mid-1920s, and O'Banion and Weiss—along with their quiet friend George Moran and the more daring Vincent Drucci—had already found a more promising career path. Together, these men developed a thriving beer business on the city's North Side. They knew that Torrio and Capone were strongest to the south and west, their empire covering everything from Calumet City to Cicero.

Within those territories there were smaller gangs—such as the Gennas, the Sheldons, and the Guilfoyles—that operated like provinces within the purview of an empire. The smaller gangs would sometimes strike out for independence, but most of the time their resistance could be easily crushed and they would return obediently to the fold. Wisely, O'Banion, Weiss, and Moran steered clear of the Torrio and Capone turf, establishing their own primacy on the North Side. As long as Torrio had been in power, they had managed to prosper without much conflict. But those days were gone. When O'Banion died pruning flowers, Weiss, Drucci, and Moran remained as the North Side's main men. Of these three, Weiss was best equipped to lead. Whenever a saloonkeep called to complain about a missed delivery, it was Weiss who took the call and tried to smooth things over. He was more diplomatic, more polished, a pragmatist. The beer business needed guys like him.

"This Weiss was a regular go-getter," recalled one of his unnamed colleagues, speaking to a newspaper reporter in the 1920s. "He got to the top of the alky racket just the way a young bank clerk gets to be a cashier—by tending to business. . . . The others . . . might go chasing women or out on drunks or picking fights, but Weiss was always right there on the job, taking orders and keeping the business going. Lots of people on the outside think the alky business is worked under cover, with customers sneaking up a back alley, laying down the jack and ducking home with a gallon or so hidden under the coat. But that's not the system. O'Banion, Weiss and the rest sold alky just the way the stockyards sell meat. They took orders over the phone or by mail and delivered the stuff like any merchant would. Sometimes they sold drum lots, sometimes they sold gallons. And they had to bustle for business like anybody else. That's where Weiss came in. Half the time . . . he'd be talking like this:

" 'Hello, who is this talking? O'Banion?'

" 'No, this is his partner, Hymie Weiss.'

" 'Well, say, Weiss, this is the Highball Drug company out in Rogers Park. We sent in a vendee ten days ago for twenty gallons, and we haven't got a drop. What the hell's the matter with you guys? O'Banion said he'd get it right out.'

" 'Listen, Highball, we haven't had a bit of stuff for a week, see? We've been getting knocked off. But there's some coming tonight. I'll fix you up in the morning.'

"That was Weiss's line—soft soap."

Whether Weiss was more intelligent or merely more ambitious, Drucci and Moran were content to let him run the show. Maybe *they* were the bright ones: By putting Weiss in charge, they put a target on his back.

Weiss was handsome in that regular-guy-with-a-crooked-smile-and-busted-nose sort of way. He wore his hair oiled to a shine and neatly parted on the left, his bow tie in a crisp, symmetrical knot. No amount of slicking up could ever make him classy, but he still seemed to enjoy the lifestyle of the high-rolling bootlegger, especially after O'Banion's death. By handing out bribes to cops, he bought himself a measure of protection that had been unattainable during his safecracking days.

The money also helped him meet a higher class of woman. Weiss introduced himself to a dancer, Josephine Libbie, blue-eyed and golden-haired, of the legendary Ziegfeld Follies. The Follies girls embodied sexiness. They burst from the seams of their gorgeously designed outfits: leggy, tiny waists cinched in, bountiful breasts thrust forward, smooth and sweet as butter. When the lighting was right, an audience member sometimes imagined he was seeing through the minimal costumes to the navel, nipples, and creamy thighs. It didn't really matter if the girls could sing or dance. They were hired to fill the costumes, and photographs of Josephine would suggest she did that quite well. Men going to see the Follies knew that at least some of the showgirls were gold diggers. It didn't matter. Weiss opened his bid to Libbie with flowers and followed up soon after with a $5,000 diamond engagement ring. Libbie got the impression that her suitor made his money in real estate. Apparently Hymie peeled the bills from his roll fast enough that she never asked questions. Soon they were married, renting a home at a fashionable address, and discussing whether to have children. "Perhaps I suspected the true state of things," Josephine later confessed. "But I didn't want to know—although . . . if he had come right out and told me, 'Yes, I'm Earl Weiss the bootlegger,' I should have married him just the same."

Already, Capone had several good reasons for wishing Weiss dead. For starters, it was most likely Weiss who'd shot Capone's mentor Johnny Torrio. The story going around in gang circles went this way: Drucci had been the driver, Weiss had fired the first volley with a sawed-off shotgun, and

Moran had been closing in with his army-issued .45 to finish the job when
the men were interrupted by a laundry truck turning on to the block.

Still, Capone made no threats. He would wait.

Not long after the attack on the Hawthorne Inn in Cicero, Capone
called for a congress of gangsters to see if they could negotiate terms that
would make for a peaceful coexistence. They did not meet in a speakeasy
or a diner, as was the custom less than a decade earlier. It was a sign of
how seriously these men were now taking themselves—and also an attempt
to find neutral ground—that they convened at the venerable, recently remodeled Hotel Sherman, at Clark and Randolph in the city's Loop. It was
the largest hotel west of New York City, and some said the handsomest.
Everything was branded with an elegant letter *S*, from the arches above
the doors to the handles of the demitasse spoons. In the lobby, polished
marble shone in all directions. In the hotel's nightclub, white jazz musicians showed off the licks they'd learned from the black musicians who
were not yet permitted to play there. Hotels offered gangs what social
clubs offered more legitimate businessmen: privacy, pampering, and hos-
pitality. Before Prohibition, Americans had done much of their drinking
in hotel bars. Now that mainstream customers patronized speakeasies, the
gangsters who ran the speakeasies used the hotels to conduct the more
civilized aspects of their business.

The Sherman, it was understood, was not a place to be sullied by
boorish behavior. Weiss and Drucci and a few of their underlings were
there, along with an unidentified police officer and an unidentified politician. However, after convening this congress, Capone decided to stay
away, perhaps fearing that he might face another assassination attempt.
Tony Lombardo took his place.

Lombardo was the newly installed president of Chicago's Unione Siciliana, otherwise known as the Italo-American National Union. By some
accounts, the Unione Siciliana was a fraternal organization; by others it
was a secret criminal group at the heart of the city's organized criminal
operations. In fact, it was both. Given that its presidents had an unfortunate habit of dying by bullet holes and that Capone had worked for years
to get one of his allies installed as the organization's head, it's obvious that
organized crime ranked high on the group's list of priorities. In New York,
none other than Capone's old boss Frankie Yale led the organization. But
Chicago emerged in the 1920s as the Unione's most important outpost,

with an estimated forty thousand members. Little Sicily (or Little Italy, as it later became known) occupied a huge swath of the city's near North Side, much bigger than it does today. The Unione was a central part of life in the neighborhood.

Little Sicily was a neighborhood of small brick houses, smoky pool halls, bowling alleys, churches, and tavernas. The Ferrara Pan Candy Company, on West Taylor Street, had a small factory where it made its famous candy-coated almonds, a traditional treat served at Italian weddings. But most of the neighborhood was much less sweet. Dense vapors hovered, coughed up from all the small factories on the Chicago River, Goose Island, and along the busy industrial, working-class stretches of Elston, Grand, and Clyburn avenues. Trash burned in alleys. Manure sat uncollected in the streets. Tanneries spewed chemical odors into the air. But the biggest producer of smoke and stench, by far, was the People's Gas, Coke, and Light Company, near the corner of Crosby and Division streets, where coal furnaces roared like thunder and mighty flames rose high in the sky all day and all night, "like a satanic specter," as one local resident put it.

But factories meant jobs, and jobs meant houses, and houses meant families, and families meant a shot at the American Dream, so no one complained. Little Sicily, despite its intimate association with the forces of organized crime, was in many ways a typical neighborhood of striving immigrants. Not all of its residents were Sicilian, or even Italian, but there were enough Italians to make the Unione a powerful force in local affairs. Capone had long wanted control of the Unione, and with Lombardo at the helm, he finally had it. Lombardo would prove an important ally.

At some point during the meeting at the Sherman Hotel, Lombardo and Weiss split from the group to speak privately.

Lombardo told Weiss that Capone sincerely wanted peace. He was prepared to leave the North Siders alone as long as they left him alone.

Weiss said he would agree to a truce, but only after he killed the two men who had shot at him and Drucci on Michigan Avenue. Of all the attacks, that was the one that burned him up most, even though no one but an innocent bystander had been hurt. He asked if Capone would offer the men as a sacrifice, as a gesture of his commitment to their new arrangement.

Lombardo said Capone would never go for it.

With that, the meeting ended.

Weiss didn't usually try diplomacy. If he wanted someone dead, he had him killed. This time, though, he needed Capone's help because he hadn't recognized the men who'd shot at him on Michigan Avenue. Capone was learning to delegate in his new position as chairman of the board. If indeed he had ordered the hits on Drucci and Weiss, he had probably told Frank Nitti to take care of it, and Nitti had probably subcontracted the job to guys whom Drucci and Weiss wouldn't know.

Ever since Capone's return from his summer-long exile in Michigan, Nitti, "The Enforcer," had emerged as one of the two most important men in the outfit, along with Jack "Greasy Thumb" Guzik.

The men had distinct roles.

Guzik was the chief financial officer, crunching numbers, handing out the cash, and helping set the organization's long-term business strategy. He was fifty years old: a short, fat, soft-voiced, middle-aged, double-chinned Jew who looked about as threatening as a bagel and cream cheese. He and his brother Harry had begun their criminal careers as pimps with a brothel called the Blue Goose, on the far South Side, at 119th Street and Marshfield Avenue. By signing up with Torrio and Capone, he seemed to appreciate that he was able to work one step removed from the filth of the bordello. Most of the time, Guzik sat at the St. Hubert English Chop House, on the top floor of the Majestic Hotel in the city's Loop. There, he would take in money from bagmen and hand it out to cops, precinct captains, and politicians. That's where the "Greasy Thumb" came in.

"You buy a judge by weight," Guzik once said, philosophically, "like iron in a junkyard. A justice of the peace or a magistrate can be had for a five-dollar bill. In the municipal court he will cost you ten." A calm, soothing presence, a Jew who never lost his faith in God, Guzik was gangland's rabbi. He never carried a gun, and Capone trusted him completely. Guzik, no doubt grateful to Capone for coming to his defense after the beating at the hands of Joe Howard, would remain loyal for the rest of his life.

Nitti was, as his nickname made clear, "The Enforcer." Like Guzik, he was older than Capone, at forty. Nitti was born Francesco Nitto in the Italian village of Angri, the same place where Capone's mother and father had been born and raised. Gabriele Capone came to the United

States the same year as the Nittos—1893—and the families settled on the same block in Brooklyn. A former barber, fence, and whiskey smuggler, Nitti had established himself by this time as a versatile member of the outfit. With his ink-black hair and dainty mustache, he had style, and he imagined himself a minor celebrity. Perhaps taking after the boss, he cultivated relationships with the press. He was personable and well liked among his associates. And even though he was often responsible for taking care of the organization's dirty work, he almost never got his own hands dirty. If Capone delegated to Nitti, Nitti delegated to one of his own trustworthy men.

Nitti may have had aspirations to rule the outfit himself, but if he did, he was patient. He, too, remained fiercely loyal to Capone. He and Guzik were pivotal to the organization's growing success.

———

As 1926 neared its end, Hirohito became emperor of Japan, Henry Ford introduced the five-day, forty-hour workweek, Kodak started selling 16 mm film stock, A. A. Milne's *Winnie the Pooh* and Adolf Hitler's *Mein Kampf* were published, and Harry Houdini died from a ruptured appendix. Celebrities were delighting the American populace. Prewar heroes such as Jane Addams—feminist, crusader for workers' rights, and pioneer social worker—were perceived now as fussy old grumps.

"If I am convinced by anything," wrote H. L. Mencken, "it is that Doing Good is in bad taste." Which meant Doing Bad was more fun than ever. The new generation's heroes were edgier than their predecessors. They were risk-takers, such as Charles A. Lindbergh, who was preparing to attempt the first nonstop flight from New York to Paris. They were individualists, such as Ernest Hemingway, who, having moved to Paris, published his first novel, *The Sun Also Rises*. They were overindulged, overfed, and oversexed, like Babe Ruth.

Hedonism ruled. Savings accounts were plundered and lines of credit drawn. "The future," declared Gertrude Stein, "is not important anymore." Sunday drives replaced Sunday church for many families. Victorian dance forms melted in the flame of Louis Armstrong's blowtorch trumpet. Women smoked and drank, bobbed their hair, shortened their skirts, danced promiscuously, and spoke openly of their sexual desires. It was the age of emotion, the age of pleasure, the age of jazz.

A revolution was under way, and it was Capone's great fortune, like so many pioneers of American enterprise, to be in the right business at the right time.

He held a position of responsibility now. Hundreds if not thousands of men and women depended on him for some, if not all, of their income. It wasn't that Capone served as everyone's boss. He was more like the senior partner at a law firm, albeit a very loosely run one. Capone exerted influence and lent his expertise to a vast number of smaller operations, most of them built on bootlegging, gambling, and prostitution. Not even the most brilliant business executive could have hoped to oversee every detail of such a casually constructed organization. Capone was a hustler and a negotiator, a risk-taker, and he liked the give-and-take of doing business with other hustlers and negotiators. Those skills—plus his willingness to use violence when necessary—made him a leader among crooks. His rise to power also was helped by good luck. As others were shot, arrested, or forced to go into hiding, Capone's power grew. Now that Polack Joe Soltis was on the lam, trying to avoid arrest for the hit on John Foley, only two gangs with broad power remained: the West Side outfit led by Capone, and the North Side operation of Weiss, Moran, and Drucci.

Capone seemed content for the moment. The responsibility of running the organization may have sobered him, or else the sudden splash of wealth had given him pause. Either way, things had changed, and, like all good businessmen, he'd adapted. He thought a great deal about his image now. He complained to the press at times that the gangsters would be better off if they cooperated. The gunplay was wrecking his family life, he said. Ever since moving to the Hawthorne, he saw his wife and son no more than four or five times a week. When newspapers referred to him as "Scarface," he would gripe to the reporters. When that got him nowhere, he went to their editors, phoning in advance to make an appointment, then meeting them and asking them to consider his feelings and please refrain from using the offensive moniker again. Some kindly editors would honor his request. Once in a while they would even order their photographers to airbrush the scars from Capone's pictures. But usually they ignored his pleas.

Among gangsters, anyway, everyone knew better than to call him Scarface. They called him Al, or Boss, or Snorky, which meant elegant or ritzy. But most of the time he was just plain Al.

Seven years into Prohibition, the bootlegging business was maturing. Even if the men running it remained mostly young and impulsive, there were important strategic decisions to be made and tremendous fortunes at stake. The more entrenched the bootleggers became, the more money they had to pay in bribes to keep operations moving smoothly, and the more violence they had to employ to keep the upstarts under control. Distribution was complicated. Speakeasies were everywhere and always on the move. The booze flowed to private homes, corporate offices, saloons, gambling halls, brothels, and legitimate nightclubs. Also, beer was heavy, and barrels were big. Smuggling the stuff was risky, no matter how well the cops had been greased. Running such an operation required more than cockiness and swagger and Tommy guns. It required finesse, diplomacy, and savvy.

"I tell them I want peace," Capone said in the autumn of 1926, "because I don't want to break the hearts of the people that love me—and maybe I can make them think of their mothers and sisters. And if they think of them, they'll put up their guns and treat their business like any other man treats his, as something to work and forget when he goes home at night."

Q IS FOR QUINCY

George Johnson never set out to be a hero.

Certainly, he seemed ill suited for the role.

Johnson was nineteen years old when he left his small hometown in Lanyon, Iowa, and came to Chicago. It was 1893, and he arrived as a tourist to take in the World's Columbian Exposition, popularly known as the Chicago World's Fair, commemorating the four-hundredth anniversary of Columbus's voyage to the New World. But it wasn't the dazzling variety of carnival novelties—such as George Ferris's 264-foot bicycle wheel in the sky, or the gyrating hips of Fahreda Mahzar, a.k.a. Little Egypt, the Bewitching Bellyrina—that enticed this young man. Johnson was too painfully earnest and intensely cerebral, even as a teenager, to allow whimsical or titillating sights to carry his emotions away. He wandered the fair to learn about the latest advances in art, science, technology, commerce, and industry. He listened to Thomas Edison's raspy phonograph, peeked admiringly into George Pullman's luxurious sleeper cars, and gawked at the new linotype machines that were speeding the production of newspapers. These were the fair's wonders—not the come-ons from the pretty girls or the tricks of the con artists on the Midway—that hooked sober and ambitious young men such as George Johnson.

He stayed two weeks. When he got back to his family's farm in Lanyon, Johnson did two things. First, he gave himself a middle name, something that would distinguish him from all the other George Johnsons. He could have picked Edison, Pullman, or Ford, but he didn't. He had ambition, but he remained a conservative at heart. So he settled on Emerson, honoring the nineteenth-century New England writer Ralph Waldo Emerson.

The next thing George Emerson Johnson did was somewhat bolder: He made up his mind to get back to Chicago as fast as he could.

Johnson had a few things in common with Alphonse Capone. Each man came from immigrant parents, each from large families, and each had dropped out of school in his early teens to go to work. But the similarities pretty much ended there. Johnson, tall and reedy, resembled a celery stalk. His curly head of light brown hair was neatly parted in the middle. He had thin lips, long eyelashes, milk-white skin, and a gentle voice. He was, as the writer Damon Runyon once put it, "a forensic looking man."

Johnson's Swedish-born parents—John and Mathilda Johnson—moved to Lanyon before it was even a town, simply because they'd heard other Swedes were trying to settle the place, which was in Webster County, seventeen miles south of Fort Dodge. They bought two hundred acres. Mathilda gave birth to nine children, all without the help of a doctor. George and his siblings were obedient, churchgoing children who lived by what God gave them: the seasons, the sunrises, and the Bible. The family squeezed into a tiny wood-frame house, with a narrow flight of stairs as steep as a ladder going from the first floor to the second. The furniture was wooden and sturdy. The clothes were handmade by Mathilda, who sheared the sheep and washed and spun the wool herself. The food was simple but always adequate: milk, cream, potatoes, bread, butter, lutefisk, beef, chicken, pork, eggs, sorghum, vegetables, and fruit. The children rode drafty, horse-drawn buses to school, with canvas curtains on the side to protect them from foul weather. When the snow got deep, they were pulled on bobsleds.

George was seven years old when his parents put him to work in the garden. When he was older, he would be expected to plow and till much more of the farm's acreage, which the family counted on for survival. But the lesson that he remembered most vividly from his childhood was the one learned in the small garden, at the knee of his hardworking father. "I was taught that I could not clean the garden by a method of selection," he recalled. "I was taught that I must not say, 'I will take that weed out and leave this weed in,' but that the only way to clean the garden was to pull up all the weeds by the roots and shake them out to the sun."

From ages thirteen to twenty, Johnson worked: harnessing, driving, seeding, milking, picking, husking, hauling, and shoveling. When the corn was ready for harvest, he would pick thirty bushels before noon, break for lunch, then pick thirty more before sundown. At night, he read by the light of homemade candles, committing to memory long portions of *Pilgrim's Progress, Paradise Lost,* and *The Decline and Fall of the Roman Empire.* Some middle children learned that rebellion brought them attention. Not Johnson: He was bookish, a thinker. He made no noise. He showed no trace of charisma. He was content to go about his work, remaining true to his stolid way, and hope for the best.

But the Johnson children were not encouraged to stay on the farm. For one thing, there was no room in their little house once the children started turning into young men and women. But that wasn't his only motivation to move on. George Johnson's parents were among the founders of their little Swedish town in Iowa. They were civic-minded. They wanted their children to be active participants in the community, to do something with their lives, to make at least some small piece of the world a little better. Being good and being enterprising were not mutually exclusive by this family's standards.

Inspired by his visit to the exposition, Johnson decided to go back to school, enrolling at Tobin College in Fort Dodge, Iowa. Soon this shy young man discovered that he liked public speaking, although he was not quite a natural. He had to work to overcome his deficiencies: He spoke slowly, without verve, without a passionate edge to his voice. William S. Kenyon, a Fort Dodge lawyer who would go on to serve Iowa in the U.S. Senate, saw Johnson compete in a speech contest at Tobin in 1895 and recalled that the young man "looked like a poet . . . and looked scared as he faced his audience." Still, Kenyon and the other judges voted that day to give Johnson the gold medal. Either the competition was worse or Johnson's earnest and subtle powers of persuasion carried him through.

Upon graduation from Tobin College in 1897, Johnson moved to Chicago and studied law at Lake Forest College.

Just after the turn of the century, the city once again inspired Johnson to add to his name. A poetic middle name might have been enough to separate him from the rest of the Swedes in Lanyon, Iowa, but the Chicago phone book had too many George E. Johnsons. He wanted to stand apart from the rest. Once again, he made a conservative, old-fashioned-sounding choice, becoming George Emerson Quincy Johnson. He introduced himself and signed his name as George E. Q. Johnson. He rented a desk in a shared office at 69 West Washington, paying $5 a month, and handled civil cases, bankruptcies, and estate settlements. He advertised himself as a Svensk Advokat, or Swedish lawyer, in the *Luther-Banaret,* a local newspaper serving Chicago's Swedes. If he ever took on a criminal case, it was not the sort to generate headlines.

He lived quietly. He spent nights at the marble-coated Newberry Library, north of downtown, where he studied the lives of Abraham Lincoln, George Washington, and King Gustavus Adolphus of Sweden, using his research to prepare a series of talks to legal associations, churches, and lodges such as the Knights of Pythias. In 1900 he worked on the Republican campaign to reelect President William McKinley and met some of the state's leading politicians.

Perhaps to overcome his awkward public speaking skills or perhaps because he loved the stage even if he was less than comfortable upon it, Johnson auditioned for roles in the local theater. Somehow he won the lead role in a locally produced drama, met a young Shakespearean actress, and fell in love. Her name was Elizabeth Marie Swanstrom. She was a fellow Swede, and she was fair, slender, and graceful. She wasn't famous anywhere but in the Swedish community, where everyone knew her theater work. Her solemn gaze stared out from posters that advertised her dramatic readings. "An Evening of Pathos and Humor" read one of the signs. At first they might seem like an odd couple, this delicate, beautiful woman and this man with all the spark of a bowl of oatmeal. But they had much in common. Both were small-towners in the big city, both children of Swedish immigrants, both fluent in their parents' native tongue, both active in the church and in Swedish social circles. And George E. Q. Johnson made up for his modesty with a soft-spoken passion that became apparent only to those who took the time to get to know him well. They married in 1906 and honeymooned in Colorado and Yellowstone National Park. Like Al Capone, George E. Q. Johnson came from a huge family and yet wound up having only one child himself, a son. They named him George E. Q. Johnson Jr., but they called him Gene.

In 1914, Johnson ran for judge in the municipal court but lost. In 1922, he was appointed a master in chancery, the same dreary job that Herman Melville gave to his fictional character Bartleby, a man who preferred not to engage with the world around him. As a master in chancery, Johnson processed paperwork that judges didn't have time to handle. He had his law practice, his church work, his choir practice, his neighborhood political work, his speeches before the Swedish National Association, and his behind-the-scenes support for his wife's community theater productions. If he yearned for more prestige, more action, more responsibility, he didn't say so publicly.

Then, on Christmas Day 1926, Johnson's name appeared on a short list of candidates to replace Chicago's U.S. attorney, Edwin A. Olson. It was one of the toughest jobs in the city—and, given Chicago's corruption and high crime rates, one of the toughest law enforcement jobs in the country. As the chief federal law enforcement officer in northern Illinois, the U.S. attorney served as the link between Chicago and Washington, D.C. It was a position appointed by none other than the president of the United States, Calvin Coolidge. The two other candidates were a clout-heavy judge and the assistant U.S. attorney who had handled the pending indictment of Capone and his Cicero cronies.

Johnson's name sent the city's reporters scrambling. Where did this guy come from? Who did he know? Was he corrupt? Corruptible? And what the hell did the "Q" stand for?

Somewhere in his low-key social networking, Johnson had met and made a strong impression on U.S. senator Charles S. Deneen. It was Deneen, a Republican and one of the most honest politicians in the state, who recommended Johnson to the Department of Justice. Maybe Deneen wanted a fellow Republican with no connections to the city's corrupt public officials. Maybe he wanted someone who would stand up to Robert Crowe, the state's attorney, a publicity hound who loved to strike dramatic poses for the photographers and who had tried and failed so many times to stop Chicago's gangsters. Maybe it was enough, in the cesspool of corruption that was Chicago, that Johnson had practiced law for thirty years without attracting any attention or committing any crimes.

"I come of Swedish farmer stock," Johnson once said, "and my bringing up made the thought of taking money when in office abhorrent. . . . It merely had no attraction for me."

While unexciting, Johnson was no milksop. He impressed those he met as fiercely principled. He may have looked like a poet, especially now, in middle age, as his curly hair turned gray and he allowed the locks to hang a little lower around his gaunt face. But he was a fighter, too. Finding a man of such high morals in Chicago was a bit like finding a mature chestnut tree growing from the urban asphalt. The wonder wasn't really that it had grown but that no one had ever cut it down.

While the newsmen searched unsuccessfully for dirt, the U.S. attorney general, John G. Sargent, sent letters from his office in Washington, D.C., asking a few of Chicago's most prominent lawyers and businessmen if they thought Johnson would be a good appointment. The attorney general's cousin, Fred W. Sargent, president of the North Western railroad company, responded with a Western Union telegram that read, "PARTY MENTIONED EXCELLENT QUALIFICATIONS FINE CHARACTER AND STANDS VERY HIGH HERE AMONG MEMBERS OF THE CHICAGO BAR." The telegrams poured in, with one glowing review after another from Chicago's leading businessmen and legal minds. A few weeks later, President Coolidge appointed Johnson to the job.

When a reporter phoned Johnson to get his reaction, the only thing he managed to say was, "It's all a surprise to me."

Upon taking office, Johnson delivered a speech remarkable for both its brevity and its modesty: "I come to this office with an open mind and with no policy to announce," he said. And that was *all* he said. If he had a plan for going after Capone, he wasn't telling anyone about it. Later, he would say that he preferred to let his indictments and convictions do the talking. If some aldermen, police captains, and other hacks tried to reach out to him and let him know that his modest $15,000-a-year salary could be supplemented with under-the-table cash, Johnson was having none of it.

He began keeping a scrapbook filled with stories about the Chicago underworld and recognized that the city's newspaper reporters were the best source—far better than the police—for the real dope on the gangs. As Johnson began to comprehend the complexity of the bootlegging business, he gained respect for Capone's skill, telling his son several times that he thought Capone could have been a success in a number of legitimate fields if he'd chosen to go straight. Johnson wasn't angry about it. He wasn't consumed, just saddened that a decent mind had gone to waste. He pursued the gangster not out of obsession but because it was his job.

Capone and seventy-eight others were already under indictment for bootlegging violations, part of the investigation launched by Johnson's immediate predecessor, Edwin A. Olson. It was up to Johnson now to bring them to trial. But two prominent federal judges were already criticizing the indictments, saying they were too broad. In pursuing so many

small-time hoods, the judges said, court dockets would get congested and
no one would ever go to jail. Already, Chicago's courts were hopelessly
backlogged. The judges urged Johnson to drop the indictments and start
over, focusing exclusively on the kingpins.

At first the new U.S. attorney had no comment. He said he needed
time. Then, after a few weeks, he concluded that he had neither the fund-
ing nor the manpower to pursue the investigation of Capone and his
men that had been launched by Olson. He decided to wait. And while he
waited, his potential witnesses—the low-level grunts of the booze business
who might be leaned on to testify against Capone—kept turning up dead.

SORRY ABOUT THAT, HYMIE

Hymie Weiss kept an office at 738 North State, above Schofield's flower shop, where Dean O'Banion had been assassinated. From his desk, Weiss could follow the cars zigzagging along State Street, watch the flower shop's customers coming and going, smell the heady perfume of roses and lilacs, and see the priests and parishioners filing into and out of Holy Name Cathedral, directly across the street.

Next door to Weiss's office, at 740 North State, was a boardinghouse run by Anna Rotariu. The place was no longer fashionable, but it was still a few years and a few dozen boarders away from decrepit.

In the first week of October, as the leaves turned to ocher and the days grew noticeably shorter, a young man named Oscar Lundin visited Mrs. Rotariu and requested a room with a window facing State Street. Told that none was available, Lundin offered to pay $20 a week instead of the usual $8. A room opened up. Lundin settled in. By day, sunlight slanted through curtained windows, revealing the room's considerable shoddiness: its tarnished brass bed, its cheap oak dresser, its chipped dishes, its threadbare rug. But Lundin, concerned only with vantage point, liked the room just fine. He informed the landlady that he worked odd hours and wished never to be disturbed. He also said his friends might be dropping by from time to time, and they, too, should be left alone. Mrs. Rotariu knew better than to ask questions.

That same day, a beautiful blond-haired woman who gave her name as Mrs. Theodore Schultz rented a third-floor room in a boardinghouse across the street. After securing the room, her job was done, and she never returned. With the two rooms—the one on State and the other on

Superior—it was possible to maintain a perfect surveillance of Schofield's flower shop.

Meanwhile, downtown, preparation was under way for the trial of Joe Soltis and his associate Frank Koncil, the gangsters accused of killing John Foley in daylight and before several eyewitnesses. It was shaping up to be a doozy.

Attorneys for the government said they had an unbeatable case, with at least three upstanding Chicago citizens set to testify that they saw Soltis and Koncil commit the crime. Yet Soltis and Koncil were hardly ready to plead guilty. A few weeks before the trial, several members of their gang robbed a mail train in Evergreen Park, escaping with $135,000. Police said the job was pulled so there would be enough cash on hand to pay Soltis's attorneys and to hand out bribes as the need arose. Not more than two weeks after the train robbery, Soltis got his first break: Two of the prosecution's key witnesses disappeared, and the *Tribune* reported that several other witnesses in the case had been approached by Soltis's agents. Prosecutors were forced to ask the court for a postponement.

When jury selection finally began, on October 6, 1926, there were other, bigger headlines in that morning's paper: President Coolidge said he saw no need to campaign for his fellow Republicans in the upcoming elections because the nation's prosperity spoke for itself; the St. Louis Cardinals shut out Babe Ruth and the rest of the New York Yankees in the third game of the 1926 World Series; Benito Mussolini told a huge crowd in Italy that he was "looking for a fight" and wouldn't quit looking until Italy's Fascists dominated all of the Mediterranean.

But in Chicago, the Soltis-Koncil trial was the story everyone talked about. The *Tribune* marveled that a gang leader was actually going to face justice, calling it "something new, something novel, something perhaps marking a new era." During the jury-selection process, Soltis, appearing confident and calm, sat beside his lawyers. He was built like a butcher, with hands big as rump roasts, but he dressed for court like a banker: in a dark gray suit with a blue silk shirt, his massive neck handsomely fettered in a crisp white collar. When the newspaper photographers pointed their big cameras at him, he turned and grinned with the élan of a leading man. Only his mouth—where a wormy mustache slunk over his twitchy lips and crooked, nicotine-stained teeth—hinted at his true character.

The city's top police officials showed up, declaring this the most im-

portant courtroom showdown Chicago had seen in years and predicting
that a pair of convictions and stiff sentences would send the rest of the
city's big bootleggers into permanent retirement. The *Trib* called it a case
"of the utmost importance," and added that the conviction of Soltis would
"do more to destroy the power of gangsters than any other case." Twenty
police officers were assigned to security, guarding not just the courthouse
but also the hotel where jurors would be sequestered.

But finding jurors proved more difficult than usual. Some of the citizens
called for duty seemed hesitant to serve. An unusually large number of
them suddenly developed moral and ethical objections to the death penalty,
which was being mentioned by emboldened prosecutors as a distinct possibility for Soltis and Koncil. Meanwhile, back in the South Side neighborhoods where Soltis controlled much of the beer traffic, bombs exploded
inside two businesses identified with a wink-wink in the press as "soft drink
parlors." Police said the bombs were delivered to punish those business
owners who had refused to contribute to the Soltis defense fund.

"No such thing," said W. W. O'Brien, Soltis's attorney, denying the existence of a defense fund in a newspaper interview. O'Brien was another
great Chicago character. He was a dapper man with a high forehead,
bushy eyebrows, and dark, mournful eyes. In 1911, while working as a
young prosecutor, he had decided to moonlight a bit and used his spare
time to defend a couple of pickpockets, or "dips," as they were sometimes
referred to. It took a certain amount of gall, of course, for a prosecutor
to moonlight as a defense attorney, but O'Brien's next move took even
more: He offered his opposing counsel a bribe to drop the case. He nearly
lost his law license for that one. Soon afterward, perhaps recognizing his
natural proclivities, he left the prosecutor's office and devoted himself full-
time to criminal defense work. In 1921, O'Brien was shot in a saloon and
refused to tell police who did it or why, which proved to be a brilliant
career move. After that, every gangster in Chicago recognized a kindred
spirit who kept his mouth shut around the coppers. O'Brien became the
go-to guy for many of the city's biggest wrongdoers.

The day after the soft drink parlor bombings, someone crept along
a window ledge and into the office of the prosecutors working on the
Soltis case. Several filing cabinets were disturbed. In all likelihood, it was
O'Brien up to his tricks again. But the cops were beginning to suspect that
he had help. None other than Hymie Weiss—the beer king of the North

Side, and Capone's peskiest rival—was seen milling around the courthouse that week and conferring with Soltis and his attorneys. Police speculated that Weiss wanted Soltis free so the two gangsters might combine forces in the war against Capone. Some said that the Capone organization was already doing more than $100 million a year in business, most of it in bootlegging and gambling. That number was wildly inflated. Still, since Capone already had the infrastructure in place—the trucks, the distilleries, the cops, the judges—he was probably eager to gobble up Soltis's turf. Weiss wanted to make sure that Capone continued to face solid competition on at least two fronts, the North and the South sides, in case he had any ideas about extending his reach.

Jury selection was finally completed on a warm, gray day, October 11, 1926, with a strong wind blowing in from across the plains. At about three thirty that afternoon, O'Brien left the courthouse for a meeting north of the river with Hymie Weiss. That morning, O'Brien had put on his trademark red tie, which was said to bring his clients good luck. One of his investigators, a part-time bootlegger named Benjamin "Buddy" Jacobs, gave his boss a lift uptown. They parked on State Street, just south of Holy Name Cathedral, less than half a block from Schofield's flower shop. Arriving at the same time via Cadillac was Weiss; his driver, Sammy Peller (a.k.a. Sam Pine); and one of the North Side gang's supporting players, a bootlegger named Paddy Murray. Weiss wore a three-piece suit with a striped tie. A newsboy cap sat shapelessly atop his head. In his pockets he had $5,300 cash, along with a set of rosary beads and a complete list of the jurors selected in the Soltis case. His shoulder holster held a .45 automatic.

The five men stepped from their cars and began crossing State Street, stepping over the trolley tracks as traffic weaved around them. They all appeared headed toward Schofield's, with its striped awning and its simple neon FLOWERS sign. Halloween pumpkins and floral arrangements in red, yellow, and orange decorated the shop's window.

The men had not quite reached the sidewalk when machine-gun bullets ripped from the second-story window of Mrs. Rotariu's boardinghouse. Bullets pinged everywhere. The screams of terrified pedestrians pierced the air. Shoes scraped the concrete as people dashed for cover. Car engines roared and vehicles slalomed haphazardly as their drivers maneuvered to avoid human bodies slumping heavily to the ground. Clouds of gray black smoke and the smells of gunpowder and spilled blood hung in the air. The machine-gun fire kept coming.

Sammy Peller took a searing bullet in the groin, and Buddy Jacobs had his tendons and hamstrings snapped and frayed by one in the leg. O'Brien took four: the first one in the right arm, then three in the side and stomach, until he lay flat on the sidewalk, eyes and mouth open wide, panting like a racehorse. Somehow, after a few moments, he managed to get up and clamber into a nearby building. Paddy Murray got hit seven or eight times, mostly in the head and torso, and never rose again. But it was Weiss, the apparent target of the attack, who absorbed the greatest damage: a dozen bullets in all. Blackish blood spewed from his mouth, splashing over his face, as if he'd coughed up a bottle of ink. He lay splayed on his back, legs kicked out at unnatural angles from his large frame.

There had been so much gunfire that at first no one knew quite where it had come from. Everyone at the corner of Superior and State seemed to be pulling guns and firing. Bullets pocked the street and sidewalk and obliterated much of the inscription on the cornerstone of Holy Name Cathedral, which had previously read "A.D. 1874—AT THE NAME OF JESUS EVERY KNEE SHOULD BOW—THOSE THAT ARE IN HEAVEN AND THOSE ON EARTH." When it was over, the machine-gunners ran down the back stairs of their boardinghouses. One ditched a piping hot Tommy in the alley. They were neither seen nor heard from again.

A short time later, out in Cicero, reporters found Capone dressed in shirtsleeves and relaxing at the Hawthorne Inn. Police had already declared that they saw no point in arresting the big fellow. Though they suspected that the machine-gunners had been imported and put to work at his behest to eliminate Weiss, they couldn't prove it. Capone expressed surprise that anyone would plug his old friend. "I'm sorry Weiss was killed," he said, "but I didn't have anything to do with it. I telephoned the detective bureau I'd come in if they wanted me and they told me they didn't want me. I knew I'd be blamed for it."

Two days later, Capone sat for a more extensive interview with a newspaperman from the *Evening American.* Yet again he tried to portray himself as a peace-seeking man of reason. "I don't want to die," he said. "Especially I don't want to die in the street, punctured with machine-gun bullets. That's the reason I've asked for peace." The newsman who visited

Capone at the Hawthorne described him as a sentimental figure. "I've got a boy," Capone said. "I love that kid."

Others who interviewed Capone over the years, from newspapermen to psychologists and psychiatrists, found the same: a personable man, a man who seemed genuinely concerned for and fairly involved with his family, a man who seemed to have successfully differentiated his working life and his emotional life. Either he was a good actor or else he really did have a human side.

In this interview, at least, he scored a public-relations coup. He admitted he was in the beer business, admitted that Johnny Torrio gave him his start in the racket, admitted that the trouble began when rival gang members started feeling "chesty," admitted that he and Torrio knew precisely who had fired the shots into Torrio's face, admitted that he was angry about the drive-by assault on his hotel, and admitted that he tried to tell his old pal Weiss that "there was business enough for all of us without killing."

But alas, said Capone, Hymie didn't listen.

It might have sounded like an admission of guilt from Capone. At the very least, it served to remind everyone that Capone had a motive.

Now with Weiss lying in the morgue, his face contorted in a ghoulish grin, and with the newspapers tallying sixty gang killings so far for 1926, Capone yet again called for calm. He must have known that the violence would not stop simply because Weiss had been eliminated. But it was not yet clear which, if any, of the surviving North Side men would emerge as his next serious contender. Reporters were guessing it would be Bugs Moran, who was bolder than Weiss but neither as smart nor as smooth. Others were betting on Schemer Drucci, even though Drucci was nobody's idea of a genius. Drucci did his best thinking with a gun. In any case, one thing was clear: As his rivals fell one by one, Capone kept rising, his empire expanding, his fame spreading.

———

A few days after the hit on Weiss, Drucci and a couple of his men were taking in a football game at Wrigley Field, which had changed its name from Cubs Park earlier that year. It was two Chicago teams, Bears versus Cardinals. Drucci and his colleagues had terrific seats, as befitting men who carried pistols. At one point, when they stood to celebrate a score by

the Bears' superstar quarterback, Paddy Driscoll, police moved in and collared them. They were taken downtown, where they were charged with
possession of weapons and questioned about the ambush of Weiss. Drucci,
of course, said he knew nothing about it. In fact, he said he knew nothing
of the bootlegging business. "I'm a real estate man," he said, straight-faced,
"with offices in the First National Bank Building. You can come and see
me anytime." He was promptly released.

Soon after, Capone, Drucci, and Moran agreed to hold another peace
summit. This time Capone appeared in person—without a bodyguard.
When it was over, Capone announced that he would confine his business to Cicero, the nearby town of Stickney, and Chicago's West Side.
Drucci and Moran agreed to stick to the North Side of Chicago. The
South Side would be divided between Ralph Sheldon, a Capone man, and
Joe Soltis. Each gang would bear responsibility for manufacturing, importing, and distributing its own products. Small bands of bootleggers would
be allowed to operate within the larger territories as long as they didn't
push their luck. And if one gang received an order to cater a wedding
or banquet in another's territory, it would decline the order and make a
referral to the appropriate organization. Any conflicts would be settled by
a board of semi-independent arbiters. Malicious gossip passed from one
gang to another by meddlesome cops would be disregarded. And leaders
of the gangs would be held personally responsible for any violations of the
pact. With the announcement, Capone checked out of the Hawthorne Inn
and repaired to the family home on South Prairie. He declared the dawn
of a new era.

"Gangland killings have come to an end in Chicago," he proudly announced in another long interview, this time with the *Herald and Examiner*.
"A treaty of peace between our fellows and the North Side combination
was signed at midnight in a Loop hotel. Now, for the first time in two
years, I will sleep without a gun under my pillow. I believe it's peace to
stay. I know I won't break it and I don't think they will. I feel like a kid
I'm so happy."

Capone said the first thing he did was call his wife and tell her the
news. Perhaps he'd been henpecked recently for not spending much time
at home or for not paying enough attention to his son. He didn't say, but
did comment that he planned to head straight home now that it was safe
to do so—right after he joined his pals for a couple of celebratory beers.

"I didn't want to die," he continued. "I told them I didn't want them to die, either. . . . I had sent that word to them many times before Hymie died. They thought I was kidding. But when they saw in the *Herald and Examiner* that I said the same thing for publication, they sent word to me that they wanted to talk things over. That was Monday night. . . . I went there alone—they were three to one, but I figured they were on the square. So I went in . . . and finally we were all talking at once and smiling and remembering the old days when we were all in one mob and happy. And after two hours we all shook hands and made up. And when I came home I rode alone. That's something I haven't done in two years. When I used to go out in my car it looked like a funeral. It had to look like that so it wouldn't be one. But tonight I rode alone, and I was like a guy all of a sudden let out of prison. I don't want to talk foolish, but the air was different. I wasn't thinking that any minute I'd get a machine gun in my face, and it felt great.

"I'm going home to my wife and kid happier than I've been for a long time. It isn't only that I'm glad I'm safe. Now I can look at my family and not think that any day they may be called on the phone and told I've been shot. It's a great feeling and I guess the other fellows have it, too. They were grinning like kids when we shook hands and separated. Our fight was never over business. It was all bad feeling between one man and another. . . . And now we're going to forget all these old grudges and start over. I haven't any business on the North Side and they haven't any in Cicero. They'll stay in their backyard and I'll stay in mine. If anything ever should come up that makes us mad, we're going to call each other on the phone and make a date to talk it over. That's our bargain and I'm going to stick to it."

A SMILE AND A GUN

Capone and his men were just beginning to give Chicagoans evidence of the strange double standards that would define the glory years of gangstering: As the organization grew bigger and more established, their crimes became more blatant. But the criminality became so widely accepted that it was glamorized at times. Corruption and violence were rampant, and the men behind it became heroes. They were cold-blooded and greedy, but in their willingness to boldly break rules that others broke only on the sly, they earned the public's fascination.

"We're big business without high hats," the late Dean O'Banion once said, which summed up nicely why such men would gain admiration. But Capone offered the quotation that best reflected the essence of the gangster life, saying, "You can get a lot farther with a smile and a gun than you can get with just a smile."

It's not clear when he made the remark or even *if* he made it. It could have been invented by an enterprising journalist. Still, it captures Capone's career to this point. He had ambition, he had flair, he had a rebellious streak wider than the American continent. And he had a gun.

The gangsters were entrepreneurial, rebellious, and competitive—solid American traits. If they tended to go too far at times, that only added to their mystique. The social worker Jane Addams worried that teenagers were "tremendously aroused by the bootleg and hijacking situation." When Capone's bulletproof car was spotted in Chicago, " 'There goes Al,' would fly from lip to lip," wrote Fred Pasley in his 1930 biography of Capone, and pedestrians would crowd the sidewalk, "craning necks as eagerly as for a circus parade."

In the early months of 1927, the sound of machine guns all but disappeared from the city. The peace treaty was holding. The effect on the culture was subtle enough, at least for a little while, that no one noticed. It was as if the winds off the lake had gone from a howl to a whisper.

Capone was so firmly convinced of the treaty's sanctity that he deemed it safe to transfer his headquarters permanently from Cicero to Chicago, taking a suite at the Metropole Hotel. The Metropole was not to be confused with the stately Sherman or the glamorous Palmer House. The Metropole was seven stories tall, standing plainly at the corner of South Michigan Avenue and Twenty-third Street, in the heart of Automobile Row. A huge American flag fluttered from the hotel's roof. The hotel's nicest touch—which wasn't saying all that much—was a first-floor sundeck where guests could sit in rocking chairs and look at the side of a church.

The Metropole tended to attract traveling shoe salesmen and farmers making the infrequent drive to the big city to trade their old vehicles for new ones. It hosted Kiwanis Club meetings. It was the sort of place where retired men in casual clothes could sit in the lobby chewing toothpicks and talking about the White Sox's latest failures. For Capone, it was conveniently close to his house on South Prairie Avenue and central to most of his business interests.

One day, a reporter dropped by the Metropole to see if he could get his questions answered. Capone obliged. The reporter stated that the new chief of the Illinois Highway Police, Michael "Go Get 'Em" Hughes, had been bragging to reporters about how he had driven Capone out of Cicero. Capone got a laugh out of that. "Nobody drove me out of Cicero," he said, "least of all Mike Hughes. . . . Does he think he throws that long a shadow before him? I have merely transferred my headquarters. I found that my business took in a bigger area than it used to, and I needed a central headquarters. That's why I moved to this hotel, which, as you can see for yourself, is well within the boundaries of Cook County. Can you blame for me for getting mad at these guys using me for glory? Why, I never met Hughes, and I never even had a telephone call from him." The reporter asked him to respond to rumors that police pressure could soon force Capone to quit and flee for Europe. "I'm not leaving Chicago," he said. "I'm a businessman and I've got plenty to keep me here. I'm staying in Chicago—that is, unless Mr. Hughes decides to chase me out like he chased me out of Cicero."

Capone seemed to be enjoying his return to Chicago and the calm that accompanied it. On one mild afternoon in January 1927, a reporter knocked at the door of Capone's house on South Prairie Avenue and found the gangster dressed in nothing but a pink apron, silken-wool underwear, and a pair of bedroom slippers. He held a pan of spaghetti in one hand. The fact that he appeared to be mortal—He cooks! He eats!—was enough to make headlines.

If Capone adjusted easily to the lull in violence, some of the city's cops did not. John Stege, the chief of detectives, found himself uncomfortably out of the headlines. Stege was an honest man, pudgy and harmless-looking. His eyes were framed by thick, round glasses. But even honest men have egos. When the gangsters were clashing, Stege always knew that he could summon the press to his office, wave around a seized machine gun or shotgun, and get his picture in the next day's papers, thus reminding the good citizens of Chicago that he was on the job. That he seldom made an arrest mattered little. Chicagoans wanted to read about the *crimes,* not the arrests. So while Stege might have used his free time in the early days of 1927 to gather evidence against bootleggers and gamblers, he chose a different tactic: He took up freelance journalism—while keeping his job with the police department. The newspapers got crime stories, Stege was once more covered in ink, and Capone could sit back and watch his legend grow.

"More than fifty murderers are roaming the streets of Chicago," wrote Stege in the first of his ten articles for the *Herald and Examiner,* accompanied by a photograph of himself cradling a Tommy gun. Stege opened with a challenge to Chicagoans, urging them not to become complacent, not to make the excuse that most of the city's homicides were tolerable because they were gangster-on-gangster crimes. If anything, he said, the citizenry should be more enraged by these crimes:

"[T]he killer of yesteryear was one who slew first of all in the heat of passion or under desperate stress of personal risk. And in either case the hand of every decent man was turned against him. Consider our present-day murderers. Are they affected by conscience? It is to laugh! Instead of seeking concealment they flaunt their badness, boast of their bloody conquests, jeer at the widows of their victims, scoff at the suggestion of retributive justice." He went on to complain that these rich, selfish, and ignorant criminals had attained "czar-like power," allowing them to buy or shoot their way out of almost any mess.

Then he offered a stunning admission: "Is it strange that we of the police department, who honestly are actuated by a sense of duty, prefer to kill the killers rather than to subject them to a mockery of jury trial?" He bragged of the number of gangsters killed by cops: "In 1924 we killed thirty-six," he said. "In 1925, the number killed was sixty-one, and last year we shot fifty-two to death."

Even in this period of tranquillity, engendered by Capone's peace conference with the North Siders, there was still an occasional gangland killing. Hillary "Hittie" Clements, a beer seller, was beaten, shot three times in the head, and dumped beside a deserted cottage on West Sixtieth Street, where his corpse turned to blood-caked ice. Joe Soltis was a prime suspect, but even Capone came out in defense of his rival. "Clements' death won't affect our peace treaty with the North Side crowd in any way," he said. "Clements was not a member of our crowd. . . . He was not killed in any outbreak of hostilities at all. A fellow like him might have a lot of enemies in a lot of places. And I don't believe he was killed by Soltis or any other fellow that is in our peace treaty."

For now, Capone could afford to protect rivals such as Soltis. Business was booming and, just as he had promised, there was money enough to go around. The Capone outfit began to take on an increasing air of professionalism. The big fellow expected the men who worked for him to conform to certain standards. For one thing, he wanted them to dress well. The typical uniform included a pearl gray felt hat with a black band, a dark, double-breasted suit, white shirt, striped tie, and spats. Fred Pasley, Capone's first biographer, wrote in 1930, "The picture of a furtive, sallow-faced creature with cap with pulled-down visor and cigarette drooping from listless lip, gives way to that of an upstanding, square-shouldered fellow, in his teens or twenties, keen-eyed, ruddy-cheeked; a smart dresser, with a flair for diamonds and blondes; always occupying choice seats at prize fights, wrestling matches, football and baseball games, the racetrack, and the theatre; knowing the night-club head waiters and receiving their deferential ministrations."

At the Metropole, Capone set up a gymnasium with punching bags, horizontal bars, trapezes, rowing machines, and more, and expected his employees to use the equipment. It was yet another example of Capone's progressive thinking. He understood that employees who took the time to fortify their bodies and mind would be more efficient killers.

THE GRINDER

While Capone was getting comfortable in his new digs at the Metropole and enjoying the most peaceful period in his still-young career, George Johnson, the man appointed by President Coolidge to destroy Chicago's gangs and bring an end to bootlegging, continued to do just what he'd promised. Nothing.

On April 10, 1927, the *Tribune* reported:

> No important criminal cases in the federal court will be called for trial until next fall, according to an announcement made yesterday by United States District Attorney George E. Q. Johnson.
>
> Shortage of funds and vacations will prevent trial of this class of cases unless an emergency arises, Mr. Johnson said.

It wasn't that Johnson didn't care. In fact, he'd developed a complete abhorrence for the men referred to in the newspapers as "crime kings," "beer barons," and "leaders in the alky aristocracy." The thought of them made him physically sick at times, he said, and when he spoke of them his face sometimes puckered as if a gust from the stockyards had blown his way. Johnson feared that gullible Chicagoans, and particularly new immigrants, had been duped into believing that these men were "brilliant emblems of success" and that their career paths ought to be emulated. "The cause is slack thinking" on the part of the entire public, he said. "Politically, socially, and economically, we have been groping. Slack thinking on the part of citizens leads to slack conduct on the part of officials." And

Chicago was so rife with slack thinking, he continued, that it had earned a reputation as a wide-open town where the law was a joke, where politicians and gangsters worked from the same agenda, where morals and ethics had lost all meaning.

Still, for the time being, Johnson did nothing. Maybe he thought that if he waited long enough the violence would resume and the gangsters would eliminate themselves. Perhaps, though, he was simply taking his time to learn which attorneys in his office were trustworthy, which cases on the court's bloated docket were worth pursuing, and which charges were most likely to stick. "Yes, George E. Q. is slower than the Second Coming," U.S. senator Charles Deneen once said, "but he grinds and grinds and grinds all the time." Johnson's immediate predecessor had indicted every whiskey-breathed outlaw in sight during his final months in office. But with an annual budget of just $90,000 (equivalent to about $1 million), Johnson couldn't try them all, and he seemed less than eager to clog the courts with cases he hadn't developed himself and wasn't certain he could win.

The most pressing case on his desk was not the one involving Capone. The U.S. attorney's first concern was Chicago Heights, an industrial suburb twenty-three miles south of downtown Chicago and six miles from the Indiana border. Johnson's preoccupation with Chicago Heights would prove fortunate for Capone. Johnson had no idea when he began his investigation what a mess he'd find in the Heights. And while he no doubt had entered the investigation hoping it would lead him toward Capone, he would wind up with almost nothing to show for his efforts.

The founders of Chicago Heights designed their town in the hopes of attracting big industry, knowing that workers would follow. Inland Steel built a plant, and the famous architect Louis Sullivan constructed an impressive hotel, the Victoria. Within a couple of decades the place was packed with immigrants in search of jobs, the largest contingent of them Italian. With the onset of Prohibition, three major gang factions developed. As usual, businessmen with transferable skills rushed to take advantage of the whopping profits. The Costellos—Sam, Nick, and Tony— had a confection business. That meant they already had warehouses, trucks, drivers, and strong connections to the area's soda shops and drugstores. They transformed easily into a booze-dealing outfit. Another gang formed around a former alderman named Antonino "Tony" Sanfilippo, pool room operator Joe Martino, and nightclub operators Phil Piazza and Jim Lamberta. Theirs was the more established outfit, with the strongest ties to the powerful Italian-American community organization Unione Siciliana, and to Capone. The third gang was run by Dominic Roberto—a Capone friend and the husband of Rio Burke, a popular nightclub singer who, in her prime, had entertained at Colosimo's—and Jimmy Emery, who also was pals with Capone. Roberto and Emery, both natives of Italy, both ostensibly grocers, were less experienced than some of their competitors but no less ambitious.

It didn't take long for the Heights gang with the strongest Capone connections to emerge as the mightiest. Sanfilippo and Piazza grew so powerful, in fact, that even some of their rivals opted to pay them for protection. But Sanfilippo was killed, shot four times in the back of the head. Piazza continued taking money from local businesses for protection, but he didn't do much protecting, and soon the whole system collapsed. The Roberto-Emery faction forged an alliance with the Costellos, and the newly allied gangs turned to Capone, asking him to abandon Piazza and support their cause instead. While all this was developing, the feds launched a huge raid on Chicago Heights, hitting the Milano Café on Sixteenth Street.

The Milano was Phil Piazza's place. When it opened in 1924, State's Attorney Robert Crowe was among the guests spotted in attendance. An electric sign in the shape of a peacock flickered in the window as an indication of when the joint was open for business, which was almost always. The raiders struck at midnight on a busy Saturday in June, nabbing some of the town's most prominent citizens and shutting down what they claimed was the state's biggest still.

Piazza was not around at the time of the raid, but Alfred "Jake" Lingle was there. Lingle was a legman for the *Tribune*. He never got the bylines; he got the news. The phone would ring in the middle of the night, or at the crack of dawn, or in the middle of the afternoon, and an editor would tell Lingle to get to the scene of a drive-by or a fire or a murder-suicide or a distillery raid. Lingle would grab his fedora, his pen, and a pocketful of coins for the pay phone and jump in his car. No matter the time of day or night, he'd arrive looking like he just rolled out of bed and grabbed someone else's clothes by mistake. Once on the scene, he'd phone the city desk and talk to a rewrite man, who would shape Lingle's words into a story, yank it from the typewriter, and hand it to a copyboy. Lingle was one of the city's great newshounds, a man with a thousand friends. He knew more cops than the chief of police and more gangsters than Capone, and he got along nicely with folks on both sides of the law. Everyone understood Lingle's complicated arrangements, and no one griped about them because Lingle was on the square, or so it seemed.

But on the night of the raid and the shutdown of the Milano in the Heights, Lingle wasn't working. He and two of his coworkers and a couple of women were out for a night of fun. When the feds came in the front door of the Milano, Lingle and his pals went out the back, taking with them twenty gallons of alcohol, six bottles of vermouth, two bottles of Scotch, thirteen table shades, four boxes of bath salts, one linen tablecloth, one apron, a pair of fur mittens, a silk shirt and collar, and a dozen wineglasses. Their car's springs bent almost to the axles by the weight of their larcenous load. Were Lingle and his friends tipped that the raid was coming? Given that it must have taken time to assemble such a collection of goods, it would seem likely. But if the feds were complicit in Lingle's theft, the Chicago Heights police were not. As the newsmen rumbled off in their car full of stolen goods, one of the local coppers stopped them and took them to jail.

The case had been assigned to Assistant State's Attorney William McSwiggin. In no hurry to prosecute, he requested several continuances. When McSwiggin was assassinated a month later, the case was forgotten.

Three months later, the Milano was back in business while more than a dozen Chicago Heights bootleggers awaited trial. Bootlegging trials were rare in Chicago, but when they did come around, the city's gangsters were not happy. They didn't want to see their peers cutting deals and blabbing to the feds. Nor did they want to see their peers taking the witness stand and testifying in court to what they knew. Better knocked off than singing like a canary. That's why so many gangsters who survived for years on the street tended to die soon after falling into the custody of the authorities. *Omerta* could be counted on to keep some men quiet; others required silencing.

Victor "Humpy" DeFrank was first to die, shot in the head while driving down State Street early one morning; followed by Jimmie Lamberta, who was blasted through by a sawed-off shotgun while drinking at the Derby Inn, a schlocky gangster hangout; followed by Phil Piazza, owner of the Milano, who was coming out of the club when a bullet caught him in the neck and continued upward into his brain; followed by Joe Salvo, Lamberta's nephew, who was shot four times in the side by a gunman who fired from a moving car at the corner of Fourteenth and Arnold streets; followed by Joe Catando, whose link to the other men was unclear to police but who nonetheless was deemed connected somehow, and who took a swarm of bullets to the arms and head while he was listening to records at a party; followed by Tony "The Cavalier" Spano, a part-time bootlegger and part-time hit man, who lost a one-sided gun battle, opposition unknown, in broad daylight on Chicago's North Side; followed by one of Spano's associates, Frank Cappello, who was shot so many times in the back of the head that his skull collapsed in a stew of bone and fluid; followed by Antonio DeStefano Pelledrino, who was strangled with a rope, soaked in alcohol, set aflame, and dumped in a ditch on Cottage Grove Avenue alongside an onion field.

These murders, all occurring within four months of one another, sickened and disgusted George Johnson, who had never before led a criminal investigation. Johnson recognized that he was a long way from chancery court, where the most violent act was the thump of a rubber stamp. Every one of his potential witnesses and informers was turning up on a slab. His case was going cold before his eyes. And Capone could say he had nothing to do with any of it.

When Capone had announced the new spirit of cooperation in the fall of 1926, a few journalists had noted that one pocket of the city would be particularly susceptible to flare-ups in violence: the southwest territories controlled by Polack Joe Soltis and his men. Soltis at the time had been busy defending himself against charges of murdering beer runner John "Mitters" Foley and could not be brought to the table. Soltis faced two trials for the Foley murder and walked away from both of them, but by the time his legal affairs were wrapped up, his business enterprise was falling apart. One of Capone's allies, Ralph Sheldon, had been creeping into Soltis's territory. Other small-time operators probably had the same idea. But Soltis wasn't going to let that happen. "We're down," said Frank "Lefty" Koncil, a top aide to Soltis, assessing the state of business in an interview in early March. "We're broke. But we won't stay that way. We're going to get back what we used to have. We won't be pushed around anymore. And if anybody gets in the way we'll take care of him." Capone and his men were not involved in all this tough talk, but it was only a matter of time before they got into it. Gang fighting, like fireworks, had a way of shooting sparks in all directions.

On the evening of March 11, 1927, Koncil and one of his men, Charles "Big Hayes" Hrubeck, were driving through their territory in a long black Cadillac, visiting the saloon owners who had recently switched suppliers. They were trying to pressure them to come back to Soltis. Koncil was at the wheel. At about eleven forty-five, a night watchman at a piano factory spotted Koncil's car fishtailing around the corner of Thirty-ninth and Ashland, another sedan giving chase. Soon the two cars were side by side. That's when the night watchman saw a blaze of orange fire and heard a rapid flurry of gunshots, probably from a Tommy.

Koncil and Hrubeck stopped their car, got out, and started running uphill toward a set of railroad tracks. Their pursuers followed on foot as well, shooting as they ran. Koncil and Hrubeck returned fire without looking where they were shooting, still scrambling to find cover. Sharp reports from pistols and shotguns rang out again. Hrubeck didn't make it to the tracks. He was cut down by a volley of bullets to the spine, ripping apart his nervous system one instant before killing him. Koncil somehow staggered on, reaching the crest of a small hill, his bloodied clothes lit by the headlamp of a switching engine half a block to the north. He staggered across the tracks and angled his wounded body through thick grass, toward the shelter of the C. G. Spring and Bumper Company on Thirty-eighth. He fell raggedly, panting and perspiring as he tried to reload his gun. Koncil managed to get on his feet again, but that was as far as he got. Another bullet caught him. Down he went and down he stayed. When the undertaker counted later that same night, he found six bullets in Koncil's back and one behind his left ear.

While the cops and rum runners were gunning it out in Chicago and the feds were trying to build a case against a bunch of small fries from Chicago Heights, Capone was vacationing in Hot Springs, Arkansas, with not a worry in the world beyond his crummy gambling skills. He was spotted in Arkansas by reporters as he tossed chips around in a casino and played golf with his former North Side rival Schemer Drucci. One night at the tables in Hot Springs, Capone reportedly lost $50,000. The next night he dropped $58,000. Only one problem: After losing the first fifty grand, he had run out of cash. So he wrote an IOU for $58,000 and handed it to the casino's croupier. "I've gone broke here," he said. "But you know your money's as good as in your pocket. When I get it, I'll send it to you. What could be fairer than that?"

The bookmaker, perhaps unaware of Capone's power, or believing that the crime boss's power extended only in and around Chicago, had a pretty good idea what could be fairer than that: cash.

The next day, he gathered his friends, hopped in a car, and went looking for Capone. They spotted him on the road and pulled up alongside his car. Capone, who had seen enough drive-by shootings to be justifiably panicked, opened the door of the moving sedan, jumped out, and tumbled down a hundred-foot hill. He was shaken but not hurt. The next day, after one more round of golf, he boarded a train to Chicago.

THE BETTER ELEMENT

Mayor William E. Dever couldn't catch a break. Though his administration had shut down thousands of speakeasies and destroyed hundreds of distilleries, it hardly mattered. Getting a nip of the sauce in Chicago was as easy as getting a book from the library. Maybe easier. Even when murder rates dipped from 1925 to 1926, down from 394 to 356, the newspapers gave the mayor and his police department no credit whatsoever. They said it was probably thanks to Capone and his cease-fire.

Dever loved the job's ceremony. He loved welcoming foreign dignitaries, cutting ribbons, making speeches, handing out keys to the city, attending grand openings, posing for photographs, putting on ten-gallon hats when cowboy actors came to town, and talking business over golf with the city's moguls. But Chicago was hopeless, he'd decided, and running the place was a thankless job.

He was a big, sturdily built man, Irish Catholic, with a thick head of iron-colored hair and a mustache to match. He was sixty-five now, and the job felt like a burden. Dever's meaty frame seemed to sag. The gleam in his eyes vanished behind drooping lids. He tired easily. He preferred to spend his evenings at home, where he would roll up his shirtsleeves, smoke a cigar, and read pulp fiction. His wife, Kate, would serve him breakfast and give him the rundown on current events in the morning papers. But politics bored him. Playing the games required to get reelected held little appeal. He was tired, too, of being forced to defend Prohibition. He liked a drink as much as the next man.

Civic leaders urged Dever to run for one more term. If his efforts had not remade the city, at least he had tried. At least the rest of the world

could see that some of the people in Chicago cared. And if he hadn't succeeded in destroying the city's criminal organizations, at least he hadn't
been corrupted by them. He had managed to harass the outlaws a little
bit. "You have redeemed the city, Mr. Mayor, from the effects of the terrible ravages it underwent for eight years," said Julius Rosenwald, a phi-
lanthropist and part owner of Sears, Roebuck & Company, referring to
the eight-year administration of Dever's immediate predecessor, Big Bill
Thompson. "Chicago faces a tremendous political crisis. You're the one
man to save the day."

There was a good reason why Rosenwald made reference to Thompson. He knew that Big Bill was thinking about trying to recapture the
mayor's office. To the city's reformers, Thompson's return would be nothing short of a disaster. It would mean a complete surrender to the forces
of greed and vice. It would deal a devastating blow to the city's sullied
image. It would make a mockery of everything the reformers had fought
for during Dever's administration.

Dever relented. He agreed to run again.

The mention of Thompson's possible candidacy set gangland buzzing. As if the democratic process had not been good enough to the gangsters already—giving them the great gift of Prohibition, and allowing this
tragically flawed and thoroughly unenforceable law to stay in place for
six years and counting—the possible return of Thompson seemed almost
too good to be true. After his vacation in Hot Springs, Capone returned
for the campaign season, intending to do everything he could to help his
candidate.

Since leaving office in 1923, Thompson had not exactly draped himself in glory. He had lost a bid for the U.S. Senate, and made national
news with a series of bizarre and ridiculous publicity stunts. For example,
he debated a pair of caged rats in a political rally at the Cort Theater, and
arranged a short-lived expedition to the South Seas to hunt tree-climbing
fish. No matter. With all those stunts and misadventures Thompson had
managed to keep his name before the public during his absence from office, and now he believed he had the perfect issues on which to build his
campaign for reelection: He would attack Dever for invading the privacy
of ordinary Chicagoans in his pursuit of bootleggers and moonshiners.

Thompson was able to make this allegation because Dever had ordered his police chief to make arrests anywhere and everywhere. Because

it wasn't easy to arrest well-protected gang leaders such as Capone, and because it was even more difficult to convict them, the cops took to making easy busts—invading homes and arresting the citizens found there for possession of small amounts of alcohol. Gradually, in the minds of many Chicagoans, the police had become the enemy. Law-abiding citizens had come to feel imposed upon. They accused the government of sticking its nose where it didn't belong. So strong were the sentiments that when a tall, slender hoodlum named Martin Durkin killed a police officer, fled, and avoided capture for several months, Chicagoans cheered. When Durkin was finally arrested and brought back to the city, crowds greeted him so warmly that Mayor Dever banned the showing of the newsreel films depicting the event.

Thompson promised to do things differently. In announcing his campaign for reelection, he vowed to represent the people, not the police, and said he would fire any cop caught "crossing the threshold of a man's home or place of business." He also promised to reopen the businesses Dever had shut down and open ten thousand new ones. Thompson did not specifically say those businesses would be speakeasies, but he didn't have to. Capone and everyone else knew that speakeasies were the only businesses Dever had shut down.

Thompson's opponents in the Democratic primary were Thompson's former protégé, Fred Lundin, and Edward Litsinger, a reform candidate who had the backing of U.S. senator Charles Deneen. Both men tried to make crime the campaign's central issue, saying Thompson was the candidate for gangland Chicago. But Big Bill mocked the notion that Chicago should or could enforce the laws of Prohibition. In addition to promising to keep Chicago soaking wet with booze, Thompson made ridiculous promises designed to appeal to voters' patriotism, saying he was the only candidate strong enough to stop King George of England from sticking his nose in American affairs, the only candidate who would fight the League of Nations and the World Court, the only candidate strong enough to preserve American independence. "America first, and last, and always!" he shouted. "That's the issue of this campaign!"

The crowds went for it like free beer. Voters were fed up with the city's elite.

Capone went to work on behalf of Thompson once again, collecting campaign contributions from the saloonkeepers who bought his beer. The minimum contribution was $40. Those operating slot machines in their saloons were expected to kick in at least $250 each.

Thompson won easily in the primary, setting up a showdown with Dever in the general election. The *Tribune* was not impressed with Capone's candidate, editorializing, "Thompson is a buffoon in a tommyrot foundry, but when his crowd gets loose in the City Hall, Chicago has more need of Marines than any Nicaraguan town. No one is obliged to guess as to Thompson or as to Dever. The city has had experience with both and knows exactly what to expect. It is not exploring unknown territory. Both regions are mapped and sign-posted. The issue is between common sense and plain bunk. It is between decency and disreputability, between sensible people and political defectives, between honesty in administration and the percentage system."

An association of Protestant ministers endorsed Dever, calling Thompson the worst mayor ever to rule any city. Another preacher accused Thompson of throwing a stag party in which naked women performed lewd acts for members of the Good Roads Association. Jane Addams and Harold L. Ickes, a powerful lawyer and future U.S. secretary of the interior, were among the righteous souls who stood up for Dever. So did the eminent political scientist Charles E. Merriam. George Brennan, a Democratic party strategist, made the declaration that "not all supporters of Thompson are hoodlums, but every hoodlum is supporting Thompson." The *New York Times* reported that Thompson's cynical campaign was designed to appeal to "the illiterate portion of the electorate, including most of the negro voters." None of it mattered. Thompson drew enormous crowds at his campaign events. The public mood seemed to be in his favor.

"Think of Chicago's future," pleaded Dever, sounding as desperate as a crazy man who can't make others see what he sees. "Think of the best interests of our city."

"Hooray for Big Bill! Hooray for beer!" shouted the crowd at one Thompson rally.

Estimates varied on Capone's contribution to the campaign. Some pegged it at $100,000. Others went as high as $260,000. In the days before the election, bootleggers and their money were seen often at the stately Sherman Hotel, where Thompson made his headquarters. "I'm for Big Bill hook, line, and sinker, and Bill's for me, hook, line, and sinker," said

Jack Zuta, a gang leader and pimp who often clashed with Capone but who had been cooperating since the truce took effect.

Schemer Drucci also was reported to be playing an active role in the Thompson campaign. Still in mourning for his old pal Hymie Weiss, Drucci kept a framed picture of the recently departed gangster in his hotel room, along with a machine gun, a shotgun, a few pistols, and a bullet-proof vest.

On April 4, the day before the election, some North Side gangsters, possibly including Drucci, raided the offices of Alderman Dorsey R. Crowe, a Dever supporter from the Forty-second Ward. They knocked over file cabinets, kicked out a window, and scared the daylights out of Crowe's secretary but didn't hurt anybody or take anything. Later that day, police caught up to Drucci in front of the Belair Hotel, at the corner of Pine Grove and Diversey. They put him in a police sedan and drove off toward the courthouse. Drucci didn't like the way the cops were treating him and let them know it. "You take your gun off and I'll kick the hell out of you," he told one of the cops, a big guy named Dan Healy, with whom he'd tangled before. A few months earlier, Healy had tried to kill Joe Soltis during a saloon raid. Only the intervention of another officer prevented it. Now Drucci kept jawing at the big cop. Shoving started. Drucci managed to push Healy out of the car. When the driver stopped to retrieve the fallen officer, Healy drew his gun, shoved it through the car window, and started firing, hitting Drucci in the arm, leg, and stomach. Drucci died en route to the hospital. He was twenty-six.

Election day was quiet, to almost everyone's surprise. Some accounts said that Capone's men were on guard at polling stations across the city, making sure Thompson got all the votes he needed. But the daily newspapers made no mention of gang activity. The papers did report, however, that the police assigned two hundred fifty officers, including thirty-five machine gunners, to guard the polling places, and that Mayor Dever's allies supplemented this force by sending out every available City Hall employee to monitor polling places for signs of cheating.

Thompson defeated Dever by a wide margin. Though Capone may have helped swing the election, he didn't vote. In all his years in Chicago, he never even registered.

The reelection of Big Bill Thompson reminded the world again of Chicago's seemingly limitless tolerance for corruption. The humorist Will

Rogers, in one of his regular syndicated newspaper columns, summed up the election this way: "They was trying to beat Bill with the better element vote. The trouble with Chicago is that there ain't much better element."

The morning after his election, Big Bill was roaring, "Officially we have arrived!"

So had Capone. With an ally in control of City Hall again; with Drucci, Weiss, and O'Banion all dead; with Prohibition enforcement all but abandoned; with the breweries and distilleries and transportation networks running smoothly; with the stock market soaring; and with no end in sight to the nation's giddy mood, Chicago's top gang boss was fully in command, his wealth and power still rising, his prospects seemingly limitless. At age twenty-eight, Capone was king.

PART TWO

KING CAPONE

"THERE'S WORSE FELLOWS IN THE WORLD THAN ME"

Al Capone called his organization "the outfit," small *t*, small *o*. He referred to it casually, and, despite the organization's Byzantine structure and bountiful cash flow, he ran it fairly casually, too. The word "mafia" never crossed his lips. The term usually applied to Sicilian criminal groups, and Capone was not a Sicilian. He was also nondiscriminatory in his hiring practices. His closest aides were Jack Guzik, a Jew; Tony Lombardo, a Sicilian; and Frank Nitti, who came from Angri in Calabria. Brother Ralph Capone supervised beer distribution (thus his nickname "Bottles"), assisted by Capone's cousin Charlie Fischetti and another Italian business associate, named Lawrence Mangano. Pete Penovich, a native of Austria, ran much of the gambling business. A pair of Irishmen, George "Red" Barker and William "Three-Fingered" White, along with a Welshman named Murray "The Camel" Humphreys, took care of the labor unions and rackets. The outfit's principal gunman was Jack "Machine Gun" McGurn, a Sicilian, whose real name was Vincenzo Antonio Gibaldi.

The Capone empire reached every corner of the city, and yet, like Lake Michigan, it was nearly impossible from almost any single angle to comprehend its depth and breadth. With his wife and mother, Capone owned the house on South Prairie Avenue. But that house was all the property he owned. He didn't want to be tied too closely to any of the illicit businesses he helped to supervise and supply. Members of his organization, on the other hand, had their own hotels, casinos, speakeasies, lower-class speakeasies known as "blind pigs," cabarets, restaurants, breweries, bakeries, and brothels. Capone would get a slice of the profits from each of those operations, but at least on paper, he had nothing to do with them.

In effect, the outfit was a collection of synergistic partnerships. No board of directors called the shots. No committees set down rules and regulations. "Rather," wrote Robert Hardy Andrews, a journalist who covered the city in the 1920s, "it was a confederation of utterly conscienceless dictators bound together by two things: their total distrust of each other, which was totally justified, and their adaptation of Benjamin Franklin's maxim that hanging together is preferable to hanging separately. Always, just below, there were thrusters reaching up for more of the loot."

Members of the confederation shared their influence and expertise. They shared the risk. And, when arrested, they pooled their resources and hired the best lawyers. As a result, when Capone's men went to war with other gang members or got themselves in hot water with the cops, it was often a result of one partner's freelance business activities and not connected directly to Capone. That separation gave Capone a degree of plausible deniability when crimes occurred within his sphere of influence, as they so often did. Nevertheless, those small freelance operations became key parts of the Capone enterprise and excellent sources of revenue. Capone's associates bought their whiskey, beer, and wine from the outfit. They got their slot machines from the outfit. They bought their protection from the outfit. Of course, they paid a big chunk of their income to the outfit, too. Or else.

The Hawthorne Smoke Shop in Cicero, for example, sold tobacco but did a much bigger business in gambling. It closed, relocated, and reopened several times over the years, mostly because of raids, but the money flowed steadily when its doors were open. Frankie Pope, a West Sider sometimes known as "The Millionaire Newsboy," ran the bookmaking there, while Pete Penovich ran the casino-style betting. Each man had a partnership interest in the operation. In 1924, the smoke shop's books showed net income of $300,000, or roughly $3.6 million by today's standards, according to the federal government. The next year was not as good; the books showed only $117,000 in income. But in 1926, the shop performed well, bringing in $170,000 in the first four months of the year before a raid shut it down. How much income went unrecorded is anybody's guess.

Then there was the Harlem Inn, a brothel or bawdy house, as they called it, in Stickney, where a dozen or so girls worked seven nights a week. On a good Friday or Saturday night, the prostitutes there brought in more than $1,200. The top earners—referred to as Edna and Ruth, according to house ledgers—earned more than $100 each on good nights. The girls kept half of what they made; the rest went to the house. Over the course of a year, the brothel probably took in more than $230,000, or about $2.7 million by today's count. Capone and his men operated sex parlors and gambling halls like these all over Chicago and the suburbs, but neither the feds nor anyone else ever accurately measured the size of the enterprise. Did Capone have ten such operations? One hundred? One thousand? No one knew. At one time, the government estimated the outfit's income to be $50 million a year from bootlegging, $25 million a year from gambling, and close to $10 million each from prostitution and narcotics, for a total of about $95 million a year, or $1.2 billion in today's dollars.

The federal government had every reason to exaggerate its estimate of Capone's economic power and probably did. But even if it was accurate in pegging the figure at $95 million, there's no way to know how much of that money settled into Capone's wallet. For starters, the feds estimated that roughly $15 million a year went to paying off cops and politicians. In Cicero for 1925 and 1926, the feds said Capone grabbed 52 percent of all gambling income, which he split evenly with his three principal partners: his brother Ralph, Jack Guzik, and Frank Nitti. After that, about 20 percent went to town officials, and the rest went to the local operators of brothels, saloons, and casinos.

But no one ever knew about the disposition of Capone's income with any certainty, which was in part the genius of Capone's business. If he really was making as much money as the authorities said, he showed few signs of avarice. He recognized that he had to spend money to make money, and he never tried to cut back on the lavish bribes to cops and public officials. He was unbothered when partners within the organization grew independently wealthy. And while he no doubt had access to large supplies of cash, there is no evidence that he ever amassed monumental personal wealth. He built no mansions in Chicago, opened no bank accounts on- or offshore, or funneled large amounts of money to his mother, as far as anyone could tell. He treated himself to an armor-plated Cadillac Town Sedan, green and black, with reinforced bulletproof side panels and glass, a steel-hooded gas tank, and a gun box behind the backseat. The car supposedly weighed seven tons and cost more than $20,000, or about ten times the price of an ordinary Cadillac sedan. He gambled like an addict. He entertained well. He wore custom suits made by Chicago's finest tailors. He purchased expensive gifts—diamond-encrusted belt buckles, for one—and handed out generous tips.

Still, if Capone possessed the phenomenal wealth the government alleged, he could have lived much more opulently. In 1927, he still hadn't even paid off the $4,400 mortgage on the family's South Prairie Avenue home.

This was not the behavior one would expect for one of the nation's richest, most famous, and most powerful men, and certainly not in the 1920s, when the stock market was minting fresh millionaires daily and everyone had a tip on a hot stock. Capone's conservative wealth management suggests that he was either devilishly smart and recognized that the accumulation of excessive wealth and property would one day land him in trouble with the government, or that his enterprise, like a drunk with money, was so volatile and so precariously balanced that the best he could do was keep it on its feet and moving in the right direction. Either way, he was clearly a careful man.

———

In the spring of 1927, thanks in large part to Big Bill Thompson's stunning reelection victory, the national press began to notice how much power Capone had amassed. A year earlier, Chicago reporters were not consistently spelling his name correctly. Now he was gaining national and international renown. He may have been gaining respect, too. When the transatlantic pilot Francesco de Pinedo flew to Chicago, the city of big shoulders, as part of his world tour, Capone was among the city dignitaries invited to greet him. And when Edward J. O'Hare, a St. Louis lawyer, went looking for a partner to open a dog-racing track, he turned to Capone.

In truth, O'Hare, who owned the patent on mechanical rabbits used at dog tracks, wasn't looking for an upstanding citizen to join his enterprise. Dog racing was gaining in popularity, thanks largely to the advent of O'Hare's electric bunny, which kept the greyhounds going fast in the right direction. Dog racing was much cheaper than horse racing. The dogs ate less and didn't require jockeys. And these races were much easier to rig; hungry dogs almost always ran faster than full-bellied ones. O'Hare was big, tough, and loudmouthed. He was quick with a joke and quick to pick up a bar tab. The gamblers loved him. He also was wickedly smart. With help from bootleggers, he built tracks all over the country. The booters, he figured out, could always be counted on to come up with cash. They had strong political connections and hearty appetites for gambling, too. Capone would eventually get more than he bargained for from his partnership with O'Hare. But in the short run, Capone loved owning a stake in a semilegitimate business.

Increasingly, the world wanted to know about Capone. And while Capone managed to be on guard in most other departments, he could never say no to requests for interviews—especially when approached by women. Generally, reporters and bootleggers came from the same neighborhoods. But the real reason Capone talked was that he enjoyed the gabbing and sensed that newspaper readers would have empathy for him. The common man knew that the whole world (or at least the whole city) was corrupt. And the common man wanted beer.

Patricia Dougherty, a reporter for the *Herald and Examiner,* landed one of the most extensive interviews, which she sold to the popular women's magazine *Cosmopolitan.* The story had no particular angle designed to appeal to women, although Capone was portrayed more humanely and more roundly than he was accustomed to. For many Americans, this was the first glimpse of Capone as a man, as opposed to the monster they'd been reading about in the headlines of their local newspapers. In the article, Capone admitted that the bootlegging business required a certain amount of violence, including an occasional murder, and confessed to bribing public officials.

"I violate the Prohibition law—sure," he said. "Who doesn't? The only difference is I take more chances than the man who drinks a cocktail before dinner and a flock of highballs after it." He went on to castigate others he deemed hypocrites. "There's only one thing worse than a crook, I think, and that is a crooked man in a big political job, a man who pretends he is enforcing the law and is really making dough out of breaking it. Even a self-respecting hoodlum hasn't any use for that kind of fella. He buys them like he'd buy any other article necessary to this trade. But he hates them in his heart."

Capone continued on the sentimental streak: "What does a man think about when he's killing another man in a gang war? Well, maybe he thinks that the law of self-defense, the way God looks at it, is a little broader than the law books have it. Maybe it means killing a man who'd kill you if he saw you first. Maybe it means killing a man in defense of your business, the way you make your money to take care of your wife and child. I think it does. You can't blame me for thinking there's worse fellows in the world than me."

The writer went on to describe the state of calm Capone had brought upon Chicago, where beer trucks rumbled without fear of hijacking and men such as Capone could travel with "only a single bodyguard instead of a score." Scarface Al, she said, claimed credit for the happy state of affairs. He even restated his regret that Hymie Weiss had to die for peace to come to the city. "That killing was unnecessary," Capone said.

Now, though, he had at last found serenity. It was, he said, "just like the old days." The North Siders stayed on the North Side. The Cicero men stayed in Cicero. "And if we meet on the street, we say hello and shake hands.

"Better, ain't it?"

Though he admitted to surprise at the direction his life had taken, he gave no sign of regret, even when he admitted that Mae had had no idea what she had been getting herself into when she had agreed to marry. "I was just a nice little boy that grew up with her in Brooklyn," he recalled, "and she was a sweet little Irish kid who took me for better or for worse. What do I want my boy, Albert, to be when he grows up? Well, first of all, I want him to be a man. A brave man who can look anyone in the eye and stand his ground no matter what comes. I like a man with nerve—even if he's on the other end of a gunfight. I want him to have all the things I never had. I want him to go to college. I went to work when I was thirteen. I want him to know about nice things in the world. I don't want him to be a bootlegger or a reformer, either. I'd rather like him to be a professional man, a doctor, a lawyer, or a businessman. Anything that'd give him an easier time than his old man's had.

"What do I want him to think about me? I want him to know that I loved him enough to risk my life to work for him. I want him to remember that I had a different kind of life than I made for him and I expect him to repay me by playing the game straight. And most of all, what I want for that boy is a wife like mine and boy like mine to make whatever game he picks out worth winning. And if he'd ever get to be a public official, I'd want him to be the squarest one that ever lived."

As Prohibition matured and as his wealth and might grew, Capone diversified the outfit's operations.

Late in 1925, a dry cleaner named Morris Becker was approached by a racket called the Retail Cleaners and Dyers' Association, which collected dues and assessments, helped set prices in the industry, and promised to protect its members from trouble. What sort of trouble might befall a mom-and-pop dry cleaner business? Those who declined to join the association found out fast. Windows were smashed. Homemade bombs were tossed. Lives were threatened. Nevertheless, Becker decided to take his chances. South Side shops that had joined the association were raising prices, charging $1.75 to clean men's suits and $2.25 to do women's dresses. Becker, who charged $0.50 less for each item, made up his mind to fly solo and hold his prices steady. That brought a visit from a representative of the association.

"You are going to raise prices," he told Becker.

"The Constitution," the merchant replied, "guarantees me the right to life, liberty, and full pursuit of happiness."

"To hell with the Constitution," said the union man. "I am a damned mite bigger than the Constitution."

Three days later, a bomb exploded in Becker's store. He filed a complaint with the police, which led to the indictment of sixteen leaders of the cleaners' association. But the men were never tried. A few years later, no longer relying on the Constitution, Becker consulted a higher power. He talked his way into Capone's office and asked for help. Capone saw a chance to get in on the rackets, and, perhaps thanks to the size and profitability of his business, was able to offer Becker better terms than his blackmailers had offered. "I now have no need of the state's attorney, the police department, or the Employers' Association," Becker boasted to the press upon securing Capone's help. "I have the best protection in the world."

Capone did not invent the protection racket, or racketeering, as it came to be known in the 1920s. The custom—nothing more than organized bullying, really—dated back ages. But now that Capone was the most powerful man in the city, he was uniquely positioned to serve and protect, and the rackets enhanced his image of importance. Before long, other dry cleaners were signing up with Capone for protection. When asked, he started telling people he was getting out of beer and going into dry cleaning.

Becker was not the only one seeking Capone's help. When real estate men feared a strike among elevator operators, twenty-five of them paid $1,000 each for Capone's help in averting the action. A year or so later, according to one of Capone's men, Capone helped put down a strike by some of the city's newsboys and newspaper delivery truck drivers. Legend has it that Capone, as a reward for his efforts, got a meeting with the *Trib*'s publisher, Colonel Robert R. McCormick, and used the occasion to request that the newspaper go easy on him.

"You know, you are famous, like Babe Ruth," McCormick supposedly said. "We can't help printing things about you, but I will see that the *Tribune* gives you a square deal." Whether McCormick made promises or not, one thing is clear: The *Trib* did in fact go easy on him in 1927. Babe Ruth, in the course of hitting sixty home runs and leading the Yankees to win the World Series, was mentioned in nearly three hundred *Trib* stories, while Capone drew ink only twenty times. And not all the stories were negative. On August 29, when police were called to the Hawthorne racetrack to put down a riot by angry bettors after race officials posted the wrong list of winning greyhounds, the *Trib* noted that "Al Capone, who is said to be one of the owners of the Hawthorne track, and several of his followers aided the police . . . in quelling the disturbance." They didn't even call him "Scarface."

Capone's other racket was jazz.

He didn't make money directly on the music business, but jazz, often referred to at the time as Negro music, gave the 1920s its sound, and there were bands in almost every one of the city's best speakeasies. The music could be raw or romantic, sexy or sweet, heraldic or hedonistic, and much of it was made up on the spot—perfect for the bacchanalian 1920s, which F. Scott Fitzgerald labeled "The Jazz Age."

The nation hadn't lost its taste for harmless ditties such as "Blue Skies" and "Ain't She Sweet," but audiences also hankered for more daring rhythms and timbres. They wanted to hear Jelly Roll Morton's Red Hot Peppers playing "Black Bottom Stomp" and Bessie Smith singing "Downhearted Blues." Chicago's booming entertainment market encouraged competition among artists and pushed them to innovate. And the innovations, fueled with booze and drugs, produced mind-blowing, pulse-pounding sounds. "Jazz has come to stay," said the conductor Leopold Stokowski, "because it is an expression of the times, of the breathless, energetic, superactive times in which we are living."

In May 1927, Louis Armstrong and his band went into a studio and recorded twelve tracks that would forever change American music; one of them, "Potato Head Blues," became an instant hit, thanks in part to the black Pullman porters who bought stacks of the record in Chicago and delivered them to friends and relatives across the country. This was a radical, electric, sexually and racially charged music. It was a joyous escape from custom, from authority, from boredom, from hardship, from pain, and it could not have flowered, could not have reached such a wide and well-integrated audience, had it not grown up from the lush soil of the speakeasy.

Joe Oliver, Bessie Smith, Johnny Dodds, and Jimmy Noone were regulars at South Side clubs such as the Dreamland Café, the Deluxe, the Sunset, and the Plantation, the last of which was reputedly owned by Capone. Up-and-comers such as Milton "Mezz" Mezzrow and Eddie Condon earned their chops at south suburban clubs such as the Arrow-head and the Martinique, where Capone may have supplied the booze or held an ownership stake. Mezzrow liked to say that he received his jazz education at "Capone's University of Gutbucket Arts" (Mezzrow's name for the Arrowhead). When the band wasn't playing, Mezzrow and his boys were put to work pouring a concoction of ginger ale and alcohol into barrels of Capone's near beer in an attempt to duplicate the real thing. "Al always showed up surrounded by a gang of trigger men—they sat in a corner, very gay and noisy but gunning the whole situation out of the corner of their eyes. Al's big round face had a broad grin plastered on it and he was always good-natured." Once, though, when Capone ordered Mezzrow to fire a singer named Lillian who had been getting flirty with one of Capone's brothers, Mezz challenged him. The saxophonist was one of the jazz world's greatest pot smokers and distributors—so great that musicians for decades would refer to the highest-grade weed as "mezz." Maybe the fact that he was high explained his boldness.

"I won't fire her," Mezz said, according to his memoirs.

"She can't sing anyway," answered Capone.

"Can't sing?" Mezzrow complained. "Why, you couldn't even tell good whiskey if you smelled it and that's your racket, so how do you figure to tell me about music?"

Capone laughed and let it go.

Almost every musician and comedian who performed in Chicago in the 1920s had a story about Capone. Some of them may have even been true. Fats Waller, composer of the hit songs "Ain't Misbehavin' " and "Keepin' Out of Mischief Now," claimed he was kidnapped and made to play for Capone's birthday party one year. Milton Berle claimed he was strong-armed by Capone's men into performing for Big Bill Thompson at the Cotton Club in Cicero. When Capone offered the comedian a wad of twenties for his trouble, Berle supposedly refused, saying, "I don't need this." To which Capone replied, "I don't need it, either." George Jessel, who turned down the chance to star in *The Jazz Singer,* the most celebrated movie of 1927, claimed that Capone once took him out to the Midnight Frolic, a nightclub owned and operated by Ike Bloom, one of the founders of Chicago's bawdy Levee District. "Call me Snorky," the gangster told Jessel by way of introduction, and continued, "Anything happens to you or any of your friends, let me know." In one of the few verifiable stories, the comedian Joe E. Lewis got in trouble with the Capone gang when he decided to abandon his gig at the Green Mill, a North Side club where he was making $600 a week, for a better deal at the Rendez-Vous Café, at the corner of Clark and Diversey. Jack McGurn, of machine-gun fame and rumored to be one of the Green Mill's owners, warned Lewis not to go. Lewis didn't listen, and one day there came a knock at the door of his hotel room. He opened the door and three men rushed in. Lewis was beaten, stabbed, and left for dead. But when police picked up McGurn, Lewis wised up and said he couldn't identify the men who attacked him and couldn't think of why anyone would want to hurt him.

By all accounts, Capone was a lover of the arts and a benefactor of musicians. He especially loved the opera, which he usually attended with bodyguards seated all around him. In fact, he was seen in the company of his bodyguards much more often than with his wife. Mae was almost never photographed, or even mentioned, in the papers during Capone's reign over the city. None of the celebrities who bragged about their encounters with Capone ever mentioned meeting his wife. Mae's acute shyness kept her home, away from glittering public nightlife. She became more involved in the church and less involved in her husband's life. To some in the Capone family it seemed as if Mae had cocooned herself, emerging only to engage with her son or her family back in Brooklyn. Nevertheless, Capone kept a busy social calendar, often in the company of paramours, and enjoyed the access to great music and theater that his wealth and fame enabled. Later in life, when he had more time on his hands, he would teach himself to read and transpose music and to play the mandola, a larger version of the mandolin. "There isn't a song written I can't play," he would boast in a letter to his son.

It was summer 1927, Charles Lindbergh was taking victory laps around the country after his solo flight across the Atlantic. The whole city seemed to stand still and gaze skyward as he buzzed Chicago on a cloudy afternoon. That same day—August 13—Captain John Stege resigned from his job with the Chicago police department when it was revealed that his real name was John Stedge and that he had been convicted of murder at age fifteen. Elsewhere, Mae West was found guilty of obscenity in New York. The famous anarchists Sacco and Vanzetti were executed in Massachusetts. President Coolidge shocked the nation with a terse announcement that he would not run for another term in office. The South was reeling from the Great Mississippi Flood, which killed more than two hundred and displaced at least seven hundred thousand. But the secretary of commerce, Herbert Hoover, was doing heroic work in organizing relief to what was described as the greatest natural disaster in the nation's history. "Yes, sir," said a farmer from Pine Bluff, Arkansas, where flood victims gathered to present Hoover with a loving cup, "they think a lot of Hoover down here, both white and colored. I read the other day where a fellow said Benjamin Franklin was the first civilized American and the most useful man of his day. We think Hoover is the most useful American of his day. Why, he'd make a fine president."

Earlier in the year, Mayor Thompson, for the sake of appearances if nothing, had named Mike "Go Get 'Em" Hughes his new chief of police. This was the same Mike Hughes, former head of the state's highway police, who had boasted of running Capone out of Cicero. Showing no obvious signs of corruption, Hughes began putting his stamp on the department by taking cops out from behind desks and putting them on the street. He said he would need another three thousand officers to give the city's gangsters a fair fight.

At the same time, he announced that he intended to put science to use in the pursuit of prominent criminals. A great debate raged at the time as to the true causes of crime. A growing number of scientists believed that criminal behavior might be explained—and perhaps even eradicated—through psychoanalysis. Endocrinology, or the study of the secretions of the endocrine glands, was said to be the key. Once researchers fully grasped the effects of hormones, they hoped they might be able to adjust the secretions in the mentally ill and the criminally inclined. Hughes suggested that the gangsters get "psychopathic examinations," and that those who failed be assigned to the state hospital in Chester, more affectionately known as the loony bin.

The first man tested was Capone's top bodyguard and assassin, McGurn. On August 17 he took a seat in a City Hall office that had been converted to a laboratory. He drew triangles within circles. Asked what the word "bear" called to mind, he answered "bathing beauty," perhaps thinking the word had been "bare." He looked at pictures of men without heads and cars without wheels and correctly identified their flaws. While he was taking the Binet-Simon intelligence exam, or "IQ test," the secretary administering the test left the room momentarily. McGurn got up and tried to crib the answers from the papers on her desk. Caught in the act, he said he had only been looking for his handkerchief.

"I may have been all right when I went in there," he told a reporter upon completion of the exam, "but I'm sure nutty now."

One day that summer in Chicago, when about four hundred agents and prospective agents were taking a civil service exam at Lane Technical High School, the men administering the exam noticed an unusually large number of snazzily dressed test-takers. Would-be civil servants, as a rule, did not come so well attired. When exams were handed out, the well-dressed men didn't touch their pencils. It turned out that scores of bootleggers had applied to take the test just so they could get into the auditorium to get a good look at the faces of the agents who would soon be coming after them.

In the early days of Prohibition, bootleggers would not have cared enough about the Prohibition agents to stake out one of their exams. But that summer the agents had been making more busts than usual. On

August 5 they burst into an old livery stable at 217 East Thirtieth Street, where they found eight fifteen-hundred-gallon vats, five fifteen-hundred-gallon storage tanks, and a double-armed racker that enabled handlers to fill two barrels at a time from one vat. Forty-seven barrels of beer were already on a truck and eight barrels more were about to be loaded when the raiders arrived, led by Patrick Roche and Clarence Converse of the Internal Revenue bureau. A couple of men escaped by climbing down a rope that hung from a second-floor window. One of the men who didn't escape begged the federal agents to let him go. "Give me a break," he pleaded. "Lemme call Al—wait a few minutes and everything'll be squared." Before the bust, Roche and Converse had observed two police cars and two motorcycle cops patrolling the area, clearly in the employ of the bootleggers, making sure no rivals attempted to hijack the shipment. The revenue men said they knew the cops' names and would soon issue warrants for their arrest. They said they hoped to find proof that Capone controlled the operation. But charges against the big fellow never came.

Even so, Capone seemed to be feeling the effects of the raids. At about this time, he called one of his competitors, Roger Touhy, saying he was low on beer and wanted to buy some. Touhy, working out of Des Plaines, fifteen miles north of downtown Chicago, ran one of the area's most efficient operations and produced some of its best-tasting beer. He considered himself a cut above the city's other booters, including Capone. "Capone wasn't my kind of person," he wrote in his autobiography. "People around him—or against him—were all the time getting murdered." Given their long-running rivalry, Touhy might have been trying to make Capone look bad. In his story, he made Chicago's most legendary gangster sound like a petty chiseler. Capone wanted beer and Touhy had surplus at the time, according to his story, so he agreed to make a deal. Touhy told Capone he would sell five hundred barrels at $37.50 per. A few days after taking delivery, Capone called and asked for another three hundred barrels. When it came time to settle his bill, he complained that fifty barrels had been "leakers," so he would pay for only 750. Touhy, who had his barrels custom-built and air-tested for leaks, knew he was being chiseled.

"You owe me for eight hundred," he told Capone.

"Well," Capone waffled, "the boys told me there were fifty leakers. I'll check on it."

The next day Capone paid $30,000 cash for all eight hundred barrels. When Capone called the following week to see about acquiring another five hundred barrels, Touhy said his regular customers had already taken his full supply. "That wasn't exactly true," recalled Touhy, "but what was the use of needling him by saying I didn't do business with weasels?"

Summer went on. The beer flowed. The cops looked away. The mayor snickered. The courts remained clogged. The gangland truce held, give or take a couple dozen shootings. And a young Prohibition officer named Eliot Ness made his first meaningful bust—nailing a small-town mayor as he delivered two barrels of beer to a roadhouse in suburban Lyons—but no one, including Capone, paid any attention. Neither did anyone make much fuss about this item in the May 17 edition of the *Chicago Tribune*:

"Washington, D.C.—Bootleggers must file income tax returns, the Supreme Court of the United States held today."

UNEASY LIES THE HEAD

Early in November 1927, the federal government dropped all the charges that had been filed a year earlier against Cicero's leading gangsters and politicians. The indictments had been too broad, the evidence too thin. Seventy-four indictments vanished in the stroke of a pen when U.S. Attorney Johnson announced he couldn't make the charges stick.

To celebrate, Capone went shopping.

He decided to redecorate his hotel suite, ordering lamp shades, bookends, a sofa, a table, a couple of walnut chairs, and three elephant figurines. Capone had a weakness for elephant figurines. He collected them in all shapes and sizes, mostly with upturned trunks, which were said to be symbols of good luck, like horseshoes. While he was ordering the items for his hotel suite, he also ordered some for the family home on South Prairie Avenue: a walnut dining room set, including a table, chairs, a china cabinet, and buffet; a new mattress and bedspring; a couple of pillows; a lamp; Chinese rugs; and a few other odds and ends. He made the selections himself, seemingly without help from his wife, and once again he paid cash; the tab came to $2,000. He also dropped in at Marshall Field & Company, where he picked up three sets of silk underwear ($12 a set), six new suits ($135 each), twelve custom-made shirts (about $25 a shirt), eighteen collars ($2 or $2.50 each), twenty-four monograms (at $1 each), twenty-eight ties ($4 or $5 each), and twenty-eight handkerchiefs ($3 each). Altogether in 1927, he purchased a total of twenty-seven suits from Marshall Field.

By now his suite at the Metropole had grown to eight rooms, occupying most of the fourth floor. He paid $1,200 to $1,500 a week, depending on the size of his bar and restaurant tab. In September, when all the world's attention had turned to Chicago for the heavyweight championship fight between Gene Tunney and Jack Dempsey, Capone had rented the hotel's banquet room and tossed a two-day party for friends, relatives, and some of the out-of-town celebrities and underworld figures who had come to town to see the fight. The charges for food and drink totaled $3,000. Capone was rumored to have bet $45,000 on Dempsey. As the boxer told it, Capone had offered to ensure a favorable outcome. When Dempsey refused, Capone supposedly sent him a floral arrangement with a note that read, "In the name of sportsmanship."

About one hundred and twenty-five thousand fans jammed Soldier Field on Chicago's lakefront to watch the fight. Dempsey knocked Tunney to the canvas with a left hook to the chin in the seventh round, then stood over his opponent, glowering, as he always did, apparently forgetting about the new rule that required him to retreat to a neutral corner. Tunney spent at least fourteen seconds on the mat, and probably should have been counted out, but managed to rise before the referee could call it a knockout. Dempsey failed to move in for the kill. Tunney recomposed himself, danced away, hit Dempsey, danced, and kept on dancing and hitting, hitting and dancing, until Dempsey looked old, soft, and thoroughly beaten. Tunney won by unanimous decision.

Capone may have lost a bundle on Dempsey, but he had no trouble paying his hotel bills. He always settled his tab in cash, pulling a big wad from his pocket. Only rarely did the hotel's manager need to remind him to pay up.

———

Meanwhile, over in Chicago's Little Italy, a long-running, internecine battle was threatening to become a citywide problem—and the biggest challenge yet to the truce that Capone had forged among his gun-toting peers.

It had started in May when someone fired two hundred rounds from a machine gun into the Aiello & Company Bakery on West Division Street. In the back-and-forth that followed during the next few weeks, sixteen men died. The man at the heart of the dispute was Joe Aiello, a big, tough, sad-eyed Sicilian immigrant. For years, Aiello and his brothers had been content to run their family bakery and to sell a little bit of pure alcohol on the side. For bakers and grocers, alcohol production was simple, because they already possessed the necessary ingredients, namely large amounts of sugar and yeast. But when Aiello had begun pushing to expand that part of his business, he ran into firm opposition from the Genna brothers, also known as the Terrible Gennas. The Gennas—once there were six of them; now, several gangland clashes later, there were three—were early allies of Torrio and Capone. Dozens of Little Italy residents operated stills in their basements and garages, and much of the alcohol they produced went to the Genna brothers. They sold it to the bootleggers, thus assuming most of the risk in exchange for the biggest chunk of the profit. With their ranks depleted, the Gennas had turned for help in running the business to a couple of murderous brutes: Albert Anselmi and John Scalise. It was said that Anselmi had a left eye that didn't properly align with the right and that Scalise had a right eye made of glass. But between them, the story went, they could shoot straight.

The Gennas also had the support of the Unione Siciliana, the fraternal organization that operated like a shadow government in Little Italy, getting out the vote, muscling favors from politicians, and settling disputes. They thought that was enough to ensure the smooth operation of their business, which is why they began spending more time out of the city and leaving Anselmi and Scalise in charge.

But they underestimated the anger and resentment of Aiello. For years, Aiello had worked closely with the Unione, and he had hoped one day to run the organization. In many ways, the president of the Unione was the most powerful man in Chicago's Italian community. Aiello believed the job belonged to him. When it went instead to Capone's pal Tony Lombardo, Aiello fumed. Lombardo was thirty-four years old, square-jawed, thick-chested, and tight-lipped, with a magnificent head of brown hair that he combed straight back. He was described by one newspaper as "a merchant, a commission man, a dealer in sugar," which was not-so-subtle code for a bootlegger, a shotgun man, and a gangster. Still, Lombardo was one of the friendliest bootleggers around, levelheaded and perpetually calm.

Aiello, a former ally but now a rival for power, was one of the only men in town who hated him enough to want him dead. Aiello sensed the time had come to make his push. His plan was an ambitious one—to kill Capone and Lombardo and to knock the Gennas out of business. To strengthen his position, he forged an alliance with the North Side gang formerly run by Dean O'Banion and then by Hymie Weiss and then by Schemer Drucci, and at present by Bugs Moran. If it worked, Aiello would be the most powerful underworld figure in Chicago.

For starters, Aiello put out word that he would pay $50,000 to any man who killed Capone. Four executioners came in from out of town, each intending to do the job on his own. But Capone's top hit man, McGurn, learned of the plots and killed the would-be assassins before they could get close to Capone. Another story has it that Aiello offered a chef at the Bella Napoli Café $35,000 to put drops of prussic acid in the food served to Lombardo and Capone. The chef, after agreeing to do the job, lost his nerve and ratted to Capone.

That was enough to make Capone forget about cooperation.

Three days after his shopping spree, Capone gave the order to kill Aiello. But when the cops heard about it, they reacted with a force that must have shocked Capone, because in all his years in Chicago nothing like it had happened before.

William O'Connor, the new chief of detectives, ordered every one of the department's 105 squad cars on the street to look for known gangsters. He told his men to bring the thugs into the police station regardless of whether they had broken the law. Beat them if they complain, he said, and shoot them if they resist. "It has come to pass, men," he told his officers in exhorting them to action, "when we've got to show that society and the police department are running this town, and not a bunch of dirty rats." Anyone killing a "notorious gang feudist," he said, will be in line for a reward or promotion.

O'Connor asked for officers with experience firing machine guns, "honest-to-God men who will be loyal to the police department and the public in this matter." If his machine gunners were to encounter a gang, he said, "I hope to arrive on the scene with the top of their car shot off and the hoodlums all dead. We're not going to stand for any gang war in Chicago!"

The weather was unusually warm, but a big chill was forecast in time for Thanksgiving. The cops, working on a tip, raided a flat at 4441 West Washington Boulevard, opposite Tony Lombardo's home, where they found two shotguns and ammunition. From there, they hustled to the Rex Hotel, where they arrested a man from Milwaukee who had allegedly been hired to assassinate Capone and Lombardo. After taking the man to jail, they motored to the Atlantic Hotel, where, in room 302, they found still more rifles and more ammunition. The room's window overlooked a Clark Street saloon owned by former alderman Michael "Hinky Dink" Kenna, and where Capone and Lombardo were said to be regular customers. Later, when the killer from Milwaukee confessed that it was Aiello who'd hired him, the police grabbed Aiello and took him to the detective bureau.

Yet despite aggressive law-enforcement activity, Capone was not cowering. If anything, he may have been grateful to the cops for taking so many of his would-be assassins off the street. Still, he wanted Aiello dead. To see if he could make it happen, he sent some of his men downtown to the police station to see if they could get to Aiello there.

Given the liberties the cops had extended him over the years, Capone might have been justified in thinking he could get away with ordering a hit at the detectives' headquarters. But the police were operating under new orders, and they came from a surprising place: the office of the mayor, Big Bill Thompson.

Thompson had been having a good year. He'd won favorable headlines by pushing schools and libraries to purge themselves of history books containing "anti-American" propaganda. New bridges and roads had opened all across Chicago, always with parades. Work had started to straighten the southern branch of the Chicago River. Plans had been launched for a lakefront airport, with the mayor saying he hoped to see the city make its fortune by winning "the business of the skies." The Dempsey-Tunney fight had created a huge spectacle, drawing worldwide attention, and Thompson had been congratulated for bringing it off smoothly. Responding to the devastating flooding along the Mississippi earlier that year, he had called for a comprehensive federal flood control plan and traveled the nation promoting the idea, to glowing reviews. Thompson's press clippings were so good, in fact, that he was being mentioned as a possible candidate for president. Herbert Hoover, the secretary of commerce, was considered the Republican Party favorite, but he faced powerful pockets of opposition, especially from leaders of big business and opponents of the dry laws, who didn't care for Hoover's rigid approach to Prohibition and strict moral codes. Thompson's larger-than-life personality and strong campaign skills might be enough to help him defeat Hoover, his backers theorized, but only if he could first show the nation that he was not in bed with Chicago's criminal element.

In particular, he would have to make an example of Capone.

Thirty minutes after Aiello reached the police station, three of Capone's bodyguards were arrested for loitering in front of a courthouse a few doors away on South Clark Street. Some of the newspapers described it as a routine arrest; others made it out to be high drama, suggesting that dozens of Capone's men had surrounded the police station, intent on murdering Aiello even as he remained in custody. But whether there were dozens of armed thugs or a mere three, all the papers agreed on what happened next.

Inside the station, one of Capone's bodyguards, Samuel Marcus, managed to conceal an extra pistol in the waistband of his pants. While under interrogation, Marcus leaped to his feet, pulled the weapon, and aimed it at O'Connor, the chief of detectives. Jumping from his chair, O'Connor ran toward the gunman and grabbed his arm. A scrum followed, with cop after cop piling on until the gun was wrested away and Capone's men were tossed in a cell that was conveniently located next to that of Aiello. There, Aiello pleaded in Italian with Capone's men, according to a police officer who overheard the men.

"Can't we settle this?" Aiello asked. "Give me just fifteen days, just fifteen days, and I will sell my stores and house and leave everything in your hands. Think of my wife and baby and let me go."

The men laughed. Control of the Unione was vital to Capone's business. Anyone who challenged Capone's clout with the Unione had to go.

"You dirty rat," one of the Capone men said. "You're as good as dead."

While all this was taking place, Capone was down the block in a courtroom, facing a charge of vagrancy. When the judge asked what evidence they had to support the charge, the prosecutors admitted they had none. Capone was released. Presumably he made his way home without the service of his three bodyguards.

Later that night, Aiello posted bond, and he, too, was released. But he was not sure he wanted to go free. With his wife and eight-year-old son at the station, he begged Chief O'Connor to provide them with a police escort.

"We haven't enough policemen to protect honest citizens," O'Connor told him, "and we certainly aren't going to assign any to protect hoodlums. However, I'll send a squad with you to New York, if you'll agree to board a boat and go back to where you came from."

Aiello refused. An officer was assigned to escort the criminal and his family home. On his way out, Aiello looked over his shoulder at the Capone men still in their cell and spat on the ground. When he got home, he packed his things and fled the city.

The next day, a bomb destroyed an Aiello brothel on West Adams Street. The day after that, dynamite ripped apart a gambling den on South Halsted. It wasn't clear if the dynamite attack was aimed at Aiello, but the newspapers treated it as if it was part of the same ongoing war. The public became so frightened that an Evanston woman called the police at one point to say someone had fired a shot—possibly from a machine gun—into her home, when in fact the only explosion had been the popping of a cork on a fermented jug of cider.

As police continued to round up gangsters, one officer was shot and killed by one of his own men during a Washington Boulevard car chase. It was a messy way to fight crime, but Mike Hughes, the chief of police, said his men were beginning to gain control of the city. "We have this gang situation in hand now, and the first move toward further violence is going to be regretted by somebody," he announced. As part of his plan, the chief said he had identified five key gang leaders—Capone, Moran, Barney Bertsche, Bill Skidmore, and Jack Zuta—and had told his officers to arrest the men any chance they got. If the charges proved too weak and the men were released, he wanted them arrested again immediately.

At least eleven bombs exploded that week, most of them doing nothing more than property damage. But a couple of gangsters died, and the police paid frequent visits to the Metropole Hotel, where they pinched anyone who even looked like he might be associated with Capone.

When Capone was asked to identify some of the men corralled by the cops, he refused. That led the officers to charge Capone with disorderly conduct. But when the court clerk called his name, Capone wasn't there.

"Mr. Capone was here and looked over the docket and did not see his name," explained his lawyer, Tyrell Richardson, "so he left."

"Well, here it is," said the clerk, pointing to the docket, which read " 'Scarface' Brown"; Al Brown and "Scarface" Brown being among Capone's aliases.

"Mr. Capone did not recognize that appellation," the lawyer said.

The next day, the docket corrected, Capone, surrounded by seven bodyguards, returned to face the same charge. His right hand stayed in his pocket, and his left tugged on a cigarette as he walked into the courtroom.

A crowd of two hundred Chicagoans gathered on the sidewalk to get a look at him. He covered his face with his hat when photographers tried to take his picture, but he did stop briefly to make small talk with reporters.

"Have all your friends been denatured?" a reporter asked, referring to Capone's bodyguards.

"I denatured them before we came," he answered with a grin. "There's not a rod in the crowd."

Only after Capone's grand arrival did prosecutors tell the court that they had decided not to bring charges, whereupon Capone walked out as serenely as he had walked in. Clearly, the cops' strategy was to harass him. Police pressure was costing the gang leaders $300,000 a day, by one estimate, as dance halls and gambling shops all over the city temporarily shut their doors and turned out their lights. There also were reports that the Aiello gang might have picked up the support of some New York City gangsters, including Capone's old friend Frankie Yale, who wanted to see Lombardo forced out as the leader of the Unione Siciliana. On the night of November 28, a Monday, when the cops went to the Metropole to see what Capone and his men were up to, they found that Capone's place there had been evacuated. Capone and his men had left town, heading to Wisconsin for some duck hunting. They returned to Chicago after a few days, but when they discovered that the pressure from the police had not slackened, Capone decided once more to disappear.

"I'm leaving for St. Petersburg, Florida, tomorrow," he told reporters at the Metropole, where he sat in one of his newly purchased easy chairs, still dressed in his hunting clothes, his fleshy face carrying six days of dark beard.

He said he owned property in St. Pete and wanted to check it out. Capone didn't play the stock market, which was going like gangbusters at the time. It was one of the few gambles he didn't like. But he was doing nicely with his real estate investment in Florida, and he was thinking that it might be time to sell. "Let the worthy citizens of Chicago get their liquor the best way they can. I'm sick of the job—it's a thankless one and full of grief. I don't know when I'll get back, if ever. But it won't be until after the holidays, anyway."

Clearly, the mayor's new approach to government was irritating Capone. "I've been spending the best years of my life as a public benefactor. I've given people the light pleasures, shown them a good time. And all I get is abuse—the existence of a hunted man. I'm called a killer. Well, tell the folks I'm going away now. I guess murder will stop. There won't be any more booze. You won't be able to find a crap game even, let alone a roulette wheel or a faro game. . . . 'Public service' is my motto. Ninety-nine percent of the people in Chicago drink and gamble. I've tried to serve them decent liquor and square games. But I'm not appreciated. It's no use.

"Say, the coppers won't have to lay all the gang murders on me now. Maybe they'll find a new hero for the headlines. It would be a shame, wouldn't it, if while I was away they would forget about me and find a new gangland chief? I wish all friends and enemies a Merry Christmas and a Happy New Year. That's all they'll get from me this year. I hope I don't spoil anybody's Christmas by not sticking around."

By that he referred to his habit of making lavish Christmas gifts to the politicians, police, and precinct workers who had served him well throughout the year. One paper said he usually dished out $100,000 a year in bonuses.

"My wife and my mother hear so much about what a terrible criminal I am. It's getting too much for them, and I'm just sick of it all myself. The other day a man came in here and said that he had to have $3,000. If I'd give it to him, he said, he would make me beneficiary in a $15,000 insurance policy he'd take out and then kill himself. I had to have him pushed out. Today I got a letter from a woman in England. Even over there I'm known as a gorilla. She offered to pay my passage to London if I'd kill some neighbors she'd been having a quarrel with. The papers have made me out to be a millionaire, and hardly an hour goes by that somebody doesn't want me to invest in some scheme or stake somebody in business. That's what I've got to put up with just because I give the public what the public wants. I never had to send out high pressure salesmen. Why, I could never meet the demand!"

He claimed that he had no criminal record, that he had "never stuck up a man in my life," and that none of his men robbed or burglarized while working for "the outfit," as far as he knew. For Capone, it was an astonishing monologue. Whether he intended it as a valedictory or merely a cry for understanding, it revealed with no uncertainty a shift in dynamic. "Uneasy lies the head that wears a crown," wrote Shakespeare in *Henry IV,* Part II. Capone was king of Chicago's underworld, which meant any number of smaller criminals might gain from his demise. At the same time, his cozy relations with the Chicago press corps had made him an international celebrity and a leading symbol of lawlessness, which meant that ambitious cops and politicians had incentives to take him down.

The month of November had delivered warm temperatures, but a massive cold front was sweeping down across Canada to the Great Lakes. Coal trucks rolled slowly through the city's neighborhoods as families loaded up. Light snow fell, and the mercury nosedived toward zero. Once the cold hit town, everyone knew it would hang on with a vengeance until the whole of Chicago started to feel bleak, gray, and lifeless.

With that in mind, on the morning of December 8, Capone, his wife, and two of his men boarded a train. But it was several days before the newsmen realized he'd gone not to St. Petersburg, as he had promised, but to Los Angeles. He set up shop at the Biltmore and kept quiet. He visited a movie studio. He took a tour of the stars' homes and concluded that Mary Pickford's old digs were nicer than her new ones. He took Mae to Tijuana to see the horse races. The *Los Angeles Evening Herald* caught up with Capone and found him "an extremely healthy looking young man." He told the reporter, "I am just a peaceful tourist and I want to take a rest and look over this country, which I have heard so much about. I had no reason for leaving Chicago other than I wanted to get away for a rest." But after a couple of days, the newspapers started paying Capone more attention than he preferred, and on December 13, the manager of the Biltmore politely asked him to leave. "They're picking on me," he complained at the train station as he boarded the Super Chief to head back to Chicago. "I wanted to stay here awhile and rest. But I didn't get a break. I don't want to get into any arguments, here or anyplace else, so I'll do my resting in Chicago."

A columnist for the *Los Angeles Times* expressed sympathy, saying that if officials couldn't bring charges against Capone, they ought to leave him alone. "Now, really, the U.S.A. ought to have some system of taking care of its men like Capone. It isn't fair to let them amass $2,000,000 and then harry them from pillar to post and deny them the rewards of their sparkling diligence. . . . Here he is at once a free citizen and not a free citizen."

Meanwhile, the police in Chicago were saying Capone would not be allowed to return home, that he'd be locked up if they spotted him. In Chillicothe, Illinois, just north of Peoria, a reporter from Chicago intercepted Capone's train and managed to get an interview. "I am too mad to talk about it," Capone said, reflecting on his experience in California. "They asked me to leave. I had paid my bills and acted like a gentleman. They told me it was a tourist town. I am a tourist, but they chase me out."

By then, everyone on board knew the infamous gangster was traveling in their midst. He could no longer leave his quarters. Capone said that he knew Chicago police would be laying for him at the train station, so he decided to get off in Joliet, fifty miles outside of town, spend the night there, and drive home the next morning. But his plan was ruined when police in Joliet, working on a tip, intercepted Ralph and some of his buddies. When a Joliet cop approached Ralph and his boys, the men tried to toss their guns in a trash can. Too late. The weapons were taken away, and the men were arrested. When the train puffed to a stop in Joliet's Union Station at 9:45 A.M. on December 16 and Capone stepped off, he was greeted not by his brother but by a Joliet police captain.

"You're Al Capone," he said.

"Pleased to meet you," said Capone.

Asked to turn over any weapons in his possession, Capone gave up a pistol and two magazines of cartridges. He spent the next eight hours at the Joliet jail, charged with possession of a concealed weapon. When his cell mate started to get on his nerves, Capone asked his jailer if he could pay the stranger's $22 fine from the $2,945 Capone had in his pocket when he arrived. The request was granted and Capone had a private cell for the rest of the afternoon.

He posted bond shortly before 6:00 P.M. and left Joliet for Chicago. That night, police surrounded his house on South Prairie Avenue, threatening to arrest him again if he emerged. But neighbors told reporters that Capone had already come and gone. Later, he was spotted downtown, walking into the Weinstein jewelry shop on State Street, where he purchased thirty diamond-studded belt buckles at $275 apiece, and twenty beaded purses at $22.50 each. Capone was still angry at the way he'd been treated, and in all likelihood not everyone would be getting a gift that year, but he wasn't going to be a complete Scrooge.

DEEPEST IN DIRT

Though its economy was roaring, its arts scene thriving, and its skyscrapers scraping more loftily than New York's, the Windy City was known primarily for one thing: crime. Chicago had developed a bad reputation.

On January 18, 1928, a Wednesday night, more than 250 of the city's leading citizens met at the Hotel LaSalle in the heart of the business district to chew over the problem. After a mild afternoon, the temperatures were falling fast, nasty winds were blowing from the west, and the water along the shore of Lake Michigan was starting to freeze. Stepping into the walnut-paneled lobby of the LaSalle, the men could feel the blood returning to their cheeks. The air inside smelled reassuringly of cigar smoke. Judges, business executives, and merchants shook hands and exchanged greetings. They talked about the headlines in that afternoon's papers: Three more bootleggers in Chicago Heights had been taken for a ride, all dead. Capone's involvement was suspected but unproved.

In the 1920s, as today, people clamored for news, especially news of crime. They bought at least two newspapers a day, one in the morning and one in the afternoon. If an unusually big story broke, the papers would print special editions, and young hawkers would canvass the city streets screaming headlines. Even personal news traveled pretty quickly. A man could hand a note to the headwaiter at his favorite restaurant or the clerk at his club and know it would be sent by courier across town immediately; often, he would have his reply before he finished his meal or his massage.

Big crowds used to turn out to hear dynamic speakers such as the larger-than-life attorney Clarence Darrow expounding on themes such as civil liberties, religion, and free thought. On this evening they came to hear State's Attorney Robert Crowe and Chief of Police Mike Hughes, as well as some of the city's top businessmen, discussing a specific issue: crime in Chicago. Hughes opened the meeting by boasting that crime was down 41 percent through the first ninety days of Mayor Thompson's latest term. Not everyone was buying it.

Silas H. Strawn, one of the city's most respected lawyers and president of the American Bar Association, summed up the issue: "All over the world," he said, "we hear about the crime situation in Chicago. . . . I do not believe crime is greater in Chicago than in any other large city of its size. The trouble is, people don't seem to take into consideration many vital elements—the growth in population and wealth. Then there is the improved methods of transportation, which enables the up-to-date criminal to escape, and the improved method of distributing crime news all over. I've lived here thirty-six years and never been held up, robbed, molested, nor racketeered, and I think the same can be said for most of you gentlemen."

Strawn's remarks rang true. The city's rapid expansion—it grew tenfold from 1870 to 1930—had indeed made it difficult to govern. Many gangsters were in fact better equipped for their jobs than the cops who chased them. And most Chicagoans really did go about their day-to-day lives without fear of being victimized.

But Strawn was wrong about one thing: Violent crime in Chicago really *was* worse than in most other large cities. In fact, the city's murder rate was roughly double that of New York's. Not all of the violence involved gangs; much of it occurred in the city's African-American neighborhoods, where poverty ran high and police presence low, but statistics showed that Chicago had more than its share of bootleg-related murders. Killing had simply become a routine part of the beer business. Why were Chicago bootleggers more apt to kill than Cincinnati bootleggers or Milwaukee bootleggers? The answer was simple: They were more likely to get away with it.

In Chicago, an astonishing 48 percent of all felony charges were dropped during preliminary hearings, according to a 1926 survey. In Milwaukee during the same period, only 17 percent of all cases were so quickly dismissed. In Chicago, only 15 percent of all felony cases ended with executed sentences, compared to 36 percent in Milwaukee. Murderers were brought to justice in Chicago during the 1920s, but not many. During Crowe's first two terms in office, the number of murders in Cook County nearly doubled. There were 349 murder victims—215 of them gangsters—yet Crowe's office won only 128 convictions for murder, none involving gangsters.

The problem was chronic. Chicago's police department still didn't have enough officers on the street, and it was especially lacking in qualified detectives. Plenty of beat cops were promoted to detective, but most of them remained beat cops at heart, with little of the knowledge or training required to conduct complex criminal investigations. Many of them took routine payoffs from gangs. And if the cops were corrupt, the courts were more so. Judges were elected to office, and to get elected they needed to stay on good terms with ward bosses and precinct captains, many of whom ran their offices from the back rooms of saloons. Getting elected also took money, and gangsters were always willing to make donations to judges who might one day return the favor. Once in office, the judges found their dockets hopelessly crowded. They had no choice but to dismiss or delay massive numbers of cases, so if a judge just happened to dismiss a case involving a criminal who had contributed to his campaign fund, the judge could justify it in his own mind as a case that probably would have been dropped anyway. Judges were never required to explain how they decided which cases to assign for trial and which to dismiss. That helped explain why poor African-American criminals were more likely to be tried and convicted; they lacked the clout to make the charges disappear. It also helps explain why a man such as Capone could operate so freely for so long.

The booming economy should have lowered Chicago's crime rate. Jobs were abundant, investments flowering, wallets fat. Crime rates tended to fall during good times, but this time it didn't happen. Chicago was too corrupt, and the backlash against Prohibition was too strong. By 1928, the Eighteenth Amendment remained overwhelmingly unpopular, and most Chicagoans had learned to tolerate a certain level of crime as long as they got their beer. It was the above-average citizens—the Strawns and the Julius Rosenwalds—who had the most reason to complain about the bootlegging business and its effect on the city's reputation. They could tolerate drinking. They could tolerate murder. But losing money was another matter, and the city's reputation was getting to be bad for business.

Chicago had always been known as a gritty city of slaughterhouses and switching yards. "First in violence, deepest in dirt," wrote the journalist Lincoln Steffens in 1904. It was dirty and tough and crooked, and much of it stank. But a man still could make an honest living and even get rich if he worked hard. That was the image the titans of industry wanted to perpetuate.

Lately, though, the world seemed to be increasingly under the impression that gangsters ran the town and that machine-gun shoot-outs on Michigan Avenue were routine occurrences. It didn't help that the newspapers loved gangsters. They loved the language of bootlegging: *Tommy guns, pineapple bombs, death cars.* They loved the nicknames. And they especially loved the ever-accessible, charismatic Capone.

A few speakers at the meeting tweaked the press for wrecking Chicago's image, and damaging tourism and business. Thomas E. Donnelley, the president of the R. R. Donnelley printing company, however, stood that night to say that the men gathered before him were wasting their time if all they wanted to do was blame the newspapers, the police, and the courts. He suggested that the city's legitimate businesses fight the illegitimate ones at their own game. "We will not get far with the courts as they are organized," he said. "We can ask the judges to do something about continuances and to use ordinary common sense in administering the law and not to look for sophistries and technicalities to let criminals off. Crime is much complicated with politics. We find men with political pull going to the front for criminals. The only way out is to get some politics on the other side. This meeting should be the beginning of a movement to get behind officials, show that we have more pull than the criminals. Let them know that decent Chicago is going to organize to the task and take ten years if necessary, putting pressure on officials so that crime will be punished speedily and justly."

Donnelley and the others didn't know much about fighting crime, but they did know about power. Soon after the meeting, the city's business leaders began lobbying Charles G. Dawes, who may have been the most powerful Chicagoan of them all, to come to their aid. Dawes was vice president of the United States, serving under Coolidge at the time. Three years earlier, in 1925, he'd won the Nobel Prize for his work in stabilizing Germany's postwar economy. Under President McKinley, he'd served as budget director and comptroller of the currency. If Chicago's justice system couldn't stop the city's crime problem, perhaps the federal government might help.

"The public is at last aroused," Dawes wrote in his journal in 1928. He told his friends in Chicago that he would see what he could do.

PINEAPPLES AND COCONUTS

After experiencing a rude reception in Los Angeles, and a ruder reception upon returning to Illinois—with one police harassment after another—Capone decided to try another city: Miami.

He arrived in January 1928, settling into a furnished bungalow on the beach, at 3605 Indian Creek Drive. He paid for six months of rent up front, pulling C-notes from a wad of cash and handing them to the real estate agent until they added up to $2,500. Of course, it was never enough to have one home. If his wife and son were to stay at the bungalow on the beach, Capone would need another place to do business. For that, he chose the Ponce de Leon Hotel, one of the grandest establishments in all of Florida, where he registered under the name Albert Costa. Days were spent playing tennis and golf. Nights were devoted to prizefights, dog races, and horse races. He stayed in touch with his associates in Chicago, but he made no attempt to build a southern satellite operation. He was simply looking to relax. He gave no indication of how long he planned to stay.

Miami's elite reacted to Capone as if an alligator had crawled into one of their backyard parties: They screamed, backed away, and tried not to do anything that would anger the beast. But the city's rank and file didn't seem to mind him much. Capone was hardly the biggest problem facing most of the locals that winter.

Between 1920 and 1925, the city's population had shot up from thirty thousand to seventy-five thousand, and it had seemed, at times, as if one in every two of those residents had been peddling real estate. Homes had been selling and reselling, prices rocketing ever higher. A salesman making $4,000 a year and renting a modest apartment was suddenly confident, thanks to easily available mortgages, that he could afford a home with an ocean view. And if that same salesman happened to earn $6,000 a year, he may have been persuaded to invest in a real estate development that everyone said would turn to gold a few years down the line. Everywhere, new hotels, new housing complexes—even whole new cities—were rising from the swampy soil. Miami Beach itself was less than a decade old. It was the new Gold Rush, and promoters said it would never end. The economy surged relentlessly, in wave after glorious wave, carrying with it not just the hopes and dreams of Floridians, but also of dreamers everywhere. The *Miami Herald* sold so many ads one day in the summer of 1925 that it needed 504 pages to print them all, setting a record at the time for American newspapers.

But by 1926 it had become clear that many of the men and women gobbling up land and investing in developments had overextended themselves. Some had been duped by con artists into buying worthless and even nonexistent parcels. Real estate values multiplied and multiplied again, but when prices showed the first sign of weakness, many buyers pulled out, and projects went into default. Life savings were lost. Then came a couple of vicious hurricanes to remind everyone that life in South Florida was not without risk. That's when the money started flowing in reverse: out of the town. Housing prices tumbled, families lost homes, and the region slumped into an economic depression. By the time Capone arrived in 1928, most of the city's real estate offices had closed. Half-built subdivisions lined the coast. Suddenly Miami had trouble collecting enough taxes to meet its expenses.

Capone might not have been the sort of citizen the city fathers had hoped to attract, but at least he had money to spend. The *Miami Daily News,* in reporting Capone's arrival, mentioned that he and eight friends had visited a nightclub and left their waiter a $20 tip. The paper also said the Chicago mob boss was interested in opening his own nightclub or gambling hall in Miami.

To assure his new neighbors that he intended to be a law-abiding citizen, he requested a meeting with Miami's police chief, Leslie Quigg. A press conference followed. "Miami's climate is more healthful than Chicago's and warmer than California, that's why I'm here," said Capone to the press, shoving both hands deep into the pockets of crisply pressed blue serge trousers and smiling for all he was worth. "Yes, I like Miami so well that I'm going to vacation here all winter. In fact, I expect my wife, mother, and child in on the train this afternoon and we plan to buy a home either in Coral Gables or Miami Beach." He noted that he might purchase additional real estate now that there were bargains to be had for the patient investor. He said he expected the market to turn around in about five years.

"Let's lay the cards on the table," Capone said straightforwardly to the police chief. "You know who I am and where I come from. I just want to ask a question. Do I stay or must I get out?"

"You can stay as long as you behave yourself," Quigg said.

"I'll stay as long as I'm treated like a human being," answered Capone.

Then he turned to the gathering of reporters. "Gentlemen," he said, "I am at your service. I've been hounded and pushed around for days. It began when somebody heard I was in town. All I have to say is that I'm orderly." He praised Miami as "the garden of America, the sunny Italy of the New World, where life is good and abundant, where happiness is to be had even by the poorest." He vowed to join the local Rotary Club, if they would have him.

But when newspapermen took a negative view of Capone's adoption of a new hometown, some members of the city council complained that the gangster should be driven out. Capone continued his public relations campaign, this time meeting with the mayor of Miami Beach, Newton Lummus Jr. Afterward, Lummus—perhaps persuaded, perhaps bought off—told the press: "Mr. Capone was one of the fairest men I have ever been in conference with. He was not ordered to leave Miami Beach, but after our conference yesterday he decided it would be to the best interests of all concerned if he left. It was a mutual agreement." Capone didn't leave, though. In fact, he decided to put down roots, and Mayor Lummus helped him.

Capone developed a friendship with Parker A. Henderson Jr., who ran the Hotel Ponce de Leon. Henderson was the son of a former mayor of Miami, which meant he had useful connections. More important, he liked doing favors for Capone. Three or four times a week, Capone would give Henderson a batch of Western Union money orders, with "Albert Capone" or "Albert Costa" listed as the payee. Capone would endorse the money orders in Henderson's presence. Then Henderson, accompanied by a Capone bodyguard, would take them to the Miami Beach Bank and

Trust Company, where he would exchange them for cash. He delivered more than $30,000 over the course of that first winter in Miami.

When Capone told Henderson that he was interested in buying a house in the area, Henderson told Mayor Lummus, and Lummus, a real estate developer like almost everyone else, offered to broker the deal—in exchange for a commission, of course. With Lummus's help, Capone picked out a house on Palm Island, a cigar-shaped sliver of land that sat roughly halfway between the mainland and Miami Beach in Biscayne Bay. It was a two-story, neo-Spanish-style house built of white stucco and surrounded by a dozen tall palm trees with coconuts growing beneath their branches. The beer magnate from St. Louis Clarence Busch had built the place in 1922. It contained fourteen rooms. The master bedroom was at the rear of the second floor, overlooking the water. The property was three hundred feet long and one hundred feet wide, with a small guesthouse over the garage. At $40,000, the price was steep enough that Capone chose to arrange an installment plan. He agreed to pay in four annual installments, at 8 percent interest. But the transaction was not quite straightforward. Capone had been careful throughout his career not to leave a paper trail. Since the purchase of his family home on South Prairie Avenue, he had put almost nothing in his own name—no bank accounts, no business licenses, no real estate. His discretion had proved a vital part of his success. Now he had Henderson front the deal, paying a $2,000 binder and an additional $8,000 on his first annual payment, both in cash. After the purchase, on April 2, 1928, Henderson deeded the property to Mae Capone.

Quickly, Al and Mae started making improvements to the place. They built a small water-lily pond with an arched bridge across it, à la Monet. They added a dock on the bay. They installed one of the biggest private swimming pools anyone had seen, sixty feet long and thirty feet wide, built of concrete, with green tiles around the edge. At the north end of the pool, Capone built a two-story cabana so that guests could change their clothes without dripping water through the house. The cabana also served to keep boaters on Biscayne Bay from peering too easily into the estate. To further ensure his privacy, he had eight-foot-high concrete walls built around the property's perimeter—tall enough to protect against drive-by shootings and thick enough to stop a tank—and an iron gate erected across the driveway to keep out oglers, enemies, and the press. Mae decorated the interior, installing new curtains, drapes, and brass lighting fixtures.

The first-floor bathroom, the one used most frequently by guests, was done all in black and gold tile, Art Deco–style, with a black porcelain toilet and brass sconces on the wall.

Sometimes Henderson would write checks from his own account to cover the Capones' purchases and home improvements. Sometimes Jack Guzik would sign the checks. Otherwise, everything was handled with cash. Revenue agents estimated that the improvements cost $50,000 to $75,000, although the *Miami Herald* put the number at only $20,000.

At one point, Capone entertained the notion of joining the American Legion post in Coral Gables. Club officials contacted police in Chicago to see if the applicant had ever been convicted of a crime and were told that he had not (despite numerous arrests). Still, he and Mae did not try to become part of the city's upper crust. When they invited guests, they tended to invite the same types of mugs who had come to Sunday night dinners at Capone's place on South Prairie Avenue in Chicago. In fact, many of the invitees were precisely the same mugs, having been imported from Chicago for the Capone family's amusement.

When Capone bought his first boat, he didn't go for a yacht, he went for a speedboat, and he didn't christen it with a hoity-toity name. He named it the *Sonny and Ralphie,* after his son and his nephew. It was a sign of Capone's humble roots that he enjoyed his wealth and fame but still didn't imagine that he belonged, suddenly, in high society. In the 1920s, anybody could get rich, anybody could get famous, and anybody could refashion his image. A man could change a lot about himself, but he didn't forget where he came from. Capone seemed pleased with all that his wealth had brought him. He had delivered his family a long way from the slums of Brooklyn. But he no doubt would have been more pleased had he been left alone to enjoy his new lifestyle. Once he had craved celebrity as much as he craved power. He was finally learning that notoriety and fame were different.

"If I were guilty of all the newspapers accuse me of," he told one reporter in Miami, "I would be afraid of myself."

While Capone was remodeling and decorating and trying to be polite in Miami, an election was under way in Chicago, and this one was explosive–literally.

The first bomb rocked the home of Charles Fitzmorris, a former newspaper editor, former chief of police, and now the city comptroller under Big Bill Thompson. The next blast shattered the windows at the home of Dr. William H. Reid, the commissioner of public service. After that came another explosive attack on the funeral home operated by John Sbarbaro, a former prosecutor. Yet another bomb tore through the apartment building of Lawrence Cunio, who was the brother-in-law and secretary to State's Attorney Robert Crowe.

Thompson and his men were stunned. Homemade bombs—known as "pineapples," a slang term for hand grenades—had been exploding at a rate of about a dozen a month in Chicago during the past year, but usually they were directed at ordinary citizens who had angered bootleggers, racketeers, or neighbors. If you were a cash register repairman who declined to join a local association of repairmen, for example, or if you refused to place an order for beer with a bootlegger who had come to expect your loyalty, or if you complained to police about the foul odors coming from a neighbor's still, you knew there was a chance someone might throw a homemade bomb through your window. It was the price of independence and free speech. But it was unusual for political figures to come under attack, and it was especially unusual that the attackers would target the powerful regime of Big Bill Thompson.

Big Bill had given up on the idea of running for president, but he continued traveling the nation and making speeches. He enjoyed the attention. And he thought having a high national profile would help him and his candidates win reelection back in Chicago. Usually Thompson could count on his fellow Republicans to put up little or no opposition in the primaries. But this year, reformers from his own party were coming after him, led by U.S. senator Charles Deneen, the same man who had elevated the unheard-of George E. Q. Johnson to the position of U.S. attorney. For years, Deneen had been hoping to take apart Thompson's machine. Now he saw an opportunity. He was especially eager to replace State's Attorney Crowe with his own man, a circuit court judge named John Swanson. Deneen, Johnson, and Swanson were all Swedes, all moderates, all impassioned reformers. They were all neighbors in the city's South Shore section, too. Was it possible that these good-government men had finally decided to fight dirty? The man who held the answer was anything but a goo-goo. His name was Diamond Joe Esposito, and he was a powerful man.

Diamond Joe was the most important figure in the city's Nineteenth Ward—also known as the Bloody Nineteenth—in the city's Italian ghetto. Once, the Terrible Gennas ruled the Nineteenth. But now that gang wars had eliminated several of them and weakened the rest, Esposito was the man with the most clout. He ruled from his restaurant, the Bella Napoli, where heaping plates of spaghetti and hot bread were served while underworld deals of every sort were made. Esposito's was the place to which gangsters retreated after an emotional funeral to inhale the heady aromas of garlic, marinara, and cigars, and to toast their fallen compadres with brimming glasses of Chianti. Politicians mingled with constituents. Judges mixed with lawyers. Capone was a regular.

Esposito, or "Dimey," as friends called him, got along with everyone—hoodlums and politicians alike—and he made noncelebrities at his restaurant feel just as important as the big shots. He sent gifts when babies were born. He arranged jobs for men who lost theirs. He paid people's doctor bills and rent. At Christmas he distributed baskets of food and toys and handed out dimes to neighborhood tots. And if you crossed him in any serious way, you were likely to be found floating facedown in a canal. "If Dimey wants it," went the expression in the Nineteenth, "it can be done."

Esposito was a big, round man, fifty-five years old, with wavy hair the color of a brand-new nickel. The papers had a habit of quoting him in a heavy Italian accent. "Well, I no hava da college edukashe," recorded the *Trib* in 1926. "I been a poor man all my life. I can read and write a leetle bit. But no-body can say Joe ever do any-body a bad turn. My frens are da beegest and highest men een da ceety of Cheecago, and I got more frens in my ward than any man in Eellinois." While he appeared to avoid any direct involvement in bootlegging, he almost certainly supplied political protection to some of the city's top gangsters, and probably sold sugar to many of Little Italy's alky cookers, too. Esposito married a woman twenty-four years his junior, and in 1926 they named their youngest child Charles, in honor of Esposito's good friend Senator Charles Deneen. They were an odd couple, Esposito and Deneen, but somehow they worked together well—so well that Esposito could not refuse when Deneen asked him to run against one of Thompson's men for ward committeeman. This put Diamond Joe in a dicey spot: He was thoroughly enmeshed in the criminal culture and yet running for office, ostensibly on the reform ticket. Soon after getting in the race, Esposito received a visit from one of

Thompson's heavies. Some have suggested that the messenger was really one of Capone's men working at the behest of the mayor.

"Get out of the ward," the visitor said. "It'll be healthier for you."

"I can't cross 'em," Esposito said, according to a newspaper account of the conversation related some weeks later. "The senator's my fren."

A few days later, Esposito received a phone call, this time with a more stern suggestion.

"Get out of town or get killed," said the voice on the line.

On the night of March 21, 1928, Esposito, campaign still going, met with his precinct captains. On his walk home from his office, accompanied by two unarmed bodyguards, he stopped to chat with one of his neighbors, Rose Seego, who was an election clerk. He told her he didn't think he had much chance of winning the election. All of Thompson's candidates were running strongly. Chicago yet again appeared unready for reform.

"It won't make much of a difference," Esposito told his neighbor. "If I lose, I'll move out of the ward—then I'll be missed."

He walked on, paused to talk to another neighbor, then turned toward home. But before he could get there, a blue Dodge tore around the corner. The first shotgun blast knocked Esposito to the ground. "Oh, my God!" he yelled, knees buckling, and hands clutching his chest, which was suddenly emblazoned with a soaking stain of his own blood. The next blast was fired at such close range that powder burns charred Esposito's suit. His bodyguards, however, were unhurt. In fact, their clothes were not even dirty or torn, which later raised suspicion among police that they might have been in on the hit. Esposito's wife ran from her home to her husband's side in time to see him die. Police found on his body a $5,000 diamond ring, a diamond belt buckle with the initials J E glittering on its front, and about $700 in cash.

Two days later, one of the witnesses to the shooting, John Infantino— a thirty-year-old alky cooker and cousin of Samoots Amatuna, former Unione president, who was gunned down three years prior in a barber's chair—was shot three times in the back of his head, execution-style, while kneeling beside his bed, perhaps in prayer.

Police didn't know why Esposito had been killed, and they still couldn't figure out why Thompson's men had had their houses bombed. But there seemed little doubt that these incidents were politically motivated—and probably connected to Capone's mob. The reformers wanted badly to strip Thompson of his power. Though they didn't have the stomach to toss bombs of their own, they were nonetheless willing to employ characters such as Esposito who played dirty. And if Esposito employed a few pineapple tossers of his own, well, at least the reformers could kid themselves that their hands were clean.

In this wildest of political seasons, the lines between the parties—between the good guys and the bad guys—had been hopelessly tangled. Politics in Chicago was always a mess. Now it had become pure chaos—a knot of corruption so thick the strands were impossible to follow, much less untie—and the whole nation took notice. A couple of days after Esposito's murder, the *Tribune* ran a front-page report on how outsiders had come to view recent events in Chicago. The headline read:

"CHICAGO" WORD OF TERROR
ALL OVER WORLD
Evil Fame Blazoned Far and Near

The story's author, a former drama critic and war correspondent named James O'Donnell Bennett, filed his report from Washington, D.C., writing that his hometown had developed a reputation as "The City of Crime." He quoted from a story in the *Washington Post* that said: "The ill fame of Chicago is spreading through the world and bringing shame to Americans who wish they could be proud of that city." He quoted a *London Evening News* story with the headline "Bomb a Day Keeps Chicago Gay." And he cited the *Arkansas Gazette,* which wrote: "Chicago today is America's worst advertisement. . . . The whole country is humiliated by the spectacle of America's second city overrun by hordes of dirty rats that could be driven out within 24 hours by honest and courageous officers."

The out-of-town journalists put in perspective what many in Chicago failed to see: that the bootleggers and politicians were one and the same. If bootleggers needed the support of politicians, and if politicians needed the support of bootleggers, it was no great surprise that violence would become part of the election process. In fact, it was inevitable.

A few days later, Bennett reported on another wave of unfavorable press clippings: The *Baltimore Sun* said Chicago had fallen victim to "terrorism that startles the country"; the *Washington Star* ran an editorial under the headline "Terrorism and Politics" that described the city as "the scene of lawlessness that has no parallel in the world's history."

And the outcry was about to grow louder. The violence had just begun.

Four thousand people attended the High Requiem Mass for Diamond Joe Esposito, and four thousand people left the church and stood outside in the sleet, snow, and icy rain to watch pallbearers carry his bronze casket to the hearse. The funeral cortege ran a mile and a half long, with three cars of mourners, twenty-five cars of flowers, and hundreds of policemen. The plan called for two airplanes to fly overhead and scatter rose petals along the procession, but the foul weather grounded them.

However, the solemnity of the occasion did not inspire a season of introspection in Chicago. Nor did it bring about a lull in the violence. That night, March 26, 1928, two more bombs exploded—the first at the home of Senator Deneen, the second at the home of Judge Swanson.

The first came at 11:20 P.M. Neighbors said they saw a man in a gray fedora (which was no help at all, since almost every man wore one) jump out of a slow-moving car, bound across the senator's snow-covered lawn to the front porch, then run back to the car, which was still rolling slowly past the senator's house. A black-powder bomb exploded moments later, obliterating the front porch, shattering every window in the twelve-room house, and knocking both the senator's sister and her maid out of their beds. Senator Deneen was on a train bound for Washington at the time of the blast.

A few minutes later, Judge Swanson, just returned from a speaking engagement, steered his car into his driveway. A dark sedan tailed him. It sped quickly, then someone in the car tossed a bomb in the direction of his house. It exploded in midair, knocking out all of the windows and destroying part of the roof. Swanson's wife and two grandchildren were in the house, unhurt. Swanson, still in his car, also was unhurt.

George Johnson, who lived a few doors away, heard the blast and rushed to Swanson's aid. After a series of death threats, Johnson had recently been assigned a full-time Secret Service agent. His house was the safest on the block, so he took the judge and his family home with him and called the police to arrange for additional protection.

"There is no doubt who did this," said Judge Swanson. "It was some of the same crowd who are fighting against my election. It was done by the crooks I want to put out of business. . . . It has come to a pretty pass when a man cannot run for office without endangering the lives of his family."

But rather than condemning the violence, Swanson's election opponent, Robert Crowe, took offense, as if he were being blamed personally for the bombing. He went so far as to accuse Swanson and Deneen of bombing their own homes to make the Thompson administration look bad. Crowe said, "They are resorting to desperate means. . . . After having bombed the homes of friends of mine and made no headway, they are now bombing their own homes in an effort to create the impression that the forces of lawlessness are now running this town." Mayor Big Bill agreed, saying, "I think Bob Crowe has the right slant on what's going on." Chicago's "fake reformers," he said, wouldn't fool anyone by "traveling in sheep's clothes in the daytime and operating with bombs at night."

The campaign of terror continued.

Someone phoned Judge Swanson's adult daughter, whose children had been sleeping at the judge's house at the time of the bombing, and made another threat: "You can tell the judge that we will do a better job next time." A Deneen candidate for committeeman received a letter saying "there is a plot to get one of your babies before the primary." Grace Missionary Church in Elmwood Park, where Swanson was scheduled to speak, received a bomb threat and asked the judge to guarantee reimbursement for any damages that might occur. Swanson agreed to the terms, and no bombing occurred.

Mayor Thompson once more blamed Deneen and his men for bringing on the trouble by forging alliances with gangsters, which would have struck some as funny—coming from Thompson—if the city's nerves hadn't been so thoroughly jangled by that time. Twelve days before the primary election, a commodities trader discovered a massive bomb—sixteen sticks of dynamite wrapped in black tape—sitting in front of a market on South Water Street. It was a big enough explosive to take out everyone and everything within half a block. The fuse on the bomb had already been lit, but falling snow had snuffed it. A federal marshal asked the U.S. attorney general for troops to guard Chicago's ballot boxes on April 10. The attorney general, not inclined to set a precedent or make a move that might tilt a local election, rejected the request.

Killing gangsters and restaurateurs was one thing, but tossing bombs at the homes of a judge and a U.S. senator and trying to blow up half of a city block was quite another. No one knew exactly what had motivated the bombings. Some said they were connected back to the murder of Diamond Joe Esposito, to intimidate the men who were promising to investigate the attack and to put the city's gangsters behind bars, while others believed they were meant to influence the outcome of the election. Either way, as Chicago hung on until Election Day and hunkered through the last weeks of winter, the murmur of national disapproval over conditions in the Second City grew to a thundering roar.

President Coolidge discussed the bombings at a cabinet meeting, and Senator George Norris of Nebraska urged the president to pull U.S. troops from Nicaragua and reassign them to Chicago. The *Cleveland Plain Dealer* wrote that Chicago had become a slave to crime. "Nowhere else in America has the inevitable relationship between fetid politics and lawlessness been better illustrated in recent months. A community willing to endure the kind of administration that rules over Chicago must expect, whether willing or not, to endure the kind of underworld domination that finds logical expression in the bombing of a senator's home." The *Indianapolis News* pronounced: "It stands to reason that the gangs that are operating so notoriously in Chicago could not continue unless they were supported in high places." And the *Boston Globe* wrote: "Gang-rule is supreme. It is only a question of which gang? When the decent citizens of Chicago are really aroused, they will take control. Until then Chicago will remain a joke on all America—on democracy itself."

The terror campaign and the public response stung Thompson. Business leaders who had supported him throughout the campaign began switching sides. A coalition of religious leaders endorsed the Deneen slate of candidates, as did the Chicago Bar Association. Thompson, furious, threatened to resign if his candidates were defeated in the primary. "I ate regular before I became mayor," he said, meaning that he had no trouble making money, "and I will eat regular after I'm mayor!"

Election Day—April 9, 1928—came with the usual assortment of allegations—ballot-stuffing, intimidation of voters, beatings, and so on. When it was over, Thompson's men were routed. The mayor sat slumped in a chair, clenching a cigar in his teeth, his shirtsleeves rolled high enough to reveal elbow-length underwear. "Smile?" he asked when a photographer asked him to put on a happy face. "You'll have to tell me a funny story." In the months and years ahead, he drank heavily, "gabbled hysterically and spoke irrationally," as one biography put it, and "stared through rheumy eyes at men he had known for years." He appeared to be collapsing like a weather-beaten old house, and taking the city with him.

Throughout most of the Pineapple Primary, as it came to be known, Capone remained in Miami, although some accounts suggested that he returned on Election Day to help get out the vote for Thompson. Remarkably, he was never directly blamed for the season's violence. When the local elections were over and the race for president heated up, pitting the Republican Herbert Hoover against the Democrat Al Smith—a supporter of Prohibition against one of the law's most vocal opponents—Chicago emerged as an important issue in the campaign, with Capone the leading symbol of the problem. Chicago was held hostage by gangsters, the bombs and accompanying headlines had turned the nation's second-largest city into an international embarrassment, and pressure was growing on the federal government to do something about it.

THE GRADUATION
OF FRANKIE YALE

Capone commuted between Miami and Chicago throughout the spring and early summer of 1928. At times, playing the benevolent boss, he would bring men from Chicago down South to discuss business and to treat them to a bit of sunshine and fishing. His former mentor, Johnny Torrio, made weekly visits to the Capone estate. Capone threw big dinner parties at his house on the bay, with fifteen or twenty guests invited at a time, the food prepared by one of the former chefs from Colosimo's Restaurant in Chicago. There were cocktail parties, too, with fifty or sixty guests traipsing about the house, sweeping drinks off silver trays, plucking hors d'oeuvres from gleaming dishes, and admiring the wealth of their host. Most of the guests were Chicago gangsters, including Charlie and Rocco Fischetti, Rocco DeGrazia, and Frankie Rio. Capone treated them all well. One day he might pack salami sandwiches and take them fishing; the next he might organize an outing to a swank nightclub, where he would foot the whole bill.

By necessity, he relied on his associates in Chicago to manage more of the business back home. The cops in Chicago still hadn't made any serious attempt to convict him of a crime, but they'd made up their minds to harass him, if nothing else. He'd been operating in the spotlight for two years, ever since the McSwiggin murder, and trying to convince newspapermen that he was only *somewhat* criminal. But fame took its toll. His movements were watched constantly. Each time he attended a horse race or a prizefight he knew there was a chance someone would snap his picture. Each time he traveled from Miami to Chicago, or Chicago to Miami, headlines accompanied him. Newspapers coast to coast were beginning to treat him like a celebrity, so that it didn't matter, really, whether he did anything to warrant attention. There were certain names, such as Lindbergh, Ruth, and Chaplin, that the public hungered for, and once Capone's name was added to the list, newspaper editors did all they could to satisfy that hunger.

It wasn't just the newspapers taking an interest in Capone. On March 24, Lelia Russell, an assistant U.S. attorney in Miami, sent a letter to Mabel Walker Willebrandt, an assistant attorney general of the United States. Willebrandt was one of the most powerful women ever to serve in federal government, and—having been in charge of Prohibition enforcement for the entire decade—one of the most frustrated. Russell reported that Capone and about thirty of his gangsters were "becoming established in Miami to conduct a liquor business on a large scale."

Russell was tall, blond, and slender, and wore her hair in a fashionable bob. She'd started her career as a schoolteacher, became a secretary in a law office, then earned a law degree and worked for the government. Very quickly, she'd earned a reputation for toughness. In the Capone case, she probably got her information from federal agents or from Miami cops she chatted with at the courthouse. The first part of Capone's plan, she told Willebrandt, was "to supply the Shrine and Elks Conventions, which will meet in May and July respectively." Willebrandt assigned a special agent from the Treasury Department to investigate Capone.

The feds would dog him for the rest of his life.

Capone was beginning to realize the mistake he'd made when he had decided to conduct his business openly, to establish a public identity as an overlord of the underworld. Lucky Luciano controlled New York as thoroughly and as profitably as Capone controlled Chicago, but Luciano didn't talk about it, and his name seldom appeared in the papers during the 1920s. The same went for Capone's former boss from Brooklyn, Frankie Yale, who ran a big bootlegging mob but rarely called any attention to himself or his operation. Trying to charm the newspapermen had gotten Capone nowhere. Now the reporters expected him to be accessible, if not accountable. Perhaps Capone should have recognized that it would be difficult to run a criminal enterprise while being held accountable to the press, but it was too late. As a result, he found himself relying more heavily on men such as Guzik, Nitti, and Louis "Little New York" Campagna, a talented gunman often assigned to handle the mob's biggest hits, who was back on the street after doing time for bank robbery. The men were his frequent guests in Miami, and they stayed in touch by telephone when they were in Chicago.

Late in June, Capone was expecting a visit from several of his men. A few days prior to the meeting, he had asked his friend Parker A. Henderson Jr. to get him weapons. Henderson went to a nearby pawnshop and purchased at least half a dozen guns. Capone told him to bring them to a certain room at the Ponce de Leon. Henderson, finding the room empty, left the weapons on the bed. When he went back later to check, the guns were gone. Henderson assumed that Capone had taken possession and distributed them.

By the summer of 1928, bootlegging was a sophisticated operation, international in scope and requiring considerable planning and coordination. In America, farmers, brewers, distillers, truckers, sailors, money launderers, and gunmen all were players in the game. But a big bootlegger such as Capone also would need to do business with legitimate merchants, including bankers and brokers, in countries outside the United States, where the production of alcoholic beverages continued without interruption. Much of the booze in the United States during Prohibition flowed in from Europe, Africa, Canada, and Latin America, with stops along the way in Mexico, the Caribbean, or the French islands of St. Pierre and Miquelon, off the coast of Canada. Al Capone remains a hero in St. Pierre and Miquelon even today for bringing a sudden fortune to a small group of islands that had previously depended heavily on fishing. On St. Pierre, one house built entirely of Cutty Sark whiskey crates still stands, a tribute to the age of Prohibition, and it is not unusual for builders doing demolition and repair work there today to come across walls constructed largely of champagne and whiskey crates.

Booze peddlers conducted their traffic in much the same way drug peddlers do today, with falsely labeled cargo, shipments addressed to fictitious destinations, and ships flown under false flags. Then as now, American investors bankrolled many of the deals. And then as now, the job fell to immigrant workers on American shores to unload and distribute the illegal goods.

Capone was hardly the only big operator. Bill McCoy was a rum runner who operated a sloop named the *Arethusa*, making runs between the Bahamas and Martha's Vineyard, carrying some of the highest-quality liquor on the market, which became known as "the real McCoy." A reporter who accompanied him on one excursion said McCoy spent $100,000 on each trip ($40,000 for whiskey and $60,000 for his crew) and hauled in a $300,000 profit. Avoiding pirates and Prohibition agents, he thrived for a few years until the U.S. Coast Guard finally caught up with him in 1924. Then there was Roy Olmstead, a lieutenant on the Seattle police force who moonlighted as a bootlegger, using his police credentials to cross into Canada to buy supplies. Fired from the police department in 1920, he used his connections in law enforcement to become one of the most efficient and canny bootleggers in the country, with net profits estimated at $200,000 a month. He kept going until 1926, when he was finally convicted and sentenced to four years in jail for "conspiracy to possess, transport and import intoxicating liquor."

But the richest and smartest of them all was probably George Remus, who worked as a criminal lawyer in Chicago at the start of Prohibition, but soon after moved to Cincinnati. "Remus was to bootlegging what Rockefeller was to oil," wrote the *St. Louis Post-Dispatch* in 1926. After selling his law practice, Remus used his cash to purchase at a discount some of the shuttered distilleries and government-bonded warehouses where millions of gallons of alcohol were stored. He soon became the largest owner of distilleries in the country. Next, he petitioned the government for permission to sell his alcohol to drug companies that were licensed to market medicinal whiskey. Then, in perhaps his most inspired moment, he set up his own drug companies so he could sell the booze to himself. As he moved the alcohol from one place to another in a series of complex and highly fictitious transactions, the government lost track of where it was all going. Of course, only a small amount of the alcohol wound up serving medicinal purposes; most of it was siphoned off to bootleggers at sensational prices. Within a few months of Prohibition, Remus was ridiculously rich, with an array of bank accounts in his own name and under aliases. He purchased a farmhouse in Westwood, a suburb of Cincinnati, and made it the hub of his operation, with a fleet of trucks running in and out, and with Cincinnati police providing protection for a price. Some say that Remus, who once gave away fifty new Pontiacs to the women attending one of his lavish parties, inspired F. Scott Fitzgerald's Jay Gatsby. But the feds got to him relatively quickly, raiding his operation and finding all the evidence they needed to make a case. Remus was tried and convicted in 1922 and, after exhausting his appeals, he was jailed in 1924.

Society viewed these big-time bootleggers as both ambitious and morally corrupt. In that sense, they were archetypes of the 1920s. McCoy, Remus, Capone, and countless others were at war with the rules of American society even as they worked to put together the wealth, power, and status that loosely defined the American Dream. America had always had a certain fond admiration for its criminals, but the feeling grew stronger in the 1920s, when moral values were especially low and frustration with the law especially high. Bootleggers were not Robin Hoods. They were not taking from the rich and giving to the poor. But they were defying the government and delivering beer to the masses, and that was good enough to put many Americans squarely on their side.

"I couldn't look upon the gangs of the Prohibition period as criminals," said one unnamed sociologist who mixed with the Capone crowd. "The people of Chicago wanted booze, gambling, and women, and the Capone organization was a public utility supplying the customers with what they wanted. It couldn't have operated one hour without the public's consent. . . . The big civil leaders and industrial moguls would get up at a meeting and denounce corruption—and then go straight to a cocktail party, or back to the office to argue with their bootleggers about the quality of the last delivery of liquor." An unnamed lawyer at the time said much the same: "Capone was relatively innocent compared with some of the men who dominated business and public life then—and I'm thinking particularly of Samuel Insull [the utility and railroad magnate], who conducted his financial operations like a ruthless brigand. . . . It was the general abandonment of honesty and integrity in public life brought about by Insull that had as a by-product the moral climate in which Capone ascended." The Chicago writer Nelson Algren, who grew up on the South Side and filled his stories with street characters, put it more succinctly: "Corruption begins at the top. I have known a lot of racket people and people who have done time. . . . Morally, they are sounder than the 'good' people who run Chicago by complicity."

Morally sound or not, most of the high-profile bootleggers were tightrope walkers; they performed exhilarating feats, but not for long. Capone carried on longer than most because he kept his operation so loosely organized and because he left little evidence of his involvement in the business.

Everyone knew what he was doing. He admitted it, and even bragged about it. But his booze came from innumerable sources, and, unlike Remus, he never attempted to corner the market or control his supply lines.

Of course, there were challenges associated with Capone's approach, too. He could count on fairly steady income from his gambling and brothel operations, where supply and demand were virtually infinite, but not in the booze business. From one week to the next, Capone never could be certain where he was going to get his alcohol, how much he was going to pay for it, or how much he would be able to get. Breweries were raided and shut down all the time. Shipments were intercepted. Allies were bumped off or jailed. The true nature of his art was improvisation. Day by day, week by week, for almost two years, he had kept the thing going, like a long, loud Louis Armstrong trumpet solo, never sure where or exactly how it would end. Remus was ravenous, insatiable, and egotistical to the extreme; Capone had the same tendencies, and others that were perhaps even less attractive, but at his core he was a businessman.

For years much of Capone's supply came through Detroit, courtesy of an organization of Jewish hoodlums founded by Sammy "Purple" Cohen. The Purple Gang, as it was known, grew out of Detroit's East Side, when a coterie of teenagers shrewdly decided to give up shoplifting and extorting in favor of selling their own alcohol. The Purple Gang supplied Capone with Canadian Club whiskey, changing the labels on the bottles to read "Old Log Cabin," which became one of the most popular and reliably high-quality drinks on the Chicago market. Even before Prohibition, much of America's alcohol had come from Canada, and in particular from the border cities of Windsor, Walkerville, and Sandwich. But once the American producers shut down, the Canadian liquor industry grew fantastically. The Detroit River, which separates the United States and Canada, is only a mile wide, with several islands in its middle that provided convenient docking for smugglers. Hundreds of private homes and boat docks, many of them hidden behind fences, lined the American side of the river, which made for secure landing points.

When Prohibition took effect, Canadian customs officials noted a huge increase in demand for motorboat licenses, and at one point the *New York Times* estimated that a fleet of thirty to fifty "mosquito boats" delivered more than fifty thousand pint bottles of beer a day to Detroit. Bigger loads arrived by train, thanks to railroad workers who were bribed by bootleggers to put false labels on carloads of beer. Of course, it was no secret that much of Capone's whiskey was coming from Canada through Detroit and across Michigan, which assured there would be frequent attempts at hijacking and at least occasional arrests by Prohibition agents. But such were the costs of doing business. Capone lost a few men and lost a few cases of whiskey, but in the long run lost very little money.

Capone's booze also came cross-country from New York, with the assistance of Frankie Yale, among others. Yale was thirty-five, a ripe old age for a man in his line of work, and fat. He had his hand in some legitimate businesses, including a funeral parlor and a cigar company that printed his picture on every box of cigars. But primarily he was still a goon. His bootlegging business was not all that different from the ice racket he built as a young man in that both depended on violence, threatened and actual. For a price, Yale would ensure the safe transport of booze, and Capone happily paid. But beginning sometime in 1928, the quality of Yale's service deteriorated. Given that there had been friction between the men in recent months, Capone grew suspicious.

It's not clear why Capone and Yale were bumping heads. Details are sketchy. Some accounts suggest that Yale was angry at Capone for installing Tony Lombardo at the helm of the Unione Siciliana in Chicago. Yale, who ran the Brooklyn chapter of the organization, had preferred Joe Aiello for the job. With Lombardo in charge, according to some versions of the story, the Chicago chapter failed to contribute dues to the New York office at the same generous level to which Yale had become accustomed. Was Yale dipping into Capone's booze supply to make up the difference? Was he hoarding money in an attempt to finance a campaign to oust Lombardo? Or was he merely being greedy, assuming that Capone was too preoccupied in Miami to keep track of every bottle and buck? Whatever his intentions, Yale's actions were perilous, as a man of his experience should have known.

On the Sunday afternoon of July 1, 1928, the sun was shining and a cool north wind was blowing over Brooklyn. Frankie Yale was cruising along Forty-fourth Street in his new Lincoln. He was moving slowly through a busy residential neighborhood when a big black Nash with Illinois plates pulled up behind, trailing by about 150 feet. As the Nash drew closer, shots rang out, shattering the rear window of Yale's car and scattering pedestrians. Yale stepped hard on the accelerator, but he could not outrun the black sedan. The Nash pulled alongside Yale's Lincoln, and more bullets flew. Yale lost control and crashed through a cluster of hedges. His vehicle came to rest on the stone stairs leading to a ground-level apartment on Forty-fourth Street. By the time the police arrived, he was already dead. Later, a few blocks away, the cops found the Nash, which contained a Thompson machine gun, a shotgun, and a revolver. Some accounts suggested that Yale was the victim of New York City's first machine-gun attack. Police traced the serial numbers on the guns and learned that at least one of them had been purchased by Parker Henderson Jr., of Miami. When contacted by police, Henderson wasted no time proving his extraordinary serviceability: He told the cops precisely where he had purchased the guns and for whom.

It looked like bad news for Capone. He had a long-running association with the victim. He had a motive. He had a connection to at least one of the guns used in the shooting. And police also heard a report that three of Capone's top men had left Miami, perhaps headed to New York, shortly before the assassination.

Yale received a beautiful send-off, packed up in a silver coffin as part of a $50,000 funeral that drew ten thousand mourners. But as the days and weeks went by, no charges were filed in the case. One day, the *New York Times* ran three stories on the investigation, and yet the newsmen had no idea where Capone could be found. One newspaper declared he was in Cicero, another said Chicago, and yet another said he was fishing in Florida. When police in Miami interviewed him about Yale, Capone listed the names of the men who had left his Palm Island home shortly before the attack and assured the officers that the men went to Chicago, not to New York.

While he had their attention, Capone asked the officers if they could do anything about the excessively bright streetlamp the city had recently installed near the entrance to his home.

In Chicago, it had been relatively easy to explain why Capone so often avoided arrest and conviction: He owned the place. But how to explain his immunity from punishment in Miami and New York? The problem was that criminals had become more sophisticated than the criminal justice system. Laws were administered unevenly, with little to no federal intervention. In most cases, anyone with enough money for a bribe or a competent attorney could beat the rap.

Corruption ran through police stations and courthouses like veins through marble. Prohibition agents were too few and too weak. The Justice Department's Bureau of Investigation (it was not yet referred to as the FBI) was a strangely inconsequential institution, more like a detective agency than a police force, with no clear mission and no great powers. Its young director, John Edgar Hoover, was attempting to reform the agency, but he had a long way to go.

New York City police might have had enough evidence to charge Capone with conspiracy to murder Yale, but detectives in New York didn't have the knowledge or the resources to run an investigation that would have required them to gather evidence in three states. In 1928, fighting crime was a local affair, and if a criminal escaped the scene of his transgression, it was a pretty safe bet he would never be caught.

George Johnson summed up the state of affairs in a speech to a group of businessmen at the Hotel LaSalle. As usual for the U.S. attorney, it was a less than rousing oration, but it nonetheless encapsulated precisely the problem with American law enforcement:

"The year 1928 is a political year," Johnson began. "The minds of many statesmen and politicians are engrossed in the question, 'What is the paramount issue?' Tax reduction, national defense, flood control, are each discussed with reference to our common welfare, and by different groups each is held to be a paramount issue. In my judgment the paramount issue today in the United States is enforcement of law."

Johnson then appealed to his audience's business instincts. Because of high crime in Chicago, he said, insurance rates were rising for all sorts of businesses. In 1920, for example, he noted, a fur dealer or jeweler paid $10 to insure every $1,000 of merchandise against theft. In 1928, he paid $16.50. In 1920, a drugstore or service station operator paid $20 for every $1,000 of theft insurance. In 1928, he paid $66. And why were criminals in Chicago running amok? Johnson answered the question with more numbers: Police arrested twenty thousand people on felony charges in 1926, but only 647 of them were sent to the penitentiary. Of the two thousand six hundred men with "major criminal records" who were arrested, only 164, or 6 percent, did time behind bars.

It didn't have to be so, he insisted. After the war, said Johnson, when robbers started targeting railroad cars carrying mail, the government faced a choice: Put armed guards on every mail car, or bring down the full force of the law on those mail thieves who had already been apprehended, making examples of them, and sending the message to would-be robbers that the government had zero tolerance for such criminal acts. As conviction rates rose, robberies of mail cars all but stopped. Postal inspectors became the most feared law enforcement officers in the nation, which is why the Treasury Department hired so many of them when it came time to toughen up the enforcement arm of the Bureau of Internal Revenue.

Prohibition was a failure, Johnson said, but Prohibition was not to blame for the lawlessness; loose morals were. Morality can't be legislated, he said, but it can be taught. He called for a system of education that reinforced moral values, reminding children that gangsters were not heroes, that "the bandit king who is paraded in the press and comes before the court is ugly and loathsome, a person not fitted into the scheme of things, not prepared for the problems of life, and therefore a derelict." He called for the removal of crooked politicians who corrupted whatever they touched. The 1920s were an age of privilege, but "today that privilege has grown out of hand," he said, so much so that criminals who are challenged by the system of law fight back "with a sawed-off shotgun and a bomb" and get away with it.

Johnson concluded his speech with solid logic and no great emotional climax, saying, "We may disagree on the wisdom of some law, but we can all agree on this principle: That a horde of undesirables . . . are not to be tolerated in a civilized community."

In his newspaper column, the poet and journalist Carl Sandburg praised Johnson for a speech containing "more wisdom than sophistry or bunk." And soon Johnson would gain a far more powerful ally who agreed entirely with his theory on fighting crime. Together they would launch an offensive to take down the nation's most notorious bootlegger.

HOOVERIZATION

One month after Frankie Yale's assassination, seventy thousand people filled Stanford University's football stadium to hear Herbert Hoover accept the Republican Party's nomination for president of the United States. Hoover was the heroic do-gooder who had saved the Belgians from starvation in 1914 and had rescued the victims of the Mississippi flood in 1927. He wasn't the most exciting candidate to make a charge at the presidency; in fact, he was probably one of the dullest. He larded his speeches with statistics and theory, like George Johnson. Hoover spoke with all the thrill of thawing ice. It seems ironic that in the 1920s, when Americans were so enthralled with glitz and glamour, they would choose such a lackluster politician to lead. Perhaps, amid all the upset, voters sought a laxative.

Hoover was everything the movie stars of the day weren't—efficient, moralistic, righteous, unflappable, and selfless. Like Henry Ford, he blended modernism and tradition. He sold himself as a master of efficiency. Since the start of his career in public service, his goal had never been to accumulate power. All he had ever wanted to do was make government work better. As secretary of commerce he had developed a simple and effective system of government. He would summon the leaders of an industry—big or small—to a meeting, call their attention to certain problems besetting their work, then guide them painstakingly through the search for solutions. In eight years, according to his biographer Eugene Lyons, he convened three thousand such meetings, and almost every one resulted in reduced waste, enhanced profits, or improved working conditions. He was a tinkerer, not a radical reformer, and he was probably best suited for the job he already held: commerce secretary. Yet there he stood, a step away from the presidency.

"I do not favor the repeal of the Eighteenth Amendment," he said on a cloudless California afternoon, taking a characteristically conservative stand on one of the few issues that deeply divided voters. "I stand for the efficient enforcement of the laws enacted thereunder. Whoever is chosen president has under his oath the solemn duty to pursue this course. Our country has deliberately undertaken a great social and economic experiment, noble in motive and far-reaching in purpose. It must be worked out constructively. Common sense compels us to realize that grave abuses have occurred—abuses which must be remedied. . . . Crime and disobedience of law cannot be permitted to break down the Constitution and laws of the United States."

He was a big, strong man with a squarish head and an eave of gray-brown hair that drooped nonchalantly from the left side of his face to the right. He seldom smiled, and he dressed as conservatively as was humanly possible, in shades of black and gray—perfect bureaucrat camouflage—as if the last thing he wanted was to call attention to himself. He spoke as cautiously as he dressed. Even before a crowd of seventy thousand, with marching bands and cheerleaders surrounding him, and with an audience of millions listening coast to coast on the radio, he made no attempt to jazz up his delivery. Hoover's idea of a good time was to work with industry to standardize the thread sizes on nuts and bolts, which he listed as one of his principal achievements as secretary of commerce. In fact, it was a brilliant move, in that it made countless factories more efficient and promoted collaboration among independent businesses. If the voters thought him dull, he would not argue. If they saw his life story as the embodiment of the American Dream, he wouldn't argue with that, either.

Hoover was born in 1874 in a whitewashed wooden cottage outside West Branch, Iowa, a village founded by Quakers. His father was a blacksmith, a pious man, but with a hot dash of American ambition. His mother worked as a teacher and a seamstress and served as a minister in the church. She expected silence from her three children when she sat them for hours at a time with the elders at the unheated Quaker meetinghouse. Herbert Hoover grew up in a community of shared values, where citizens learned that hard work, temperance, and careful planning led to a guiltless, untroubled conscience. His reading was limited to the Bible, schoolbooks, and novels that taught the dangers of "demon rum," but he occasionally risked the ire of his elders by partaking in certain forbidden acts, such as sledding.

When Herbert was six, his father died from typhoid fever. For eight months after his father's death, Herbert was sent to live with an uncle who worked as a federal agent on an Osage Indian reservation in Arkansas, where Herbert and his cousin were the only white boys around. There he learned to hunt with bow and arrow, build fires, and cook on them. When he was eight and living back in West Branch, pneumonia killed his mother. The three siblings were split up. After two years on an Iowa farm with one uncle, Herbert was gently told, "Thee is going to Oregon," to live with the most respected of his uncles, a country doctor and missionary named Henry John Minthorn, who had recently lost his only son and all but insisted that his sister's boy be sent as a replacement.

Hoover never overcame his natural shyness; it just hardened, like bread crust, leaving him with a thick shell that made people think of him as closed and dispassionate.

After studying geology at Stanford, he found work as a miner among low-paid, hard-living, dirty-lunged men. He didn't drink or curse to impress them; he merely worked harder than the rest. If this highly educated, principled young Quaker did not cower before such rough characters and was not resented by them, wrote biographer Lyons, "it was because he was the best miner of them all."

Before long, Hoover was moved up to management, traveling the world, evaluating mines for purchase by the big companies that employed him. In 1899, between trips, he returned home to marry the only girl he'd ever dated—and probably the only one with whom he'd ever danced: Lou Henry (her parents had been counting on a boy and couldn't bring themselves to come up with a feminine name for their child). A stunning beauty, tall and lean, with a love of the outdoors, Lou could have charmed any man on campus, but she was drawn to Hoover by his confidence; his quiet, sturdy charm; and by his legendary status as the most brilliant geology student in the college. She, too, had chosen geology as her major.

In 1914, the Hoovers were living in London when war erupted in Europe.

For years, Hoover had been nagged by the sense that he ought to be contributing to society, but his antisocial personality and poor speaking skills held him back. With the war raging, the U.S. embassy asked Hoover to help stranded American travelers get back home. He jumped at the chance. He found he was well suited for such behind-the-scenes work, where results counted far more than style. As the war went on, German soldiers occupied Belgium, and the British navy blockaded the tiny nation's ports. The defenseless Belgians, who imported almost all their food, began to starve. Again, the American embassy asked Hoover to help. First, he negotiated with the British and Germans to allow emergency food supplies to reach civilians. Then, calling on wealthy donors, corporations, and government agencies, he began building a network of boats, trains, and trucks to deliver them. Through four years of war, Hoover's Committee for the Relief of Belgium raised $1 billion and fed more than eleven million people. Hoover, ever righteous, took no salary and hired an accounting firm to audit his charity's books. The audit showed that the organization spent less than half of 1 percent of its money on administration.

When America entered the war in 1917, President Woodrow Wilson asked Hoover to come home and serve as the nation's food administrator, leading America's effort in conservation so that more could be sent overseas. Once more, Hoover found the work immensely satisfying. Children were taught to finish their apples ("Be Patriotic to the Core," went the slogan); bakers cooked up coarser breads to conserve ingredients; and families were urged to institute "meatless Mondays" and "wheatless Wednesdays." Hoover had the government start buying wheat and sugar crops. He set hog prices so high that farmers were motivated to double production. He called it conservation, but many Americans referred to it, with no trace of scorn or ridicule, as "Hooverizing." One cartoonist's Valentine at the time read:

> *I can Hooverize on Dinners*
> *And on lights and fuel too*
> *But I'll never learn to Hooverize*
> *When it comes to loving you!*

It was, as the historian William E. Leuchtenburg noted, the first time America had acted as a nation. And it worked. Though he intended to return to the mining business after the war, Hoover never made it. In 1920, President-elect Warren G. Harding named him secretary of commerce. Though Harding's administration would prove one of the most thoroughly venal in American history, notorious for its Teapot Dome scandal, a bribery racket involving oil-field reserves, Hoover came through with his reputation unsullied. When Vice President Calvin Coolidge took office upon Harding's death in 1923, Hoover held on to his job, and the economy took off on a white-hot streak, beginning a period of prosperity unlike any before.

Throughout his years in Washington, Hoover had never acted like a man who burned to be president. He just sat at his rolltop desk, appointing committees, analyzing statistics, scheduling meetings, and reading reports. Asked to name the most important task he faced, he usually picked waste reduction. And if waste reduction wasn't the sort of issue that tended to thrust a man into a position of power, so be it.

When it came to running for president, Hoover decided that the best thing he could do, given his drab personality, was to let the American people come to their own conclusion that he would make a fine leader before expressing any desire of his own for the job. It was modest. It was risk-free. And it was effective.

So as Coolidge made vague statements about his intention to seek reelection, Hoover and his friends started building an informal, nearly invisible campaign organization. All over the country, labor unions, small-business associations, miners, railway workers, social workers, engineers, and religious leaders went to work on Hoover's behalf. Men and women who had toiled with him in flood relief efforts and on international food programs formed clubs to promote his campaign. Newspapers declared that this humble technocrat, this genius of organization, might be better qualified for the presidency than any first-time candidate the nation had ever put forth. Here was an experienced candidate with no great ego and no obvious appetite for power who managed to make it appear as if he'd been propelled into a position of national leadership by a force of nature and through no doing of his own. Nothing like it had ever happened before in America.

Yet even as it had become clear that a great wave of support was building behind him, Hoover, cloaking his confidence in a kind of humility, declined to commit. With the exception of a brief letter he sent to party leaders in Ohio giving them permission to enter his name in the state's primary, he made not a single public pronouncement prior to the party's national convention. On his way West to accept the nomination, his train stopped in Fort Wayne, Indiana, where he was greeted by a crowd that beseeched him to offer a few words. "This is not an occasion for a political speech," he said. "It is Sunday morning. However, I do appreciate greatly the sentiment and courtesy of your coming down to the station."

That was all he had to say.

At his next stop, in Chicago, he was not even recognized as his small motorcade rolled through the city's Loop. When reporters met him in suburban Evanston, at the home of Vice President Dawes, Hoover excused himself, saying, "I will get into the background," leaving Dawes to handle the newsmen alone.

The campaign centered on a few themes. First, there was the ethnicity and religion of Hoover's Democratic opponent, New York governor Al Smith. An Irish-American and practicing Roman Catholic, Smith made many voters in the South uncomfortable. Smith also was a drinking man, and unafraid to admit it. He came out in opposition to Prohibition, while Hoover promised to enforce and maintain the law. Hoover knew that the ban on drinking was unpopular in big cities. He was bothered by the fact that the law had corrupted the nation's justice system and turned petty criminals into violent tyrants. But he also knew that the majority of American voters still wanted Prohibition to work. They still wanted to believe that Americans were a God-fearing, law-abiding, hardworking people capable of kicking their bad habits.

Had he been more audacious, Hoover could have campaigned against Al Capone rather than Al Smith. He could have made the gangster his scapegoat for the failures of Prohibition and vowed to take him down. It would not have been much of a stretch, given that Hoover spoke often of his intention to reform the nation's criminal justice system. But the Republican candidate was not prone to hyperbole. It would appear that he never mentioned Capone on the stump. But then again, he didn't have to. He had the economy on his side.

By the late 1920s, the national income of the United States exceeded that of Great Britain, Germany, Japan, Canada, France, and seventeen other nations combined. Americans worked less, earned more, and got more for their money. Henry Ford had instituted the five-day workweek (as opposed to the previous six), and the agricultural machinery manufacturer International Harvester started offering its employees something fantastic and all but unheard-of: a two-week annual paid vacation. The manufacturing sector was exploding. Cars, telephones, and radios led the way. Then came new products such as cigarette lighters, paint spray-ers, wristwatches, book matches, Pyrex cooking utensils, cellophane. The economy was flying high, like Lindbergh over the Atlantic. All anyone really wanted was more.

Hoover and the Republicans claimed credit for the nation's prosperity and warned voters that there was still a bit of tinkering to be done before economic bliss could be achieved and locked in. The stock market had hiccuped a few times during the campaign season, but as Election Day drew near, the big bull market was back. People were starting to believe the Irving Berlin lyrics, "Blue skies smiling at me . . . nothing but blue skies from now on." Schoolteachers, plumbers, and all sorts of modestly paid Americans were investing in stocks or at least following the daily shifts in prices, a habit once largely reserved for the privileged. It was only a matter of time, it seemed, before poverty was completely eliminated and wealth blanketed the land from coast to coast. American business leaders were driving the nation toward the greatest age of good fortune the world had ever seen.

"Big business in America is producing what the Socialists held up as their goal: food, shelter and clothing for all," wrote the muckraking, left-wing journalist Lincoln Steffens. "You will see it during the Hoover administration."

"I DO NOT STAY UP LATE"

"Miss Parsons?"

The voice on the telephone seemed alarmingly low.

It was Al Capone, on a call with Hollywood's leading gossip columnist, Louella Parsons, of the Hearst newspaper chain.

"Yes," she said flatly, not really believing that the big fellow himself was on the line.

"Al Capone speaking," he said. The voice was strangely subdued. To Parsons, it sounded like a tone one might hear in a library, or around a sick person. It gave her the creeps.

She was not the sort to be afraid. In Hollywood, Parsons had a reputation for being as ruthless as any gangster, a "bitch goddess," as the actress Mamie Van Doren would later describe her, with the power to make or break careers. According to film industry lore, Parsons had been aboard the yacht of William Randolph Hearst when the producer Thomas Ince died. Hearst supposedly found his lover in the arms of Charlie Chaplin, tried to shoot Chaplin, and hit Ince instead. In exchange for her silence, the story went, Parsons received a lifetime contract from the newspaper magnate. True or not, the legend certainly enhanced Parsons's image. The gossip columnist had met Capone a year earlier, when she had come to Chicago, along with seemingly half of the American populace, for the Dempsey-Tunney fight. Capone had gone on and on at the time about his son, and Parsons doubted if "even the most chicken-hearted would have been 'scairt' of Al" on that occasion. Now she was in town again, making a recreational stop on her way to New York. Capone had recently returned from Miami. Parsons asked if she could stop by the Metropole that evening for an interview.

"Come early, I do not stay up late," Capone said, his voice still hushed.

Later, when Edward G. Robinson, Jimmy Cagney, and Humphrey Bogart started playing gangsters on the silver screen and speaking in low monotones that hovered just above a mumble, Parsons would swear they'd all copied the style from Capone. Their wardrobe ideas came from him, too.

On the train from Los Angeles, Parsons had met a young doctor named Harry Martin. She became infatuated. Showing off, she invited him to come along to meet Capone. The doctor thought it was a gag, but off he went to the Metropole with this dazzling, fascinating, fearless woman.

"Al Capone doesn't live here," the hotel desk clerk told Parsons.

"I would advise you to call room four oh eight," she snapped.

They rode the elevator, knocked at the door, and withstood a screening by three of Capone's men. At last, the door opened to reveal Capone in a combination office–sitting room. To Parsons's eye, the furniture looked too cheap for a man of Capone's stature. If not for the photos of family and friends, one would never have known that the suite had been Capone's more or less permanent residence for nearly a year. Other, more self-aggrandizing reporters tended to describe Capone's hotel suite as an imposing chamber, darkly paneled and majestically accoutered. But Parsons was not impressed.

"The gangster chief was a dark, squat man," she recalled, "under medium height, but immaculately groomed in a soft gray suit. His eyes were small but rather pleasant. It was his mouth that was his bad feature—too full, purple rather than red in color, and his lips shone so they seemed to be polished. Purple too was the scar on his cheek which gave him his nickname."

He rose slowly and easily to greet his guests, and "with the poise of an actor," began discoursing about European antiques he had recently acquired, then about how much his son enjoyed riding horseback through Lincoln Park each morning. Like any celebrity, it seemed, he was eager to impress. "The more Capone talked," wrote Parsons, "the more obvious it became to both his nervous guests that there was absolutely no thought in his mind that he had ever done a thing to harm society."

Only after several minutes of chitchat did Parsons come to realize that Capone wanted something in return for the access he'd granted his interviewer. "That paper that runs your column, the *Chicago Herald and Examiner*," he said, his voice betraying the first hint of petulance, "is particularly bad to my dog races." He was talking about the Hawthorne Kennel Club, where he had a stake in the greyhound action, in partnership with Fast Eddie O'Hare. "Look at the play they give the horse races. Why do they ignore my dogs?"

At this shocker, Parsons should have been greatly relieved. If Capone's biggest beef was newspaper coverage of the dog races, she held pretty fair standing. But as Capone went on, it was clear that he was not joking.

"Well," he said, in that same level tone, which by now was getting on Parsons's nerves in the extreme, "you are the girl who can fix it! Speak to the editor about it."

Parsons sensed this was an order, not a request, and decided to change the subject. She said she was only in town for a day, on her way from Los Angeles to New York.

"Los Angeles," Capone said. "There's a lousy town!"

He went on to tell how he'd been run out by the district attorney and forced to return to Chicago last year around Christmastime and how someone had swiped a jug of wine from one of his suitcases. Then, as he had approached Chicago, he griped, he had given a hundred bucks to a newspaper reporter and asked the fellow to send a telegram to one of his associates with details on when and where he wished to be met. But instead of wiring his associate, the reporter had wired the police. The cops had met Capone at the station in Joliet and locked him up for the night.

"What burned me up," he said, "was that the guy kept the hundred dollars. The cheap crook."

THE ENFORCER

"Oh! Look at the airplane!" said Tony Lombardo to his two bodyguards. He stepped out of the Hartford Building, a steel skyscraper built in the burst of industry before the 1893 World's Fair, and stood for a moment on the sidewalk near the busy intersection of Madison and Dearborn. A thickly packed crowd had gathered in front of the Boston Store, where workers with pulleys and ropes were hoisting a real airplane up the department store's exterior wall and in through an enormous window on the eleventh floor.

The downtown Loop's brick buildings were lit orange in the fading sun, its streets soaked in shadows. It was four twenty-five on a mild Friday afternoon, September 7, 1928, the kind of crisp autumn day you longed for through the long Chicago winter. Electric streetcars buzzed up and down Madison Street, their bells jingling. Delivery trucks ground their gears and coughed gray smoke into the air, while the amused crowd ogled at the amazing sight of the suspended aircraft.

Americans in the 1920s, more than ever, defined themselves by how they dressed, the movies they viewed, and the games they played. It was part of being stylish and modern. The Boston was one of those department stores that helped explain the latest fashions and helped make those fashions available to the masses at marked-down prices. But it wasn't enough for stores to offer low prices and a stunningly vast variety of products. And it wasn't enough to advertise, even though American businesses in 1928 would spend a record-breaking $1.2 billion doing so. Now in the age of indulgence and spectacle, department stores took extreme steps to outshine the competition. Today it was a plane.

After watching the slowly climbing aircraft, Lombardo and his body-guards began walking west on Madison. Lombardo was a busy man. As president of the Unione Siciliana, now referred to as the Italo-American Union, he was routinely besieged by requests for favors, but just now he was under greater than usual pressure. For starters, there were the rumors that gunmen from New York were looking to knock him off to make way for a member of the Aiello faction.

Capone, too, was "on the spot," gangster parlance for under contract or facing heat. But Capone could hide. Lombardo didn't have that luxury. He was expected to be out among the people he served. He was expected to attend baptisms, weddings, and the endless array of religious festivals that seemed to go on for days. He also kept regular office hours to help settle feuds among neighbors and to listen to pleas from men who needed a hand finding work. Most recently he had been asked to help save a ten-year-old Italian boy who had been kidnapped. The story was making banner headlines, in no small part because it evoked memories of the kidnapping and murder of fourteen-year-old Bobby Franks by Leopold and Loeb a few years earlier. The kidnappers were demanding a ransom of $60,000. The boy's father, a stubborn and independent man, said he would pay, but not that much. And he wanted the police to stay out of it. He was counting on Lombardo with his connections to win his son's release.

Without Capone, Lombardo never would have ascended to the posi-tion of power and wealth he inhabited with such grace. Yet Capone's be-neficence had turned out to be like the storied monkey's paw: It brought great fortune and greater complications. That was why he surrounded himself with bodyguards and tried to confine his public activities to the Loop, where the crowds afforded him a sense of safety. As Lombardo left his office after a long meeting, his clothes reeking of cigarette smoke and his eyes still adjusting to the light, one of those complications followed Lombardo down the street.

He was a tall man in a brown suit, hatless, and seemingly alone. Walk-ing quickly along the crowded sidewalk, he closed in behind Lombardo and pulled a gun. Lombardo saw the man coming out of the corner of his eye, and reached in his pocket for his own revolver—but not fast enough. Four shots rang out, echoing in the canyon of tall buildings. Lombardo and one of his bodyguards fell in front of the Raklios Cafeteria. Pedestri-ans shrieked and scattered chaotically, ducking behind taxis and darting into shops. Streetcars screeched to a stop, bells jangling. The man in the brown suit took off running, briefly chased by the surviving bodyguard. He ducked into a Regal Shoes store and went out the back, never to be seen again. When it was clear the shooting had stopped, men and women came out from cover to see the bloody bodies, ignoring the airplane overhead.

By the time police arrived, it was clear that Lombardo, thirty-six years old, was a goner, the blood pouring like syrup from two small holes behind his left ear, and spreading across the sidewalk. His wounded bodyguard, shot in the back, his spinal cord shattered, would die three days later.

Lombardo's murder once again put Chicago in the national news. Police speculated that the hit was payback for the assassination of Frankie Yale and connected to the struggle for control of the Italo-American Union. Though there were hundreds of witnesses to the crime, including the bodyguard who gave chase to the gunman, police were clueless when it came to identifying the murderer. They did say they believed it looked like a professional job. Dumdum bullets, points blunted to dull their impact and to make a more gaping wound, had been used to make certain that the shots wouldn't go through Lombardo and strike any unintended civilians.

Now, the newspapers said, it wasn't just a bunch of local idiots shooting one another over kegs of beer. It was bigger than that. It was, as the *New York Times* put it, nothing less than the "bloody struggle for the right of dictatorship in the criminal empire, of which Alphonse (Scarface) Capone now seems the titular head." The papers were stoking fears, suggesting that gangster-fueled terrorism was spreading and would soon plague every city in the nation if something wasn't done.

It's difficult to say for certain whether Americans were less safe in the late 1920s than they were prior to Prohibition. The government was not yet compiling national statistics on crime. One study estimated that murders and assaults increased 37 percent during the Prohibition years, but other studies concluded that the crime wave was a myth and that the nation was enjoying a long-term decline in serious crime that would carry through into the 1960s.

Either way, there was no doubt that American fascination with crime had reached its all-time peak. That much could be blamed on the press. News and entertainment were no longer purely local, thanks to the emergence of national newspaper and radio companies and the growth of big-circulation magazines. Crossword puzzles and Kellogg's Corn Flakes and dozens of other products were becoming national phenomena, too, thanks to coast-to-coast marketing campaigns that hadn't existed a decade earlier. The gangster became a cultural icon as newspaper writers began looking for stories with national appeal. Crime stories were perfect. They were about morality, about money, about profit and loss, success and failure, good and evil. Crime stories had powerful images, too: fast cars, gushing wounds, rattling gats, big hats, and catchy nicknames. Writers such as Damon Runyon and Ben Hecht spotted the appeal right away and cashed in. The newspaper chain boss and fan of splashy tabloids William Randolph Hearst also recognized the trend and capitalized. These men knew that life in America in the 1920s was wild and reckless. The country was changing fast and in often frightening ways. But everyone could relate to the tale of the American gangster. It was a story that boiled down many of the day's most complicated matters—crime, poverty, Prohibition—into simple, action-packed narratives. And best of all, it offered Americans a bogeyman—an object of fear that managed to frighten without doing much real harm to the average citizen.

"The hoodlum of 1920 had become page one news, copy for the magazines, material for talkie plots and vaudeville gags," Fred Pasley wrote in his 1930 biography of Capone, in which he ranked the gangster with American legends such as Will Rogers, Henry Ford, Babe Ruth, the corner of Broadway and Forty-second Street, and Bromo-Seltzer. "Chicago's Exhibit A had become America's Exhibit A."

After returning to Chicago late in the summer of 1928, Capone had moved his headquarters from the Metropole to the Lexington Hotel. Same neighborhood, but one block north. The Lexington was a little bit classier than the Metropole, but it wasn't the Palmer House, which had grand ballrooms, Tiffany windows, and muraled ceilings. The Lexington was still well south of the city's center, much closer to the old Four Deuces than to the city's imposing skyscrapers.

He registered under the name George Phillips and took room 230, which consisted of three rooms connected to form a single suite. Later he moved to the fourth floor, where he used part of his suite as living quarters and part as office. The office looked like any other: filing cabinets, adding machines, and a big desk set in the bay window. Capone sat with his back to Michigan Avenue. On his desk sat a framed portrait of Sonny. On the office walls were two engravings—one of George Washington and one of Abraham Lincoln. At some point he added a portrait of Big Bill Thompson. At another, between the presidential portraits, he hung a cartoon image of himself dressed in golfing togs and holding a driver.

For now, this was his home and office. Eight years in Chicago, a city of neighborhoods, and Capone had never really had a neighborhood to call his own. He'd never had a local saloon, where the bartender knew his order, never had a regular shoe-shine stand, never had a barbershop where the fellows had already heard his jokes but laughed anyway. Hanging out in saloons was too dangerous, and the shoe-shine men and barbers all came to him. This was the life he'd chosen, or else the life that had chosen him. There was nothing normal about it.

On September 11, 1928, when Lombardo was buried, Capone and his men emerged en masse from the Lexington, all in dark suits and big hats, and drove out to Cicero to pay respects. The sky was mackerel gray. It looked like all of Cicero and a good part of Chicago had collected around the dead man's humble brick house: housewives, old women with shawls covering their heads, taxi drivers in dirty shoes, teenage girls chewing gum, tailors, assembly-line workers, chauffeurs with machine guns on the floorboards of their cars, cops, precinct captains, judges, streetcar conductors, newspaper reporters, and a handful of men who didn't know the dead man at all but had made a grotesque hobby of showing up at gangster funerals.

Cars were parked two deep by the curb, stopping all traffic and forcing mourners to walk. Flowers filled the front yard of the Lombardo home with Amazonian density. One wreath spanned the entire width of the home: "T. LOMBARDO," the flowers spelled, the "T" fashioned from pink carnations, the "LOMBARDO" from white. A clock built of pink gladiolas marked the time of Lombardo's last breath: 4:25. Capone sent something a bit more tasteful, sort of: a heart made of red roses, roughly eight feet in height, with white roses around the edge and white roses at the center spelling "My Pal." Friends and neighbors wandered about the driveway and backyard, swapping stories, while waiting for the family to join them on the trip to the cemetery. A buzz went through the crowd when Capone arrived. But he disappointed the gawkers by taking not the bulletproof Cadillac—which was said to weigh nine thousand pounds under all that armor—but the automobile of a friend. A soft gray fedora tilted on his head. He wore a black suit of fine wool, patent leather shoes, black tie, and a plain white shirt, unlike some other gangsters who tried to show off with their colored shirts, flashy ties, and tan shoes. Capone chatted with Frankie Rio, his principal bodyguard and full-time companion, as well as with Jack McGurn. The noted assassins Albert Anselmi and John Scalise may have been strolling the backyard, but the reporter who thought he spotted them couldn't say for sure. Capone and his men tugged on cigars thick as billy clubs and chatted about their wives and kids. A *Chicago Daily News* reporter asked Capone if the stories were true that Lombardo had been killed in retaliation for the death of Yale, that the gangs of New York and Chicago were going to war.

"Honest," Capone said, "it's all a puzzle to me. I don't know nothing about New York connections. I'm all up in the air. It all seems like a dream." He went on to say, straight-faced, that he had thought Lombardo and Yale had been friends. He couldn't imagine why either of them had been killed.

Some of the photographers asked Capone for permission to snap a few shots. "There'll be no trouble about taking pictures if you just take crowd pictures," he said. "Don't try to get any close-ups." They obeyed.

Then the big man got sentimental, saying, "I've tried to treat Tony Lombardo, who is dead, as Tony Lombardo would have treated me were he alive today and were I in his place." The polished language, better suited for Julius Caesar than the Brooklyn-accented Capone, was almost certainly created by the unnamed "girl reporter" for the *Evening American* who interviewed Capone that day. He continued, "He was my best friend, the truest friend any man on earth ever had. Now he is dead. In death I won't forget or forsake him, or those of his who live, as long as I live, as long as they live, as long as live those who will carry on my orders after I am gone."

Sodden skies and sadness seemed to soften the light in Capone's gray green eyes, the reporter noted.

"Tony Lombardo," he continued, repeating himself, "was one of the best men who ever lived. They don't make them any better than Tony Lombardo. Just say for me that he was a prince among men."

With that, Capone led his men into the Lombardo living room. "Boys," he ordered, "let us pray." And they knelt.

Moments later, Lombardo was transported to the cemetery in a $3,000 bronze coffin. Seventeen carloads of flowers accompanied the body to the grave, as did a bevy of police squad cars, countless crooks, and a dozen tuxedoed pallbearers. Once more, the spectacle thrilled Chicagoans, who lined up by the thousands to watch.

In a hearing held shortly after Lombardo's funeral, the latest man to serve as Chicago's police commissioner, William F. Russell, was called to the bar by Judge Frank Comerford.

The commissioner stepped forward.

"How many men have you on your police force?" the judge asked.

"There were 5,641 when I counted last," the commissioner said.

"Very well," the judge answered sternly. "Now, Commissioner. I say to you that a few hundred cutthroats, described as the mafia of Chicago, have challenged and threatened the right of three million people in this city to live happily in peace and security. Five thousand six hundred policemen can subdue those lawless few hundred without difficulty and restore the safety of our homes and children. . . . So I suggest to you, Commissioner Russell, that you use all the power of your department, thousands of your men, if necessary, in concentrating against these mafia gunmen. Remove by annihilation the few hundreds [*sic*] who challenge the three million."

The giant headline stripped across the top of the next day's front page of the *Chicago Tribune* read: "ANNIHILATE MAFIA—JUDGE."

Until then, the Chicago papers had seldom used the term "mafia" to describe local underworld operators. Capone and his men had been "bootleggers," "rum runners," "goons," "gangsters," and, occasionally, "Black Handers." But now for the first time, officials in Chicago were making an attempt to link his outfit to the organized criminals of Italy. Never mind that Capone's crew contained plenty of Irishmen, Englishmen, and Jews, too. Never mind that some of Capone's biggest enemies were Sicilians. He was a mafia kingpin, not some ordinary criminal. In years to come, the term would be applied to Capone with increasing frequency, in part to make him sound more menacing, in part to invoke ethnic stereotyping, and, perhaps most of all, to make his reign of terror seem less of an American phenomenon.

In October 1928, with another municipal election approaching, Chicago's leading businessmen and crime fighters were eager to avoid a repetition of the Pineapple Primary, when bomb blasts had echoed through the city and headlines had spread across the country. So in the interest of fair play in democracy, Frank J. Loesch, president of the Chicago Crime Commission, paid a visit to Capone at the Lexington Hotel.

In that same year, Loesch had all but given up his lucrative law practice to take over leadership of the privately run, quasi-governmental crime commission. The move suggested to his contemporaries that Loesch was nuts—or at the very least nuts for publicity. Loesch was, in fact, quite fond of attention. But he also was a deeply religious man, a Sunday school teacher, and a passionate lover of Chicago. He'd seen the city burned to ashes in 1871, when he was nineteen, and figured then that the place was gone forever. "I had only two dollars in my pocket and had the impression that Chicago would, of course, disappear as a business place," he recalled. "Then, I saw a score of men at work in the ruins of the Chamber of Commerce at the corner of Washington and LaSalle streets. They were actually removing debris, smoking hot, preparatory to rebuilding." Loesch walked through the smoldering city, found a pie shop still selling pies, bought one for twenty cents, and resolved in that moment "that Chicago would come back and I must stay right here." At age seventy-five, he saw his city threatened once more, and he resolved to do something.

Capone's guards ushered Loesch into the boss's suite at the Lexington. Capone gazed at Loesch. He was a strange-looking man, small and bald, with great folds of skin sagging from his face. His nose and ears were monstrous. They looked like they'd been hastily removed from a man twice his size and stuck on his small, shiny skull. His left eye was considerably higher than his right, so that he looked at all times as if he were raising one brow in skepticism. It was such a freaky mug that strangers speaking to Loesch for the first time often found themselves disoriented and unable to read his mood. So at least he had an aura of mystery about him as he sat down with Capone. He had age in his favor, too. He was too old to be afraid of anybody. And having made his money as a lawyer in the railroad business, he was well accustomed to dealing with thugs and frauds.

This day, Loesch found Capone to be in good spirits. Loesch asked

Capone if he would help ensure a clean election. There wasn't much worry about the presidential race. Hoover was expected to beat Smith easily in Illinois, but there were several city elections that mattered. Thompson's machine was trying to bounce back from its losses in the March primary. Loesch wanted to see the reformers continue to make progress in routing the forces of corruption. It was either a sign of his great pragmatism or the hopelessness of his long-term cause that he turned to Capone for help enforcing the law.

Loesch was under no illusions about Chicago's crime boss. He knew that Capone was not the superwealthy, all-powerful being that the press liked to make him out to be. He once told a gathering of business executives, "When they talk about Al Capone being rich, I don't believe them. He may take in much money, but every man surrounding him is a blackmailer preying upon him. If Al Capone is not murdered, the law will get him, or he will die in poverty. He is just as certain to go down as God lives."

But Loesch also understood that Capone was a community organizer, in his own fiendish way, and that this mob boss commanded the best-connected network in the city. Chicago was organized by neighborhoods, precincts, and parishes, and there were many politicians with strong local organizations. But not even Big Bill Thompson had yet built a machine that could match Capone's for its ability to work block by block, neighborhood by neighborhood, across the entire city.

"I'll have the cops send out squad cars the night before the election," Capone promised Loesch, sounding like the mayor or the chief of police. "They'll throw the punks into the cooler and keep 'em there until the voting's over."

A municipal judge, John Lyle, addressing a church group during the campaign, warned of Capone's might: "If you doubt the political sway of this man," he said, "let me inform you that at the last election he elected a State senator to protect his interests at Springfield—a man of his own race who has been in my chambers time and again on behalf of gangsters in police custody. . . . Capone has in the City Council an alderman completely under his dictation, who will front for him and his boys in case anything affecting them comes before the Council. Furthermore he elected a congressman. The money element in crime is linked up to official posts to a greater extent than the public realizes."

Whether Capone had anything to do with it, the November 6 election was the calmest Chicago had witnessed in years. "No Violence," read the subhead on the *Tribune*'s story, "Not Even a Kidnaping Reported." Nothing like it had happened for a generation, the story said. Loesch was beaming. "Today will stand out as the most remarkable Election Day in Chicago's history since it has been a great city," he said.

Thompson's machine took another hit as reformers won more positions of power. In the presidential election, Hoover won in a landslide, taking 444 electoral votes to Smith's 87. As if in celebration, the stock market rocketed into record territory. On November 12, the *New York Times,* reporting on the most active day of trading in the market's history, attributed the wave of optimism to "Herbert Hoover and the promise of 'four more years of prosperity.' "

THE FORMIDABLE ALPHONSE

Abraham Lincoln created the income tax in 1861 to fund the Civil War. The law called for a 3 percent tax on any U.S. resident with annual income of more than $600. Lincoln and his tax collectors didn't care how the money was earned—whether it came from "property, rents, interest, dividends, salaries or from any profession, trade, employment or vocation carried on in the United States or elsewhere, or from any source whatever." Income was income, and the government wanted a cut.

The law was simple but not popular. And it didn't take hold right away. It was overturned in 1872, brought back in 1894, and ruled unconstitutional in 1895. In 1913, Wyoming ratified the Sixteenth Amendment, creating the three-quarter majority of states required to make that amendment official. The amendment provided the legal basis for a federal income tax. That same year, a 1 percent tax was imposed on Americans with income higher than $3,000, and a 6 percent surtax was added for those who earned $500,000 or more. From that moment, the income tax became a permanent part of American life. There were only two ways to avoid it: by death or by fraud, the latter being the more popular choice. "The income tax," quipped the cowboy humorist Will Rogers, "has made liars out of more Americans than golf."

American honesty, like auto sales, tended to rise and fall with the economy. When money was tight during World War I, cheating flourished. In response, Daniel C. Roper, commissioner of the Bureau of Internal Revenue, which was part of the Treasury Department, hired half a dozen of the post office's most meticulous inspectors and turned them loose in pursuit of tax evaders. Postal inspectors at the time continued to be some of the most respected and feared men in government, known across the land for their honesty, perspicacity, and determination. Thus was formed the Special Intelligence Unit. Almost instantly, compliance rates improved.

But what about criminals? Were they supposed to file 1040s and report their illicit gains? The question was paradoxical. If one's money is illegally earned, is one legally required to pay taxes on it? Criminals, of course, were not engaging in philosophical discussions about their moral and constitutional duties. But they were smart enough to know that it didn't make sense to fill out forms providing the government with details of their illegal activities. They might as well have monogrammed their bullets and sent the cops photographs from their robberies while they were at it.

The question became more than merely philosophical in 1921, when a bootlegger named Manley Sullivan was arrested and charged with income tax evasion. Sullivan argued all the way to the U.S. Supreme Court that income from illegal transactions should not be taxable and that reporting such income amounted to self-incrimination. The Court didn't buy his argument, though, and that decision, in 1927, cleared the way for the Bureau of Internal Revenue's aggressive pursuit of bootleggers.

In Chicago, the Special Intelligence Unit dispatched one of its young, inexperienced agents, Eddie Waters, to see if he could get gangsters to report their income. "Occasionally, he would succeed, believe it or not," wrote his boss, Elmer Irey, the man in charge of the Special Intelligence Unit. And how did Agent Waters select his targets? From the newspapers, of course, which reported daily on the big bootleggers. Newspapermen loved nothing more than a bloody shoot-out on Michigan Avenue, but when they couldn't find one of those to write about they often settled for an account of the lavish spending habits of the city's leading hoodlums. Waters pestered Ralph "Bottles" Capone long enough that he finally agreed to file a return, listing his income as $20,000 a year for four years and his profession as "gambler." But to the government's great fortune, Ralph never got around to paying his income tax, or at least not all of it. Finally, on September 22, 1928, a collector for the Bureau of Internal Revenue filed liens for $11,000 against his property. Newspaper accounts said the investigators pursuing Ralph were also gathering evidence against his well-known younger brother. The stories didn't say whether Al Capone had been contacted by the feds or if charges against him might be coming soon.

The case against Al Capone would eventually become the most important income tax investigation in American history, but for now the big fellow had more pressing problems.

Ever since his arrival in Chicago in the winter of 1920, Capone had made his living catering to Chicagoans' vices. But eight years is a long time to stay in the same business, especially when the business involves so much shooting, stealing, bribing, and bomb-tossing. Over time, his operation evolved. In 1927, authorities in Chicago reported the birth of more than two hundred new rackets, and Capone was said to have a hand in many of them.

The rackets were simple operations. Suppose a dozen men on the West Side were selling fruit from sidewalk carts. One day a big guy with hairy knuckles wrapped around a crowbar would start paying visits to the fruit peddlers. "Are you with us?" he would ask. The confused peddler would soon learn that his peers had formed a union. Thanks to the union, the goon would inform him, prices for peaches and plums would be rising sharply, and police would no longer be bothering the pushcart men. The fruit peddler would need only to pay a small initiation fee of two bucks—plus a dollar-a-month membership charge—and do what he's told. His life would get easier. His wealth would grow. If the fruit peddler expressed hesitation, the gangster would tell him, with a laugh and a gentle punch in the arm, about what happened to the last man who decided not to join the organization. Inevitably, the fruit peddler would decide to pay.

The racketeers had broad reach. They had their hands in the pockets of window washers, bootblacks, soda dispensers, table girls, photo finishers, chicken killers, tire workers, candy jobbers, milkmen, taxi drivers, miniature-golf-course operators, pinball machine suppliers, and dozens of others. The hoodlums tended to pick on the small and powerless, and they looked for segments with a lot of competition so they could help to regulate them. As a result, Chicago residents contributed to the rackets in small, often unnoticeable increments. It was a great business for the gangsters, who had learned from bootlegging that there were better ways than larceny to get rich. Safecracking and house prowling belonged now almost exclusively to the desperate and degenerate. That stuff was too risky for the bootleggers, who had come to think of themselves as serious businessmen with steady customers, regular payrolls, and substantial capital investments. Racketeering was simple and steadily profitable. Thanks to the utter dysfunction of local government, it was fairly safe, too. As with any business, its success depended on strong management, clear operating principles, and well-organized, low-paid field operators who were willing to perform the dirty and dangerous work. The racket leaders, just like the leaders of legitimate industries, got the bulk of the money while taking little of the risk. By the late 1920s, racketeering became the hot new business for bootleggers.

Maxie Eisen, for instance, who got his start with Johnny Torrio and Capone, controlled the city's kosher butchers. Eisen set chicken prices at thirty-eight cents a pound, and when he found out that a butcher named Sam Trabush was refusing to go higher than thirty-five cents on his birds, Eisen fined him fifty bucks. When Trabush refused to pay, Eisen and his pal Jack "Knuckles" Cito beat the butcher with a crowbar, turning his head to chopmeat.

Gangsters already had thugs working every corner of the city and already had control of the speakeasies, where they maintained the flow of beer and the installation and maintenance of slot machines. Moving into the rackets required a redeployment of certain resources and the addition of a certain number of brass-knuckled enforcers, but it hardly called for reinvention.

In fact, when Capone got into the dry-cleaning racket, newspapers described him as a hero riding to the rescue of the small businessmen who had fallen under the oppression of other, greedier racketeers. "What police have attempted unsuccessfully for months to do—stop racketeering among cleaners and dyers of Chicago—today became the chore of Al Capone, vice lord and 'big shot' among the gangsters," wrote the *Chicago Daily Journal.* "The formidable Alphonse has become a principal partner in the Sanitary Cleaning Shops, Inc." The story went on to say that Capone, in exchange for his muscle, would receive a "$25,000 interest" in the shops he represented.

The *Tribune* recognized Capone's growing power as a grave concern. "We have here a situation as shameful as that created by the *Camorra* and Mafia in southern Italy," the paper editorialized.

In racketeering as in bootlegging, Capone's arms reached wide, but his grip was loose. He didn't rule the Coal Hikers Union, his associate William White did. He didn't supervise the Bill Posters and Billers Union, his pal Jack McGurn did. But Capone surely got a cut of the income from those and other organizations.

Of course, Capone's rivals were not rolling over and letting him have a monopoly. Bugs Moran, heir to Dean O'Banion's North Side throne, got into the dry-cleaning business the same as Capone did.

Moran was a big man with a beautiful head of highly sheened brown hair and a jowly face. In addition to dry cleaning, he had a hand in the taxi business, helping the Checker Taxicab Company put pressure on the Yellow Cab Company. Two Yellow cabs were tipped over on Lower Wacker Drive, two of the company's garages were bombed, and a barn in the countryside belonging to a Yellow Cab attorney was destroyed, killing eleven Thoroughbred horses. Suddenly, thanks to racketeering work, the North Side gangsters, who had been almost invisible since the death of Schemer Drucci, were raising hell again. They still didn't have the strength or the size of Capone's outfit, but they were big enough to cause trouble.

The North Siders no longer had their headquarters above Schofield's flower shop on State Street. Now they moved from place to place, like vagabonds. One of their hideouts was a dingy garage at 2122 North Clark Street, identified by the letters on the front window as the S. M. C. Cartage Co., on a block full of low-rent boardinghouses and greasy-spoon diners. It was a useful place, big enough to stash cases of whiskey and barrels of beer, even if it lacked the comforts enjoyed by Capone and his entourage at the Lexington Hotel.

Part of the trouble with the North Side gang was its chief. Moran hardly impressed anyone as a born leader. He was a great guy to have a drink with. He was quick with a joke. He remembered names. And he told thrilling stories of his horse-thieving and safecracking days. But he had a low-watt bulb for a brain—so low that it's not even clear he appreciated that his fantastic fortune had accumulated mostly because he'd been in the right place at the right time and had avoided the bullets that had, one by one, knocked off each of his partners. There was a reason beyond dumb luck, though, that Moran had survived while the others had died: It was because they'd posed a threat and he hadn't. He wasn't bright enough to scare anybody. But by the late 1920s, Moran's hands-off management style had left his outfit in a sorry state of disorganization. His men were operating almost randomly, and often with laughable results.

Peter Gusenberg, one of Moran's top guys, was proving to be a particular problem. On October 31, 1928, Gusenberg stuck up a couple of well-dressed women in the Loop, snatching from them an estimated $14,000 in jewelry. It was a nice haul, but it was a low-class move. Less than a week later, Gusenberg and a couple of other North Side goons—Leo Mongoven and Frank Foster—decided to score a little quick cash by picking on a former bootlegger who now worked as a stockbroker in the Loop. Their proposed victim, Abe Cooper, looked like an easy mark. He stood five feet two and weighed just a shade over a hundred pounds, much of that weight seemingly concentrated in the ears and eyelids, which drooped cartoonishly. He had the look of a man in perpetual need of a nap. Cooper was at work in the Rookery Building when Mongoven, a big galoot, went in, pulled the little fellow from his desk, and dragged him toward a car parked at LaSalle and Adams. "Get in and we'll take you for a ride," the thug offered. Cooper had a better idea. He pulled a revolver and started firing. Mongoven was hit twice. He fell but didn't die. Foster froze. Gusenberg, built like a washed-up footballer, took off running as fast as his chunky legs would take him. When the story hit the newspapers, Cooper was a hero, the trio of gangsters sat in jail, and Moran's entire gang was the joke of Chicago.

At roughly the same time, a former firefighter named William Davern Jr. was shot in the stomach during a tussle with some Moran men at the C & O Restaurant, at 509 North Clark Street, a popular nightspot where the beer and whiskey flowed. No one ever told what sparked the fight. The gangsters took Davern's bleeding body and dumped it at the corner of Rush Street and Austin Avenue. It was about four in the morning. Davern found the strength to reach a fire alarm call box. He died six weeks later in the hospital. While he never told investigators who shot him, he may have told his father, who was a Chicago police sergeant, and he also may have told his first cousin. Psychopathic criminal, part-time gangster, part-time bank robber, friend of Capone, and former cop killer, Davern's cousin was William White.

Davern's murder warranted only a few paragraphs in the local papers despite his being the son of a policeman. It was just another gang shooting to the ink-stained set, just another dirty rat "taken for a ride." But for the Moran gang, and for Capone, it may have had enormous ripple effects.

––––––

The Moran outfit was spinning out of control. Robbing wealthy women of their jewels? Blowing up horses? Getting beaten to the draw by a stockbroker? Knocking off a cop's son? Capone's men knew better than to engage in such amateurish stuff.

And what was the big fellow doing while Moran was reminding everyone how *not* to run a criminal organization? Playing golf, for one thing. It seemed like a safe sport. But one day in September, after shooting eighteen holes in northwestern Indiana, Capone was getting back into his car when the gun in his right hip pocket discharged. The bullet ripped through his flesh, and blood began soaking his golfing togs immediately. The pain was excruciating. His golfing partner, Johnny Patton—the mayor of suburban Burnham and an investor in some of Capone's gambling operations—drove his friend to a hospital in Hammond. The wound wasn't life-threatening, but Capone remained hospitalized for a few days. When the *Tribune* reported the accident, he issued a denial. "A man who has been shot in the leg can't dance!" he declared, getting up from his desk to do a little jig for an *Evening Post* reporter.

In fact, he hadn't been shot in the leg. Years later, during a routine physical exam, Capone revealed the truth. The bullet, he told his doctor, had put a hole in his scrotum.

LITTLE CAESAR

For Herbert Hoover, the first days of 1929 were filled with hope and high spirits. He began by drawing up plans for the reorganization of the federal government's ten largest departments, with the goal of eliminating overlapping functions and reducing waste. He asked experts across the country to submit proposals on how better to go about flood control, pricing regulation, child welfare, manufacturing, home building, military disarmament, job creation, and crime control. Once that work was under way, he traveled aboard American battleships to ten countries in Central and South America, touting what he called his "good neighbor" approach to diplomacy, and helping to settle a forty-six-year-old territorial dispute between Bolivia and Peru. He fished for marlin from the battleships' decks, and when a powerful storm flooded his stateroom one night, he went topside and watched the dark skies unleash their torrents, standing there in his soaking pajamas and trench coat even after most of the sailors had sought shelter below.

From Latin America, Hoover's ship plowed north toward Washington, D.C., where he stopped briefly to interview potential cabinet members and meet with the committee planning his inauguration, which was to be held on March 4. He reminded them to keep it plain, simple, and cheap.

Then, with two months remaining before taking office, he headed to Miami for a working vacation. In Miami, schools and businesses were closed to celebrate Hoover's arrival. Thousands of people lined Flagler Street in the heart of the business district on a bright blue afternoon to catch a glimpse of the president-elect and his brilliant and forceful wife, Lou Henry. Boy Scouts held back the crowds with ropes. Former heavyweight champ Jack Dempsey was on hand, as was Mary Elizabeth Baird Bryan, the

Bible-thumping lawyer and wife of William Jennings Bryan. Al Capone was in town that day but was home in bed with the flu. Miami's mayor, E. G. Sewell, presented Hoover with a key to the city and two new fishing rods. The parade ended at Belle Island, where Hoover would spend the next month as a guest in the home of the department store magnate J. C. Penney.

The Penney mansion was simple yet elegant. It was three stories tall and built of white limestone, with overhanging eaves of sun-faded, apricot-colored tiles. A rich frieze of red and brown skirted the roof. Like every home on the island, it had its own boat dock and broad views of Biscayne Bay. When he wasn't fighting sailfish from the deck of a borrowed yacht, Hoover answered mail and continued making plans for the reform of government. His thoughts returned again and again to Prohibition, which he referred to as "a cloud over all our problems." Years later, in composing his memoirs, he would write, "I should have been glad to have humanity forget all about strong alcoholic drinks. They are moral, physical, and economic curses to the race. But in the present stage of human progress, this vehicle of joy could not be generally suppressed by the Federal Law." As Hoover saw it, the nation's cities and states had given up almost entirely on holding citizens to the law. Even the states that had most aggressively sought the ban on alcohol had gradually abandoned the law's enforcement, leaving it to the overmatched federal government. E. B. White—a new writer at the *New Yorker* who later wrote *Charlotte's Web* and other classic books—joked that the government could fix the problem by taking control of speakeasies. "In that manner," he wrote, "the citizenry would be assured liquor of a uniformly high quality and the enormous cost of enforcement could be met by the profits from the sale of drinks."

Not since slavery had a moral, legal, and ethical issue so thoroughly engrossed the American public. It was the favorite topic of barbershop debates and Sunday sermons. It divided husbands and wives, sisters and brothers, bosses and workers. It was the rare piece of public policy that touched almost every adult life almost every day.

Hoover liked to think of himself as government's Mr. Fix-It, but he knew he would have a difficult time fixing this problem. Bootleggers, moonshiners, and still owners were pumping money into police departments and city councils across the land, corrupting all they touched. Anyone with twenty-five cents in his pocket could get a drink virtually anywhere and anytime he wanted. Jails were overcrowded and court dockets were as slow and unreliable as hundred-year-old plumbing. Clogs and leaks made it simple for lawyers to game the system, so that even convicted criminals managed to postpone or completely dodge their prison sentences by stalling for time. Why not simply scrap the law and admit it had done more harm than good? Most congressmen wouldn't think of it. They didn't want to capitulate. They didn't want to let their political opponents cast them as supporters of sin. Of course, there was one final reason that federal lawmakers weren't in too great a hurry to repeal Prohibition. Like so many others, they were having no difficulty getting their booze. Bootleggers roamed the halls of Congress and kept crates of liquor in the cellars of the Senate and House of Representatives. In Hoover's case, though, it seemed to be more a matter of pride: The law was the law, and it ought to be made to work, he believed.

Corruption was everywhere, but, as Hoover well understood, Chicago had an especially pronounced problem. Chicago had produced Al Capone. It had planted him and watered him and fertilized the ground around him and watched him grow. Chicago had given him everything he had wanted, and now he was so big that the city was helpless to stop him.

Profligacy seemed stamped on the city like a lurid tattoo. It was the first thing—sometimes the *only* thing—people talked about when they discussed the Second City. When a tourist or businessman returned home after a trip to the city by the lake, his friends could be counted on to joke, "Where are your bullet holes?" or "Did you see Scarface Capone?"

By 1929, gangsters were the subjects of a growing number of books and movies, many of them modeled at least partially on Capone. The most popular among them was *Little Caesar,* a novel by W. R. Burnett, which would soon become a movie starring Edward G. Robinson as the gang kingpin Rico Bandello. Writers and directors in the late 1920s presented these gangsters in much the same way Horatio Alger presented his heroes: urban success stories, heirs to the legacy of Benjamin Franklin and Andrew Carnegie, ambitious men willing to take great risks in pursuit of wealth and power, entrepreneurs whose tools of the trade just happened to be Tommy guns. That's why the writer Fred Pasley, in publishing the first Capone biography in 1930, subtitled it *The Biography of a Self-Made Man.* Wrote Pasley: "Capone was to revolutionize crime and corruption by putting both on an efficiency basis, and to instill into a reorganized gangland firm business methods of procedure." In a country built on rawboned capitalism, what could be wrong with that?

But to Hoover, who understood a few things about efficiency and organization, the celebration of Capone's talents was galling. Capone stood for everything Hoover opposed, beginning with bootlegging but hardly ending there. And if the president-elect needed any reminder of Capone's growing stature in American culture, all he needed to do was look across Biscayne Bay. Capone's home on Palm Island sat less than a mile away from Hoover's borrowed place on Belle Island. Did their fishing boats ever pass under a mid-afternoon's sun? Did their paths cross in the lobby of the Biltmore Hotel? Did members of their respective entourages rub elbows at the racetrack? One report, written years later, claimed that Hoover complained of noise from a party at the Capone house. Though Capone did throw several big parties that winter, and though it's conceivable that the racket could have reached the president-elect if the wind had been blowing the right way, the story seems apocryphal. When Hoover wasn't on a boat, his every move was covered by newspapermen and movie camera operators, and Capone was getting a fair bit of attention at the time, too. If a party thrown by America's best-known gangster had disturbed the sleep of America's president-elect, the story probably would have been picked up by one of the reporters camped on Belle Island. Nonetheless, in the years ahead, Hoover would pay a great deal of attention to Capone—far more, probably, than either man liked.

————

Capone made it known upon his arrival in Miami in the early days of 1929 that he intended to stay "indefinitely," and not just because he liked the weather. The beer business back in Chicago was getting tougher. The cops were cracking down again, in large part because the city fathers were planning a world's fair to honor the city's centennial. The hundredth anniversary wouldn't come until 1937, but Big Bill Thompson wasn't going to let a little thing like the Gregorian calendar keep him waiting. The city needed a boost fast. It needed something to remind the world that the machine gun was not Chicago's only cultural contribution. So the decision was made to celebrate the centennial in 1933, which meant preparations would begin at once, and part of those preparations included yet another shakeup of the police department. A new line of politically appointed chiefs and detectives came to power, and some old ones returned to the fight. Business leaders with strong connections in Washington were urged to lobby for more federal crime-fighting muscle for Chicago. The city had but four years to turn around its reputation or else risk scaring off tourists who might come for the fair.

As the city's crackdown began, suburban bootleggers such as Roger Touhy, who boasted of making the best beer in northern Illinois, were flourishing, while city-based gangs struggled. Gangs displayed less respect for turf lines. The rackets were big business now and tended to be run by the same men who ran the bootlegging, but not all the players were the same. There were unions involved, some of them quite strong and quite hostile to the intervention of gangsters.

On top of all that, tempers in Little Italy were still hot over the battle for control of the Unione Siciliana. So hot that New York City police were making a much greater effort than usual to find the men responsible for the murder of Frankie Yale. So hot that Tony Lombardo's successor as president of the Unione, Pasqualino "Patsy" Lolordo, lasted only four months on the job. Lolordo, whose brother Tony had been of dubious service as bodyguard to Lombardo, was at home one afternoon—January 8, 1929—in his flat over a harness shop when three men knocked at the door. They came in, sat down in Lolordo's well-appointed living room, and raised four wineglasses in a toast to his health—before ruining it with a bunch of bullets. It was, as the Chicago writer Walter Noble Burns put it, an "amazingly friendly murder." By one account, Lolordo was the fifteenth man to die in the war for control of the Unione. Lolordo's wife identified Joe Aiello as one of the friendly men who'd been drinking with her husband before his death. Other reports said the killers were Bugs Moran's men. The killing was done in daylight, the killers presumably left fingerprints all over their cocktail glasses, and Mrs. Lolordo claimed that she got a good look at them as they ran past her on the way out of her house. The cops said they agreed with Lolordo's wife that it looked like the work of Joe Aiello and his men. And yet as usual, the crime was never officially solved.

The *Herald and Examiner* summed up the news with the opening paragraph of one story on the Lolordo attack: "Forecast for Chicago: More gang murders."

Though Capone was no doubt concerned about the war for the Unione, he was not exactly leading the life of an outcast or a wanted criminal. When he wasn't on the phone to Jack Guzik in Chicago, keeping tabs on business there, or consulting with his lawyers, he dined in fine restaurants, gambled heavily at the Hialeah Park racetrack, and entertained his guests aboard fishing vessels in the Caribbean. Capone loved the company of men. He liked to smoke and drink and talk and bet. If he also loved the company of beautiful women, as might have been expected for a man of his wealth and fame, he hid it well. He was never photographed in the company of a woman other than his wife. For that matter, he wasn't seen in Mae's company very often, either. Even as federal agents began to pick up his trail in the early part of 1929, as part of the ongoing investigation of business interests and income tax liability, no witnesses ever reported seeing the boss with a woman.

Capone's winter vacation in Miami started badly, though. Sonny got the flu, and then Al got it, too. The virus hit him so hard that two nurses were hired to provide constant care, and a Miami doctor named Samuel D. Light was called to the house sixteen or seventeen times over the course of nine days. Eventually Capone's doctor was brought from Chicago to Miami to look after him.

By the middle of January, he had at last made a full recovery. He began visiting Hialeah Park nearly every day it was open. At Hialeah, he would slide a ten-dollar bill into the palm of the parking attendant to make sure his car was looked after, then find a seat in one of the boxes near the front of the grandstand. Betting on the horses was illegal in Florida, but some tracks had developed a new system called the "buying option," which allowed interested parties to purchase stock in the horse he expected to win a race. If the horse did in fact win, the stockholder received a dividend in line with the odds the horse had faced. If the horse lost, the stockholder's investment was wiped out. This was January 1929, the stock market was booming (most of the time), and horse racing benefited by mimicking the workings of the U.S. stock exchanges.

On February 2, 1929, Capone and three pals chartered a seaplane for a day trip from Miami to Bimini, in the Bahamas. Six days later, aboard the SS *New Northland,* Capone sailed for Nassau, in the Bahamas, where he remained for nearly a week. Accompanying him were his brother Albert (known as Boots or Bites), who had only a marginal involvement in his criminal activities; Philip D'Andrea, a former trucker who made the transition to bootlegging and became one of Capone's top bodyguards; Fred Girton, a Miami newspaper editor; Kenneth Phillips, a local physician who had consulted with Capone's doctor from Chicago during Capone's bout with the flu;

and William McCabe, a big-time gambler. Given the presence of Capone's doctor, the newspaper editor, and Al's brother Bites, who almost never got into any serious trouble, it would appear that the trip was recreational.

On February 11, Hoover traveled to Fort Myers, Florida, to help celebrate the eighty-second birthday of his friend Thomas Edison. The titan of automobiles, Henry Ford, and the titan of automobile tires, Harvey Firestone, joined the party, as did the inventor's neighbors. But Hoover declined a request from Fort Myers officials to participate in a parade, saying he didn't want his presence to distract from the birthday festivities. Nearly fifty years after filing the patent on his revolutionary lightbulb, The Wizard of Menlo Park still looked spritely and still spoke of his ongoing experiments. He wore a black three-piece suit with a bow tie. While there was no entertainment at the party, some of his favorite musicians performed songs in his honor during a national radio broadcast, and Edison tuned in throughout the day. After showing President-elect Hoover and his other guests around his property, he walked briskly inside to meet a group of reporters and answer their questions. His hearing was bad, so the reporters submitted their questions in writing, and Edison barked his answers. "We don't know a millionth of 1 percent about anything," he remarked in an answer to a question about the future of scientific discovery. When asked if the Hoover administration would bring "greater national prosperity," Edison replied simply, "Yes."

After bidding farewell to Edison, the president-elect had intended to spend a day fishing for tarpon off the coast of Fort Myers. But he was turned back by strong winds and choppy seas and forced to return to Miami.

Capone returned to Miami Beach the same day as Hoover, February 12. It's not clear if the weather forced Capone to cut short his trip, too, or if he had planned to be back by the twelfth all along. Most of his time in Miami was unstructured. He went to the track when he felt like it, took off on fishing trips with little or no warning, and went to see the prizefights in Miami Beach whenever there was one worth watching. But this time he had an appointment to keep: Louis Goldstein, a hard-hitting assistant district attorney from Brooklyn, was coming down to Florida to ask Capone a few questions about the slaying of Frankie Yale. The meeting was set for St. Valentine's Day, February 14.

ST. VALENTINE'S DAY

Back in Chicago, the early-morning skies were gray, and the air was cold and snappish. A light snow powdered the city's sidewalks, windowsills, and rooftops. Bakers, candy merchants, and florists woke earlier than usual to prepare for the expected crush of customers. At the stately Hotel Sherman, the catering crew began setting up tables for the big St. Valentine's Day party thrown every year by the Kiwanis Club. Children put the finishing touches on cards for their classmates before leaving for school.

Of course, not everyone was thinking about hugs and kisses that morning. Over at the Cook County Jail, guards prepared for the midnight execution of three convicted killers. On La Salle Street, bankers and stockbrokers, whiplashed the day before by stock prices that plummeted and only partially recovered, nervously watched their stock tickers as trading began in New York. And inside a humdrum garage at 2122 North Clark Street, an unusually large gathering of Bugs Moran's men came together for purposes unknown.

Except for a single white lightbulb dangling from the ceiling, the big S.M.C. Cartage Co. garage on North Clark Street was dark, the parked trucks and cars almost lost in the vast shadowed spaces. A little bit of light filtered through the grimy front window, but it barely made a dent in the darkness or the cold. It was a facility meant for vehicles, not humans, and the presence of only one small table and a few chairs would suggest that it was unusual for so many men to congregate there at the same time. The Moran gang used the garage to park and repair trucks and store booze. But it was not a hangout. The men arrived at the garage for a meeting, not for camaraderie, and certainly not to exchange Valentines.

Inside the garage were seven men: Johnny May, dressed in greasy brown coveralls, was lying on his back under a jacked-up truck, repairing a wheel. He was a former safe blower hired by Moran as an auto mechanic and one of the countless Chicagoans who could thank Prohibition and the bootlegging business for giving him a good, steady, and relatively safe career. May lived with his wife, his seven kids, and a dog named Highball, who was tied by leash to the axle of the truck May was trying to fix. Six more men milled about, trying to stay warm in the unheated garage. There were the Gusenberg brothers, Frank and Peter, two of the city's most troublesome goons; James Clark (real name: Albert Kachellek), a convicted armed robber, and a reputed killer; Adam Heyer, a.k.a. Frank Snyder, an accountant and embezzler; Albert Weinshank, a nightclub owner and a newly appointed official of the Cleaners and Dyers Association; and an optometrist named Reinhart H. Schwimmer, who hung around the Moran boys mostly so he could brag to friends about his underworld connections. These were some of Moran's top men—with the exception of the mechanic and the optometrist—and they were well dressed this morning in expensive suits, ties, tiepins, and street shoes. One of them wore a carnation. Moran, who lived little more than a block away, at the Parkway Hotel, may have been on his way, too. All of this suggested that the men had not come to the garage to unload crates of whiskey. This was a meeting of higher purpose, or at least a rendezvous that would lead them to an appointment elsewhere.

At about ten that morning, Elmer Lewis steered his Nelson-LeMoon delivery truck through Chicago's North Side. The wind blew snow dust across his windshield and the big steering wheel shook in his hands as he navigated the slippery pavement along Clark Street. Watching the road and scanning for the address of his delivery, he almost didn't notice the black Cadillac peeling out from Webster Avenue, which ran perpendicular to Clark, until it was too late. He slammed on the truck's mechanical brakes, but he couldn't avoid a collision. His truck's left front bumper clipped the sedan's left rear fender.

Lewis pulled to the curb and stopped. When he got a good look at the Cadillac, he became frightened. It looked like a police car, with curtains covering the rear windows. One could never be sure in Chicago, because cop cars weren't clearly marked. But this one had a bell on the driver's side running board, which was usually a pretty reliable gauge, and detectives sometime drove Caddies. There were four or five men in the car; Lewis wasn't sure. The driver was not in uniform—he had on a fancy chinchilla topcoat and a gray fedora—but he still could have been a detective. Lewis never found out. He got out of his truck and walked toward the Cadillac, but the driver waved him off. The Caddie zoomed up the street full of two- and three-story brick buildings, past a drugstore, a barbershop, and boardinghouses, and stopped in front of the S.M.C. Cartage Co.

It was about 10:30 A.M. as the men got out of the car and entered the garage through the front door. Two of them wore police uniforms, and two or three wore street clothes. The cold air in the garage smelled of truck tires, engine grease, and gasoline. The temperature outside held at about eighteen degrees, and inside wasn't much better.

If Moran's gangsters were worried by the new arrivals, they didn't show it. Most of the Moran men were armed, but no one reached for his weapon. Maybe they had been expecting the company. Maybe they knew their guests. Or maybe, seeing two men in police uniform, they decided to play it cool and see what had prompted the visit. Experienced gangsters such as these men were not unaccustomed to dealing with the cops. There was no reason to overreact. If it was money the cops wanted, Moran's men had plenty of it.

But this visit wasn't about money.

The intruders raised their weapons—two Tommys and one twelve-gauge shotgun—and ordered Moran's men to move away from the doors and windows. They lined them up shoulder to shoulder against the wall on the garage's northern side. To the left of them stood a table with a hot plate, a coffeepot, and a couple of boxes. To the right of them sat a beat-up truck with a tarp stretched over its bed. They were made to face the wall.

What happened next took no more than two minutes.

The armed men raised their guns.

In a haze of sprayed machine-gun fire, brick dust, and smoke, seven men were viciously executed. Bullets tore through flesh and sinew and lodged in the wall. Shells pinged to the ground and spun. Bodies fell like bowling pins, every which way. Blood dark as motor oil surged across the cold concrete floor and slid thickly down a drain. Some men died instantly, some gasped briefly for air.

Out on Clark Street, neighbors heard popping noises, which some took for the sound of a backfiring car. Others heard the desperate howling of a dog. A few of them peered out of their windows in time to see men leaving the garage and getting into a car. It looked as if two cops were leading two or three other men into a Cadillac police car, possibly at gunpoint, the witnesses said. The Cadillac sped south on Clark Street, zigzagging to avoid a trolley car, and disappeared from view somewhere around Armitage Avenue, a wide residential street of thickset trees and tall, handsome homes.

One of the neighbors walked over to the garage and pushed open the door. He saw smoke and smelled gunpowder. He saw hideously mutilated bodies on the floor and inhaled the nauseating stench of blood. Smoke still hung in the air. The dog, Highball, was still howling, driven to a frenzy by the thunderous noise and the bloody scent of the freshly slain.

Pete Gusenberg was lying farthest west, slumped over a chair, bloodied head and shoulders on the seat of the chair. Next to him, on the floor, was Weinshank, who had toppled straight back, arms by his sides, blood spurting from his eyes and nose, his hat perched tidily on his chest. Next to Weinshank was Heyer, whose scarf flowed from his neck in the same direction as the blood flowing from his cracked head. Next to Heyer lay the mechanic May, who was flat on the floor with a splintered skull and a mass of his own brain tissue sitting next to his face like a clump of oatmeal. Next to May was the optometrist Schwimmer, his hat still on. Clark's body lay at the feet of the others, along the wall, facedown in a warm, spreading puddle of blood, cartilage, and nerve tissue. The seventh victim, Frank Gusenberg, gurgling blood, was still alive.

"Who is it?" the wounded man asked when he heard someone enter the garage.

"I just come in to help you out," the neighbor said, according to his testimony to police and reporters.

The neighbor then raced outside and shouted for someone to call the police. Sergeant Thomas J. Loftus, a veteran of the Thirty-sixth District station, responded to the call first, reaching the garage at about 10:45 A.M. In thirty-eight years on the force he had never seen anything like this. No one had. He moved a bunch of neighbors away from the bodies and told one of his colleagues to call for help. Then he spotted Frank Gusenberg, shot fourteen times, entrails soaking his woolen suit, and still breathing.

One newspaper account said that Gusenberg staggered over to Loftus and collapsed into his arms; others said Gusenberg remained on the floor, trying in vain to crawl away from the grotesque scene.

"Do you know me, Frank?" the sergeant asked.

"Yes, you're Tom Loftus," the gangster said between gulps of air.

Then Gusenberg added: "I won't talk," as if he knew from experience the copper's next question.

But after sucking more air, he did talk, briefly.

"Cops did it," Gusenberg said.

Loftus pressed for details but got none.

"For God's sake," said Gusenberg, "get me to a hospital!"

He got to the hospital, but it didn't matter. He died there, still not talking.

In Miami, Capone sat in a Dade County office building, wearing a checkered sport jacket, white flannel trousers, and a light gray fedora. He had arrived for an interview with Louis Goldstein, the prosecutor from Brooklyn. Also present were Dade County's prosecutor, Robert Taylor, and the county sheriff, M. P. Lehman. Ruth Gaskin, a stenographer, took down every word. Capone was so confident that he came without an attorney, but he may have regretted his decision when the first questions came not from Goldstein but from Taylor, the Dade county solicitor.

"Do you remember when you first met Parker Henderson?" Taylor asked, as the session began.

"About two years ago," Capone answered.

"That was when he was running the Ponce de Leon Hotel?"

"Yes."

"Can you remember who was staying there with you that winter?"

"I don't like to disclose their names unless you tell me what this is all about."

The interrogator persisted.

"I don't remember," Capone said.

"Under what name did you register?"

"My own name."

"You didn't register under the name of A. Costa?"

"No."

"You left money with Henderson, $1,000 to $5,000 at a time, didn't you?"

"I don't remember."

"You didn't receive any money by Western Union from Chicago?"

"I don't remember. I'll try to find out."

Capone had been expecting questions about the murder of Frankie Yale, not about his finances. He grew defensive.

"Then you keep a record of your money transactions?"

"Absolutely."

"How long has Dan Serritella been living with you?"

"He's not living with me. He's just a friend of mine."

"How much did you give Parker Henderson to buy your home?"

"Fifty thousand dollars."

"Was that in cash?"

"Yes."

"Besides gambling, you're a bootlegger, aren't you?"

"No, I was never a bootlegger."

"Do you know Jake Guzik?"

"Yes."

"What does he do?"

"He fights," Capone answered with a chuckle.

"And do you know anybody who sent you money under the name of A. Costa?"

"No."

"But you did receive it from Chicago?"

"That is correct. All of it comes from Chicago, from my gambling business."

"Are you going to buy Cat Cay [a small island in the Bahamas]?"

"I don't know. I don't think I will get it."

"How much do they want for it?"

"Half a million."

"Who is Mitchell of Oak Park, Illinois? He called your home three times on January 20." Police in Chicago and Cicero had run a series of raids on pool halls, casinos, and brothels that day, which might explain why someone in Oak Park would have needed to speak to the boss.

"He commissions money on racetracks for me."

"Did you get any money from Charlie Fischetti while you were staying at the Ponce de Leon? Henderson said you received various sums from $1,000 to $5,000."

"What has money got to do with it?"

With that, Capone may have finally understood that the interviewer was more interested in his income tax liability than his suspected role in the Yale assassination. Perhaps Capone had dropped his guard because no representative of the Bureau of Internal Revenue had been present.

By the time Capone finished his interview, news of the massacre in Chicago was spreading like flames through dry timber. Huge, block-lettered headlines screamed across the top of every paper in Chicago. The *Herald and Examiner*'s writer topped his story with: "Chicago gangsters graduated yesterday from murder to massacre." The article continued succinctly, powerfully, and accurately: "They killed seven men in a group. There was just a few seconds of machine gun and shotgun fire. Then six of them lay dead and the seventh was dying. It was like the precise work of the Mexican army, [or] like the assassination of Csar Nicholas and his family." All over the country, the bloodletting made page-one news. The black-and-white photos accompanying the stories, showing a tangle of bodies and pools of blood, were among the most graphically violent ever to appear in the American press. In one image, the mechanic John May's brain was clearly visible, lying in a creamy lump against his left cheek.

Chicago may have already been known as the nation's gangland murder capital, but this crime was shocking even by Chicago standards. It was not only because of the number of men murdered all at once, but also because of the cold-blooded manner in which they were gunned down. Almost instantly it became known as the St. Valentine's Day Massacre.

Capone, still feeling cocky, would brag that he had an airtight alibi. He had a sheriff, a prosecutor, and a stenographer to prove his whereabouts. But it didn't matter.

This crime stirred people in a way they had seldom been stirred before. From coast to coast, people seemed suddenly to be reaching the conclusion that a line had been crossed, that the violence had become too much to bear, that the experiment known as Prohibition had blown up once and for all.

Herbert Hoover's letters and diaries offer no clues about when he became aware of the Valentine's Day Massacre. He spent the day at the Penney mansion on Belle Island, where he had sixteen meetings scheduled prior to lunch. He posed for a portrait that would hang in New York City's Union League Club, led a meeting on tax policy, and gave several interviews. That afternoon he did some fishing, and that evening he dined with Charles Lindbergh. If he spoke of the horrific crime in Chicago, none of the newspapermen who met him reported it.

It would soon become clear, however, that the president-elect was paying attention. The day after the assassination, Hoover administration officials announced that the incoming president would appoint four hundred more federal Prohibition agents and would ask Congress for an additional $2.5 million in Prohibition enforcement funding. A consensus was beginning to emerge, both in Chicago and Washington, that Capone and his type had to be stopped.

PART THREE

CAPONE FALLING

"AN UNSOLVED CRIME"

Two days after the St. Valentine's Day Massacre, Capone threw a party at his home on Palm Island, hosting eighty guests with "the prodigality of a Medici," as one writer put it. Two heavyweight fighters, Jack Sharkey and William "Young" Stribling, were preparing for a big bout at Flamingo Park in Miami. Jack Dempsey was promoting the event. Walter Winchell, Babe Ruth, and Connie Mack would be ringside. With Miami's economy in a depression—the result of cratering real estate prices and recent hurricane damage—the city needed big sporting events like this one to boost its image and pump cash into local businesses. Capone did his part. He encouraged friends from New York and Chicago to come down for the fight. He took them to nightclubs and invited them to splash in his pool. He organized fishing trips. He hosted a boxing exhibition at his home. He even granted an interview to a reporter who showed up, seemingly unannounced, on Palm Island.

Greeting the newspaperman, Capone climbed out of his swimming pool and wrapped himself in a bathrobe. "I am sick and tired of publicity," he said with no hint of irony, in a story that would appear in hundreds of newspapers across the country. "I want no more of it. It puts me in a bad light. I just want to be forgotten."

He was asked if he always carried a weapon.

He answered, "I am a peaceable citizen. No, I do not carry a gun. If I did I would be breaking the law, and I am not breaking the law."

Capone said he had no idea who had killed Moran's men in Chicago. He said he still kept tabs on his dog track and other business interests in Illinois, but he gave the writer the impression that he was otherwise not all that engaged in day-to-day affairs back home. He seemed to be a man in transition. He volunteered that he had recently purchased thirty-five acres of land in St. Petersburg. Beyond that, his attention was focused on the poor health of his boy, Sonny, who was ten years old. Sonny had recently undergone another operation for mastoiditis, an infection that caused swelling and pain behind the ear. Capone talked about the fact that he'd never had much education and how badly he wanted to see Sonny go to college. On the subject of the upcoming prizefight, which was what had prompted the reporter's visit after all, Capone predicted Stribling would win, although he admitted that his hunches had not paid off lately; at Hialeah, he said, he had recently lost $27,500 on a single race.

The reporter finished his story intent on making his subject seem more mysterious: "One leaves the dark-complexioned, heavy set Capone with the feeling that here is a man who is an enigmatic, a man who nobody knows, not even his closest intimates." It was a common theme among Capone's chroniclers. None tried to interview his closest intimates. None tried to get a word with his wife or mother. Capone did everything possible to make himself accessible, to answer questions, and to promote the illusion that he led something resembling an ordinary American life, even as he complained that he was sick of all the publicity, while the newsmen did everything possible to make him seem dark and mysterious.

Meanwhile, in Chicago, George Johnson called the St. Valentine's Day Massacre "the most amazing crime in Chicago's amazing criminal history." Detectives, federal law-enforcement officers, and newspapermen blanketed the city's North Side, talking to neighbors, searching for the killers' black Cadillac, trying to make sense out of what had happened. Nobody knew.

Sure, Capone might have wanted to hurt Moran, given their competing interests in booze and gambling, but Moran also had trouble with rivals in the dry cleaning rackets, and, for that matter, he was not on the best of terms with Joe Aiello. Besides, Moran wasn't even in the garage at the time of the killing. There remained a strong possibility that the massacre had nothing to do with him whatsoever. Maybe the killers were gunning for the Gusenbergs, who certainly had plenty of enemies. Or maybe the motive was something much simpler altogether: revenge for a hijacking. Every hour, more clues and more theories emerged among cops and newspaper reporters until no one could possibly keep them straight.

Only a handful of facts seemed solid. Police learned that a phone call was received at the garage ten minutes before the shooting. The call came from a phone booth at the Webster Hotel, a little more than a block away, at 2150 Lincoln Avenue. There seemed to be no dispute about that. It would have been easy for the killers to make the call, get in their car, and drive to the garage in ten minutes or less. It seemed clear that the men there had been expecting company. Why else would so many of them have come together, so smartly dressed, in the cold, dank garage? Why else would there be coffee set out on the table? Why else would they have failed to draw their weapons when their assassins came in the door?

Investigators initially pursued the simplest and most obvious of all possible explanations: that Frank Gusenberg had been right in blaming the cops. If Moran's men had double-crossed police officers, retaliation would have been inevitable. The investigators quickly dispensed with that theory, though, announcing that Gusenberg must have been mistaken and that the men in uniform must have been impostors. The investigators never said why they decided this. Their next theory was that the murder had been the work of the Purple Gang, an outfit from Detroit, acting in retaliation for the recent hijacking of a $50,000 truckload of whiskey. A woman who ran a boardinghouse across from the garage on Clark Street was said to have identified photographs of three members of the Purple Gang who had rented a room, presumably so they could watch for the arrival of Moran's men. Then came the notion that the killing might have been connected to a vicious aldermanic election in the Twentieth Ward, where Capone supported one candidate and Moran another. Investigators also considered the possibility that the killing was tied to the fight for control of the dry cleaning rackets. Albert Weinshank, one of the dead men, was a central figure in the laundry business.

Police also listed Moran himself as a suspect. The gang boss was seen driving past the garage at about the time of the murder. Why didn't he go in? Was it possible that he had tired of the Gusenbergs' insubordination and decided to get rid of them? It was possible, but police weren't sure. So they considered one possibility after another. They searched for Jack McGurn on the hunch that he was always a strong suspect when multiple shots were fired in Chicago. He'd been feuding of late with the Gusenbergs. The cops also searched for Sam Giancana, a twenty-three-year-old hit man who had been firing and ducking a lot of bullets recently. They searched for Rocco Fanelli, another Capone underling, probably out of pure habit.

After five days of hopping from one theory to another, police officials reverted to their original notion, saying they had new evidence suggesting that the killing had been the work of police officers. Moran's gang had stolen a truckload of liquor from a cop, according to a story in the *Chicago Evening Post,* and the cop had retaliated. The *Evening Post* quoted a witness who said that the car seen in front of the garage was "a police squad automobile beyond any doubt. It even had a gun rack fastened on the rear of the front seat."

John Stege, deputy police commissioner, had probably investigated more murders than anyone in Chicago. If he hadn't solved many of them, it wasn't entirely his fault. He was in Miami at the time of the St. Valentine's Day Massacre, although it's not clear if he attended the Sharkey-Stribling fight or if he ran into Capone at any time. He interrupted his vacation and came back to Chicago to help lead the investigation.

"It seems funny to me," he announced upon his return, "that all of the big men in this gang escaped. . . . Just suppose that some of Moran's lesser men had been double-crossing him, dealing with a rival booze-peddling outfit. . . . And suppose Moran found it out. What would Moran do? Think it over."

A week after the crime, cops found a stripped-down, burned-out Cadillac that may have been the one used in the St. Valentine's Day Massacre. But it didn't help them much. The investigation was still going in circles. "I can name fifty motives for this crime," complained David Stansbury, the lead investigator for the state's attorney's office, "but no one stands out as being important enough to be called the probable cause of the murders. If we could eliminate all theories but the true one, and concentrate on that, we could solve this thing in a hurry." One would hope. The only thing Stansbury seemed fairly sure of was that Al Capone had *not* been involved.

When police finally located McGurn, Machine Gun Jack didn't seem the least bit worried. "Me, mixed up in that gang killing? Don't make me laugh! The Gusenberg boys would have plugged me if they saw me a block away. Even if I was dressed up in a police uniform they would have recognized me. I would never have got past that garage door!" He cheerfully informed investigators that he'd been at the Stevens Hotel, in room 1919A, with a woman the entire morning of February 14. The woman in question was Louise Rolfe, forever after referred to in the press as "The Blonde Alibi." Rolfe was the perfect image of a gangster's girl: long-legged, pouty-mouthed, and luscious, the kind of voluptuous siren who would drive even the toughest mug nuts. Indeed, now, with her moment in the spotlight, Rolfe turned on the charm. She flashed a smile, stuck to her story, and told anyone who would listen that her Jack was a true gentleman who wouldn't—and, indeed, didn't—hurt a fly.

"I didn't even know about the murder until the afternoon papers were brought up to my room," said McGurn. No further evidence emerged to link Capone to the massacre. Asked by an *Evening Post* reporter for his own theory on who'd killed Moran's men, McGurn did not hesitate: "It was coppers," he said flatly. "Some squad had been dealing with the Moran mob and they had a fight about a booze deal—that's the answer."

A good answer, too, although not a perfectly satisfying one. For starters, it didn't explain why the men had gathered in the garage that morning, why they were so well dressed, or why their boss, Bugs Moran, was not among them. If the cops had indeed wanted to kill Moran's men, why didn't they do it in the usual way—by arresting them, shooting them while in custody, and claiming subsequently that the men had tried to escape?

Also, it would appear that at least two of the men killed—the mechanic, Johnny May, and the optometrist, Reinhart H. Schwimmer—were merely peripheral members of the mob, accidental victims. For innocent men to have died, someone must have been acting in anger, with little time for or little interest in precision. Likewise, if Moran had wanted the Gusenbergs eliminated, it's difficult to fathom why he would have wiped out all the others. Nothing in Moran's history suggests that he was given to such rash behavior. The speed, fury, and thoroughness suggested the work of gangsters. Angry gangsters.

The Purple Gang from Detroit could have done it. They had reason to seek revenge if the Moran men had hijacked their whiskey. And given that they were from Detroit, they probably would not have differentiated among members of the Moran mob. It's also possible, as police speculated at one point in the investigation, that Egan's Rats, a gang from St. Louis, came to Chicago to make the hit to settle a score on yet another hijacked shipment of booze. The Gusenbergs and their crew had ripped off so many bootleggers that there was no end to the list of suspects. Unfortunately, though, these hypotheses also were riddled with holes. If the attack was intended in retaliation for the theft of whiskey, why didn't the killers empty the pockets of their victims and recapture some of their lost revenue? The dead men had thousands of dollars in their pockets, and not a dime was taken.

It didn't add up. There had to be another explanation—and there was. But it was not yet forthcoming.

"THE MOST SORE NECESSITY
OF OUR TIMES"

The St. Valentine's Day Massacre fascinated and horrified the American public like no crime since that of Leopold and Loeb. For weeks, stories from Chicago ribboned the front pages of newspapers across the nation. But the news accounts began to frustrate readers as one lead after another evaporated. Crime stories were supposed to unfold like movies, with explosive openings, followed by the slow ratcheting of suspense, then the satisfying resolution in which good triumphs over evil and the bad guys die or go to prison. In this case, though, there was no suspense and no resolution—just an endless drone of theories. As days turned to weeks and the crime went unsolved, blame gradually drifted to Capone. As the largest object in the gangster universe, dispersed matter tended to coalesce around him by force of nature.

He wasn't exactly helping his own cause as he continued to dish out interviews. Walter Winchell, America's most popular newspaper columnist, reported just two weeks after the Valentine's Day attack that "Scarface Capone may have retired but his phone bill at Miami last weekend for Chicago and New York calls was four and a half grand." Another New York newspaperman described Capone as "one of the authentic big men of Miami now, receiving royalties on all the slot machines within twenty miles and obviously on certain terms with the sheriff."

Indeed, Capone had attained such prominence in the social order that some of the city's leading legitimate businessmen came to call. R. B. Burdine, owner of the city's biggest department store, and G. C. Stembler, an insurance salesman, visited Capone at 10:00 A.M. one day in early March. They sat down to breakfast. Champagne bottles were popped open. "He had a colored man to do the serving," recalled Burdine. Only after the drinks began to flow did the department store owner bring up the purpose of his social call: He was looking for a donation to the Community Chest, a fund that local business leaders collected to boost their pet projects. Capone, no doubt pleased at being treated so respectfully by one of the city's elite, handed over a check for $1,000. Later, in light of sour publicity surrounding the St. Valentine's Day Massacre, the money was returned.

Another newspaper article, filed at about the same time, claimed that Capone had already established firm control of the bulk of the city's underworld activities. The story, which appeared in papers across the country, listed no sources and contained few if any solid facts, but it showed how much of a bogeyman Capone was becoming: " 'Scarface Al' Capone may be the next boss of Greater Miami," the story read. "The man who is reputed to have solidified the beer running activities in Chicago and hooked up a nationwide chain with ramifications from New York to Los Angeles, daily is becoming a factor in the life of America's greatest winter resort."

Intelligence files from the Bureau of Internal Revenue show that agents looked into allegations that Capone had begun importing liquor from Cuba and the Bahamas; flying it into Elliot Key, the northernmost of the Florida Keys; and driving it north with a fleet of thirty cars and trucks. Agents examined Capone's phone records and found he was in contact with an interesting mix of political figures and criminals, including Glenn B. Skipper, a leading Republican Party official from Florida; a man identified only as "Dr. Ford—Negro doctor said to sell narcotics"; and Gertrude Webster, who was described as the "Queen of Miami bootleggers" and a "sales agent for Bahama Island dealers." Still, the investigating agents concluded there was little evidence to support claims that Capone was involved as anything more than an investor in Miami booze-running operations.

Back in Chicago, newspaper editorials and elected officials continued to blame police for the murder of the Moran mob members. Some writers claimed they had new, anonymous sources in the police department telling them that the crime was the work of at least two real cops, not just thugs in disguise. But even if police officers didn't perform the executions themselves, the stories said, the culture of corruption on the force and the lawlessness fomented by Prohibition had surely made the crime possible.

In response, the department's leaders announced yet another campaign to shut down the city's vice dens. "The speakeasy, the soft-drink parlor, and the backstairs beer club are all rendezvous for the loafer, the thief, the thug, and are the only sources of income to the beer racketeer, the alcohol agent, and the wholesale bootlegger," said Cook County state's attorney John A. Swanson. "Those rascals will not linger in a community which does not support them." The *Evening Post* pointed out that the police would have to board up at least ten thousand speakeasies to carry out Swanson's order. Yet Swanson said he expected nothing less than full compliance. Cops who didn't heed his call, he warned, would find *themselves* behind bars.

Police Commissioner William F. Russell echoed the remarks in an address to captains and deputy commissioners from all across the city, saying, "An unwavering drive against booze is to start the minute you leave this room. Booze running and booze selling must be wiped out in Chicago—wiped out to stay." He told his men to proceed forcefully but deliberately, making sure they gathered strong evidence and applied sound warrants for arrest so that charges would be made to stick. "It's a war to the finish," Russell said.

Chicago cops had heard this sort of talk before, but nothing had ever changed. As long as Chicagoans wanted to drink, they would find thousands of speakeasies ready to serve them, in the neighborhoods where they lived and on the blocks where they worked. If Swanson and Russell hoped that anger over the St. Valentine's Day Massacre would compel citizens to forswear alcohol, they had badly misread the public mood. Chicagoans were shocked by the crime, but not *that* shocked, and there's little evidence to suggest that even this hideous act of violence made the average citizen more concerned for his own safety. If it had been seven schoolteachers or even seven Loop lawyers mowed down by mobsters, it might have been different; but these were hoodlums, and Chicagoans were well accustomed to their violence, and considered all of them seasoned murderers.

The biggest worry seemed to be the effect of the crime on their city's image. "What a wonderful advertisement to be broadcast all over the world, to boost Chicago for the world's fair in 1933," wrote one sarcastic

Chicagoan in a letter to the editor of the *Tribune* submitted the day after the massacre. Another letter writer reminded his fellow citizens that Chicago's bootleggers were a well-organized bunch who supplied a far better caliber of beer than the bootleggers in New York. "So let's give Soltis, Moran, Capone and the others their due," he wrote. "They may war with one another, but they are extremely careful not to hurt any of the general public—perhaps in fear of losing a few customers."

Others stressed that Prohibition was to blame for the killing, and that clamping down more firmly on drinking without making fundamental reforms in government would only lead to more violence. Religious leaders throughout the city blamed their flock for failing to take responsibility for their actions as violators of the Prohibition law and enablers of the bootleggers responsible for so much carnage. "The world is not to be blamed if it believes Chicago unsafe," said Rabbi Gerson B. Levi of Temple Isaiah-Israel. "If we had read a news report from Moscow stating that four people had invaded a place of business, two of them wearing uniforms of policemen, and had shot down seven persons, we would either assume that the Soviet government was implicated in the crime or that it was time that another government be established which could maintain order. Is Prohibition working when in Chicago and other cities we have encouraged the formation and have paid indirectly for the maintenance of gangsters whose business it is to circumvent for supposedly respectable people this 'noble experiment' of ours?" Yet while some pushed for tougher enforcement, others thought it best to give up entirely. In the Illinois legislature, a bill was introduced to cease enforcing liquor laws. Similar measures were proposed in Michigan, Wisconsin, and Missouri. The nation was more outraged than ever, but just as divided.

––––––––

On the morning of February 27, 1929, in Miami, a government process server delivered a subpoena to Capone, ordering him to appear before a federal grand jury on March 12, 1929, in Chicago, where he was wanted for questioning in an investigation of Prohibition violations in Chicago Heights. That night, Capone, tuxedo-clad, attended the Sharkey-Stribling fight. He sat beside Jack Dempsey, who bent over to clean Capone's seat for him. Stribling won, just as Capone had predicted. Asked about the subpoena, Capone told reporters he would be happy to answer the government's questions, but he wasn't about to commit to appearing on March 12. He would get around to it, he said, when he was finished with his vacation. As for the massacre, he said, "I wasn't mixed up in it, and neither were any of my men."

———————

Three weeks after Valentine's Day, on March 4, Herbert Hoover, rain lashing at his face, stood on the eastern portico of the U.S. Capitol and recited the oath of office, becoming the nation's thirty-first president. More than two hundred thousand visitors came to Washington, helping to form the largest crowd ever gathered thus far for a presidential inauguration. They stood on the streets, under dripping, blowing umbrellas, to catch a glimpse of their new president. Hoover, dressed in gray with a high, stiff collar, stepped to the podium with his nineteen-page typewritten speech clutched in one hand. He gazed out at an ocean of shiny black umbrellas and soggy gray hats.

"My countrymen," he said in a monotone, beginning the first inaugural address carried nationwide by radio. "This occasion is not alone the administration of the most sacred oath which can be assumed by an American citizen. It is a dedication and consecration under God to the highest office in service of our people. I assume this trust in the humility of knowledge that only through the guidance of Almighty Providence can I hope to discharge its ever-increasing burdens. It is in keeping with tradition throughout our history that I should express simply and directly the opinions which I hold concerning some of the matters of present importance."

Hoover went on for thirty minutes, speaking simply and directly, the only way he knew how, describing the "many satisfactions" enjoyed by Americans: a strong economy, a respected position of moral and military leadership in a peaceful world, a world-class system of education, and a level of poverty so scant that complete eradication of suffering and need seemed close at hand. But Hoover being Hoover, he still preached caution: "The strong man must at all times be alert to the attack of insidious disease," he said, and went on to describe the most treacherous agent of that disease. "The most malign of all these dangers today is disregard and disobedience of law," he said. "Crime is increasing. Confidence in rigid and speedy justice is decreasing. I am not prepared to believe that this indicates any decay in the moral fiber of the American people. I am not

prepared to believe that it indicates an impotence of the federal government to enforce its laws. It is only in part due to the additional burdens
imposed upon our judicial system by the Eighteenth Amendment. The
problem is much wider than that."

While promising to remake the nation's criminal justice system and to
strictly enforce the law, Hoover also asked Americans to help by ceasing
their support for the nation's bootleggers and speakeasy operators. If you
don't like Prohibition, he said, work to change the law. But until the law is
repealed, every American who drinks should recognize that he's abetting
the gangsters and contributing to the spiritual decline of the nation. As for
the gangsters, or "those of criminal mind," as Hoover labeled them, it would
not be necessary to ask them to obey the law; it was up to the government
to make them obey it. "Their activities must be stopped," he said.

In conclusion, he said, "I have no fears for the future of our country.
It is bright with hope." One line captured best the spirit of his inaugural
address: "In no nation," he said, "are the fruits of accomplishment more
secure."

As he finished, the rains grew heavier. Still, Hoover insisted on riding
to the White House in an open car. He would not disappoint the thousands who had withstood the ghastly weather all morning to see him. He
arrived at the White House soaked to his skin but feeling fine.

Capone's court date in Chicago came and went. He sent a note from his
doctor saying that he'd been confined to bed for six weeks, beginning in
mid-January, and that his illness had made travel impossible. "I'm really
an invalid," he told one reporter. "For me to go north . . . and face the
raw winds and possible snow in Chicago would be too much of a risk."
Besides, he said, there was no point in bringing him all the way to Chicago
to ask questions he couldn't answer.

Given how many newspaper interviews he'd given and how many
times he'd been photographed in those past six weeks, Capone's excuse
seemed worse than weak; it seemed contemptuous. And that's exactly
how it looked to U.S. Attorney George Johnson, who wrote to his superiors in the Justice Department and asked for help in launching an investigation that would bring contempt of court charges against Capone.

Johnson made his plea to Mabel Willebrandt, an assistant attorney general, who forwarded the letter to the director of the Bureau of Investigation, John Edgar Hoover, who was no relation to the president. Only years later would he start calling himself J. Edgar. John Edgar Hoover was young, only thirty-four, but he had the eyes of a much older man and seemed to have been around the Justice Department forever. When he took over the bureau, it was a small, poorly organized agency, with a lot of loose-cannon detectives running around answering to no one in particular. But young Hoover had an ambition that burned like a high fever and a toughness that surprised those who took him lightly. Immediately, he started cleaning house, firing the hacks and political appointees, and replacing them with men who pledged their unwavering loyalty. He wanted energetic young men working for him—men who still lived with their mothers, as he did, if possible, because those men made work, not family, their priority. And he wanted men with expertise in accounting and law. With a new president taking office and promising to make crime control the focal point of his administration, John Edgar Hoover sensed an opportunity to expand his power and boost his stature within the administration.

Quickly, he assigned agents to get down to Miami and check out the story about Capone's illness. They filled their notebooks with reports from people who'd seen Capone at the track, on fishing trips, and at nightclubs, accounting for almost every day of his time in Miami, and discovered that Capone appeared to be in robust health. No one had seen him so much as sniffle or cough, and certainly he had not been stuck in bed. Johnson began preparing to have Capone arrested and charged with contempt of court. Capone's lawyers began negotiating, asking if Capone might be granted immunity if he agreed to talk about the crimes in Chicago Heights.

Meanwhile, on March 20, as Johnson, Willebrandt, and John Edgar Hoover were building their case, President Hoover met at the White House with a group of prominent Chicagoans, including Frank Loesch, president of the Chicago Crime Commission. The civic leaders asked the president to get personally involved in restoring civility to their city. "They gave me chapter and verse for their statement that Chicago was in the hands of the gangsters," the president recalled years later in his memoirs, "that the police and magistrates were completely under their control, that the governor of the state was futile, that the federal government was the only force by which the city's ability to govern itself could be restored."

Hoover knew that most of Capone's crimes were local and none of the federal government's business. He knew that stopping Capone would not solve the nation's broader law enforcement problems. But he also knew that Capone, thanks to his great appetite for fame as much as for his villainous deeds, had made himself a leading symbol of lawlessness. Surely the president, an avid reader of newspapers, had noticed the attention paid in the press that winter to his Miami Beach neighbor. "Probably no private citizen in American life," wrote the *New York Times* in reference to Capone, "has ever had so much publicity in so short a period." The president knew that if the government could convict Capone, it would send a strong message that a new era had dawned, that such brazen criminality would no longer be allowed, and that the American system of law was bigger and stronger than even the biggest hoodlum. So he gave the order to the top officials in every relevant agency: Get Capone.

The business leaders who had gone to the White House were elated with Hoover's response, and they pledged to do their part. They agreed to pick up the tab for activities that the federal agencies couldn't afford or wouldn't authorize. And they pledged to pay for the creation of a scientific crime laboratory—the nation's first—to see if new technology used to analyze bullets and guns could help determine who had been responsible for the St. Valentine's Day Massacre.

Hoover made no public announcement after his meeting with the businessmen from Chicago. But his Prohibition commissioner, James M. Doran, announced to reporters that the Treasury Department would soon assign additional agents to certain cities, including Chicago, where enforcement had been lax. A massive assault would soon be under way. Not since the manhunt for John Wilkes Booth, Abraham Lincoln's killer, had so many resources been brought to bear in an attempt to jail one man. But the search for Booth had been short and relatively simple: It was just a matter of finding the man and dealing with him (in Booth's case he died of a gunshot wound during his capture). Capone's crimes were more subtle, and he would prove to be a more elusive target.

THE BRIGHTEST DAYS

Capone could have called it quits then. He could have taken off for the Bahamas or Havana. These were civilized places where a man could drink a highball without breaking federal law, as he coyly commented. They also were places where a man stood a pretty fair chance of dodging the law. He could have gone on the lam and never returned.

Though he hardly could have realized it yet, the St. Valentine's Day Massacre had changed everything. Before the bloodbath in the garage, he'd been a well-known criminal; now he was a star of the highest order, his name a synonym for "gangster." The *Tribune,* in an editorial, noted that he had had "most of the breaks and must regard his career as a success. Even the police attention is in a way flattering. Life has not held much out on Mr. Capone and as he sees it the brightest days are still ahead." Unfortunately for "Squire Alphonse," as the *Trib* playfully called him, he had no clue that a vast and powerful machine was lining up to ensure that his best days were well behind him.

After missing his court date, supposedly on account of his illness, Capone continued to bellyache about being forced to abandon his palmy environs, telling one reporter that "the raw spring climate of Chicago at this time will be dangerous for one in my weakened condition." His lawyers appeared in federal court on March 10 in Chicago and asked for a delay of thirty days. The judge granted ten. Although the subpoena said Capone was wanted for questioning on charges related to bootlegging in Chicago Heights, the U.S. attorney had the power to ask him about anything. At the time, police investigating the massacre were focusing most of their attention on four of Capone's men—Jack McGurn, Fred Burke, Rocco Fanelli, and John Scalise—and prosecutors wanted to see how much Capone knew about their connection to the slaying on North Clark Street. George Johnson promised that "Capone will be handled like the hoodlum that he is," but he declined to say if the feds intended to arrest the gangster upon arrival.

Finally, on March 20, he returned, and he did so with uncharacteristic stealth. No phone calls to reporters and no press conferences this time. Since the newspapers didn't know when he would appear, neither did the public, and there were no crowds gathered on the sidewalks around the courthouse. Wearing his trademark pearl gray fedora, Capone strolled into the federal courthouse through the rear entrance on Dearborn.

Only after he reached Johnson's office did word reach the city's newsrooms that Capone had arrived. Reporters scampered in pursuit and caught up to him outside Johnson's office. "How did you get here?" they asked, as if feeling snubbed.

Capone said he and his brother Ralph had driven up from Florida and spent the night in Indiana. He said he'd left his brother and a few pals on the other side of the state line and had come to town alone this morning.

The reporters fired more questions.

"I'd rather not talk," he kept saying politely, although he did let slip a few harmless comments and did agree to pose for a few photos with his attorneys, Ben Epstein and William Waugh. Capone looked good: snappily dressed, of course, but also tanned, well fed, and with an easy smile on his face. He'd lost hair and gained weight since his appearance in the same building three years earlier for the McSwiggin investigation, and the effect made him look older than his thirty-one years, but he still appeared rugged and hale, every bit in his prime, without a trace of gray hair or a wrinkle on his forehead. As word spread through the Federal Building and out into the Loop that the city's most famous figure had returned home at last to answer the government's questions, crowds began to cluster, first filling the halls of the courthouse, then crowding the sidewalks and streets around it. Police were called to help control the throng, which was estimated at about fifteen hundred people. Most of the gawkers were well mannered. They were workingmen in suits and ties and hats. They hoisted no cameras, shouted no crude remarks. One asked for—and received—an autograph. But the rest wanted only to catch a glimpse so they could go home to dinner and tell their wives and children that they'd seen the great Capone.

The earliest known photo of Al Capone (center), probably taken in Brooklyn around 1918. The men on either side of him are not identified. (Courtesy of Deirdre Marie Capone)

Capone got his first job in Chicago here, at the Four Deuces, named for its vice district address: 2222 South Wabash. (John Binder Collection)

His first employer was the suave and dignified gangster Johnny "The Fox" Torrio. (John Binder Collection)

Capone in his prime, with scars visible. (Library of Congress)

Before Torrio and before Capone, Chicago's biggest gangster was Big Jim Colosimo (left), pictured here with the attorney Charles Erbstein. (Chicago History Museum)

Frankie Yale of Brooklyn may have given Capone his start in organized crime—and may have helped bump off Big Jim Colosimo, too. (Chicago History Museum)

Mae Capone was shy, deeply religious, and eternally devoted to her husband, Al. (Arthur Nash Collection)

Mae and Al had only one son, Albert Francis "Sonny" Capone. (Arthur Nash Collection)

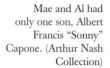

Al's mother and sister—
Theresa and Mafalda
Capone—were part of a large,
tightly bound family.
(Arthur Nash Collection)

Soon after establishing himself in Chicago, Capone bought a home in a middle-class
section of the city, at 7244 South Prairie Avenue. (Chicago History Museum)

Jack "Greasy Thumb" Guzik got his nickname because he handled payoffs for Capone's outfit. He was one of Capone's most loyal and long-serving aides. (John Binder Collection)

"Machine Gun" Jack McGurn was good with a gun and also with a golf club. He dressed smashingly, too. (Chicago History Museum)

Ralph "Bottles" Capone (left), Al's older brother, was a key figure in the organization, running much of the gambling and booze business. (The man next to him is Anthony Aresso, a member of the Capone outfit.) (Chicago History Museum)

Frank "The Enforcer" Nitti served loyally under Capone but had both the talent and the ambition to run the outfit himself. (Library of Congress)

In 1926, Capone appeared in court on a Prohibition-related charge with (from left to right) "Three-Fingered Jack" White, Red Barker, and the defense lawyer Michael Ahern. (Chicago History Museum)

In the 1927 election for mayor, Big Bill Thompson (left) ousted the reformer, William Dever (right). Here, the candidates are seen with their wives, Mary Thompson and Kate Dever. (Chicago History Museum)

Paddy Murray, bodyguard to Hymie Weiss, was gunned down in an attack that also took the life of Weiss, in front of Schofield's flower shop at 738 North State Street. (Chicago History Museum)

When Weiss died, the dim-witted George "Bugs" Moran took over the North Side bootlegging business. (John Binder Collection)

Members of Moran's gang were gathered in a garage on Clark Street when assassins dressed as police officers lined them up and mowed them down on St. Valentine's Day. (Library of Congress)

New evidence suggests that the St. Valentine's Day murders may have had nothing to do with Capone, despite widespread perceptions that he was behind them. (Library of Congress)

Capone with Captain John Stege, one of the many Chicago cops who failed to take down the city's biggest criminal. (Chicago History Museum)

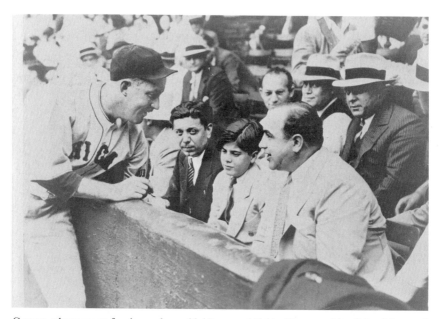

Capone, a huge sports fan, is seen here with his son and Gabby Hartnett of the Cubs. (Library of Congress)

This Palm Island estate, purchased in 1926, would become Capone's primary residence. (Library of Congress)

Capone, seen here with an unidentified boy, occasionally hosted parties for friends of his son and for his Miami neighbors. (Arthur Nash Collection)

When the Great Depression hit, Capone opened one of the biggest and best soup kitchens in Chicago. (Library of Congress)

Though he received much of the credit, Eliot Ness did little of the work in catching Capone. (Cleveland State University Library)

During daily games of Hoover-Ball on the White House lawn, Herbert Hoover would ask for updates on the case against Capone. Here the president is flanked by his secretary, Lawrence Richey, left, and Supreme Court Justice Harlan Fiske Stone. (Hoover Presidential Library)

This cartoon from the *Washington Star* captured the public sentiment: Capone seemed to have the authorities tied in knots. (Library of Congress)

Judge James H. Wilkerson seemed determined to help the government make its case in his court. (John Binder Collection)

Mild-mannered, modest, and "forensic-looking," in the words of Damon Runyon, U.S. Attorney George E. Q. Johnson was the real force behind the campaign against Capone. (Library of Congress)

Chicago police captured Capone's mug shot several times but never a conviction. (Library of Congress)

Frank Wilson, special investigator for the U.S. Bureau of Internal Revenue, played a key role in building a tax case against the gangster. (Library of Congress)

Capone's lawyers had good luck in Cook County court cases, but had little experience with federal crimes. Here, William Waugh confers with his client. (Chicago History Museum)

Capone is flanked by his two lawyers: Michael Ahern, left, and Albert Fink, right, at his 1931 federal trial. (Chicago History Museum)

Capone carrying law books at the courthouse near the end of his 1931 trial. Despite the wink, he knew the trial wasn't going well for him. (Library of Congress)

Alcatraz Island as it appeared at the time of Capone's arrival. (National Archives)

Shortly before Capone's release from prison, one of the men who helped put him away—Edward J. "Fast Eddie" O'Hare—was brutally gunned down. (John Binder Collection)

Capone was buried in Chicago on a bitterly cold day in 1947, with only a few of his old friends and family on hand. (Library of Congress)

"I ought to go into vaudeville," Capone said. "Look at the crowd I get. . . . I seem to be a sort of freak."

At one point, a custodian for the building came into the waiting room where Capone and his lawyers sat and reported that a gaggle of reporters was standing in the hall. He didn't want them there and wondered if Capone would consent to having his picture taken in the anteroom of George Johnson's office. Capone said to bring them in. A shuffle of footsteps came down the hall, and the anteroom filled. Capone turned his right cheek toward the cameramen and began to smile. He was still preening and smiling when Johnson heard the commotion and burst into the room. He shoved his toothpick frame past the photographers and stood in front of Capone.

"Get out of here! Get out of here!" he shouted at the cameramen, angrier than anyone in the press corps had ever seen him before. "This isn't any photograph gallery for hoodlums!"

The photographers lowered their shoe-box-size cameras and turned to leave.

"So long, boys!" Capone said with a laugh.

––––––––

Johnson went back into his office. He would keep the mob boss waiting. All day Capone sat, his lawyers' fees rising by the hour. If the tactic was intended to harass, it worked. Capone had hoped to answer Johnson's questions and head back to Miami. That wasn't happening. Lunch came—Capone retreated to his attorney's office on the ninth floor of the Marquette Building for a kosher corned beef sandwich and a glass of milk—and when he returned from lunch he waited some more. After almost a full day spent waiting, late in the afternoon he was finally summoned to the grand jury room, where he answered questions for about eighty minutes. An assistant U.S. attorney announced that Capone had in fact been granted immunity in exchange for his testimony.

No one outside the room would have ever known what was asked or what he said. One newspaper said Capone's answers were mostly "I don't know" and "I don't remember." When it was over, Johnson ordered him to return six days later to answer more questions. Capone was furious. For another week he would have to remain in Chicago. For another week he would have to guess what Johnson was up to. Were the feds trying to tie him to the St. Valentine's Day Massacre? Were they trying to get him for contempt of court on the suspicion that the note from his doctor had been bogus? Were they planning to ask him questions about his taxes? Capone read such speculation in the newspapers but didn't know. Neither did his lawyers. They continued to say that their client had no connection to the slaying of Moran's men; they swore that he had truly been sick; and they further offered that if Johnson wanted to make an issue of Capone's tax debt, they would be happy to negotiate a payment.

But Johnson wasn't showing his hand. The truth is that he didn't have enough evidence to bring charges of any kind against Capone. He had no proof that Capone was involved directly in any of the Chicago Heights bootlegging operations. And he knew that the Bureau of Internal Revenue had not made much progress in its investigation of Capone's tax liability. If Capone had filed false returns, a case could have been built quickly and easily, but Capone had filed no returns at all, which made matters more complicated. Johnson's best bet, he felt, was to charge Capone with contempt for failing to appear in court in March, but he was politically astute enough to realize that arresting the nation's most infamous criminal for submitting a false note from his doctor would seem ridiculous, like locking up Jesse James for jaywalking. He needed more time and more evidence. For now, the best he could do was make Capone uncomfortable.

————

Chicago was thawing out from another wicked winter. Chunks of bobbing ice on Lake Michigan grew smaller by the day, and mounds of soot-blackened snow melted from even the darkest alleys. The spring of 1929 was a time of great hope for most Chicagoans, the last great spring of hope they would enjoy for many years to come. The Cubs, now twenty years without winning a World Series, had picked up Rogers Hornsby, one of the game's all-time best players, and seemed like strong contenders for baseball's championship. Three grand new structures—the Civic Opera House, Chicago Stadium, and the Palmolive Building—containing the city's most prestigious set of offices—were set to open. Planning for the big fair continued, too, of course. At the same time, the pursuit of Al Capone was becoming something of a local obsession, an entertainment for newspaper readers, a terrific career opportunity for the scribblers assigned to the story, and a booming industry for Hollywood screenwriters.

For the law enforcement officials determined to stop the gangster, all the attention was embarrassing. While U.S. Attorney Johnson proceeded deliberately, others pushed for quicker action. Some of the city's business leaders thought Johnson was being too cautious, that the feds ought to take their best shot at Capone, even if it wasn't precisely aimed, just to score the public relations victory and to get him off the street. A few of them decided to see what they could do to speed things up.

They sent for a man in New York who had recently quit his work as a doctor because he had become obsessed with guns.

His name was Calvin Hooker Goddard. He was a slender man, his head pale and oval-shaped, like an egg, and he wore wire-framed pince-nez spectacles. He had graduated with honors from Johns Hopkins medical school, served as a first lieutenant in the Medical Reserve Corps during World War I, and returned to New York to teach medicine. But he'd always been fascinated with weapons, and in 1925 he quit teaching and signed on with Charles Waite, founder of the Bureau of Forensic Ballistics, in New York.

Waite believed, as did a number of scientists before him in Europe, that forensic ballistics would soon revolutionize police work. It was a simple concept: Waite and Goddard would examine two bullets simultaneously using a comparison microscope. If the bullets were marked with the same dents and grooves, they said, then it was a sure bet they came from the same gun. Forensic ballistics would revolutionize crime fighting in much the same way fingerprinting did, they said. But bullet identification had several advantages over fingerprinting. Fingerprints smudged and could easily be wiped away with a rag or a handkerchief. Bullet markings, on the other hand, were permanent and unchangeable. "[O]n the subject of bullets and shells and powder," Goddard told a convention of fingerprint identification experts in 1927, "there ought not be any guesswork; it is so or it isn't so; and there are instruments that have been devised to bring out absolute proof one way or the other."

But like so many trailblazers, Waite and Goddard had the right idea but little notion of what to do with it. They tried selling their services to local law enforcement agencies, but the cops didn't like being humbled by these fast-talking New Yorkers with their fancy microscopes. They tried training police officers, but they found that most departments couldn't afford the new equipment needed to make use of the science and, in any case, didn't see the wisdom in taking cops off the street to give them science lessons. When Waite and Goddard did receive assignments, they often wound up working for nothing. Police departments called them in to help with cases and simply neglected to pay when they received the bills. When Waite died and other partners abandoned the work in frustration and poverty, Goddard plugged along, seemingly in despair. But then along came the St. Valentine's Day Massacre to give him the break he needed.

Days after the incident in the North Clark Street garage, he received a call from Bert A. Massee, a member of the coroner's jury and president of the Colgate-Palmolive Company, asking Goddard to come to Chicago at once to investigate the killing. He would have unlimited access to the evidence gathered by police and the coroner, and all his expenses would be paid by Massee and another Chicago businessman, Walter E. Olson, owner of the Olson Rug Company. Goddard packed his microscope and boarded a train for Chicago.

Upon arrival, Goddard asked to see the evidence. Seventy empty shells were recovered from the floor of the garage. He examined them one at a time, scratching numbers on the inside and outside of each shell so he could keep them carefully organized. He knew from marks on the shells that they all had been fired from .45-caliber automatic weapons and that the weapons had all been of the same make. Figuring out the make was easy. Only two American-made weapons held such shells: the Colt automatic pistol and the Thompson submachine gun. But the tiny dents on the shell heads were so deep that only the superfast bolt of a machine gun could have produced them, so Goddard concluded that all the shells had come from Tommys. Then he studied the lines scratched in the shells and detected two different patterns. That told him two Tommy guns had been used. Fifty bullets had come from one of them, twenty from the other. In all likelihood, he noted, one of the gunmen had loaded his machine gun with a fifty-shot drum while the other had loaded a smaller, twenty-shot clip. Both of the gunmen had fired until their weapons were empty. Turning his attention to the two empty twelve-gauge shotgun shells found on the floor of the garage, Goddard was able to discern from the dark splotches on the inner walls that they had been loaded with buckshot and smokeless powder.

At that point he began considering the victims. Adam Heyer's body, he noted, had absorbed fourteen bullets or bullet fragments; James Clark's, seven; Alexander Weinshank's, six; John May's, three; Pete Gusenberg's, one; Frank Gusenberg's, seven; and Reinhart Schwimmer's, one bullet and seven pieces of buckshot.

Convinced that he had a good sense—ballistically, anyway—of how the men had died, he began the more difficult job of trying to determine who had fired the weapons. If the gunmen really had been police officers, he theorized, they still might have the weapons used in the attack. So he rounded up as many Tommy guns as he could, ultimately getting hold of five from the Chicago police department, one from the suburban Melrose Park police department, and two from the Cook County highway police department. He loaded the guns with the same kind of bullets used in the massacre, fired them into trash cans filled with cotton, and removed the bullets so they could be compared to the ones recovered from the garage. He did the same with more than a dozen shotguns. None of the marks on the bullets or shells matched. Police boasted that Goddard's tests proved that cops hadn't perpetrated the massacre, even though Goddard had said no such thing; all Goddard had proved so far was that the guns used in the massacre had not been found.

Next, he tested more than two dozen weapons that police had confiscated from criminals. Again, no matches. By the cops' logic, this would have proved that hoodlums had not committed the crime, either. But as Goddard knew all too well, this new science was much better at eliminating suspects than identifying them.

He had half the evidence he needed to identify the killers, but the other half would be much more difficult to come by. And worst of all, it was completely out of his control. If Chicago police had done a better job of sweeping the streets and collecting weapons on February 14, it might have been a different story.

Frustrated, he returned to New York. From time to time, police in Chicago would send him another machine gun for testing, but none matched. "We seemed to have reached the end of a blind alley," Goddard wrote.

The banner headline in the *Chicago American* trumpeted "U.S. ARRESTS CAPONE" on the afternoon of March 27, 1929.

Never mind that America's most notorious villain was arrested for the trifling contempt-of-court charge stemming from his bogus doctor's note, punishable by no more than $1,000 and a year in jail. Never mind that he spent a mere ten minutes as a prisoner before winning his release. And never mind that he needed only $500 to post bond.

It was still a great headline.

Capone ducked his head as he left the courthouse. The photographers trying to take his picture got nothing but hat. He snared a taxi, went back to his room at the Lexington, and packed for the trip to Miami.

It must have galled Johnson to see Capone go free, to see him packing for another Florida vacation. It must have frightened him, too, that Capone might take off for Cuba or Mexico and never return. Had Johnson blown his chance? Had he been too conservative in charging Capone with nothing but contempt of court after all these years of cat-and-mouse pursuit? Why not go for conspiracy to commit murder? Why not force Capone to answer questions? Why not press him under oath to tell what he knew about the murder of his rivals? Even if it was a stretch, why not take a shot at connecting him to the St. Valentine's Day Massacre?

Maybe it was because Johnson and others in the federal government knew Capone had nothing to do with it.

"HAVE YOU GOT CAPONE YET?"

Every morning but Sunday, in all kinds of weather except the nastiest of rains, President Hoover liked to go out on the White House lawn with members of his cabinet and toss around a medicine ball for exercise. Over time, the White House physician helped the president establish a set of rules to formalize a game they called Hoover-Ball.

The court was sixty-six feet long and thirty feet wide, divided by an eight-foot-tall volleyball net. The ball weighed six pounds. Teams consisted of two to four players, with one or two substitutes allowed on each team. Points were scored when a team failed to catch a ball, failed to get it over the net, or sent it thudding out of bounds. Running with the ball was not allowed; it had to be thrown from where it was caught. "Good sportsmanship is required," the last of Hoover's rules stated. "Points in dispute are played over." The president compared his game to tennis or volleyball, but said his invention made for more vigorous sport than those other, better-known games. "Stopping a six-pound ball with steam back of it, returning it with similar steam, is not pink-tea stuff," wrote the *New York Times*.

At the start of his administration, Hoover was still refining his game and still teaching it to his cabinet members. But he also used the time on the grass court to shape his administration's agenda. At the start of each morning session, according to a 1931 *Chicago Herald and Examiner* account, Hoover would ask, "Have you got Capone yet?"

And when each game was over and the men, weary-armed and soaked in sweat, went back inside, the president would reiterate that he wanted Capone in jail. The *Herald and Examiner*'s account of the dialogue was confirmed years later by Elmer Irey, head of the Internal Revenue Bureau's investigations unit. Irey claimed that he heard of Hoover's daily exhortations from Andrew Mellon, the silver-haired and much-esteemed Treasury secretary, who was probably too old to catch a medicine ball but may well have stood on the sidelines and jotted notes on the president's orders. Wrote Irey: "I couldn't help wondering why a Treasury Department unit charged with fighting tax, customs, and narcotics frauds should be assigned to nab a murderer, a gambler, a whoremonger and a bootlegger." But Irey knew the answer: Hoover, a pragmatic man, understood that the federal government had limited jurisdiction and little experience when it came to busting murderers, gamblers, whoremongers, and bootleggers. Tax cheats were another story.

Hoover wanted Capone imprisoned to reinforce two points central to his mission as president: that he was serious about reforming America's dilapidated justice system, and that Prohibition would be enforced as long as it remained the law. Hoover, who enjoyed a cocktail before dinner, had declared that he would abstain from all alcohol in the White House and expected abstinence by his cabinet members at all government meetings and social functions. (Under Coolidge, alcohol had been served at informal gatherings, although not at official White House events.) Hoover also had announced that he would not bring his pre-Prohibition wine and liquor collection with him to the White House.

On April 22, 1929, speaking to a room full of Associated Press editors at the Waldorf-Astoria Hotel in New York, Hoover gave the first major policy speech of his presidency, calling for a nationwide campaign against crime. It was one of the most powerful speeches of his career, perhaps suggesting that the White House staff was no longer trusting him to write his own material. He called crime "the dominant issue" facing the nation and said solving the problem "is more vital to the preservation of our institutions than any other question before us."

He was careful not to blame the gangsters and bootleggers. "A surprising number of our people, otherwise of responsibility in the community, have drifted into the extraordinary notion, that laws are made for those who choose to obey them," he said. To support his argument, he cited statistics: Nine thousand murders a year resulted in only five thousand arrests and a pathetic three hundred convictions. The murder rate for the United States was twenty times greater than for Great Britain, he noted, and the nation's disregard for the rules of Prohibition did not entirely explain the problem. "What we are facing today," he said, "is something far larger and more fundamental—the possibility that respect for law is fading from the sensibilities of our people."

The president vowed to do his part. He would order his staff to weed out the corrupt, the negligent, and the incompetent from the federal law-enforcement machinery. He would appoint a committee of the nation's brightest men to recommend fundamental changes to the nation's system of law. He asked the press to stop treating gangsters as glamorous heroes and concluded by quoting Abraham Lincoln: "Let every man remember that to violate the law is to trample on the blood of his father and to tear the character of his own and his children's liberty. Let reverence for the laws be breathed by every American mother to the lisping babe that prattles on her lap. Let it be taught in the schools, in seminaries, in colleges. Let it be preached from the pulpit, proclaimed in the legislative halls, and enforced in courts of justice. And, in short, let it become the political religion of the nation, and let the old and the young, the rich and the poor, the grave and the gay of all sexes and tongues and colors and conditions sacrifice unceasingly upon its altar."

The speech was broadcast nationwide by radio and was reprinted in newspapers everywhere. Hoover had always believed in the power of public relations. If he could make enough symbolic gestures, he believed, such as appointing a committee, locking up Capone, or drying up Capitol Hill, the American people might start to follow his lead. They might treat the laws with more respect. Collective action, as Hoover's Quaker upbringing preached, was society's greatest tool for change. Government should provide the guidance and oversight, the president believed, but the people themselves should carry out most of the work. Hoover wanted to see more Americans voluntarily give up drinking. That was the surest and easiest way to put bootleggers out of business. And in the early days of his presidency, when his popularity soared and he could seemingly do no wrong, support for abstinence seemed to grow.

In Chicago, for example, George Johnson met with the city's social club directors and encouraged them to put an end to drinking in their dining halls and lounges. Some clubs had assumed that they were immune from punishment because they weren't selling alcohol; they were merely permitting their members to bring in their own booze, store it in their lockers, and imbibe as they saw fit. But Johnson, himself a member of the Union League Club, one of the city's finest, told them it wasn't enough for the clubs to look the other way. Of course, everybody got a good laugh about it. Prohibition was nine years old, and people had gotten used to it in the same way they might have gotten used to a persnickety mother-in-law or a finicky boss; they knew it wasn't going away anytime soon, and they had found ways to deal with it.

Still, many businesses in Chicago responded to the pressure applied by Hoover and Johnson. Managers at the Stevens Hotel announced that they would no longer be providing ginger ale, seltzer water, and cracked ice, commonly known as setups, routinely ordered by guests who wished to assemble their own cocktails. The Morrison said it would provide setups only after guests agreed to sign a pledge that they would not be used in conjunction with liquor. The booze wasn't going away, but for the moment people tried to show a little more respect for the law. They believed in the new president and wanted to get behind him.

After his court date in Chicago, Capone disappeared. He was last seen at the Lexington, packing his bags for the return trip to Miami. But that was on March 27. For the next month, he dropped completely from sight. Neither the newspapers nor the Bureau of Investigation marked his whereabouts.

In mid-April, one Chicago paper quoted Jack Guzik as saying that the police crackdown had created a heavy drag on the bootleg business and "the chief" was looking for a way out. "Chicago, his biggest outlet for alcohol, is practically a closed market," Guzik said, perhaps hoping to garner sympathy and, in turn, take the heat off his boss. "Sales are off to almost nothing, because the little fellows, who made the direct contacts with the consumers and bought wholesale from us, are getting out of the racket. . . . Bootleggers still operate, of course, but not one-third as many small-time boys are going now as were three months ago. . . . The cabarets and nightclubs, whether they admit it or not, are doing a tenth the business, or consuming a tenth the liquor, of even six months ago. Capone has a tremendous daily payroll. Just how much would startle the country. He has to meet it, whether the income is rolling in or not. Right now he's in actual difficulty about raising $30,000 to meet notes due on his house in

Miami. He doesn't own that, in spite of all the stories that come in about his tremendous wealth. He paid $5,000 down to a real estate dealer, and it's mortgaged to the hilt, with the $30,000 now due. He entertains a lot. He had to, to keep up appearances, and that costs plenty. He is always being asked for loans—loans that are never paid back, and he invariably grants them. If he could, today, he'd turn it all over to anyone, let them assume the responsibility for the payroll, and get out."

If Capone wasn't out, at least he was out of the spotlight for most of the spring, until another multiple murder put his name back in head-lines.

On the morning of May 8, 1929, a couple of cops were driving south on Sheffield Avenue in Hammond, Indiana, transporting prisoners to the Hammond jail. It was one in the morning when they spotted two fast-moving cars on a residential street that should have been quiet at that hour. They made a note to circle back that way after dropping off their prisoners. When they returned, their suspicions were rewarded. They found a Cadillac coupe with two dead bodies in it. The backseat of the car had been removed to make room for the corpses, which were covered with blankets and still warm, probably dead for no more than three hours. When police peeled back the blankets, it looked like the men had been beaten with bats or crowbars and then shot, or perhaps shot and then beaten. Either way, it looked at a glance as if twice as much effort as necessary had been exerted in making sure these men were dead. Skulls had been smashed to mush, noses reversed, ears beaten to bloody scraps. Nearby the car, they found a third body in much the same condition.

After going through the victims' pockets and making a few calls, the police determined that the men were Albert Anselmi, John Scalise, and Joseph "Hop Toad" Guinta. Anselmi and Scalise were well-known Capone bruisers and among the many rumored to have been in on the St. Valentine's Day Massacre; Guinta was said to have been in line to replace Tony Lombardo at the helm of Unione Siciliana, which meant he probably wasn't going to live long anyway. Immediately, cops and reporters speculated that the three men had been killed by the Moran gang in retaliation for the North Clark Street killings of February 14.

But over time another story took hold.

The scene was first described by Walter Noble Burns in his 1931 book *The One-Way Ride*. Burns tried to understand how a pair of ruthless killers such as Anselmi and Scalise, who should have been perpetually alert to attack, could have been killed "like sheep in a slaughter pen." He speculated that the men must have been lured into a trap by friends, and then, with a flourish of literary license, he imagined the scene in which such a trap might have been sprung. "Imagine a little diner in a private room in some café," he writes. "Scalisi [*sic*], Anselmi, Guinta, the guests of honor. Perhaps the banquet is given to celebrate Scalisi's recent release from jail. Or his triumph of brilliant strategy on St. Valentine's Day." He goes on to imagine the men drinking and enjoying themselves. Perhaps their wine is drugged to cloud their minds and slow their hands. As they try to rise from the table, pistols flash from across the table, shots flare, and the three men fall backward.

Four decades later, in 1975, the journalist George Murray added another imaginative flourish in his book *The Legacy of Al Capone*. In Murray's version, Capone himself stands over the chairs of Scalise and Guinta, smiling, thanking the men for their fine service, and holding in each hand a pair of long, narrow objects—the men at the table assume they are magnums of champagne—wrapped in tissue paper. But suddenly the smile vanishes from Capone's face. He raises his arms high, holding the gift-wrapped packages above his head, and crashes them down atop the heads of Scalise and Guinta. Now the men at the table can see he's not holding bottles of bubbly but a pair of wooden clubs. He swings again and again, both arms going at the same time, until the men lay motionless. When Anselmi gets up and points a pistol at Capone, McGurn disarms him. Capone, still clutching the bloody clubs, proceeds to lecture Anselmi on the importance of loyalty. The boss says he knows that Anselmi, Scalise, and Guinta were planning to kill him. Anselmi objects, "No, Al, please," as the first blow of the wooden club smashes his raised arm. The club snaps but Capone keeps swinging until his victim stops moving. Then McGurn places his pistol in Capone's beefy paw, and Capone fires an exclamation point into each body.

Murray's tale appears to have been the inspiration for a scene in the 1987 movie *The Untouchables*. Robert DeNiro played the role of Capone. "A man becomes preeminent," says DeNiro, fleshy face in a scowl as he stands over his men at an elegantly appointed dinner table, "he is expected to have enthusiasms. . . . Enthusiasms. . . . Enthusiasms. What are mine? What draws my admiration? What is that which gives me joy? Baseball!

A man . . . a man stands alone at a plate. This is the time for what? For individual achievement. There he stands alone. But in the field, what? Part . . . of . . . a . . . team." His speech over, he raises a baseball bat in both hands, grimaces, and brings it down like a tomahawk: wood hitting bone with the thundering crack of a double off the left-field wall. The victim's cigar is crushed into the plate first, followed by his face, sending silverware and glasses clattering. A spray of blood shoots across the table. The bat slams again and again. Blood pours across the white linen tablecloth in lurid red waves. The rest of the gangsters look on, horrified, but well schooled on the importance of teamwork.

How much of the scene is true? Did Capone kill the men himself? Would so famous a man, already under intense scrutiny, have taken so great a risk? Would he have acted in front of so many witnesses? Did he actually need, at that point in his career, to teach his men a lesson in teamwork? Then there are the more practical matters: Could Capone really have battered three men with baseball bats, as Murray suggests? Even if he was strong enough and coordinated enough to strike two blows at a time, would the third man have sat still and waited his turn? Finally, is there any evidence placing Capone at the scene, or even suggesting that he might have wanted the men dead? Newspaper reporters covering the triple murder searched for Capone after the discovery of the bodies and couldn't find him. They said it was not clear if he was in Chicago, Miami, or somewhere else entirely.

Ten days later, though, everyone would know exactly where he was.

LOCKED UP

The first meeting of the nation's top crime lords, later known as the Commission, began on May 13, 1929, in Atlantic City. The roster of attendees reads like an encyclopedia of crime: Albert Anastasia, Dutch Schultz, Frank Costello, Moe Dalitz, Louis Lepke, Lucky Luciano, Abner "Longy" Zwillman, Bugsy Siegel, Bugs Moran, Johnny Torrio, Frank Nitti, Jack Guzik, and, of course, Al Capone. The men, most of them only in their twenties, stayed at the city's finest hotels: the Ritz, the President, and the Breakers. Thanks to payoffs arranged by one of the local racket bosses, the cops in Atlantic City left them alone.

Still, the mafia men seemed uncomfortable. They met on the boardwalk, in small, rotating groups. Dressed as usual—pinstriped suits, two-toned shoes, and cantered hats—they made no attempt to fit in among the hoi polloi. They took their meals at pushcarts and strolled along the beach, amid the crowds in their ballooning bathing costumes and swimming caps. At night they drank and smoked and attended prizefights.

Capone was not only the most important mafioso on the beach, he also was one of the most important topics of conversation. The big fellow was getting to be a big problem. Most of the other overlords managed to operate quietly, keeping the banner headlines to a minimum. Not Capone. And it wasn't just his chatty nature that kept him covered in ink. There was also the matter of all those corpses: seven wiped out in the North Clark Street garage; three wiped out on the side of the road in Hammond; Tony Lombardo wiped out; Diamond Joe Esposito wiped out; Frankie Yale wiped out. Then there was the November 1928 slaying of Arnold Rothstein, one of New York's biggest gamblers and bootleggers. And while no evidence linked Capone to the murder—word on the beach had it that Rothstein had welched on a huge poker debt—that didn't stop the speculation.

Whether Capone was directly responsible for the violence, it had happened on his watch. The gangsters who gathered in Atlantic City were not squeamish. What bothered them wasn't the spilled blood but the fact that Capone and his gangland territory had become so infamous. These men knew how to control the local police in their respective cities, but now Capone had gotten the feds involved. He'd poked a hornet's nest. They didn't know exactly what to do about it, but they knew, at the very least, that they needed to stop him before he poked it again.

When the summit in Atlantic City ended, reports varied on what had been accomplished. Some newspaper reports said that Capone and the other gangsters had agreed on a power-sharing arrangement and that the Commission, headed by Johnny Torrio, would serve as a governing body to settle the group's internal disputes. Other reports said that Bugs Moran had refused to go along with any deal involving Capone and had made it clear that he would not be satisfied until Capone was lying facedown with a bullet in his head. But if that was the case, why hadn't Moran taken care of the job in Atlantic City, where Capone would have been an easy target?

Early in the afternoon on May 16, Capone, Frankie Rio, and two other bodyguards left Atlantic City by car, headed for New York City, where they intended to catch the Broadway Limited train back to Chicago. It was cold and gray, as if February had knocked off May and taken its place. Capone wore an overcoat; into the right front pocket he slid a .38 snub-nosed revolver.

Fifteen miles south of Camden, New Jersey, Capone's car conked out, forcing the gangsters to take a commuter train to Philadelphia, where they purchased tickets for another train to Chicago. Scheduled departure was 9:05 P.M.

With time to kill, Capone and his men decided to take in a movie. A detective story, *Voice of the City,* starring Willard Mack, was playing at the Stanley Theater on Nineteenth Street. Just as the men were about to enter the theater, two real detectives, James "Shooey" Malone and John Creeden of the Philadelphia Police Department, happened to drive by on their way to work in Creeden's car. It was Malone who spotted and recognized Capone. They circled back around, but by the time they could park their car and get out, Capone and his men were inside. The cops didn't want to make a scene in a crowded theater, so they called for backup and waited.

When the picture was over, the movie-house lights came on, and Capone and his men got up to leave. It was about eight thirty, still plenty of time for them to make their train. But before they could get out of the lobby, Malone and Creeden approached.

Malone flashed his badge. Creeden grabbed Rio, which was ordinarily no easy task because Rio was a bull of a man. Rio didn't put up a fight. Malone noticed that Capone had his right hand in his overcoat pocket. The detective grabbed Capone by the hand and together, slowly, the men pulled out the .38. Capone's other two bodyguards, seeing the cops, disappeared into the crowd.

The men were booked on weapons-possession charges. They were fingerprinted. They were photographed, Capone with his hat on. After the picture, Capone lit a cigarette. Then the men stood before a magistrate judge, who ordered them held on $35,000 bail. All this before Capone could get an attorney. With less than $30 in his pockets and no quick way to come up with more, he would have to spend the night in jail.

"Phew," he said, wiping his forehead with his hand. "This is some city. They work fast here."

It was 11:35 P.M. by the time he managed to find a lawyer, but still, his mouthpiece wasn't able to get him sprung. At midnight, he received a visit from Lemuel B. Schofield, Philadelphia's director of public safety, whose duties were much the same as a police commissioner's, except that he also supervised firefighters, building inspectors, and elevator repairmen. Now presented with the chance to show the world that Philadelphia meant business when it came to fighting crime, Schofield brought a stenographer to his meeting with Capone. The purpose of the wide-ranging chat primarily seemed to be to get Schofield attention. Capone, for his part, made his usual plea for compassion and understanding.

"I went into the racket four and a half years ago," he told Schofield, referring, probably, to the point at which he became Torrio's top lieutenant. "During the last two years I've been trying to get out. But once in the racket you're always in it, it seems. The parasites trail you, begging for favors and money, and you can never get away from them, no matter where you go. I have a wife and an eleven-year-old boy I idolize, and a beautiful home at Palm Island, Florida. If I could go there and forget it all I would be the happiest man in the world. I want peace and I'm willing to live and let live. I'm tired of gang murders and gang shootings. . . . Three of my friends were killed in the last two weeks in Chicago. That certainly is not conducive to peace of mind. I haven't had peace of mind in years."

"What are you doing now?" Schofield asked.

"I'm retired and living on my money," Capone answered.

"You should get out of the racket and forget it."

"I can't," he complained, "because of the parasites."

Capone and Rio spent the night on benches at the detective bureau, sleeping as best they could until about eight. Later that morning, while awaiting trial, Capone chatted with a bystander.

"What's the weight of that ring?" the bystander asked, referring to the bauble on Capone's pinkie.

"It's exactly eleven and a half carats," he answered politely.

"Worth about fifty thousand, eh?"

"Well, you made a good guess," Capone replied amiably.

Ten big Philly cops guarded the courtroom, halting all who tried to enter. The trial started, and after a sidebar conference, Capone's lawyer, a Philadelphian who must have been recommended to Capone by one of his attorneys in Chicago, said his clients had decided to plead guilty. Capone's face reddened but he said nothing. Almost anyone else would have received a light sentence—a month or two behind bars, or perhaps merely a fine of a few hundred dollars—but the judge surprised Capone and everyone else in the room with his announcement: "All right," he said. "Each of the prisoners is sentenced to one year's imprisonment."

For the first time in his life, Al Capone was a convicted criminal. He pulled the diamond ring from his finger and handed it to his lawyer, asking that it be sent to his brother in Chicago.

A bailiff led him away.

"It's the breaks, kid," Capone said in the general direction of Rio. "It's the breaks."

The fantastic speed of Capone's conviction—sixteen hours from arrest to sentencing!—led many in the press to conclude that Chicago's crime boss must have wanted to go to jail, that the peace pact forged in Atlantic City hadn't lasted five minutes, and that Capone sought refuge in a prison cell.

Pat Roche, chief investigator for the state's attorney's office in Chicago, called it "a desperate measure . . . to escape death." The newspapers decided that Capone would never have been so foolish as to carry a gun unless he'd wanted to go to jail, overlooking the more likely possibility that he'd been carrying the gun because he thought he might have to use it.

Capone sister's, Mafalda, in a rare interview, mocked the notion that her brother would want to be arrested. "He never gets in jail," she said. She showed the reporter around the family home on South Prairie, which was decorated "luxuriously . . . but in good taste." In Mafalda's bedroom, a golden crucifix hung on the wall between two tapestries, and the bed was draped in rose-colored satin. "If only people knew him as I know him," Mafalda said, "they would not say the things about him they do. I adore him. And he is his mother's life. He is so very good, so kind to us. You who only know him from the newspaper stories will never realize the real man he is."

Capone's wife agreed that Al would never let himself be arrested intentionally. "What would he want to go to jail for?" Mae asked. "He liked to talk of Europe, of Palm Beach, of the famous racetracks, of the scenes at the big fights—but jail—oh, no, not for Al." She went on: "I didn't even know he was in Atlantic City, or Philadelphia. The last I saw of him was in Chicago after we returned from Miami. He said he was going away for a while, but he didn't say why or where." And, presumably, she didn't ask.

If Capone did want to spend time behind bars, his colleagues told reporters, he probably would have chosen a federal prison in the Chicago area, so he could receive visits from his friends and family. Given that the feds were said to be close to filing contempt charges, he might have told his attorneys to negotiate a plea bargain.

Capone, too, told a Philadelphia reporter that his arrest had not been arranged. "I'm here because I'm here," he said.

Meanwhile, Philadelphia police officers fired Capone's gun into a barrel, retrieved the bullets, and sent them to Chicago so the ballistics expert Calvin Goddard could test to see if the same weapon had been used in the St. Valentine's Day Massacre. Since Goddard had already concluded that no pistols were used, it was probably just a publicity stunt by the Philly cops, who posed for pictures wielding the famed mobster's piece. All of the hoopla no doubt left the people of Chicago wondering: If putting Capone away was so easy that Philadelphia could do it in less than a day, why hadn't cops and prosecutors in the Windy City ever managed the trick? One sly writer suggested that Chicago law officers ought to try a new approach to fighting crime: Give all the rum runners one-way tickets to Philadelphia.

But the joking only made the ridiculous seem more profoundly disturbing. Chicago in recent months had taken to arresting waiters who served ginger ale and ice, claiming that the waiters were knowingly abetting the consumption of alcohol. Restaurants had been padlocked for offering setups—tall glasses with nothing but ice and lemon wedges—on the same suspicion. And yet the nation's most notorious gangster and the man with his hand on the valve of the city's liquor pipeline had never been busted. Some city officials defended themselves in light of Philadelphia's accomplishment, pointing out that police in Illinois were not allowed to search people without a warrant or probable cause, or else they might have gotten Capone long ago on a weapon-possession charge.

In Chicago, nobody was buying it. Capone's hometown cops and prosecutors had had plenty of opportunities to put the man away, beginning in 1922 with his drunken driving arrest, and continuing more recently with his failure to respond to the grand jury's subpoena. He avoided conviction in those instances and every other because he knew how to work the system. He knew which cops, which judges, and which lawyers could be counted on to come through for him and how much it would take. He knew when to stall and when to cut and run. And he knew how to get rid of witnesses who might make charges against him stick. "I've arrested Capone a half dozen times and found a gun on him," said John Stege, chief of detectives in Chicago. "But the minute you get into court and the judge finds there was no warrant . . . he declares the arrest illegal." In Philadelphia, though, Capone was out of his element, like a speeding driver on unfamiliar roads, and everything happened too fast.

After one night at a jail for short-term prisoners, he was handcuffed to a guard and driven to the county prison at Holmesburg, "known throughout crookdom as the toughest place between the two oceans in which to take a rap," as one newspaper noted. Capone wore prison-issued black trousers and a white shirt. He was one of seventeen hundred prisoners, assigned to one of the facility's lesser cells, facing a fetid creek. The place was dark, dank, and depressing. A few weeks earlier, inmates had set their bedding afire to protest conditions. In all likelihood, given the airlessness of the place, the concrete vault must have smelled like hell—all piss and cinders and shit and armpits.

Capone acted like he didn't care.

"Not much like home here," he joked.

But he wasn't the only one feeling cocky. The prison superintendent laughed when asked if Capone might somehow manage to run his boot-legging syndicate from inside Holmesburg's walls. "Oh, yes," he said, "we are all going into the beer business in a big way."

Almost right away, Capone's lawyers began working on plans to get him sprung. On May 29, his wife and mother visited. On June 4, he gave his first newspaper interview since his arrest, although he didn't say much. "You see, I want to get out of here," he told a reporter. "If the public is constantly reminded that I still am in jail it will be that much worse for me. The less I say the quicker the public will forget me." At the same time, he made a $1,000 donation to a Philadelphia hospital and offered a $50,000 reward to any lawyer who or group that could win his freedom. Still, he didn't go free. But his lawyers and friends did pull enough strings to get him transferred to a friendlier prison.

Eastern State Penitentiary had once been even tougher than Holmesburg. The prison's history dated back to 1787, when a group of Philadelphians met in the home of Benjamin Franklin to discuss the deplorable conditions endured by America's incarcerated criminals and resolved to try something new. They wanted to see if prisoners—isolated and forced to reflect on their crimes—might become genuinely penitent. Thus the word "penitentiary," previously used only to describe a place people went to contemplate their religious transgressions, became a synonym for "jail."

From the outside, Eastern State looked like a medieval castle, built to inspire fear and awe. Inside, it was like no place else on Earth—a structure designed in every way to disrupt man's instincts of community, to force him to be alone with his thoughts. The environment was almost entirely artificial, providing just enough light, just enough heat, just enough food for survival. Prisoners were hooded when they left their cells to keep them from becoming familiar with their surroundings and to prevent them from bonding with their guards and fellow inmates. There were to be no distractions from penitence. Part monastery, part dungeon, the place became a symbol of progressive principles in criminal reform, at least for the first eighty years or so, until attitudes began to change and the tactics were gradually abandoned.

By the time Capone arrived, on May 19, 1929, the prison had been remodeled, and most of the extreme methods had been jettisoned. Officials said Capone was sent here for his own safety. Men were assigned two or three to a cell, and they were allowed to work in bakeries and kitchens. They dined communally and even published a newspaper. And when Capone asked for permission to decorate his cell, the warden, H. B. "Hard-Boiled" Smith, okayed it. Within two weeks of his arrival, Capone had made the place feel like home, with a cabinet radio, a colorful rug, a wooden desk, a chest of drawers, and a comfy bed that was clearly not prison-issue. While other prisoners got only as much light as the slanting sun sent through the small openings at the top of their cells, Capone's had a small desk lamp by which to read books and write letters late into the evening. When he wanted to make a phone call, he used the warden's line. Apparently "Hard-Boiled" Smith got his nickname from the way he liked his eggs.

When a reporter asked him if he found the new accommodations suitable, Capone replied, "Yes, very comfortable."

To another newsman he said, "I have been quoted so much that I would rather not say anything now. Let my friends talk for me. My enemies will talk enough in any case." Then, genetically incapable of shutting up, he continued, "However, I would like to tell those persons who might be interested in me that they can discount one half of what has been credited to me. . . . To my friends in Chicago, and I think I have many regardless of the stories that have been printed about me, I might say that I enjoyed a perfect night's rest. I had a good sleep and I had no worries."

A little thing like a year in the joint was not enough to wreck Capone's equilibrium. He had long ago learned to live alone in the world, apart from the family he loved, more or less happily. Whether he arranged the arrest, he recognized the benefit in taking time off and getting out of the national spotlight. He would do his time. And while he did it, perhaps other gangsters would lay off the shooting. That would help. He had the idea that he would emerge from his cell in 1930, go back to Chicago, and some of his problems would have passed. With time, he thought, he might try to remove himself from the day-to-day operations in Chicago, spend more time in Miami, and get everyone—including the feds—off his back.

"Within the next few months," he predicted, "there is to come a proper adjustment of things and conditions. And when that comes, I tell you, people will see me in an entirely different light."

ELEGANT MESS

For six months, George E. Q. Johnson had been pursuing Capone with one tender step after another, like a man hunting butterflies. He wasn't sure if he could make the income tax charges stick, so he continued to pursue the contempt case stemming from the lies about Capone's health. But he didn't want to settle for a piffling contempt charge if there was a chance the tax case could be made, so he tried to keep both investigations going until he could decide which one had the greater chance of success. And while he had not completely given up on the idea of building a case for Prohibition violations, neither had he made any progress toward it.

When reporters asked Johnson what he thought about the fact that Philadelphia had managed to put Capone away in a few hours, at almost zero expense to the taxpayers, and with no help from the federal government, Johnson surely understood that the question was not really a question at all; it was a criticism. The arrest speaks for itself, he said. And that was the end of the conversation.

If Johnson was feeling glum, he was about to feel glummer.

Word came from Miami that the U.S. attorney for the Southern District of Florida was preparing to bring perjury charges against Capone's doctor, Kenneth Phillips, for falsely stating that his patient was too sick to appear in court. For all practical purposes, Johnson was about to have a big chunk of his case stolen from him. If the prosecutor in Miami charged Capone's doctor with perjury, it was a safe bet that his next move would be charging Capone. It was beginning to look as if Johnson had equivocated too long; the butterfly had flown.

Throughout his short career in public office, Johnson had been given the benefit of the doubt by his superiors in Washington and by the political establishment in Chicago. Sure, he bore an unfortunate resemblance to the poet William Butler Yeats; sure, he lacked fire; and, sure, he had no real experience as a criminal lawyer: But he was a solid citizen, no doubt intelligent, and seemingly incorruptible. Over the course of his first two years in office it was generally assumed that, given time, he would get the job done, in his own quiet way.

In fairness to Johnson, he may have understood the prosecutor's role better than most. While the general public tended to think that prosecutors were supposed to be ferocious enemies of criminals, the law says otherwise. Because prosecutors have such great power, the law reminds them that they have a special duty to govern impartially. It's not about winning cases; it's about doing justice. Perhaps Johnson could have slapped a charge on Capone willy-nilly, but he seemed determined to wait until he had a bulletproof case; the last thing he wanted was the embarrassment of taking Capone to trial and losing. Still, some were beginning to wonder if Johnson was too even handed for the job.

He could keep adding initials to his name, the thinking went, but he would never make it in Chicago if he weren't willing to be an SOB once in a while.

Johnson tried to recover. He fired off a letter to the U.S. attorney general, William DeWitt Mitchell, politely arguing that he deserved first crack at Capone. The Miami office got involved, he reminded Mitchell, only because Chicago had initiated an investigation. Johnson asked Mitchell to have the Miami prosecutors defer their case. Give him a chance to finish the job, he said. And if he failed, there would still be time to press charges in Miami.

Mitchell granted the request.

Now Johnson had no excuses. Capone would be in jail for a year, at most. The big fellow's lawyers were working to get him out sooner—immediately, if possible—and there was always a good chance that he would get out in eight or ten months with time off for good behavior. Capone was practically running the Eastern State Penitentiary, by the way the press made it sound, so why would he misbehave? The clock was ticking. Johnson knew that he needed to push harder than ever to be ready to indict the crime boss after his release from the pen in Philadelphia. It would help that Capone was locked away. His associates were more likely to cooperate with the feds if they felt that Capone posed less of a threat. If Johnson waited, however, if he let Capone go free, there was no telling what might happen. Capone might murder the government's witnesses. He might ply the press with interviews in an attempt to rehabilitate his image. He might be killed. He might leave the country. Or he might be indicted elsewhere.

Certainly no good could come of it for Johnson. At last, this man of much thought and little action seemed determined to do something.

———————

Eliot Ness was feeling restless. He was twenty-seven years old, and for more than two years he'd been working as a Prohibition agent. What did he have to show for it? Goose eggs. No big arrests, no great fortune (not that money motivated him, but still . . .), and no great fame. It had been ages since he'd seen his name in the pages of the *Tribune,* and even then it had been an insignificant story, stuck unceremoniously in the middle of page three.

The city was cracking down on bootleggers, or at least making yet another symbolic effort at it, but the beer was flowing through the streets and alleys of Chicago as robustly as ever. Flatbed trucks with tarps draped over their tops ran into and out of the Loop day and night, and everyone knew what they were hauling. Ness felt like a loser, a pawn in a game no one was watching and no one would win. Later in life, such moods would lead to bouts of heavy drinking, to a sense of depression that weighed on him like a wet woolen coat, but if the depression this time burdened him or made him feel like drowning his sorrows in gin, he didn't say. All he allowed, when he recalled this pivotal moment years later, his words filtered by a coauthor, was that he "almost felt like chucking the whole business."

Ness was tall, lean, and broad-shouldered. He had a round face, pointed slightly at the chin, with brown hair parted in the middle and slicked down on both sides, all symmetrical. Yet he was not a classically handsome man. It might have been because his head was a bit too small for his body, or because his ears were a bit too small for his head, or because there were few sharp angles to his face, mostly soft curves. But probably it was because of his eyes. No matter what message the rest of his face or body conveyed, his eyes gave away sadness. It was there in every photograph the man ever took, from the one on his badge to the

one he would print on posters years later when running—unsuccessfully—
for mayor of Cleveland.

More or less from the day he was born, Ness was a Goody Two-shoes.
He loved his mother, respected his father, obeyed his teachers, helped out
gladly in the family bakery, and never got paddled, spanked, or severely
punished, as far as his friends and family could recall. Even as a child,
he kept his hair perfectly combed and his shirts neatly tucked. When the
boys in his South Side Chicago neighborhood invited him to play army or
baseball, he usually declined. He preferred the company of girls, or else a
detective novel. "Elegant Mess," the kids called him, because he was nice
to look at but nevertheless a misfit.

At the University of Chicago, he was an undistinguished student,
scraping by on a steady diet of Cs and C-minuses. After graduating in
1925 with a bachelor's degree in business and political science, he went to
work as a retail credit investigator. But he quickly grew bored with that
work, which involved more bookkeeping than investigating. Fortunately
for Ness, his brother-in-law, Alexander Jamie, had recently been appointed
chief investigator for the Justice Department's Prohibition bureau in Chicago. Though Ness would appear to have been entirely unqualified, Jamie
pulled strings and got his wife's kid brother a job as a Prohibition agent at
a salary that was probably about $50 a week.

Many Prohibition agents got into the work because they knew they
could supplement their incomes with bribes from bootleggers. Ness,
though, ever the straight arrow, wasn't interested in kickbacks. He had
$410 in his bank account, and that was good enough for him. Jamie, for
his part, didn't need to line his pockets with booze money. He had a much
sweeter deal. While the Justice Department paid him one salary, a group
of wealthy Chicago businessmen paid him another.

The businessmen, organized by Robert Isham Randolph, president of
the Chicago Association of Commerce, were beginning to mount a private war against the city's gangsters. Some of them had already contributed cash to set up Calvin Goddard's forensic crime laboratory. Others
had gone to Washington to lobby President Hoover for his support. And
they had made it clear to George Johnson that they were prepared to act
as a shadow agency of the government, providing whatever he needed,
legal or not, to get the job done. If there were tasks that went beyond the
strict purview of the government, or that the government couldn't pay for,

or that might have been ethically objectionable to some in Washington, all Johnson had to do was ask.

By putting Jamie on the payroll, the businessmen gained access to government information and a pipeline to Johnson's office. They also bought themselves the services of the young and ambitious G-man Eliot Ness.

Years later, when he was old, washed up, drinking heavily, and trying to cash in on the glories of his youth, he would sell his life story for $300 to a writer named Oscar Fraley. Ness typed twenty-one pages on onionskin paper and gave them to Fraley, and from those slender sheets Fraley spun a marvelous fable, with Ness as the lonely warrior battling against Al Capone, the most notorious criminal who ever lived. Fraley called his book *The Untouchables,* the term coined by newspapers to describe Ness's organization. It was utter bull, but it was some of the most successful bull $300 ever bought— even if Ness wouldn't live long enough to see it play out. Fraley's story would inspire a long-running television series and a huge hit movie. It would make Ness one of the most famous crime fighters in American history, a paragon of virtue, an archetype for the hard-nosed Prohibition agent.

But in his own twenty-one-page manuscript, Ness described his role more honestly and more modestly. He was merely along for the ride, as the junior agent on the team in 1927 and 1928, rumbling around south suburban Chicago Heights in a "large, heavy Cadillac," he wrote, looking for bootleggers and their stills. The quarry was not Al Capone at that time but Joe Martino, the last surviving member of the Chicago Heights Piazza gang. In fact, it would seem from Ness's own description that he and his men had bungled their investigation. They had hoped to infiltrate Martino's gang and learn the names of some of the cops and Prohibition agents who had been receiving bribes. But they couldn't persuade the mobsters to trust them. Ness, a taciturn university graduate, had a difficult enough time fitting in with cops. He should have known that he would never dupe a streetwise mobster such as Martino.

Finally giving up, Ness and his men decided to quit the cute stuff. They raided eighteen of Martino's stills in Chicago Heights. That move backfired, too. Now the goons knew without a doubt that the men they'd met earlier were federal agents. Ness would never again work undercover. Martino was arrested but never tried.

The next phase of Ness's career would be more rewarding. In Ness's original manuscript, he said simply that he was assigned by George John-

son to help the revenue agents who were already going after Ralph and
Al Capone. "It was my job to raid the income medium possibilities of the
Capone mob," he wrote. "I was allowed to pick a number of agents from
any government services that I wished. I was to have a squad of about
12 men." While Ness took no credit for the idea in his manuscript, Fraley
constructed a dramatic scene in which Ness complained to his brother-in-
law that all his fellow agents were either corrupt or incompetent.

"Suppose the Prohibition bureau picked a small, select squad," Ness
told Jamie according to the Fraley account, published in 1957. "Let's say
ten or a dozen men. Every man could be investigated thoroughly, and
they could be brought in from other cities, if necessary, to insure that they
had no hookup with the Chicago mobsters. No rotten apples. Get it? Now
if this squad were given a free hand—and backing, when they did make
arrests—I'll guarantee it could dry up this town. And when that happens,
and the big money stops rolling in to the Capone mob, pretty soon they
don't have that twenty-five million dollars a year to be handing out for
protection. Then everybody starts to go to work on them, like they were
supposed to do in the first place, and you've got them licked."

Unfortunately, almost nothing in Fraley's book checks out. Johnson
probably did meet with Ness, and Johnson probably did hire him to do
work on the Capone investigation. While most of Johnson's attack was focused on building income tax and contempt charges against Capone, Ness
was still interested in cutting off the booze supply and pinching Capone's
income. Late in September, Johnson went to Washington to meet with
his bosses. Afterward, he told reporters that the Justice Department had
authorized him to go after Capone's beer. "A greater effort will be made to
reach the sources of the bootleggers' supply and get at the revenue which
finances the organized gangs," he said at that time. In that way, if in no
other, Ness would be useful. But nothing in the prosecutor's comments to
the press or in his voluminous personal files suggest that Ness's work was
a priority to the federal government.

While Ness was beginning his work and Johnson continued pondering
his strategy, the third important member of the team assigned to target
Capone, Frank Wilson, was plowing ahead. He was a stark man, pale
as a sheet of typing paper, with a square jaw and a cleft chin. He was of

average height, but with broad shoulders and a bullish chest. Ever since he was a boy he had wanted to be a cop, like his old man, who had served for years on the streets of Buffalo. Wilson had the right demeanor for it but, to his everlasting disappointment, he didn't have the eyesight: His vision was so poor that he would never be licensed to carry a firearm.

Wilson didn't talk much, but he had already earned a reputation within law enforcement circles as one of the toughest and most aggressive revenue investigators in the country. He didn't mind the monotony of the work, didn't mind the loneliness, didn't mind the long hours staring through thick corrective lenses at bank ledgers and canceled checks. But whenever the opportunity presented itself for Wilson to act like a street cop, he leaped at it. He loved getting out of the office and interviewing witnesses. He would never carry a gun, but that didn't mean he couldn't carry himself the same way his father had, straight up and stern as a two-by-four. Once, he'd been assigned to check out allegations of corruption concerning one of the bureau's own agents—and a high-ranking one, at that. When he was informed that the accused agent's wife had just died and that it might be best to postpone his initial interview by a few days, Wilson refused. "Wilson fears nothing," wrote his boss, Elmer Irey. "He will sit quietly looking at books eighteen hours a day, seven days a week, forever, if he wants to find something in those books." Wilson's only vice, so far as anyone could tell, was his taste for cheap cigars.

Wilson left Washington for Chicago in the late part of 1928 or early in 1929, setting up a tiny office in the Old Post Office Building downtown at Dearborn and Adams. It was more like a janitor's closet than an office, really, with no windows, no ventilation, and peeling green walls. Wilson filled it quickly with a huge, flat-topped desk and file cabinets. "I could hardly scratch my head without sticking my elbow in somebody's eye," he recalled.

He brought with him from Washington a small team of revenue agents. One of them began hanging around the lobby of the Lexington Hotel, pretending to be a midlevel gangster from Philly, looking for action. Wilson and the others began visiting the speakeasies, casinos, and brothels said to have been operated by Capone. They also visited nearby banks, looking for financial records that would establish Capone's income. Wilson heard all about Capone as he made the rounds. He heard that the boss took a slice of the profit on every case of whiskey brought into Cook County;

controlled a thousand speakeasies, a thousand more bookie joints, fifteen gambling halls, half a dozen breweries, and innumerable brothels; spent $1,000 a week on banquets; lounged about in $50 French pajamas; ordered suits by the dozen; and employed a staff of seven hundred gunmen. Maybe it was true, maybe it wasn't, or maybe some of it was and the rest of it wasn't. Wilson never could be sure. But one thing he did know for sure was that Capone would never be convicted on tax evasion if all that the revenue agents could come up with was evidence of great expenses and a lavish lifestyle. "The courts had to see income," he said. Several months into his investigation, to his great surprise, he hadn't found any.

"He did all his business through front men," Wilson said, with a hint of admiration for Capone's cleverness. When it came to income, the nation's most conspicuous criminal was "completely anonymous."

To get the case moving, and perhaps in hopes of getting more information, on October 9, 1929, revenue agents arrested Ralph Capone, Al's older brother, on charges of filing false income tax returns. Two years earlier, Ralph, at the behest of a seemingly friendly revenue agent, had filed a return claiming that he owed only about $5,000 in taxes for the years 1922 to 1925. The government claimed that Ralph's bank balances—he allegedly maintained several accounts under false names at the Pinkert State Bank of Cicero—averaged more than $350,000 a year. Investigators also claimed he owned seven horses.

Two days after Ralph's arrest, one of Ralph's favorite horses, Azov, finished first at Hawthorne, beating Vowed Vengeance by two lengths. At twenty-six-to-one odds, the horse paid off handsomely. Unfortunately for Ralph, although he had already been released from prison on bail, he failed to make it to the track that day to bet.

For a man such as Ralph, getting arrested was bothersome, but missing out on a twenty-six-to-one shot was tragic.

The authorities were closing in on Capone from every direction. It seemed only a matter of time. It didn't hurt, either, that the big fellow was already behind bars in Philadelphia. It was much easier to hit a stationary target. But President Hoover and his team were so caught up in the pursuit of the nation's most infamous criminal that they seemed to be paying little mind to a much bigger matter, one that would soon rivet their attention.

The 1920s had been so prosperous, so thrilling, so fast, so intoxicating that Americans had been conditioned to believe the good times could only get better. They had air travel, electric refrigerators, washing machines, and department stores that offered a sultan's array of products at working-men's prices. They had talking movies, radios in every home, fruits and vegetables in cans, and cars in every driveway. Women could vote, dress the way they wanted, smoke and drink in public, take jobs, and control their own money. It had all happened over the course of a mere decade, and it had happened because the country had grown richer and richer, wealth unfurling across the land like a brilliant red carpet. Hoover had said as much in his campaign, proclaiming that America was "closer to the final triumph over poverty than ever before in the history of any land."

Thanks for this great prosperity went to the American businessman. The spirit of salesmanship and the magic of conspicuous consumption had turned the nation into a virtual paradise. To dream it was to have it. And for those Americans who had not yet attained the levels of affluence they desired, it was only a matter of time. The average working stiff made just a few thousand dollars a year, but he socked away a few dollars every week to save for a down payment on a house or a car, and if he was really brave, he bought stocks. His time would come, too.

A great bull market in stocks began in the spring of 1928. RCA, for one example, soared from $85 a share at the start of 1928 to $420 a share by the end of the year. Much of it, of course, was illusion. Pools of wealthy businessmen would invest heavily in companies such as RCA then hire publicity agents and pay off reporters to spread the word that the compa-nies in which they'd invested would soon see their values soar. Investors were reminded to "never give up your position in a good stock." To sell, big-time industrialists warned, was not only unwise but unpatriotic. Of course, the big players were selling all the time.

Late in 1928, for example, several wealthy investors started a pool to promote the stock of Anaconda Copper, even though they knew that copper prices were down and likely to stay there, even though credit was inflated, and even though consumer spending throughout the economy was stalled. So what? Share prices shot from $40 to $128 in three months. The big investors who started the promotion correctly assumed that the public would keep buying as long as prices kept going up, so they made fortunes on top of their fortunes while small investors would eventually go bust. There was no logic to it and no integrity. Greed and high hopes fueled it all. A few years later, when a Senate committee investigated the schemes, a brazen trader named Matthew "Bear" Brush was asked if the wealthy investors who inflated stock prices had behaved in a manner comparable to Al Capone. Brush just said with a snicker, "Al Capone is a piker compared to that racket."

Capone never invested in stocks. "Those stock market guys are crooked," he said in a prison interview that fall. "I won't play with them. I know lots of better ways of investing my small change." But at least a million and perhaps as many as three million Americans played the market, and the rest acted as if they did. Market talk replaced sex talk as the national obsession. Psychics peddled newsletters with stock tips. The comedian Groucho Marx, like many others, trusted everything he had to his broker. "The little judgment I had told me to sell," he later recalled, "but like all the other suckers, I was greedy. I was loath to relinquish any stock that was sure to double in a few months." Whenever confidence waned, the president or the esteemed millionaire and Treasury secretary Andrew Mellon issued reassuring statements, and the market pushed higher. The *Saturday Evening Post* sang,

> *Oh hush thee, my babe, granny's bought some more shares,*
> *Daddy's gone to play with the bulls and the bears,*
> *Mother's buying on tips and she simply can't lose,*
> *And baby shall have some expensive new shoes.*

They all managed to ignore the fact that the economy was going eighty miles an hour on broken axles. A closer inspection by an objective party would have revealed the underlying problems. Florida had never recovered from the big hurricane of 1926. Farmers had never enjoyed the good times at all. Then there was the real estate market. With encouragement from the government, countless Americans had been buying homes they couldn't afford. Mortgage debt doubled between 1922 and 1929, until it reached more than $27 billion. By 1929 the housing market was beginning to slump, auto sales were slowing, and Americans began cutting back on the madcap spending that had defined the decade.

Only the stock market barreled forward, faster and stronger. Each time it hit a bump, the whole chassis of the economy rattled and shook more violently, and each time the Americans at the wheel gave it more gas, thundering forward, faster, faster, faster. When in doubt, they purchased more shares. And increasingly, they began buying on margin, borrowing against money they didn't have but expected to make just as soon as the market shot higher yet again.

In September 1929, the market collapsed. Then it bounced back. Then it collapsed again, in early October. Brokers urged their customers to buy, buy, buy. Stocks had slipped to bargain prices, they explained. The market was merely experiencing a period of readjustment. So the suckers bought.

On October 23, the same day the dazzling new Chrysler Building in New York was fitted with its lofty silver crown, the market came tumbling down again, harder this time. Surely it could go no lower, said the brokers and the pundits: Buy, buy, buy! But the next day, sell orders hit the market like a tsunami. Traders who were overloaded with margin deals began dumping everything they owned. The stock market, built almost entirely on speculation and credit, began to collapse upon itself. Word spread by telephone across the country that this nosedive was different from the rest, that the game was over, the bottom falling out of the market, and wave after wave of selling crashed down on Wall Street. A group of business titans tried to stop the flood by investing millions of their own money, a token of their faith in the economy, but it wasn't enough.

On October 29, Black Tuesday, widespread panic took hold, and the market lost about 13 percent of its value. "The jig is up!" Groucho Marx's broker told him. The Marx Brothers were set to open their play *Animal Crackers* in Baltimore that week, but Groucho was too depressed to go on with the show. Later, when he recovered his sense of humor, he wrote in his autobiography, "All I lost was two hundred and forty thousand dollars. . . . I would have lost more but that was all I had."

Within two weeks the New York Stock Exchange had surrendered half its value. Fortunes were eviscerated, businesses destroyed, confidence in the American economy gut-stabbed. Stories of stockbrokers jumping from windows may have been apocryphal, but the suffering was not. In the months and years to follow, more banks would close, small businesses would shut down, families would lose their homes, and hunger would spread across the land as never before. It was not merely the end of the big bull market. It also was the end of the Jazz Age—and the beginning of the Great Depression.

The crash prompted a statement from Capone:

"Tell them," he joked to his lawyer, "I deny absolutely that I am responsible."

Despite all the bleak news, Americans found a measure of comfort in the knowledge that they had in Herbert Hoover the ideal man to guide the nation through a crisis. Hadn't he saved the South after the floods? Hadn't he rescued Europe from starvation? Here was a student of business, a titan of industry in his own right, a brilliant organizer, and a master in the art of public relations. Yes, Americans told themselves, Hoover would know what to do.

Hoover worked with commendable speed to address the problem. In mid-November he gathered the leaders of finance, industry, construction, labor, agriculture, and public utilities at the White House. He promised tax cuts and urged manufacturers to maintain wages—a move he believed would not only help workers but also bolster the economy. He beseeched unions to withdraw their pending requests for salary increases. At the same time, he tried to offer soothing words. He urged Americans not to refer to the economic condition as a panic. It was merely a depression, he said, an unfortunate word choice that would haunt him forever.

With his campaign of optimism under way, the president, like most Americans, believed the economy would bounce back fast, at least partially. At first, Hoover's plan worked brilliantly. State and county governments launched construction projects. The Federal Reserve boosted the money supply. Henry Ford announced that he was actually raising wages, not cutting them. Management and labor worked in cooperation to keep workers employed. The Federal Farm Board kept crop prices from falling. If Hoover made one mistake during this early phase of the Depression, it was this: He continued to insist on a limited government role in addressing the crisis. He urged Congress to spend modestly on public works and to let the private sector lead the recovery effort. As unemployment mounted and breadlines grew longer, Hoover remained convinced that the country was merely suffering from a short-term malaise.

As autumn turned to winter, Americans attempted to return to their routines. They craved normalcy and found it in the newspaper stories that reminded them of the near and dear past. A *Saturday Evening Post* reporter got everyone talking with his report that college football had become a $50 million annual enterprise, much of it built on the exploitation of unpaid student athletes. The Wickersham Commission, appointed by Hoover to investigate problems with law enforcement, buckled down to work. Charles Lindbergh settled into his marriage to Anne Morrow. Commander Richard E. Byrd and his team made their first flight to the South Pole, an event declared by the *New York Times* to be the biggest news story of 1929. Al Capone's attorneys filed one motion after another in their futile attempts to win his early release from the state pen in Philadelphia. And federal agents and attorneys in Chicago went about the task of trying to make certain that Capone never enjoyed another day of freedom as long as he lived.

Life went on.

THE NAPOLEON OF CHICAGO

At Eastern State, Capone worked as a janitor, mopping the halls outside the warden's office. Later he would earn a promotion to library file clerk. But beyond that, for the first time in years, and perhaps for the first time in his life, he found himself with time on his hands. To fill it, he picked up a copy of *Napoleon,* Emil Ludwig's popular biography of Napoleon Bonaparte, published in 1926, and settled down on his bed to read. In Napoleon's story, Capone may have found parallels to his own. Both men were natural leaders, bold tacticians, and improvising opportunists. But just how long Capone dwelled on the similarities is anybody's guess, and the quote ascribed to him in 1931 by his excitable biographer Fred Pasley sounds a little too Runyonesque to be true.

"I'll have to hand it to Napoleon as the world's greatest racketeer," he supposedly said, "but I could have wised him up on some things. The trouble with that guy was he got the swelled head. He overplayed his hand and they made a bum out of him. He should have had the sense after that Elba jolt to kiss himself out of the game. But he was just like the rest of us. He didn't know when to quit and he had to get back into the racket. He simply put himself on the spot. That made it easy for the other gangs to take him, and they were no dumbbells. If he had lived in Chicago, it would have been a sawed-off shotgun Waterloo for him."

In all likelihood, Pasley was riffing on a quote from a syndicated news story that contained a brief comment from Capone:

"Nap sure was a great little guy," said Al, by way of reviewing Ludwig's book.

In the same news story, Capone went on to say that reports of his pampered prison life had been greatly exaggerated. Prisoner no. 527 shared a dank and dimly lit cell with a convicted embezzler, according to the newspaper account. Contrary to earlier published stories, the accommodations were not decorated to resemble a suite at the Ritz. Capone and his cell mate had a phonograph and a wooden smoking stand, which was cut and painted in the form of a butler holding a tray. The only other enhancement that caught the reporter's eye was a plain vase with a small bunch of gladioli in it.

"I'm taking this rap and I'm taking it just like anybody else would," Capone told the reporter in his soft tenor. The warden said Capone was a good prisoner and received the same privileges as other good prisoners—no more, no less.

Capone underwent two minor operations during the early part of his incarceration, the first on his nose, apparently to repair a deviated septum, the second to remove his tonsils. During his treatment, he made a friend of his doctor, Herbert M. Goddard, a nationally respected ear, nose, and throat man, who served as the prison's physician. Said Dr. Goddard, "In my seven years' experience, I have never seen a prisoner so kind, cheery, and accommodating. . . . He has brains. He would have made good anywhere, at anything." Capone also was said to have earned the goodwill of his fellow inmates by spending $1,000 in the prison craft shop and shipping the purchased articles around the country as Christmas presents for friends and relatives.

Back in Chicago, the cops continued to pursue the St. Valentine's Day murderers with their usual inept vigor. Then, by sheer luck, they caught what looked at first like a big break.

On the evening of December 14, 1929, Fred "Killer" Burke, a well-known bank robber and hired gun, had the misfortune of smashing his car into another in front of the police station in St. Joseph, Michigan, a hundred miles from Chicago. When the motorist with whom he'd collided asked for $5 to cover the repair, Burke drove off. A twenty-four-year-old St. Joe cop named Charles Skelly, having seen the whole thing, leaped on the running board of the dented car and told the driver to take off after Burke. After a brief chase, Burke stopped. Skelly hopped down from the running board and approached. That's when Burke raised a gun—probably a .45 automatic—and shot the officer three times, wounding him fatally, before speeding off. Later, cops found Burke's abandoned car and traced it to a home in nearby Stevensville. There they discovered Burke's wife, along with a huge arsenal, including two machine guns, two rifles, a shotgun, seven revolvers, eleven tear-gas canisters, several bottles of nitroglycerine, and enough ammunition to support the overthrow of a small government. They also found twenty gallons of wine and bonds valued at more than $300,000, some of which had been stolen a month earlier in a Jefferson, Wisconsin, bank robbery.

Weapons and ammunition from the Burke home were sent to Calvin Goddard at his forensic crime lab. At a press conference on December 23, Goddard and coroner Herman Bundeson announced with great flourish and certainty that both guns had been used in the attack in the North Clark Street garage. He matched the guns to bullets taken from the bodies of victims Schwimmer and Clark. In an interesting footnote, one that went almost entirely overlooked in the daily press, Goddard further noted that some of the bullets recovered from the Brooklyn murder of Frankie Yale also had been fired from one of Burke's two machine guns.

The report made headlines across the country and, more than anything Goddard had ever done, helped establish ballistic science as a respected crime-fighting tool. But Goddard was never able to build a strong nationwide network or bring uniform high standards to police labs across the country. Soon after, John Edgar Hoover would order agents to create a crime lab within the bureau, a move that would effectively put Goddard out of business but bring an important element of standardization to criminal science. In more immediate terms, the Burke investigation provided the first hard evidence in the nation's most spectacular unsolved crime. Police said they were convinced that Burke had been the leader of the attack on the Moran gang, and that he had perpetrated the assault because the Moran men had been hijacking his whiskey shipments somewhere around Hammond, Indiana, as they crossed from Detroit to Chicago.

There were no eyewitnesses placing Burke at the North Clark Street garage. In fact, inconveniently, there were some who said with great certainty that they had seen Burke at a bar in Calumet City on the morning of February 14. Of course, finding the guns in Burke's home was not the same as proving he had been in on the St. Valentine's Day hits. The guns might have changed hands several times before winding up in Burke's home. Burke might have been the mob's warehouse director, in charge of storage, given that he owned a home and spent most of his time in the relatively safe environs of western Michigan. But with his long record of criminality and his long association with the other men suspected in the crime, it was not difficult to imagine a prosecutor building a decent case on the circumstantial evidence. A jury was not likely to have much sympathy for a man known as "Killer."

Unfortunately, Burke was never charged. After eluding the cops for more than a year, he was arrested on March 26, 1931, in Green City, Missouri, extradited to Michigan, and sentenced to life in prison for the murder of Officer Skelly. He died in prison in 1940 from heart disease, at age forty-seven. Like Capone, he was never pressed to answer questions about the St. Valentine's Day Massacre.

Over the years, other theories would rise and fall.

Six years after the massacre, in January 1935, a bank robber named Byron Bolton, already in custody on an unrelated charge, told the feds that the massacre had been carried out by Burke, Claude Maddox, Gus Winkler, Fred Goetz, and Murray Humphreys. Bolton claimed to have served as one of the lookouts. Capone had planned the crime to get Moran out of the way, the criminal claimed. Bolton's confession made huge headlines across the country. If anyone had doubted Capone's involvement in the massacre before, they weren't doubting it anymore.

But there were serious problems with Bolton's story. For starters, at least two of the men he identified as killers had airtight alibis. Then there's the question of why Capone would hire so many men for a job that required only one assassin. He knew where the rival gangster lived. He could have put Jack McGurn in a car across the street and had him wait until he got a clean shot. But even if Capone had ordered the hit and even if the job had gone horribly wrong, another question remained: Why hadn't he ordered the men to try again? Why was Moran still alive? In the end, Bolton's story made little sense, which is why the feds ignored his confession and let him go.

But the story doesn't end there.

When Bolton's bogus confession hit the newspapers, a Chicagoan named Frank T. Farrell composed a letter to John Edgar Hoover dated

January 28, 1935, saying he had information that might be useful to the feds in their investigation. His account—recently discovered in the FBI archives and never before revealed—offers the most logical and satisfying solution to the crime.

In cramped but tidy script, Farrell informed the director that he had been doing "Undercover Investigation" work—he gives no more detail than that—at the time of the crime. He said that if the bureau would check Chicago police logs, it would find that a forty-year-old firefighter named William Davern Jr., the son of a Chicago police sergeant, had been shot during a bar fight in November 1928, back when members of the Moran mob were running out of control and getting themselves in all sorts of trouble. Davern, the letter said, was the key to unraveling the mystery of the St. Valentine's Day Massacre. A straight line could be drawn between the two attacks, according to Farrell.

William Davern Jr. was in the kitchen of the C & O Restaurant at 509 North Clark Street, a popular gangster hangout, when a fight erupted in the kitchen and someone shot him in the stomach. Police never learned why, although the Moran mob was operating so recklessly at the time, motives seemed superfluous. Spurting blood, he was carried to a car, driven to the corner of Rush Street and Austin Avenue, and dumped there. But Davern managed to crawl to a fire station call box and ring for help. He was taken to the hospital, where he held on for six weeks. And while he wouldn't tell the police during those six weeks who had shot him, Davern did tell his first cousin, William White. White's mother and Davern's mother were sisters—so close, it would seem, that they gave their boys the same name. William Davern and William White grew up together in Chicago. Now as he lay dying, Davern decided there was only one man he could trust, so he gave White the names of several members of the Moran gang, including one of the Gusenberg brothers. In his letter, Farrell doesn't say which brother. Those are the guys who shot me, Davern told his cousin.

William "Three-Fingered Jack" White was beady-eyed, bald, and double-chinned, even tougher than he was ugly. A boyhood accident or a botched safecracking job—accounts varied—had taken two of the fingers on his right hand. For the better part of the decade he had maintained status as one of Chicago's most vicious criminals, with a rap sheet as long and as savage as the processing line at the Armour meatpacking plant.

White was a known killer of cops, a robber of banks, and a gunman for hire. When Davern died, according to Farrell's letter, White made up his mind to avenge his cousin's murder. He contacted the same Gusenberg brother who had been involved in the murder of Davern and said he was planning to hold up a factory for its payroll and wanted men to help. They were sure to oblige. White was supposed to be locked up in the county jail at the time, according to Farrell, but bribed his way out whenever business or personal matters required.

White knew both Gusenberg brothers. They'd worked together in 1926 on the $80,000 robbery of the International Harvester factory on Thirty-first Street. In that job they had used eight men, and when one of those men ratted to the cops and started naming his accomplices, White and one of his cohorts disguised themselves as police, went to the rat's home, and murdered him while he slept. White knew that when people saw police uniforms they tended to be more trusting, and they tended not to notice the distinguishing features of the men in the uniform. All they saw were hats and badges. And getting uniforms was easy. White knew plenty of crooked cops. In this case, he might have enlisted the help of his uncle, Sergeant William J. Davern, the father of the man killed by the Moran boys.

Farrell's letter solves many, if not all, of the mysteries surrounding the massacre. It helps explain why so many of Moran's men were in the garage that morning and why they never drew their guns when faced by their intruders. It also offers a clear motive—one with enough emotional power to explain the fury of the attack. It may even account for why the investigation of the crime went nowhere. Perhaps word had spread through the department that the garage killing had been carried out in retaliation for the murder of a cop's kid. That would have been enough to quell further investigation and persuade the detectives to accept this rough justice.

If White had been arrested and had confessed that he'd committed the crime in retaliation for the murder of Davern, the newspapermen certainly would have followed up with the next logical question: Was Sergeant Davern involved? Did any other cops help him commit or cover up the crime? And once those questions were asked, the reporters no doubt would have cited the dying words of Frank Gusenberg, which to this day remain the only testimony from a victim of the crime.

"Cops did it," Gusenberg had said.

When police went through the neighborhood conducting interviews after the massacre, they picked up a great deal of information, some of which slipped through the cracks.

Less than a week after the crimes on North Clark Street, an eyewitness told police he had seen some of the action on the street. His testimony seemed inconsequential at the time and was quickly forgotten, but it included this nugget of information: "Just about the time I arrived in front of the place, an automobile I thought was a police squad car stopped in front of the garage. There were five men in it. The fellow who stayed at the wheel had a finger missing. His hand was spread out on the steering apparatus, so the old amputation was apparent." Police, apparently, never followed up on the lead.

For several years in the early 1930s, White worked as a federal informant, trading information about his fellow gangsters to federal agents in exchange for their protection, according to newly released FBI documents. If John Edgar Hoover knew White was the mastermind of the St. Valentine's Day Massacre, the bureau might have helped to cover his tracks for fear of losing an informant and jeopardizing the lives of the agents who had worked with him.

In January 1934, when his peers figured out that White was a rat working for the FBI, he was executed in his home. Federal agents were seen visiting his home shortly before the murder, but White's killers were never caught.

One year later, when Hoover received the letter from Frank T. Farrell suggesting that White had been responsible for the St. Valentine's Day Massacre—a letter thoroughly grounded by logic and steeped in accuracy—the director replied that the gangland killings were a matter for local police and of no interest to the bureau. In other words, as far as he was concerned, the case was closed.

THE BIG FELLOW CHILLS

In the spring of 1930, Herbert Hoover and other government officials spoke and acted as if the economy had already rebounded. But in the real world, people turned off the heat in their houses and put on sweaters. They canceled their vacations. They abandoned their homes as mortgages went unpaid. Weeds sprouted in the cracked concrete of unfinished buildings. Some laid-off workers, too ashamed to tell their spouses, dressed for work and left home each morning, only to spend their days hunting in vain for jobs. In Cleveland, thousands of unemployed workers showed up at a meeting of the Welfare Committee of the City Council, demanding relief money. When police tried to clear the men from the steps of City Hall, punches flew and knives flashed. Firefighters with water hoses and cops with nightsticks pushed the protesters back, crushing bones and spilling blood in the process. There were similar scenes in New York, Philadelphia, and Newark.

It was just the beginning.

Still, Hoover saw no reason to panic. Philosophically, the new president was a lot like Jefferson and Lincoln. He believed Americans ought to "go it alone." As much as possible, he thought, they ought to rule themselves, pull themselves up by their own bootstraps, and organize to solve their own problems.

Yet he was smart enough to know that modern America was different from Jefferson's America. People lived in cities and worked in factories now. He was not opposed to helping those who were losing their jobs, and he certainly was not opposed to helping to revitalize the economy. He prided himself, after all, on his great skills as an engineer and a fixer of broken things. But he believed that private enterprise, not big government, would lead the recovery. Even more important to Hoover, still clinging to Quaker traditions, was the ideal that the poor could count on their neighbors for support. He was a man of principle, and he intended to stick to his beliefs.

Unfortunately, Hoover severely misjudged the depth of the Depression. He failed to see that the problem was too big for local governments and charities to solve. And his confidence in an imminent recovery quickly began to look like callousness to the millions of Americans suffering without food and jobs.

When he wasn't focused on the economy, Hoover continued to devote much of his time to the issue of law enforcement. In his December 1929 State of the Union address, after once more assuring Americans that the nation's financial system would soon return to normal, he saved for last his comments on law enforcement. Proper enforcement of the Prohibition laws, he said, required proper organization of government. For starters, Hoover wanted to transfer the Prohibition Bureau from the Treasury Department to the Justice Department, streamline court procedures, and reorganize border patrol functions. "No one will look with satisfaction upon the volume of crime of all kinds and the growth of organized crime in our country," he said with typical passivity. "We need to reestablish faith that the highest interests of our country are served by insistence on the swift and even-handed administration of justice to all offenders, whether they be rich or poor."

With Capone in jail, Hoover might have bragged. He might have vowed that he was making it his personal mission to keep the gangster on ice for years to come. It would have made huge headlines. It would have added grit to Hoover's squeaky-clean image. It also would have been true. But as usual, the president was conflicted. He continued to approach the problem as an engineer would approach the design of a new road, studying the landscape from every angle before moving the first load of dirt. "We can no longer gloss over the unpleasant reality which should be made vital in the consciousness of every citizen," he said, "that he who condones or traffics with crime, who is indifferent to it and to the punishment of the criminal, or to lax performance of official duty, is himself the most effective agency for the breakdown of society."

It wasn't much of a rallying cry, but it would have to do.

While Hoover maneuvered and Capone cooled his heels in prison, leadership of the Chicago outfit fell to Ralph Capone, Jack Guzik, and Frank Nitti. These were three men Al Capone could trust. Ralph knew the booze business and the gambling operations. Guzik was the bagman. Nitti provided the muscle.

They faced a difficult business environment. Frank Wilson of the corrective lenses and dogged determination, along with his fellow revenue agents, were investigating all three men. Ralph Capone had already been indicted. Cops were raiding gambling dens and speakeasies with unusual fervor. In one raid on the offices of Bugs Moran, at 127 North Dearborn, where the sign on the door said Acme Sales Company, cops said they found four quarts of good Scotch (which probably meant they found eight). They confiscated it, but somehow it disappeared before the officers could get back to the station. "Scotch? Scotch?" teased one of the cops who made the bust. "Impossible! Why, the country's dry and so am I. That rhymes. Can you rhyme?" That prompted the *Chicago Herald and Examiner* reporter to quip: "As the detectives are all teetotalers, it is planned to put Scotland Yard on the scent."

At the same time, Eliot Ness and his men were tapping phone lines and eavesdropping on some of the city's gangsters. Ness began with Ralph Capone, who in those days was spending most of his time at the Montmartre Café, a speakeasy in Cicero, conducting his business on a phone nestled in an alcove behind the bar. Ness rented a basement apartment three blocks from the café, where he and his men could set up their equipment. Then one day, he and four of his agents hopped in their Cadillac and began circling the block around the Montmartre. When Ralph's men got into cars and began following Ness, another one of Ness's men shinnied up the telephone pole in the alley behind the café and began playing with the wires. "My secretary made a call to the Montmartre Café and engaged the man who answered in light conversation," Ness wrote in the first draft of his memoir. "My telephone man was simultaneously raking the box. Suddenly he gave me the sign that he had found it; the bridge was made and telephone tap on the Cicero headquarters of the mob established. This tap was kept alive for many, many months, and we learned a great deal."

The transcripts from those wiretaps were only recently discovered among the personal possessions of George E. Q. Johnson. Some have Ness's name at the top, suggesting that he was listening and typing or taking notes himself, while others have the names of his men. They read like dialogue from Damon Runyon's *Guys and Dolls,* and they suggest that the police crackdown this time was more than hype. The wiretaps reveal that the Capone gang was struggling to keep the beer and whiskey flowing.

In this call, recorded at 8:45 P.M. on February 20, 1930, the caller, identified as the man on the line "out," is probably Pete Penovich, who supervised many of Capone's gambling operations. The man receiving the call "in," identified as Dutch, is most likely Ralph Capone.

Out	Is Mike there?
In	No, But Dutch is.
Out	Let me talk to Dutch [Dutch answers phone].
Out	Is Blackie still there?
In	No, I sent him away twenty minutes ago. Are you coming over?
Out	Yes, but not for some time, I've got to get a fellow out of the can.
In	I can go get his bond, you know, Pete.
Out	Oh, I can fix it, all right. Say, Dutch, I want to collect a bill in East St. Louis, have you got anyone there?
In	I might have, how much is it?
Out	Thirty-eight hundred dollars—it's not a legitimate bill, you know, the guy is a businessman, he sells what we do.
In	Will I get eight hundred if I get it?
Out	Yes, if you get the guy here we will make him pay.
In	All right, when you get here we will talk about it.
Out	Say, have you got the little one there?
In	No, Little Mike has it.
Out	What have you got?
In	My own, the one I always carry.

In another call, recorded at five thirty-five on the afternoon of February 24, Ralph complained that police raids were hurting business. His reference here to having his head examined might suggest he was speaking to Jack McGurn, who had been the subject of a well-publicized psychiatric examination a few years earlier.

Out	I'm in a swell spot now.
In	Why? What's the matter?
Out	My joints ain't working; somebody else is making all the dough.
In	Yeah.
Out	Yes, I'm getting in your class, I ought to have my head examined.
In	Well, you'll smarten up someday.
Out	Say, did you leave that short [probably referring to a sawed-off rifle] over there?
In	Yes. You coming over tonight?
Out	I don't think I can, I got to hunt up some moon.

The next night, Ralph and his men were at the Cotton Club, where jazz bands grooved all night and women paraded in flimsy gowns. The men drank until they were fried and singing like idiots. But when they woke up and went back to work on February 26, they were still having trouble finding enough hooch to satisfy their customers.

Out	Did you get any today?
In	No, it's just a push around.
Out	I've been looking for some. That's all I've been doing.
In	If you get some, hold a couple for me so I can fix up these guys.
Out	All right.

The transcripts contain no mention of Al Capone. If the big man was running his gang from prison, one couldn't tell it from the evidence Ness gathered. Was it possible that Capone's operation, described by federal and local law enforcement agencies as a massive purveyor of vice, was really so well organized that it continued to function without its head? The fact that Ralph Capone was overheard repeatedly on these wiretaps discussing individual shipments of beer to individual saloons would certainly seem to suggest that the Capone outfit was not exactly Standard Oil. Which is what Al Capone had been saying all along.

Questions of the outfit's size and strength would become more important as the government further developed its case. For now, the information obtained by Ness and his men was proving of little or no use to Johnson. In fact, it's not at all clear what Ness was doing with the information gathered from his wiretaps. While the Chicago cops were out making raids and disrupting supply lines, Ness and his team of "untouchables" never made a move. They should have been called the "inactives."

SILENT PARTNER

If you were a newspaper reporter covering the crime beat in Chicago circa 1930, you didn't waste your time hanging around the police station. Nor did you sit around the newsroom smoking cigarettes and waiting for the phone to ring or for your editor to hand you an assignment. The less contact you had with your editor the better. No; if you were a crime reporter you spent your time among criminals: in bars, at the track, in casinos, in brothels. You made connections. You got to know not only the goons but also their molls, and sometimes even their mothers. You became friendly with the cops, too, but never too friendly, or else you risked scaring off your less lawful friends. If you were a crime reporter, you occupied a special place in the universe of law and order; you could go anywhere and talk to anyone; and usually you were immune from reprisal. It was a little bit like being a diplomat, only with worn-out shoes and a soup-stained tie.

Eliot Ness never understood this. He cared too much about getting his name in the papers. He fed the newsmen tips, hoping they would show up—and bring photographers—to glorify his raids on bootleggers. But he never asked them for anything more than publicity, and he never gave them much in return.

Frank Wilson was smarter. Wilson understood that the city's well-traveled, hard-drinking newspapermen could help his team of revenue agents do their job. He knew that the reporters had access to valuable information, much of which never made print, and that they could be persuaded to turn over useful facts. Some would do it for the price of a drink, others out of patriotic duty, and still others in exchange for the promise of a future scoop. There's no loyalty among thieves, as the saying goes, and there wasn't much among the press corps.

Why did the thugs talk to reporters? First, because the reporters and the criminals had much in common. They came from the same schools and neighborhoods, lived on the same blocks in the same sort of houses, watched the same horse races, drank the same whiskey, chased the same women, and held the same low opinion of politicians. Their rapport was elemental. But the thugs also talked because they thought the newsmen would give them a more sympathetic hearing than the cops or the politicians or the courts did, and because it made them feel important to have someone listen.

So while the reporters chatted up the hoodlums, Wilson chatted up the reporters, and it was one of those reporters, John T. Rogers, who gave Wilson his first important break in the case. Rogers worked for the *St. Louis Post-Dispatch*, but he did not confine his reporting to St. Louis. He cruised all of the Midwest looking for stories. The *Post-Dispatch* was one of the nation's most aggressive papers, winner of two straight Pulitzer prizes for reporting, and famed for its role in exposing the bribery of government officials at the heart of the Teapot Dome scandal. Rogers, lanky and charming, was the paper's shining star. It was Rogers whose investigation forced the resignation of Federal Judge George W. English for abusive treatment of lawyers and litigants, a story that won Rogers a Pulitzer Prize; Rogers who broke the story of George Remus, the first big bootlegger to be arrested and tried; and Rogers who exposed and ultimately helped wipe out the Charlie Birger bootlegging gang of Williamson County, Illinois.

Rogers knew the gang world as well as anyone operating outside of its orbit. Without being coaxed, the reporter gave Wilson the name of a man who did business with Capone, a man who had long made a living walking the tightrope between legitimate business and crime, a man who—as Rogers viewed it—might be willing to supply the feds with useful evidence against the Chicago mob. His name was Eddie J. O'Hare.

No one would have dreamed of calling him Edward. In every kind of company he was EJ, Eddie, Easy Eddie, or Fast Eddie. O'Hare was a man's man—strong and tough and lots of laughs. He looked like a former football player, with a head big and round as a pumpkin. He had a high forehead with wavy brown hair. His smile was the smile of a fine politician—warm, contagious, and possibly even genuine.

Prohibition had been very, very good to Eddie O'Hare. He grew up in St. Louis and practiced law there. No one—least of all Eddie—seemed to mind that he had never been to law school. In 1925, he'd been indicted along with George Remus and more than a dozen other men for siphoning whiskey valued at $200,000 from a Jack Daniel's warehouse in St. Louis. Remus went to jail for two years, but O'Hare beat the rap. Had he been working with the feds to help make a case against Remus? If so, it was never reported. But given how badly the feds wanted Remus and how cleanly O'Hare emerged from the whole affair, it's a possibility. After that close call, he went back to work as a lawyer, but lawyering was never enough for O'Hare, a man with a taste for wealth and action. He wanted another racket, but something slightly cleaner than bootlegging.

As a lawyer, O'Hare tended to attract shady clients. If some lawyers were great scholars, crafting nuanced cases that would be read and discussed for ages, O'Hare was something different and much more useful for his client's purposes. He studied the angles for making money.

When one of his clients, Owen P. Smith, needed help with a patent application for an electric rabbit, O'Hare sniffed an opportunity. As commissioner of the International Greyhound Racing Association, Smith was top man in a sport that had many promising elements and one huge problem. The promising elements were these: Dogs ran fast. Dogs ate less than horses. Dogs didn't need riders. Dogs were cheaper to breed and haul than horses. The problem was this: Dogs weren't bright. Sometimes they ran and sometimes they sat. Sometimes they sprinted around the oval and sometimes they chased flies. One track operator had the idea of putting monkeys on the dogs' backs. Unfortunately, it didn't help the dogs run faster or straighter, and it doubled the food budget for track operators.

Enter Owen P. Smith, who decided he could solve the sport's problems by attaching an electric rabbit to a small car that hummed around the track on a rail. As long as the rabbit kept ahead of the dogs, the dogs would fly straight as arrows, with a raw intensity that thrilled spectators. Smith's clever invention would do for greyhound racing what air-conditioning did for movie theaters in the 1920s: It made business boom. O'Hare thought so much of Smith's idea that he forged a partnership with the inventor. Whether Smith entered the partnership voluntarily is anybody's guess. When Smith died in 1927, his widow agreed to sell O'Hare exclusive rights to the device. From there, Fast Eddie was off and running.

He opened the Madison Kennel Club, just across the river from St. Louis, with eight races a night every night but Sunday, "Financed and Operated by Home People," his newspaper ads boasted. When the cops shut him down for running an illegal gambling operation, he moved his operation upstate, to Cicero.

O'Hare no doubt knew that Cicero already had a dog track—the Hawthorne Kennel Club—and that it represented one of the key properties in the business empire of Al Capone. He didn't care. O'Hare had the mechanical rabbit and Capone didn't, which meant that his track would instantly overtake Capone's. Wisely, though, O'Hare never tried to put the crime boss out of business. He sent word that he was interested in a partnership, and Capone took him up on it. O'Hare would maintain a 51 percent interest in the business, while Capone and three of his associates—Nitti, Guzik, and Burnham mayor Johnny Patton (who liked the gangsters and saw no reason to restrict his business to Burnham)—would get 49 percent. O'Hare had few direct dealings with Capone. Patton served as the middleman. The match was a good one. O'Hare gained access to Capone's business and political connections in Cicero, and Capone got O'Hare's rabbit. Before long, the track was clearing more than $100,000 in annual profits. Everybody was happy, at least for a time.

The only trouble they ran into was with the law. Illinois made it illegal to bet on greyhounds. So every once in a while, the cops would raid the track and shut it down, and O'Hare would go to court and seek an injunction allowing the track to reopen. He argued that there was no gambling at the Hawthorne Kennel Club. Contributions were accepted from spectators, and those contributions were taken as investments in certain dogs. If the chosen dogs happened to win their races, investors were naturally entitled to share the prize money. But gambling? Oh, no, there was none of that. "Persons coming to the track do not wager," said Fast Eddie during one court appearance. "They make contributions for the development of better greyhounds."

"Oh," replied the assistant state's attorney, no trace of sarcasm detected, "it is something like taking up contributions in church?"

O'Hare said, "Yes. Something like that."

For all his sparring with the cops and the courts, O'Hare prospered in Cicero. And so it came to pass that he became part of the Capone corporation. Together, Capone and O'Hare ran additional dog-racing tracks in

Boston, Miami, and Tampa. In each case, O'Hare was the front man and Capone a silent partner. How they split the profits is unclear.

By 1930, O'Hare was spending most of his time away from St. Louis and away from his wife and three children. Eddie was handsome, gregarious, and very charming with the ladies. Yet while he juggled a number of mistresses and made little effort to hide his affairs from his wife, he retained a strong interest in his children, especially in his only son, the eldest of his children, Edward Henry "Butch" O'Hare.

Butch had inherited little of his father's machismo. Eddie was rough, especially on kids. He made them chew each bite of food twenty-five times, and enforced the rule like a prison warden. Yet his son, go figure, was soft and sweet, a real jelly doughnut. Eddie, hoping to toughen the boy up, sent him to the Western Military Academy in Alton, Illinois. He proved to be an average student, but, to his credit, he hung in there. When he told his father he wanted to be a pilot, Eddie O'Hare began tapping his long list of political connections to see if he could get his son admitted to the U.S. Naval Academy at Annapolis, Maryland.

Wilson and O'Hare met for lunch at the Missouri Club in St. Louis one day, along with Rogers of the *Post-Dispatch*. Wilson would later claim that he had the feeling Capone had forced O'Hare into partnership on the greyhound operation. In fact, it was probably the other way around. When O'Hare agreed to feed Wilson inside dope on Capone, Wilson asked Rogers why the businessman would take such a chance. Rogers said he was doing it to help get his boy admitted to the Naval Academy.

"Does he realize . . . he is taking his life in his hands?" Wilson asked.

"Hell, Frank," said Rogers, "if Eddie had ten lives to live he'd jeopardize every one of them for that boy Butch."

O'Hare had plenty of other reasons to cooperate with the feds, of course. For one thing, he probably had a tax liability of his own and didn't want Wilson taking too close a look. But more important, O'Hare surely knew that partnerships with Capone were perilous. His business prospects, not to mention his personal safety, would improve with the big fellow behind bars. He also knew that Capone's ownership interests were entirely off the books. That was good for Capone, because he didn't report his income, but it was even better for his partner, because it meant Capone had nothing in writing and therefore no legal claim to anything. If Capone went away, some of his dough would flow to O'Hare.

O'Hare, in Wilson's own words, would turn out to be "one of the best undercover men I have ever known." Though he probably didn't know much about Capone's bootlegging business, he knew a great deal about the gambling operation. Capone's men in Chicago wired money by Western Union to Miami, he told Wilson. In Miami, the money was picked up by Parker Henderson Jr., he said. O'Hare also gave Wilson the names of two bookkeepers, Fred Ries and Leslie Shumway. If anyone knew Capone's finances, he said, it was those two. Wilson also hoped to make a close examination of the track's betting records and corporate records with the aim of proving that Capone had been skimming off the top.

At last he had solid leads to pursue.

"LADY, *NOBODY'S* ON THE LEGIT"

On March 15, 1930, the day before his release from Eastern State Penitentiary, Al Capone sat in his cell with a reporter from the *Tribune*. He said he
was roughly twenty pounds lighter and $25,000 poorer since landing in
prison. The weight loss, of course, had come from a steady diet of prison
food. The money had been doled out to local charities and prisoners with
hard-luck stories. He was paler and wore gold-rimmed glasses, the result
of eyestrain. But otherwise he reported himself to be in fine shape.

"Of course I'm going back to Chicago," he said in the March 15 interview. "Where else would I go? I live in Chicago, my business is there,
my mother and my family are there. I'm going to call . . . the collector of
Internal Revenue and renew my compromise offer." He was referring to
overtures his lawyers had made to settle his outstanding tax bill. "The
government better take me up," he continued, "because I never kept any
books and never had a bank account. . . .

"After I get back home and visit with my family, I'll go down to Miami
for a month or so. They can't keep me out of Miami even if they want to.
I'm an American citizen, I own property there, and I'll go there like any
other citizen."

Later that day, the prison warden ordered Capone and his fellow inmate Frank Rio removed from Eastern State and taken to another prison,
thirty miles away. The warden told no one. The following morning, before
dawn, reporters, photographers, and a handful of the curious began lining
up outside the castlelike walls of Eastern State. By sunrise, the crowd began
to swell. By noon thousands of people crowded the streets and sidewalks
around the massive prison. The weather was cool and damp. Newsreel

shooters perched their bulky cameras on the roofs of their cars. Reporters sat on the curb, smoking cigarettes, and glancing at their watches. They waited and waited. As it turned out, they waited for nothing. Capone and Rio were four hours outside of town, aboard the Chicago-bound Broadway Limited, before prison officials acknowledged to the waiting mob that the men were gone. Later, the warden said he had hidden Capone in part for his safety and in part to spare him the harassment of the press.

"Try and find out where they've gone!" the warden taunted the infuriated crowd.

"How much did you get for this?" shot back one reporter.

The *Tribune* splashed a banner headline across the front page of the next morning's paper: "CAPONE SPEEDS FOR CHICAGO." The paper also reported that the Capone family had ordered two eighteen-pound turkeys from the local butcher in preparation for the homecoming feast. Angling for a scoop, a reporter had shown up at the Capone home on South Prairie and dangled a bag full of candy in front of the eyes of twelve-year-old Ralph Capone Jr.

"Where's Grandma?" the fearless reporter asked.

"Out," said the boy, already adept at handling the press.

"Is Grandma going to have a special kind of spaghetti for Uncle Al's dinner?"

"Yeah, walnut-flavored, probably," he said, before adding, "Another paper sent some people out here to play marbles with me. I won ninety cents from them and didn't tell them a thing." And with that he shut the door.

Despite the size and clarity of its headline, the *Trib* was not actually sure if Capone was speeding for Chicago. When word got out that the press crew in Philadelphia had been duped, phone calls were made quickly to Pittsburgh, and when the Broadway Limited hissed into the station there after midnight, reporters jumped aboard and stalked the aisles. Stories didn't mention whether the reporters barged into private sleeping cars and woke weary travelers, although the newsmen did seem fairly certain after the search that Capone was not on the train.

Other news agencies offered a different itinerary, saying that Ralph Capone and Jack Guzik had chartered a plane in New York, flown to Camden, New Jersey, and then driven to Philadelphia to pick up the two released prisoners. From there, according to these accounts, the four men drove back to Camden, flew to Baltimore, and traveled by boat to Miami. Yet another report said Capone had taken the train from Philadelphia to St. Louis, sneaked into Chicago from the south, stayed briefly, then departed for Indiana. Still others said he was on his way to Miami, or Hawaii, or Cuba.

The mystery made page-one news in most of the nation's newspapers. Capone was "lost in the fog," according to one wire-service story. He "may be here, he may be there, he may be riding the billowy waves to Shanghai or he may be picking daisies from the pretty green lawns of Florida," concluded the Associated Press. Was he on the run? Preparing a bold return? Was he afraid to set foot in Chicago? Was he already there?

Capone's disappearance only heightened the public's fascination. By now he had captivated the American imagination like no criminal before. He was an international star, a household name. He was royalty–the King of Crime. In just a few years, Capone became the most notorious criminal of his time. In an era devoid of international radio broadcasts, satellite television, and the Internet, he nevertheless became instantly recognizable worldwide. He enjoyed a celebrity previously experienced only by royalty or military heroes. Men and women who met him even briefly would tell about it for the rest of their lives. In most of their stories, they would recall him fondly.

It was widely understood that Capone ran the Chicago underworld, supervised brothels and casinos, splashed beer across the land, and killed countless rivals, with or without the St. Valentine's Day Massacre added to his list of credits. And yet he also was perceived as a human being, a family man, a lover of music, a sports fan, a genial host, a quiet resident of a working-class neighborhood in Chicago, and a bon vivant with a splendid winter home in Miami. He offered up the kind of moral ambiguity– the subtle charms offset by sharp edges, the smile offset by the gun–that made so many of the nation's celebrities intriguing.

The press framed his story as an immigrant boy's rise from poverty to wealth, power, and celebrity. They described him as businessman more than bruiser, although, to be sure, they never left out the latter. The message was clear: In America, anybody could rise above his roots. Even Dale Carnegie, in the opening chapter of his 1937 bestseller *How to Win Friends and Influence People,* cited Capone as proof of the power of positive thinking.

Time magazine, in putting Capone on its cover in 1930, declared, "No desperado of the old school is 'Scarface Al,' plundering or murdering for the savage joy of crime. He is, in his own phrase, 'a business man' who wears clean linen, rides in a Lincoln car, leaves acts of violence to his underlings." In short, the magazine stated, Capone was the John D. Rockefeller of the underworld.

Americans were fascinated by Capone not just because he boldly broke so many rules but also because he obeyed so many. He dressed nicely, shook hands, smiled, made polite conversation, and hosted parties. He did all the things an upwardly mobile American was supposed to do. Other criminals were photographed in shackles, or with their faces buried in the lapels of their coats. Not Capone. He posed for close-ups, politely requesting that the photographers aim from his right. Other criminals gave interviews only to deny accusations. Not Capone. He used the newspapers to tell the American people how much he loved his wife and child and how fervent was his desire to see his son go to college and have a better life than his own. In a way, he was very much a conservative.

Capone's popular appeal infuriated the people who were hell-bent on keeping him behind bars. President Hoover was promising Americans that the worst of the economic crisis would be over by the summer of 1930. He wasn't ignoring the economy, but neither was he allowing it to consume him. He continued to pay attention to Capone.

The day after Capone's release, Walter Hope, assistant secretary of the U.S. Treasury, on orders from Hoover, directed his staff to perform a complete audit on Capone's tax-paying history. The report came back quickly, and, as the investigators in Chicago already knew, it showed that Capone had never filed a return. That same day, Assistant Attorney General G. A. Youngquist phoned the commissioner of the Prohibition Bureau and asked if there were any liquor-law violations pending against Capone. The Prohibition Bureau chief told Youngquist they had no proof Capone was a bootlegger. Next, Youngquist made a call to Chicago, speaking to George Johnson, and learned that Johnson "had been much interested in Capone for a long time, but that the Federal authorities had not thus far been able to procure any tangible evidence of wrong-doing." Asked about the contempt of court charges that he had been investigating a year earlier, Johnson said, "It is not a matter of seriousness or importance." Johnson went on to say that he'd been busy preparing his tax case against Ralph

Capone, "and the Al Capone case has been delayed with others on that account."

Ten months earlier, when Capone had been arrested in Philadelphia, the feds had seemed to be closing in. Now that he was free again, they had lost their aim. No one was ready to bring charges. Capone, complained Arthur P. Madden, special agent in charge of the Revenue Bureau's intelligence unit, had "prepared himself for almost every contingency. . . . [N]o matter what has been done so far in this investigation . . . the funds have not and could not be followed through."

On March 31, Youngquist phoned the president to tell him what he had learned about the case against Capone: "He is very clever," Youngquist told Hoover. "He is two or three or four times removed from the actual operation." That same day, or so it would appear from notes in the federal archives, Youngquist phoned the president again to reassure him that his men were making progress. George Johnson in Chicago was in charge of the case, he told the president. He concluded, "I wanted you to know we are keeping after it."

On April 8, President Hoover wrote to his Treasury secretary, Andrew Mellon, and his attorney general, William D. Mitchell, urging them to adopt a more forceful line of attack in the war against the nation's illegal booze dealers: "The most important areas for the enforcement of the Eighteenth Amendment should be directed toward those larger rings and conspiracies whose operations in illicit liquor are obvious, and whose manifestations apparently cover even more than single states." He went on to say that he wanted the Department of Justice to assemble teams of prosecutors and Prohibition agents to go after the most sophisticated cartels. But then, in typically timid form, he told them not to do it at once but first to give him a report "as to the correctness of these assumptions."

For days, newspapers nationwide carried reports of alleged Capone sightings, as if he were Bigfoot in a silk suit. He was spotted arriving by yacht in suburban Evanston, Illinois; strolling the streets of downtown Toronto; stopping for gasoline at a filling station in Malabar, Florida; making calls from a hideout in Indiana; ducking for cover in Philadelphia; and sailing on a merchant marine vessel from Baltimore to Miami. Hoping to solve the mystery, Miami cops raided his Palm Island home on March 20. They arrested six men, including Al's younger brothers Umberto (a.k.a. Albert or Bites) and Amadeo (a.k.a. John or Mimi), on charges of vagrancy and possession of alcohol, but walked away embarrassed and without their real quarry.

The next day, perhaps to take the heat off his family, Capone told his lawyer, Thomas D. Nash, that he was ready to face the cops in Chicago. Nash dialed a telephone number he no doubt knew by heart: that of John Stege, Chicago's chief of detectives, who had been giving Capone the runaround and getting the Capone runaround for the better part of a decade, almost entirely to the gangster's advantage.

"Do you want Capone?" asked Nash.

"I have no process for his arrest," said Stege.

"Well, are you going to arrest him?"

"We are arresting all bootleggers, gangsters, and gunmen on sight. He is one of them and I suspect he will be brought in if any of our men see him."

"I'll bring him over," said Nash. "He wants to get it over with."

Soon after, Capone elbowed his way past a sidewalk full of oglers and into the lobby of police headquarters at Eleventh and State.

"When did you get in?" a reporter shouted at him.

"Day before yesterday," he answered.

"Did you pay your income tax this year?" asked another reporter.

Capone smiled, declining to answer that one, before adding, "Just a minute, boys; I'll be right out and then we can talk things over."

Capone and Stege chatted meaninglessly for some time, with the detective asking vague questions about the St. Valentine's Day Massacre and with Capone wondering innocently why Stege still insisted on blaming him for everything that ever happened in Chicago. When they were done, Stege still couldn't justify making an arrest. The best he could do was tell Capone he should think about leaving Chicago, permanently, that he wasn't wanted here, and that the cops had plans to make his life miserable—all of which Capone already knew. After that, Stege sent Capone to see U.S. Attorney George Johnson, and State's Attorney John Swanson, in case they had any desire to interrogate or arrest him. But neither of them had strong enough reason to keep Capone.

When he was done, Capone kept his word to the newspapermen, pulling up a chair to chat with them. "Well, fellows, what do you want to know?" he asked. When one of the reporters stared awkwardly at Capone's left hand, which was swathed in bandages, he explained, "I was roasting some ducks and I grabbed the oven instead of a duck." He loved cooking fancy food, he added.

"The sun's shining once more, boys," he said, getting up to leave. "I saw my wife just before I left Philadelphia; she looks wonderful. So does my boy. Now all I'm thinking of is being with them again. So long!"

————

Meanwhile, two more of Capone's lawyers were in court in Miami, asking a federal judge to protect their client from police harassment. Florida's governor, Doyle E. Carlton, had telegraphed each of the state's sixty-seven sheriffs, ordering them to arrest Capone on sight if he entered the state. The lawyers insisted that the state had no authority to seize a citizen who had not been charged with a crime—and the judge agreed. He issued an injunction. Capone was free to return to his home in Miami.

That evening, once again showing his preference for female reporters, the boss sat down for a lengthy interview with the *Tribune*'s Genevieve Forbes Herrick, a graduate of Northwestern University's journalism school and one of the paper's "front-page girls," so called for her knack at landing big stories. Capone was back at his big mahogany desk, photos of George Washington and Big Bill Thompson smiling down upon him. "I never had a number," Capone began, referring to his prisoner number, "until they picked me up in the City of Brotherly Love for carrying a gun, and gave me a year, not for carrying a gun, but because my name is Capone. I'd never been indicted before. Why should I be? All I ever did was supply a demand that was pretty popular. Why, the very guys that make my trade good are the ones that yell the loudest about me." He paused and then added, "Some of our best judges use the stuff."

At one point Capone stopped to answer the jangling French telephone on his desk; the receiver looked like a child's toy in his sausagelike fingers. "Sure, this is the big fellow," he said into the mouthpiece. "Come on over." He returned the receiver to its cradle and went back to the interview. He spoke in a low voice and seemed to choose his words carefully.

"They talk to me about not being on the legitimate. Why, lady, *nobody's* on the legit. You know that and so do they. Your brother or your father gets in a jam, what do they do? Do you sit back and let him go over the road, without trying to help him? You'd be a yellow dog if you did. Nobody's really on the legit when it comes down to cases. You know that.

"Whatever I did in the jail, everybody was watching to see that Al Capone didn't get any favors. When I'd been there six months I came up for parole. I had a writ of relief, they call it, before the Supreme Court. It's even more important than a writ of habeas corpus. The judge is supposed to allow it or deny it, with reasons for what he does. If I'd been plain John Smith from Oshkosh, he'd have allowed it. All I did, you know, lady, was carry a gun."

He pressed a buzzer on his desk, and a door at the far end of the room opened. A young bodyguard came in.

"Please ask my wife and sister to come here," Capone said.

The door opened again and in walked Mae and Mafalda. Pleasantries were exchanged, and the two women left.

"Did you notice my wife's hair?" asked Al, alone again with the reporter.

"We had," wrote Herrick. "It was lustrous and fluffy."

"No, I mean the streak of gray," said Capone. "She's only twenty-eight, and she's got gray hair, just worrying. . . . I'm only thirty-one, and I've been blamed for crimes that happened as far back as the Chicago Fire."

He said he was particularly irked about being blamed for the death of his friend Frankie Yale, when everyone knew Capone was in Miami, not New York, at the time of the hit. Herrick summarized, "All he ever did, he reiterates, was to ply his trade. And if his trade was so popular that it brought him a home in Miami Beach and a reputation for giving one-hundred-dollar tips, that's the fault, he claims, of the customer, not the dealer. He is quite frank about it. His theme song is: 'All I ever did was sell beer and whiskey to our best people.' "

The same day, he gave another interview, this time to the *Chicago American*. "I'm not telling anybody how to run the country, but . . . I'm giving it to you straight out," he said. "If people did not want beer and wouldn't drink it, a fellow would be crazy for going around trying to sell it. I've seen gambling houses, in my travels, you understand, and I never saw anyone point a gun at a man and make him go in. I never heard of anyone being forced to go to a place to have some fun. I have read in the newspapers, though, of bank cashiers being put in cars, with pistols stuck in their ribs and taken to the bank where they had to open the vault for the fellow with the gun. It really looks like taking a drink was worse than robbing a bank. Maybe I'm wrong. Maybe it is."

"Do you blame the police, Al?" he was asked.

"No, I don't blame the police and I don't blame the state's attorney and I don't blame the government. They have the pressure put on them and they got to move, see? Everyone you meet has a different idea of what's poison. This fellow says it's beer. This dame says it's whiskey, the next bird says it's women, and some say it's gambling. How do I know? I only got my own idea."

The more he spoke, the more his legend grew, although by now it would have grown without his commentary. His name continued to appear in newspaper stories all over the world. His monicker became like a brand—Coca-Cola, Packard, Capone—instantly recognized and iconically American.

While Capone was sitting for his interview with the *American,* Adolphe Menjou, star of the films *The Three Musketeers* and *A Gentleman of Paris,* made a brief stop in Chicago. With but a few hours to spend in the city, the world-renowned actor stepped off his train and asked, "Where can I find Al Capone? I want to meet him."

In South Dakota, the president of the Rapid City Chamber of Commerce sent word that if Capone continued to feel unwelcome in Chicago and Miami, he would be greeted with open arms in Rapid City, "where the stranger is not judged by the reports of his past record." Capone replied thanks, but no thanks.

In Monticello, Iowa, when voters went to the polls on April 1 to elect a mayor, there was only one candidate on the ballot, the incumbent, B. E. First. But that didn't stop fifty Monticellans, in a coordinated effort to attract publicity for their small town, from writing in the name of another candidate: Al Capone.

In Miami, Al's brother Albert was arrested on a charge of vagrancy while playing golf, which prompted Will Rogers to send a letter to the editor of the *New York Times.* It read, "A vagrant is a man that has no visible means of support. If they start enforcing that rule it will mean the death of golf. Maybe they searched him and he didn't have either a flask, or a gun. That would constitute vagrancy with a former Chicago resident."

In New York, at the annual meeting of the Eastern Osteopathic Association, Dr. C. G. Gaddis pronounced that Capone's life of crime was directly attributable to poor spinal alignment.

In China, said Chu Chiang-ling, director of the Richfield Oil Company, "we have our bandits . . . but the Chicago bandits and gangsters, especially Al Capone, seem to hog most of the publicity. Capone is as well known in China as Genghis Khan. But while we take our bad men as a matter of course and quietly behead them on the execution grounds, Chicago gangsters seem to be immune."

In Java and Burma, Major General Milton J. Foreman, a hero of the Spanish-American War, discovered that Illinois was no longer renowned exclusively as the Land of Lincoln. "[T]he name of Al Capone is on everyone's tongue," he said. "The Scarface is as well known in the Orient as it is here. People the world over believe that they would be shot down by machine guns five minutes after their arrival in Chicago."

And back home in Chicago, the famous preacher Billy Sunday vowed "to do my level best to give Al Capone and his gang of cutthroats the hot end of the poker" as he began a series of temperance revival meetings in the Loop.

On April 17, 1930, about three weeks after his extended interview with the *Tribune,* Capone sat down for another chat, this time with agents from the Bureau of Internal Revenue, at the bureau's office in Chicago. C. W. Herrick, the agent in charge of Chicago operations, led the conversation. Interestingly, Frank Wilson was not present, although years later, while composing his memoirs, he claimed to have been in the room. Perhaps Wilson was left out of the meeting because the feds wanted to protect his anonymity, or perhaps he attended a later meeting. Capone was accompanied by his new attorney, Lawrence P. Mattingly, who had been hired specifically for his expertise in tax cases.

Herrick began by laying out the rules: "Now, Mr. Capone, just so we all understand the situation, you and Mr. Mattingly are here in an effort to clean up your income tax liability. I want to say this, in order that there may be no misunderstanding, that any statement you make here will naturally be the subject of such investigation and verification as we can make; that is, in the nature of income or anything of that sort; and I think it is only fair to say to you that any statements which are made here could be used against you, would probably be used. I want you to know your rights."

Mattingly replied that Capone would cooperate as best he could without admitting any liability. He also said that once the session was over, he might be willing to provide information off the record about his client's tax liability to help negotiate a settlement. With that, the questioning of Capone began:

"What records have you of your income, Mr. Capone?" Herrick asked. "Do you keep any records?"

"No," he said. "I never did."

"Any checking account?"

"No, sir."

"Do you own any property in your own name?"

"No, sir."

"How long, Mr. Capone, have you enjoyed a large income?"

"I never had much of an income, a large income."

Another agent asked: "Have you ever filed income tax returns?"

"No."

"For the years mentioned [1926 to 1929], did you buy or sell any real estate?"

"No."

"Did you furnish any money to purchase real estate which was placed in the name of others?"

"I would rather let my lawyer answer that question."

Mattingly said Capone provided his wife the money to buy a home in Miami in 1928. She paid $10,000 in cash and took a $30,000 mortgage.

"What was the source of the money that you used to make your cash payment?"

"I would rather let my lawyer answer that question."

But Mattingly didn't want to touch that one, either.

"Did you purchase any securities during the years under consideration?"

"No, I never had anything like that."

"Did you have any brokerage accounts in your own name?"

"No."

"Did you have any brokerage accounts under an assumed name?"

"No."

"Did your wife or relatives have any brokerage accounts or did they purchase any securities?"

"I would rather not answer that question."

And so it proceeded, with Capone answering "no" or that he would rather not say to a long list of questions: When money was transferred to you in Miami, where did it come from? How much have you spent on attorneys during the years in question? What's your net worth? Do you own any race horses? Any canceled checks? Any safe deposit boxes? Does your wife have any safe deposit boxes? Ever done business under an alias? Do you have a financial interest in the Hawthorne dog-racing operation?

The only "yes" came when the revenue agent asked Capone if he completed most of his financial transactions with cash. And when asked where he kept all his cash for all those years, Capone replied, "Carried it on my person." (Later, when Capone's testimony was made public, the writer Damon Runyon quipped, "He must have had plenty of room on his person.")

The meeting ended. Mattingly offered to arrange a session in which he would provide the agents an estimate of his client's income, in hopes of negotiating a settlement. He asked the agents if it could wait until after Easter, and they said that would be fine. In fact, though, for reasons not clear, it would take Mattingly six months to come up with an estimate of Capone's income. He may have recognized the quandary he and his client faced: If he filed late returns or offered to make restitution on unpaid taxes, he would essentially be admitting delinquency. His only other option was an across-the-board denial of income and a principled assertion that the government wasn't entitled to a dime. But given the high style in which Capone had lived these past few years, such an argument would have been difficult to sustain. The investigators still didn't have much evidence against Capone, and great doubt remained in almost every government office whether they would ever build a winnable case. Yet government memorandums suggest that the agents were pleased, for now, merely to have engaged with Capone and his attorney. The more they talked, the more likely Capone would give them something they could use. They had cast their net, and the big fish had swum in. The trick was to see if they could land him.

PUBLIC ENEMY NUMBER ONE

On April 24, 1930, President Hoover repeated his vow to hold down taxes during this period of economic turbulence; Henry Ford promised to fire any and all employees showing up for work reeking of alcohol; a British medical journal urged England to ban the sale of the liqueur absinthe; and British troops in Peshawar, India, opened fire on supporters of Gandhi's independence movement, killing twenty. But the biggest story in Chicago's newspapers—and in countless papers nationwide—was about Al Capone. And this time he *really* didn't do anything.

The story was the brainchild of Frank J. Loesch, president of the Chicago Crime Commission and a member of President Hoover's national commission on criminal justice reform. Loesch was almost eighty, and the older he got the more worked up he became about gangsters. Sometimes he became so steamed that he couldn't keep the lid on his bigotry. "The real Americans are not gangsters," he said that spring in a lecture at Princeton University. "Recent immigrants and the first generation of Jews and Italians are the chief offenders, with the Jews furnishing the brains and the Italians the brawn."

Back in Chicago, he went to work on a press release that would prove to be his most memorable achievement. Issued on Crime Commission stationery, the press release named the twenty-eight "most prominent and well-known and notorious gangsters" in Chicago. These men, he urged, ought not be treated as citizens entitled to a fair administration of justice. Instead, they must "be relentlessly pursued in every legal way as aliens, tax evaders, inmates of gambling and disorderly houses, and vagrants." They must be hounded and harassed, Loesch said, until every last one was removed from society. Loesch listed the names alphabetically, beginning with Joe Aiello, a suspect in the Tony Lombardo murder, and continuing through to Jack Zuta, one of Capone's brothel and casino operators. Al and Ralph Capone both made the list, not surprisingly, as did Jack Guzik, Jack McGurn, Bugs Moran, and William White. Each name was accompanied by a short biography listing criminal achievements. Oddly, Frank Nitti didn't make the list. The reason he decided to name names, said Loesch, was "to keep the light of publicity on Chicago's most prominent and notorious gangsters to the end that they may be under constant observation by law enforcing authorities."

There was no real news in the pronouncement, but Loesch understood that news editors love lists the way personal-injury lawyers love slippery floors. And in this instance they especially loved the name Loesch had chosen for his list. These twenty-eight villains, he declared, were Public Enemies.

Only the *New York Times* recognized the emptiness of the phrase and the questionable ethics of Loesch's tactic. Chicago seemed to be giving up on any meaningful prosecution of its criminals, the paper editorialized, and settling for harassment instead. "The Capones and Morans are not within the law and not outside the law," the *Times* said in an April 25 editorial. "They dwell in a twilight zone where the courts cannot function but where the police department may harry them and keep them moving."

One Chicago journalist, Robert Hardy Andrews, griped to his editor that the Public Enemy list was hokum, and his editor seemed to agree, but that didn't keep them from running with the story. "Poverty wasn't a Public Enemy," wrote Andrews, a reporter for the *Chicago Daily News*, in his memoir. "Joblessness wasn't, or homelessness, or human desperation. Al Capone was PUBLIC ENEMY NUMBER ONE, in bigger type than ARMISTICE SIGNED! on November 11, 1918." What Andrews neglected to mention, or didn't know, is that Loesch probably got the idea for his Public Enemies list from the pages of the *Daily News*. Two months earlier, it was the *News* that first printed a list of prominent gangsters, along with detailed accounts of their activities, and declared, "The following article tells names and places so plainly that if officials decide to confront gangsters with intelligent determination, they will have no trouble in finding those public enemies."

Ultimately, though, it didn't matter who coined the term. Nor did it matter who was first to dub Capone "Public Enemy Number One." A resonant catchphrase had entered the lexicon. The next year, James Cagney and Warner Bros. released a hit gangster movie that made the life of crime seem fearsome, romantic, and sexy. They called the movie *Public Enemy,* and it was a huge sensation, further cementing the phrase in the American consciousness. A Public Enemy, even a raffishly charming one like Cagney, was something much more than a thug. A Public Enemy was a predator, a force for chaos, a menace, a bogeyman, a renegade, a threat to democracy. All his life, Capone had striven to portray himself as an ambitious son of immigrants who happened to be engaged in a criminal life, a businessman whose business happened to be illegal. Now brilliantly, Loesch had struck back with one deft phrase, reminding Americans still sobering up from the Roaring Twenties that traditional moral values remained in effect and that there were grave dangers to society when men such as Capone stepped so boldly outside the law.

———

Capone didn't need a Public Enemy list to know he was persona non grata in Miami. After his meeting with the Bureau of Revenue agents, he had left Chicago and headed for his Palm Island home, just as he had said he would. Traveling with him was his nephew Ralph Capone Jr., whose father was on trial in Chicago at the time for tax evasion. Capone and the boy, who had just turned thirteen, stepped off the train in Hollywood, Florida, one station shy of Miami. The date was April 20, 1930. It was a clear day, the sky bright as chrome, the air hot and humid. They were met at the station by the attorneys who had worked in advance of his arrival to assure that Capone would not face immediate arrest. Also at the station were a gaggle of reporters—their presence by now as certain as the train itself wherever and whenever he traveled. Capone tried to give them as little news as possible, saying, "I am here for a rest, which I think I deserve." He added that he planned to stay at least two weeks.

After the drive from the train station to his home, he took his son and his nephew for a ride on his speedboat. Later that day, a newspaper photographer snapped a picture of Capone in slippers, pajamas, and striped robe as he cast a line off the deck of a boat.

Two days later, Capone and seven other men—including Harry Read, city editor of the *Chicago Evening American*—flew to Cuba and checked into the Sevilla Biltmore Hotel in downtown Havana, where they stayed for a week. While they were gone, Florida governor Doyle E. Carlton, describing Capone as a "public nuisance" and calling the Palm Island estate a harbor for "all classes of criminals and desperate characters," petitioned a judge in Miami for authority to padlock the home and deport its famous occupant. "He will not establish headquarters in Florida," said the governor. "His element will not take root here. . . . Those who wish to lend aid and comfort to such an element have the privilege. For me there is but one position and in this I expect the support of every thinking, self-respecting citizen whose first interest is the welfare of the state."

The court denied the governor's request, but that did little to ensure Capone's tranquility. A week after his return from Cuba, Capone, his brother John, and two other men were stopped by detectives as they motored along Biscayne Boulevard in downtown Miami. It would seem that the cops had decided to ignore the court order protecting Capone from indiscriminate arrest. None of the men was armed. Capone was reported to have more than $1,100 cash in his pocket.

"If you agree to clear out of the state we'll turn you loose," said the city's director of public safety. "If you don't, our police will pick you up every time you show your face within the limits of the city." Capone's answer, according to the *Herald and Examiner,* his least favorite paper, was a snarl. Five days later, while watching a boxing match at the American Legion Hall, he was detained again by Miami cops, and this time spent seventeen hours in jail. Again, neither Capone nor any of his men had weapons in their possession. Then, a few days later, as he returned to the American Legion building for another night of boxing, he was arrested once more. That night at the station, he smoked a cigar and chatted with cops, taking it in stride.

In the weeks ahead, Capone and his lawyers would spend day after day in court. Capone would win most of the rulings, with judges declaring that Miami's cops had been arresting him without cause. But after each court ruling, Miami officials would find a new reason to haul him back in. At the same time, some of Miami Beach's most prominent citizens, including Carl G. Fisher, who just ten years earlier developed Miami Beach from a largely unpopulated barrier island, and the tire manufacturer Harvey S. Firestone, began meeting with city officials to request that the gate to Capone's home be padlocked and a guard stationed in front to keep him out.

If Capone had thoughts of returning to Chicago to escape the harassments in Miami, all he had to do was read the newspaper to see the storm developing on that front, too.

On June 16, 1930, his brother Ralph was sentenced to three years in the federal penitentiary at Leavenworth and fined $10,000 for income tax fraud. Testimony in the trial said that Ralph had deposited more than $1.8 million in the Pinkert State Bank over a period of six years, using his own name in some instances and his alias James Carroll in others, to endorse checks. Ralph said the money wasn't his—that it was gambling dough, that it flowed into and out of the bank when bets were made and paid off. He also claimed, quite accurately, that he had filed his tax returns with the assistance of a revenue agent. He had the impression when he filed, he said, that everything had been settled to the government's satisfaction. Indeed, in Ralph's defense it should be noted that despite the vast sums moving into and out of his account, the government still couldn't prove that the $1.8 million was his. In the end, they claimed he owed a mere $6,000 in back taxes. It was enough to put him away.

"I can't understand this at all," Ralph said upon receiving the sentence.

Over the next few days, going for a knockout blow, the feds raided more than two dozen Capone-controlled stills and speakeasies, many of them tiny operations based in bungalow basements, but all told, said to produce an impressive six thousand gallons of hooch a month. After years of missteps and delays, U.S. Attorney George Johnson had finally found a tactic that seemed to work: He would use Prohibition agents to harass the bootleggers and to cut off their income, but he would give up on trying to convict the gangsters for selling booze. It was too difficult to prove, and besides, jurors were almost always drinking men and disinclined to convict. But tax law was different: A person paid or he didn't. And jurors, who paid their taxes, had no qualms about sending cheats to jail. It wasn't sexy. It wouldn't make the best headlines. It might not have seemed, to some, as if the punishment perfectly fit the crime. But Johnson had never been much concerned with sexiness or headlines, and he was happy to settle for any kind of punishment at all. In Washington, President Hoover urged Attorney General William Mitchell to make something happen in the Capone case. "We are being criticized very severely around centers like Chicago for failure to do anything in the larger conspiracies," he wrote.

Getting Ralph Capone was one thing. Getting Al was another. Johnson knew that Al had been careful. He'd taken great care not to leave a paper trail. It wouldn't be easy, but Johnson was beginning to see how it might be done.

In Miami, Capone was under more pressure than ever. In May, the City Council passed an ordinance intended to give police more reliable cause for putting him away. The new ordinance defined as a vagrant "any person having visible means of support acquired by unlawful means or methods, or any person who is dangerous to the peace or safety of the city of Miami, or any person or persons known or reputed to be crooks, gangsters, or hijackers." Or, it might as well have said, any person named Al Capone. Violators were subject to a $500 fine and sixty days in jail.

Soon after, on a Saturday afternoon, Al and Mae hosted a party for fifty of Sonny's schoolmates. Capone, clearly anxious, insisted that the children bring notes from their parents saying they had permission to visit his home. The Capones decorated the lawn with balloons, encouraged the kids to splash in the big pool, and served fried chicken, soda pop, and cake. Ten days later, Capone held a "dinner musical" at his home, hosting fifty businessmen and leading citizens. Where once Capone's guests would have bragged to the press about their invitations, this time the list of invitees was not announced. It was a shrewd tactical move on Capone's part. Losing the public relations war, he tried to fight back by showing some of the city's elite that he was just like them: a businessman, a father, a property owner, a guy who just wanted a little peace. But the net was tightening anyway.

Frank Wilson continued pounding the streets, looking for people who knew details about Capone's business dealings. No point in hanging around the Revenue Bureau office, which smelled from cigar smoke and sweat and wasn't much bigger than a janitor's closet. Better to get out.

Somewhere in the course of his canvassing, Wilson heard that Capone had had a falling out with the *Tribune*'s ace crime reporter, Alfred "Jake" Lingle. In a city full of great reporters, Lingle might well have been the greatest of them all. He was certainly the best known among the city's cops and hoodlums. On June 1, 1930, Wilson met with editors of the *Trib,* telling them that he wanted to arrange an interview with Lingle. The editors said they would help set it up.

Jake Lingle wasn't handsome. He wasn't big or strong. He had a long, pale face with slivers for eyes, wispy eyebrows, chubby cheeks, and no discernible chin. You could look right at him and miss him completely if not for his surprisingly snazzy accessories, like his expensive snap-brim fedora, flashy cuff links, and diamond-studded belt buckle. Lingle grew up in a blue-collar neighborhood on the city's West Side. After finishing grammar school, he found work as an errand boy for a surgical supply house. In his spare time he liked to chase fire engines and hang out where cops and firefighters hung out. He learned to drink and gamble and curse. He had a "blistering tongue," as one of his colleagues put it, "and a blunt, contemptuous way of dealing with people," but he didn't bullshit anybody, and men—especially tough men—liked his company.

In 1912, when he was twenty-one, Lingle went to work as an office boy at the *Trib,* where editors quickly concluded that his gift for gab and his facile way of making friends would serve him well on the street. For the next eighteen years, Lingle chased fire trucks and police cars and hung around bars and racetracks and got paid for it. One of the beat cops he came to know well was William F. Russell. The men played golf, and went to the races, the fights, and the theater together. As Russell rose through the ranks of the department, eventually becoming commissioner in 1928, Lingle became the best-connected reporter in town. Gangsters talked to him knowing that he might put in a good word for them with the commissioner, and the commissioner talked to him knowing that he might pass along certain messages to the gangsters. But Lingle was no bootlicker. Once, when a hoodlum asked Lingle to help arrange police protection for a new speakeasy, Lingle barked, "For [expletive] sake, don't bother me with your [expletive] troubles! Go ahead and open it if you want to, but you'll probably get pushed over [raided] as soon as you do. Now get out of my way, bum!"

Not every gangster respected him, but most reckoned with him. Before Capone, Lingle knew Torrio and O'Banion and Weiss, and before those men he knew Big Jim Colosimo. He was as much a part of the Chicago speakeasy scene as ashtrays. Yet for all his knowledge and his great nose for news, Lingle never wrote a word for the *Trib*. He was strictly a legman. He stuck to the streets. When a gangster was killed, he would phone the office and, sometimes off the top of his head, dictate the victim's biography, with a complete list of arrests and achievements. Then he would explain to the editor on the desk who'd been at war with whom and what string of events had likely stoked the shooting. Back in 1926, when Capone spent a night in jail awaiting a hearing on the murder of Billy McSwiggin, it was Lingle who had brought him dinner. When Capone wound up in jail in Philadelphia, the *Trib* put Lingle on a train and told him to bring back an interview.

Lingle was married to his childhood sweetheart, Helen Sullivan, although he waited until he was thirty to marry her. They had two children. He had a house on the West Side and a summer home at Long Beach in Indiana. And when he wasn't at one of those two houses, he was living the bachelor's life at the Stevens Hotel. When anyone asked how he maintained such a lifestyle on a $65-dollar-a-week salary, Lingle said he'd been left a fair chunk of money when his father had died, and another fair chunk when an uncle died, and that he'd invested the money wisely in the stock market—at least until the market crash of 1929, in which he admitted losing some but hardly all of his fortune. From the way he bet at the track—sometimes putting a grand on a single race—it certainly looked as if he still had plenty of money. He liked long shots, and he liked bragging when they came through for him. When he lost, he never said a word. That was Jake Lingle: a guy who knew when to talk and when to keep his mouth shut.

When Frank Wilson dropped by the *Trib* to see about talking to Lingle, he hoped that this would be one of those instances in which Lingle might be persuaded to gab. The reporter wasn't in the office, as usual. Wilson left word for him.

Eight days went by and Wilson and Lingle never met.

On June 9, 1930, the newsman woke late and got dressed. At noon, he left his room at the Stevens for lunch in the hotel's coffee shop. He stopped by *Tribune* Tower, just north of the Loop, where Michigan Avenue met the Chicago River, and chatted briefly with his editor, telling him he was planning to spend the day trying to track down Bugs Moran. In truth, he was planning to spend the day at the Washington Park racetrack, although he was as likely to find Moran there as anywhere else. Leaving the *Trib,* he walked toward the suburban station of the Illinois Central Railroad, to catch the one-thirty train to Homewood. He wore a straw boater and puffed a cigar. Reaching the Chicago Public Library at Michigan Avenue and Randolph Street, he stopped at a newsstand to buy a *Racing Form.* When an acquaintance shouted that Lingle should be sure to bet on a horse named Hy Schneider in the third race, he waved and said he would. Then he ducked into a crowded tunnel that would take him under Michigan Avenue and over to the train station.

Lingle shuffled down the concrete stairs and headed toward the light at the eastern edge of the tunnel. He was halfway through when a man stepped up behind him, pulled a revolver from his pocket, and raised it to within a few inches of Lingle's head: *Bang!* The shot echoed terrifically. The cigar hit the floor first, followed by Lingle's face, and then the rest of his lifeless body.

A woman screamed. Everyone ran. A crimson puddle bloomed on the concrete around Lingle's right cheek, staining the collar of his jacket and shirt.

The killer stood briefly over the body and then took off—walking, not running—toward the eastern end of the tunnel. A few men, including a police officer, began to follow. The gunman emerged from the tunnel and paused, as if dazzled by the sunlight. Only then did he start to run: first through a busy intersection, then west on Randolph, north through one alley, west through another, south on Wabash, then back to Randolph, where he got lost in the crowd.

As gang killings go, this one was unusually bold. There had been no attempt at subterfuge and no camouflage. Witnesses were everywhere. Some said the killer looked like Sam Hunt, one of Capone's men, who had been arrested a week earlier after he'd dropped a golf bag containing a shotgun while fleeing the scene of a shooting. (The charges in that incident didn't stick, but the nickname did. Forevermore, he was "Golf Bag" Hunt.) The cops caught up with Hunt after the Lingle murder, but he convinced them he was innocent.

In all of his memos, Frank Wilson never suggested to his supervisors that Lingle might have died for talking—or just thinking about talking—to the feds. Still, it must have entered his mind. The Lingle killing made more news than any slaying since the St. Valentine's Day Massacre. Newspapers across the country were outraged, viewing it as an attack on democracy and freedom of the press. The *San Francisco Chronicle* called the murder a "warning that gangland has crossed the borderline and that every man, woman, and child in the community is in immediate peril." The *Illinois State Register* of Springfield called it a "crowning tragedy" that "ought to be tantamount to a declaration of war." The *Trib* offered a $25,000 reward for information leading to an arrest, the *Herald and Examiner* matched the offer, and the *Chicago Evening Post* chipped in $5,000.

Business officials and political leaders were enraged, too, because until now, the gangsters had confined their killing almost entirely to other gangsters. The governor of Michigan called Lingle's murder "a challenge from organized crime which must be squarely met" and offered to put Michigan police at Chicago's command. In Chicago, the police mobilized special gang-busting squads to raid every known vice den in the city. John Stege, the chief of detectives, bragged that each squad would be led by an officer with a talent for killing gangsters: "The commanders of the squads," said Stege, "are Lt. Frank Reynolds, who has killed eleven criminals; Lt. Al Booth, who has killed six; Lt. Walter Storms, who has killed five; Lt. William Cusack, who has killed four; Lt. Pat O'Connell, who has killed five; and Lt. Andy Barry, who has killed six. . . . I know these men will clean out the Loop and it is up to other squads and district police to keep the criminals running."

Commissioner Russell reminded the city's newsmen that he and Lingle had been bosom buddies. "I was fonder of him than I could be of my own son," the commissioner said.

A few days later, investigators got hold of the reporter's bank records. That changed everything. Everyone knew that reporters in general, and Lingle in particular, hardly qualified for sainthood. Everyone knew they palled around with sinister characters. Everyone knew they ran their own little rackets on the side—stroking an alderman with a favorable story in exchange for a streets-and-sanitation job for a brother-in-law, say, or accepting a case of whiskey in thanks for keeping a name out of a story. Almost everybody bent the rules of ethics from time to time. But Lingle had been bending, twisting, and tying them in knots.

For starters, he had shared a bank account with his most important legit source, Commissioner Russell. Together, they'd invested more than $20,000 in the stock market, running up huge gains and huge losses—especially losses, of late. It turned out that Lingle's father had left him only $500, his uncle only $1,150.

After wailing that his dead reporter had been a soldier on the front lines of the war for freedom in Chicago, *Tribune* publisher Robert C. Mc-Cormick pulled a U-turn and branded him an extortionist, a chiseler, and an aide to the kingpins of crime. In a personally written editorial, Mc-Cormick declared: "Alfred Lingle now takes a different character, one in which he was unknown to the management of the *Tribune.* . . . He was not, and could not have been, a great reporter." Now it appeared, wrote Mc-Cormick, "that Alfred Lingle was killed because he was using his *Tribune* position to profit from criminal operations and not because he was serving the *Tribune* as it thought he was."

Presumably the reward money was off the table.

The theory around town said that Lingle had run afoul of some North Side gangsters, and in particular Jack Zuta, who, along with Julian "Potatoes" Kaufman, ran a posh gambling joint at 621 Waveland Avenue, near Wrigley Field. The gambling place had been padlocked in the crackdown that followed the St. Valentine's Day Massacre, but Zuta and Kaufman were preparing for a grand reopening. Lingle supposedly had offered to use his influence to keep the cops away. His price: $15,000, paid up front. There were questions about Lingle's relationship to Capone, too. Some friends of the dead reporter recalled rumors that Lingle's diamond-encrusted belt buckle had been a gift from the big fellow—which seemed plausible considering Capone's fondness for that type of glittery accessory. But for the most part, Capone, still in Miami, kept his name out of the Lingle stories—until a reporter came knocking and, as usual, Capone couldn't resist the temptation to gab.

John T. Rogers, star of the *St. Louis Post-Dispatch* and the man who'd been slipping information to Frank Wilson, had been among the first to report on Lingle's underworld ties. Now Rogers's chief rival in St. Louis, Harry T. Brundidge of the *St. Louis Star,* began digging into the story. Brundidge reported that many of Chicago's leading reporters maintained unholy alliances with gangsters, paying them for information, or taking money from them in exchange for favorable coverage. "Only the dumb wits in the newspaper game in Chicago are without a racket," he wrote. Then, without invitation, Brundidge showed up at the front door of Capone's home on Palm Island, seeking confirmation of his theory. It was ten at night on July 11 when the reporter introduced himself and asked for an interview.

"Come on in," Capone said.

Brundidge was charmed, describing his host as "intelligent . . . happy go lucky . . . affable." He noted the gangster's "dark, kindly face," and "big sparkling eyes." If one didn't know the man's history, wrote Brundidge, one would be inclined to think him "a playful, lovable chap, as harmless as a big St. Bernard dog." Capone began by flattering the reporter with the suggestion that he'd been reading his work.

"You seem to have raised merry hell in Chicago," Capone said.

After a tour of the property, the men pulled up chairs on the patio.

"What brings you here?" Capone asked.

Brundidge said he wanted to know about Lingle.

"Why ask me?" came the reply. "The Chicago police know who killed him."

What about the dead man's diamond belt buckle? he asked.

"I gave it to him," he said. "He was my friend."

How many more like Lingle are in the Chicago newspaper racket?

"Phooey!" said Capone. "Don't ask."

Brundidge asked.

"How many newspapermen have you had on your payroll?"

"Plenty," Capone shot back.

He leaned over and put his big left arm on the reporter's shoulder. "Listen, Harry," he said. "I like your face. Let me give you a hot tip. Lay off Chicago and the money-hungry reporters. . . . You can't buck it. . . . No one man will ever realize just how big it is, so lay off."

Brundidge said he was going to quote Capone saying that.

"If you do, I'll deny it," he promised.

The Lingle case dragged on, unsolved. Russell and Stege were both forced to resign from the police force—as much for their ties to Lingle (Stege had vacationed with the crime reporter) as for their incompetence in solving his murder. Nearly everyone believed that Jack Zuta had ordered the hit, but no one managed to identify the gunman. On July 1, someone took a shot at Zuta while he was in his car, but the shots missed their mark. A streetcar motorman was killed and a night watchman was wounded by stray bullets. Zuta, no dummy, hotfooted it out of town.

A month later, on July 28, Capone returned to Chicago, announcing that the heat in Florida had become too much to take. This time he meant the actual temperature, not the pressure from police. A few days later, he threw a party for a hundred friends at the Hotel Western in Cicero.

Several hours after reporters in Chicago learned of Capone's return, news of a bigger story broke: At the Lake View Hotel on Upper Nemahbin Lake, near Delafield, Wisconsin, gunmen finally caught up with Zuta. The roly-poly Zuta had been passing his days in a fishing boat and his nights in a dance hall, phoning back to Chicago several times a day to check on his business interests. A few couples were out on the dance floor when Zuta turned to the jukebox and prepared to drop a nickel in its slot. That's when he heard footsteps. He turned around in time to catch a bullet in the teeth. The men and women on the dance floor dashed for the door. Just to make sure their work was done, the gunmen poured fifteen more bullets into his head and body.

Not long after Zuta's assassination, Capone sent word to the state's attorney's office that he wanted to talk.

"Here's what I want to tell you and I won't be long about it," Capone told one prosecutor. "I can't stand the gaff of these raids and pinches. If it's going to keep up, I'll have to pack up and get out of Chicago."

"So far as I can tell you," answered the investigator, "the gaff is on for keeps."

Capone swore that he hadn't killed Lingle, nor ordered the hit. But with a little snooping around, he said, he might be able to find out who had been responsible. Capone said he'd heard that Lingle had taken thirty grand from Zuta and other North Siders to help open a dog-racing operation at Chicago Stadium and to keep the cops off the track operators' backs. When their bid for the track failed and the cops continued raiding Zuta's North Side dives, Lingle took the blame for it—"and I think that's why he was pushed," Capone said.

Capone was so eager to help the cops find Lingle's killer that he told the investigator he would go to Bugs Moran and Joe Aiello to see if they would cooperate in the investigation. But he never did.

Less than two weeks later, on October 23, 1930, Aiello was coming out of a friend's house at the corner of Kolmar and West End avenues on the far West Side when machine guns fired from a building across the street. He turned and tried to run but didn't get far. Thirty-five steel-tipped bullets swiss-cheesed his body as he collapsed and died behind a small hedge of bushes.

———

By now, Capone's every move was scrutinized. All four of his closest allies—Ralph Capone, Jack Guzik, Frank Nitti, and Jack McGurn—were in trouble. Ralph Capone had been convicted on income tax evasion; Guzik had been arrested and awaited trial on the same charge; Nitti also was under investigation for failure to pay the tax collector; and McGurn was free on bond while awaiting an appeal to his conviction for gun possession. None of them had turned rat. That was the good news. But it was plain to see that the cops and feds were pushing hard. Even the most law-abiding of the Capone brothers—twenty-one-year-old Matt, who told police he was enrolled at Villanova University (school records indicate he never attended)—was held for questioning one day for no apparent reason.

Capone was walking a tightrope, and the feds were shaking both ends, hoping he'd slip. And yet he had shown time and again that he had better balance than other bootleggers. It wasn't necessarily that he was smarter or more powerful than the others, but he had two things going for him: He'd always avoided doing business in his own name, and he'd always been lucky.

Just before Thanksgiving came an example of his fortune: His baby sister, Mafalda, age nineteen, announced to the family that she would soon be married. Mafalda was big-boned, bottom-heavy, and heavily browed. But she had a lovely smile, startling violet eyes, and a sunny personality that brightened rooms. And having learned at her mother's side, Mafalda was a cook of almost magical talent. The groom-to-be was a twenty-three-year-old movie theater projectionist named John Maritote, brother of the well-known gangster Frank Maritote, a.k.a. Frank Diamond, one of the so-called Public Enemies and a longtime Capone lieutenant. The *Trib* reported that the marriage had been arranged and that big brother Al had promised the couple a $50,000 dowry, which "should provide a powerful stimulant in furthering the cause of young love." But Frank's granddaughter Regina Maritote says the Maritotes were frequent Sunday-dinner guests at the Capone home and that Mafalda and John Maritote had known each other most of their lives. Either way, Al and the rest of the Capones were delighted with Mafalda's match.

Capone still hoped to make his tax case go away. On September 20, 1930, his lawyer, Lawrence Mattingly, submitted a letter to an Internal Revenue agent in charge of the Chicago office, offering to negotiate a settlement. The letter read like the sketch of an income tax return, noting that Capone was thirty-one, with a wife and twelve-year-old son. Since 1922, it reported, he had been the primary supporter of his mother, his sister, Mafalda, and his brother (Matt). Prior to 1925, Capone was a salaried employee of Johnny Torrio, the letter continued, making no more than $75 a week. Beginning in 1926, he became a principal in a three-man partnership, but given that he had no capital to invest in the partnership for all of 1926 and most of 1927, his returns were small. For 1928 and 1929, Capone received a sixth of the organization's profits. During this period, his bodyguards were employees of the organization, not paid directly by Capone. In conclusion, Mattingly listed his estimates of Capone's annual income. For 1926, he wrote, "I am of the opinion that his taxable income . . . might be fairly fixed at not to exceed $26,000." For 1927, he estimated his client's income at no more than $40,000. And for 1928 and 1929, he said, Capone made no more than $100,000 per year.

It was an intriguing admission. The government claimed that Capone made millions, not hundreds of thousands, but in truth they had no clue. It was all guesswork, thanks to Capone's reliance on cash and his intentionally poor recordkeeping. But $100,000 was hardly chicken feed. In 1929, the last year of the economic boom, only 14,700 Americans reported incomes greater than $100,000. Even Babe Ruth, far and away the best-paid player in all of baseball, made a mere $70,000. Thomas John Watson, president of International Business Machines, made $60,000 in salary plus $258,000 in bonuses. Movie producer Irving Thalberg earned a straight salary of $200,000 from MGM. The tax rate on such a fortune was 24 percent, which meant Mattingly was essentially admitting that Capone owed as much as $48,000 in taxes for 1928 and 1929 alone.

By putting numbers on the page, Mattingly gambled. He tried to remind the revenue agents that his estimates were not an admission of income, that he was operating on the assumption that statements made in pursuit of a settlement would not be used against his client in court. But the feds had other ideas. They might never know if Capone made a hundred grand or a million, but at least they had a base number with which to work and an admission—albeit a tentative one—that Capone had in fact shirked his duty to pay taxes.

They had no intention of letting him negotiate a payment.

"THERE IS NO FRIENDSHIP AMONG HOODLUMS"

Frank Wilson was frustrated. Two years on the Capone case, and what did he have to show for it? A few promising leads, not much more. He knew that Capone hadn't paid taxes, but he had no idea how much he *should* have paid. At this point, if pressed, he probably couldn't prove that Capone had income of even $5,000 a year. Wilson knew that Capone's annual underwear budget probably amounted to more than $5,000, but it hardly mattered. He needed proof of income. He didn't have it, and at this point he wasn't sure he would ever get it.

"Some of the boys say I sweat ice water," he wrote years later. "After two years, I was in a sweat all right."

George E. Q. Johnson was sweating, too, perhaps even more than Wilson. At a meeting with the Justice Department in Washington on September 3, 1930, Attorney General William Mitchell announced that he would be sending one of his special assistants, William J. Froelich, to Chicago to oversee the investigation of Capone. The bosses were running out of patience. They were no longer certain that Johnson and his small staff could handle the task they'd been assigned.

Johnson took it as a slap in the face, which is probably how it had been intended. After the meeting, Johnson returned to Chicago, where he wrote a long reply to the attorney general, defending his performance and practically begging Mitchell not to undermine his authority. In response to the suggestion that he couldn't get the job done on his own, Johnson wrote, "[M]y reply respectfully is that I am quite able to do this, as I have an office that is well organized." Johnson, with startling bluntness, confessed in his letter to Mitchell that he was concerned with how the new man's arrival would be perceived. The newspapers would surely pick up on it, he complained. "It does not increase either the prestige nor the dignity of the United States Attorney," he wrote, "to assign a special assistant to the Attorney General to supervise or aid his work." He continued, "I frankly state that I do not see the purpose of having this done."

But Mitchell was unpersuaded. Froelich was on the way.

––––––––

Late one night, long after his colleagues had gone home, Frank Wilson sat around the office looking over notes, wondering if he'd missed anything. The more he stared at the files, the more certain he became that he hadn't missed a thing. A man like Wilson seldom did. He got up to put the folders away, but in so doing accidentally bumped the file cabinet shut. He didn't have the key. So now he had to find another place to put his papers. Though he was tired and perturbed, he wasn't about to get sloppy and leave his work materials unprotected. He found an open file cabinet in a nearby storeroom, opened a drawer to see if it had space, and pulled out some dusty envelopes. In the back of one drawer he found a heavy package tied in brown paper. Curious, he snipped the strings, revealing three accounting ledgers, black with red corners. He thumbed through one of them and saw column headings that read: *Bird cage, 21, Craps, Faro, Roulette, and Horse bets.* He took the books back to his desk and began scanning them. Quickly, he concluded that he was looking at the ledgers for a big gambling operation, with net profits that probably ran to more than $500,000 over a twenty-four-month period.

He soon learned that the books had been seized from the Ship, formerly known as the Hawthorne Smoke Shop, one of the biggest gambling houses in Cicero, during a raid in 1926. They covered part of 1924, all of 1925, and part of 1926.

"Here was a record of *income,*" wrote Wilson, adding his own italics to a magazine article he coauthored years later.

But could he tie the income to Capone?

On one page he saw a list of payouts:

$6,537.42 went to "Town," presumably meaning local police and elected officials.

"Ralph" and "Pete"—most likely Ralph Capone and Pete Penovich—each got $1,634.35.

Then came four payments of $5,720.22 each: to "Frank," "Lou," "D," and "J&A." Frank was almost certainly Frank Pope. Lou was probably Louis Alterie. D could have been Dominick "Mops" Volpe, one of Capone's men. J&A might have stood for Jack and Al, as in Guzik and Capone. But the initials were of secondary importance because, near the top of that page, Wilson read the followed note: "Frank Paid $17,500 for Al."

Wilson already knew about the Ship. Eddie O'Hare had told him about the place and had told him that Fred Ries worked there as the head cashier. If anybody could explain the notations in the ledger, it was he. Ries was bald, middle-aged, and wore horn-rimmed glasses. The pallor of his skin suggested that racetracks were his only source of sunshine and fresh air. When Wilson caught up with him, he was hiding out in St. Louis. Ries wouldn't talk, so Wilson threw him in a jail in Danville, Illinois, a small town 140 miles south of Chicago and asked the judge to sit on the paperwork so word that Ries had been detained would not get back to Chicago. Wilson didn't know what Capone's men would do: Bail him out and kill him, or just kill him in jail.

After forty-eight hours in a roach-infested cell, Ries, "who feared nothing in this world—except maybe little insects," according to Wilson, buckled and agreed to talk. At last Wilson had a source with details on the organization, a source who knew where the money had gone. On October 20, 1930, Ries signed an affidavit saying that he had taken at least $224,000 in profits earned at the Ship and exchanged them for cashier's checks, signing for the checks with the fictitious name J. C. Dunbar, at the Pinkert State Bank in Cicero. He said he'd given the cashier's checks to members of "the syndicate" who owned the establishment—Pete Penovich, Frank Nitti, Jack Guzik, Ralph Capone, and Al Capone. Capone didn't visit the Ship often, said Ries, and didn't seem too familiar with the details of the operation, although every so often he would complain that the joint ought to be churning more profits. In those instances, Ries would tell Capone that they could easily boost their profit margins if they weren't forced to employ so many of the crime king's shiftless pals, such as the washed-up prizefighter known as Knockout Brown, a Greek with a face as flat and triangular as an iron. Brown sold cigars in the front of the shop but served no real purpose other than entertaining customers with stories of his ancient glories.

Wilson took no chances. He sneaked Ries to Chicago and had him testify before a grand jury. There was no such thing yet as a federal witness protection program, so Wilson booked Ries on a trip to South America, paid for by a group of Chicago businessmen who called themselves the Secret Six. These were some of the same men who had gone to Washington to beg for the president's help in cleaning up their town. While they called themselves the Secret Six, their constant quest for publicity suggested they were not terribly interested in secrecy, only in the aura surrounding it. They were led by Robert Isham Randolph, president of the Chicago Association of Commerce, who represented the group to the press. The others were Frank J. Loesch, part-time attorney and full-time crime crusader; George A. Paddock, a stockbroker and Crime Commission member; utilities tycoon Samuel Insull; Sears, Roebuck, & Company president, Julius Rosenewald; and Edward E. Gore, an accountant and Crime Commission leader. Their fund in support of the feds may have been illegal. It was probably unethical. And it reeked of hypocrisy. After all, members of the Secret Six were not exactly giving up their own supplies of gin and whiskey. But it hardly mattered. They were businessmen who knew how to get things done.

———

Ries knew the mob's routine, but Wilson discovered in his interview with the cashier that it was another man—an accountant named Leslie Albert Shumway—who had made the notations in the newly discovered ledger. Wilson tracked Shumway to Miami. On his second night in town, he spotted Shumway at the Biscayne Bay Kennel Club and followed him home. He called on Shumway the next morning, interrupting his breakfast. Together, the men drove across the causeway to the Federal Building.

"I'm investigating the income tax liability of one Alphonse Capone," Wilson told Shumway as the men settled in.

Shumway, meek as a mouse, didn't say a word but started shaking. Wilson poured him a stiff drink, which seemed to help.

He spoke: "Oh, you're mistaken. I don't know Al Capone."

Wilson put a hand on Shumway's shoulder, as if he could empathize, as if these two bookkeeping specialists shared a special bond. "I know you're in a helluva spot," he said.

But Wilson was about to make that spot a helluva lot more unpleasant. He told Shumway he had a choice that wasn't much of a choice at all:

Come clean and tell us what we want to know about the Capone operation and we'll keep you in hiding until the trial. Or don't come clean and
force us to arrest you at the dog track, for all of Capone's men to see.

So Shumway told his wife he was going to visit a sick relative in Okla-
homa, traveled back to Chicago with Wilson, and testified before the
grand jury. Shumway stated that Capone was one of the owners of the
Ship. He also told Wilson—privately, not in his testimony to the grand
jury—that Guzik had warned him never to pay money directly to Capone.
It wasn't that they were trying to protect the big man; it was just that they
knew Capone would burn through every penny of profit, spending it on
suits and betting it on the horses, if given the chance.

When he finished interviewing Shumway, Wilson stashed his witness
somewhere in California, once more using Secret Six money, until he was
ready to use him at trial.

———————

Since the murder of Jake Lingle, Capone had disappeared. Where he'd
gone was anybody's guess. One report said he'd been spotted in Pough-
keepsie, New York, en route to Brooklyn, where it was thought he'd hide
out with Johnny Torrio. Another account had him in Miami. Another
report placed him in San Francisco, where he was said to be muscling
into the grape-concentrate business. And yet another story placed him in
Hollywood, where he was said to have been lunching with movie executives. Wherever he was, he clearly had access to a phone, because he was
continuing to direct his lawyers to get him out of his tax jam. It had been
six months since Capone's initial meeting with revenue agents and he'd
made no progress at all.

One day in early November, Harry Curtis—a Chicago attorney and the
son of Charles Curtis, vice president of the United States under Hoover—
visited the commissioner of the Bureau of Internal Revenue. This was
David Burnet, the agency's top man, and Curtis made him an offer: Drop
all the gang prosecutions, Curtis said, and he would guarantee that Chicago's racketeers would pay tax collectors at least $3.5 million. Soon after,
Capone's attorney Mattingly called on Burnet and made an almost identical pledge, suggesting that Mattingly, who also represented Johnny Torrio
in an ongoing tax case, may have hired Curtis to lobby on his clients'
behalf. "There have been other slight intimations," Burnet wrote in a con-

fidential memo to one of his assistants, "but all of such a nature that they could not be regarded as more than a very delicate hint."

Capone probably figured the feds were hard up for cash. And they were. Businesses all over the country were cutting staff and reducing wages. Even those workers who still had their jobs were worried that they might be next to go, so they curtailed spending on big-dollar items such as cars and houses. As a result, the economy spiraled lower still. Revenue from income taxes in 1930 dropped 15 percent, and it was expected to drop even more steeply the following year.

But the revenue men weren't biting.

In Chicago, meanwhile, the cops were growing more aggressive. The papers every day carried reports of one gangster or other under arrest or on trial—more often for tax evasion or vagrancy than for bootlegging or murder. But the effect was much the same. Among the busted were Frankie Rio, Murray "the Camel" Humphreys, Ed "Spike" O'Donnell, Sam "Golf Bag" Hunt, Lawrence "Dago" Mangano, Harry and Sam Guzik (the obese brothers of Jack), Terry Druggan, Red Barker, William White, James "Fur" Sammons, Danny Stanton, and Bugs Moran. Some of them were even convicted. George Johnson referred to it as his "flank attack," meaning that he would come after them from the direction they were least prepared to defend. These scoundrels had spent a decade paying off the cops and courts to insulate themselves against bootlegging-related charges, but they had not yet figured out how to fight against the more obscure and complicated charges. By every measure, Johnson's approach, which was quite novel at the time, seemed to be working.

"Ralph Capone and Jack Guzik can never again be leaders in organized crime," Johnson boasted. "Their immunity—or gangdom's belief in their immunity—is gone. That was their stock in trade. They will not be able to count on old loyalties when they come out of prison. There is no friendship among hoodlums. . . . There is no loyalty except the loyalty born of common purpose. That purpose is easy money. Take their money away and they dry up like a weed that has been cut down. . . . The work has often been slow and painful, but it has been effective." There will always be crime, Johnson continued, but certain kinds of crime can and must be stopped. He spoke of the corruption of elections, the corruption

of police forces, the corruption of the judicial system through the terroriza-
tion of jurors and witnesses. But the bottom-line message he delivered was
this: Not everything had been corrupted. Not every office of government.
Not his.

Upon taking office in 1927, Johnson had vowed to let his indictments
and convictions do the talking, and for the past three years he had kept
that vow. His flank attack was working. The only question remaining was
how effective it would be against his primary target, Al Capone.

————————

Once, Capone's reputation for violence had helped keep his men in check.
No one would have dared cooperate with the feds. Now, though, at least
three men—Shumway, Ries, and O'Hare—had been forced to make a
choice: Which force posed less danger to them—Capone or the federal
government? And they'd chosen the feds.

Michael F. Malone, an agent with the Bureau of Internal Revenue,
also seemed unafraid of Capone when he agreed to go undercover and
infiltrate the big fellow's gang. Calling himself Michael Lepito and introducing himself as a gangster from Philadelphia, Malone spent weeks
hanging around the lobby of the Lexington Hotel, hoping to pick up a few
details on Capone's whereabouts and activities. Malone failed to crack
Capone's inner sanctum, failed to get to know the boss personally, and
never seemed to be in any immediate peril. But the fact that Malone could
spend as much time as he did without facing any questioning, any threat,
or any real danger would seem to suggest that the gang was no longer at
the top of its game.

One day, shortly before Thanksgiving, Malone heard rumblings that
Capone had ordered hits on Wilson, Johnson, Pat Roche of the state's
attorney's office, and Revenue Bureau agent A. P. Madden. Five men in
a blue sedan bearing New York plates were in town for the jobs, Malone
reported. Wilson's other informant—Eddie O'Hare—phoned in the same
urgent tip. Such a strike, if it were carried out, would have badly damaged
the government's case against Capone, but it hardly would have stopped
it. It would have brought a temporary reprieve, at best, followed by a
crackdown of epic proportion. If the murder of McSwiggin four and a half
years earlier had rocked the nation, imagine the response to the murder of
three high-ranking federal officials and another high-ranking state official.

In any case, Malone never heard any more than the initial rumors. If there were in fact an assassination plot, it never went anywhere. Wilson and Malone described it years later, but even in their exaggerated accounts they admitted that they were never genuinely frightened and never felt that their lives were in peril.

A better gambit for Capone would have been to track down and murder Shumway, Ries, or O'Hare. But these never happened. As a result, in the months ahead, several more of Capone's key men would agree to cooperate with the feds. Each time one of his men testified against him, each time the feds extracted a piece of information about his business machinery, Capone took a hit.

By the fall of 1930, the economy was in a nosedive. A great summer drought had devastated farmers, especially in the South. Elsewhere, industrial production steadily slid, down 20 percent from 1929 to 1930. After a brief rally in the summer of 1930, stock prices fell again—this time to levels even lower than in the autumn of 1929. Brokerage houses that had been hanging on waiting for a rebound finally gave up, their customers gone. More than a thousand banks shuttered in 1930, including one of the nation's biggest, the Bank of the United States in New York. Wrote the historian Frederick Lewis Allen, "[A]pple salesmen stood on the street corner, executives and clerks and factory hands lay awake wondering when they, too, would be thrown off, and contributed anxiously to funds for the workless; and a stroller on Broadway, seeing a queue forming outside a theater where Charlie Chaplin was opening in *City Lights,* asked in some concern, 'What's that—a bread line or a bank?' "

The ranks of unemployed grew to an estimated 6 million, with 113,000 out of work in Chicago. In response, more than a dozen prominent Chicago business leaders met the morning of November 15 to plan a relief campaign. They would ask working Chicagoans to donate a day's pay every month—and for the city's richest to give much more—until they raised $5 million. The money would go toward emergency relief—food and coal, for starters—and toward public works that would create jobs and stimulate the local economy.

Someone mentioned that there was already at least one elaborate soup kitchen, at 935 South State, where an average of 2,200 men were fed three times a day, at an estimated total cost of $300 a day. More were needed, but this place might serve as a model. Lines snaked from State Street to Roosevelt Road, almost two blocks away. No questions were asked; anyone who wanted food got it. Smiling women in white aprons catered to diners sitting eight to a table. The kitchen, neat as a pin, served not only soup, but coffee and doughnuts, too. But who was behind it? Someone in the meeting said they'd heard that Al Capone sponsored the place. Though his participation was never firmly established, one soup kitchen attendant told a reporter that Capone was indeed behind the charitable effort. "Nobody else was doing it," he said, "and Mr. Capone couldn't stand it seeing so many poor fellows dying of starvation. Not heart failure, mind you, but starvation. . . . We serve the best of everything—the best brands of canned soup, 250 loaves of bread a day, two cases of evaporated cream every three days, and 200 pounds of coffee a week. And he's going to keep it up until this Depression business is over and the men on the streets can find jobs. Drop around here on Thanksgiving. We're going to serve turkey and cranberry sauce and pumpkin pie to everybody."

If the soup kitchen was indeed supported by Capone, he sought no publicity for his good deed. When the story went national, he made no visit to the soup kitchen. He was never photographed or interviewed there. If it was an attempt to boost his image in anticipation of an upcoming jury trial, it was an unusually subtle one for Capone. Joked the *Albuquerque Journal,* "We like to see him take an interest in the unemployed, but we hope he doesn't give 'em jobs." An editorial writer for the *Daily Independent* of Murphysboro, Illinois, wondered if Capone's next move might be announcing a run for the mayor's office. With a few more stunts like this soup kitchen, added the writer, "We are afraid he would get a tremendous vote."

But not everyone found it funny. First Capone made a mockery of Prohibition. Now he was suggesting that if the federal government didn't have the heart or the wherewithal to take care of its poor, he'd do it himself.

No wonder Herbert Hoover wanted him put away.

CONTEMPT

The wedding was held at St. Mary's Church in Cicero on December 14, 1930, a Sunday afternoon, sharply cold, with snow flurries.

Mafalda Capone, who had said she wanted the event to be "neat but not gaudy," got her wish. At two o'clock, four thousand celebrants crammed the church and a thousand more stood outside, under gray, threatening skies. The six formally dressed ushers arrived first, making their way along the red carpet leading into the church. The bridegroom, John Maritote, was next to step from a car. He was a narrow-shouldered, wide-eyed, worried-looking man, with ink-black hair and eyebrows thick as thumbs. Arriving next, to a chorus of "oohs" and "ahs," were the brides-maids in identical dresses: long, full, sleeveless, and made of seashell pink taffeta with turquoise blue accents. They looked like big billows of cotton candy. Mae Capone, Mafalda's matron of honor, followed, dressed in pink chiffon, with tiny shoulder straps of turquoise ribbon.

But it was the bride, of course, who caused the biggest stir when she finally stepped out of a sedan and into the church. She was "plump and olive skinned," in the words of the *Trib*'s reporter at the scene. Her hair was cut short (although not as short as flappers had worn it a few years earlier) and was done up in waves that clung to her forehead, just like the movie star Claudette Colbert. In her white-gloved hands she held a massive bouquet of gardenias and lilies of the valley. A frilled cap of tulle sat atop her black hair, with a filmy veil fluttering three yards behind. Her sleeveless gown was made of ivory-colored satin, draped at the bodice, snug at the hips, and fitted almost to the knees, where it gave way to a long train. The ensemble was stunning, and Mafalda carried it off well, with a beautiful smile that said she was perfectly comfortable in her own skin, in these lavish duds, and even in this marriage. More than any of her brothers, Mafalda Capone bore a strong resemblance to Al: They shared the same moon-shaped head, the same heavy brow, the same straight, large, slightly pointed nose, the same barrel-shaped torso. It was not a resemblance a woman still in her late teens would much desire, and yet on this soggy winter afternoon, she made a radiant bride. Her brother Ralph, in tuxedo and top hat, walked her down the aisle. Though convicted of tax evasion, he remained free pending an appeal. Brother Al was nowhere to be seen.

Where was he?

Given how close Al had always been to his sister, and given that the Maritotes were among his dearest friends, it was nothing short of shocking that he would miss this event. And yet unless he appeared in disguise, it would seem that he did in fact stay away. The newspapermen didn't know what to make of his absence. Neither did the feds. And the rest of the Capones weren't talking.

The day after the wedding, several high-ranking members of the Capone outfit had dates in court, including the man who may have gotten away with the St. Valentine's Day Massacre: William White, who faced a charge of carrying a gun without a permit. The others were Mike "the Pike" Heitler, charged with vagrancy, and Danny Stanton, who stood accused of the murder of Jack Zuta.

Capone himself was scheduled to appear before Judge James Wilkerson of the federal court to answer the contempt-of-court charge stemming from his feigned illness two years earlier. But when the judge called the Capone case and asked why the defendant was not present, the big fellow's lawyers were ready with an answer. The charge was a misdemeanor, not a felony, they reminded the judge, and—at least until the trial commenced—their client's presence was not required. Wilkerson—the same hard-liner who had sentenced Ralph Capone to three years in jail for tax evasion—had to agree that the lawyers were right. He set a trial date of January 19.

Meanwhile, a criminal court judge named John H. Lyle announced to the press that he thought Capone should be executed for his crimes. "We will send Capone to the chair if it is possible to do so," said the judge, who had no cases pending against Capone at the time but would soon after announce his candidacy for mayor. "He deserves to die. . . . Capone has become almost a mythical being in Chicago. He is not a myth but a reptile." Perhaps Capone's lawyers should have requested a change in venue.

The court date was postponed once when Judge Wilkerson became ill, and again on a procedural maneuver by Capone's lawyers. Meanwhile, throughout most of December and all of January, no one heard a peep from Capone. The only reporter who claimed to have picked up his trail was the famous journalist and humorist Ring Lardner, who filed this report on February 2, 1931, from Miami Beach:

> Dear Public: Al Capone has been ordered out of this neighborhood so many times that he is still here, and the other night he gave a dinner party that was novel and really a big improvement on most affairs of the kind. There were twenty-six men and four women, which is just about the right proportion. They were all friends of Al's, but none of them was acquainted with any of the others. Al didn't take the trouble to introduce them and nobody had to talk to anybody else. I saw one of the guests afterwards and got the impression that the Capone winter home is not in the drought area.

Finally, on February 25, 1931, a cool, crisp, blue-sky Wednesday morning, Capone appeared at the federal courthouse in Chicago. He entered on the Clark Street side and took an elevator to Judge Wilkerson's courtroom, on the sixth floor. He was conservatively and elegantly dressed in a dark-blue, three-piece suit, with a blue shirt and blue tie of a slightly lighter shade, but reporters nonetheless focused on his diamond ring, diamond-studded watch chain, pearl-gray spats, and the silk white handkerchief that accented the ensemble. An unnamed writer for the *Tribune* went a step beyond, describing Capone's "porcine bulk" as he settled into his chair, and noting that the gangster's evident complacency evoked the image of a "milk fattened shoat lolling in a mud puddle."

Capone, facing a maximum of one year in jail, was represented by his usual attorneys: Benjamin P. Epstein and William F. Waugh. Epstein, a graduate of Northwestern University's law school, had started his career as an aide to Judge Wilkerson and gone on to become a special prosecutor handling federal fraud cases. In 1922, he switched sides and became a criminal defense attorney. He had been representing Capone, quite successfully, at least since 1926. Waugh was an army captain during World War I and a former federal prosecutor who was said to have once rejected a $50,000 bribe from Johnny Torrio. Now he, too, had begun defending criminals. At the other table sat no fewer than fifteen attorneys from the office of George Johnson, as well as Johnson himself. The courtroom also was packed with Secret Service agents, federal marshals, Revenue Bureau investigators, postal inspectors, Prohibition agents, John Edgar Hoover's men, newspaper reporters, newspaper sketch artists, and a constant stream of secretaries from offices in the building who ducked in to catch a glimpse of Capone. For security reasons—and because so little room remained—the general public was forbidden to enter the courtroom. A thousand or more Chicagoans crowded the sidewalk outside the building, hoping to catch sight of Capone on his way in or out.

Capone chatted happily with a few reporters before the trial began. He said he had no plans to launch a Hollywood career, as some had speculated. He claimed that he'd been offered as much as $2 million for his autobiography, including film, magazine, and book rights. "But I am not going into the literary business," he quipped. A day earlier, in the Republican primary election, Mayor Big Bill Thompson had soundly defeated his main challenger, Judge John H. Lyle, who had campaigned at times as if running against Capone. Asked for his thoughts on the result, Capone said, "Lyle tried to make me an issue and the public has given its answer." When asked if the rumors were true that he'd contributed $150,000 to Thompson's election fund, Capone just laughed.

As the trial began, Assistant U.S. Attorney Jacob Grossman led the interrogation of witnesses for the prosecution. One after another testified that they'd seen Capone in Miami at the time of his alleged illness and that he'd seemed perfectly healthy.

When the court took a break for lunch, a couple of Chicago cops greeted Capone and served him with a warrant—courtesy of none other than Judge Lyle. The warrant ordered him to appear in court to answer charges of vagrancy.

Vagrancy was the vaguest of charges—contending, in essence, that Capone was an idler with no legitimate means of support. Though the charge didn't always stand up in court, law enforcement officials throughout modern history had used the charge to harass. The poet Arthur Rimbaud, blues singer Robert Johnson, and lawman Wild Bill Hickock had all faced vagrancy charges at one time or another. Now came Capone's turn. So instead of going to lunch, he was escorted by police to the detective bureau, where he was fingerprinted, photographed, and briefly questioned. The detectives offered coffee and sandwiches, which Capone accepted. Capone's attorneys arranged quickly to pay a $10,000 bond to keep their client out of jail. When the paperwork on the vagrancy charge was all done, Capone returned to the federal courthouse.

In court that day, his lawyers called only one witness: Dr. Kenneth Phillips, the physician who had signed the affidavit on March 5, 1929, saying that Capone had "bronchial-pneumatic pleurisy" and was too sick to return to Chicago for his court date. Dr. Phillips testified that he had examined Capone on January 13, 1929, and "found him acutely ill, talking incessantly, with a temperature of 104 and a pulse rate of 140. He was suffering stabbing pains from pleurisy in the left side and bronchial pneumonia in both lungs." The judge interrupted to ask the doctor if Capone had been "dangerously ill," and Phillips said, "In my opinion, he was."

The next day, Capone swapped his diamond ring for one set with a stone he referred to as a "cat's eye." He arrived thirty minutes early. As the trial resumed, Capone's nurses supported the doctor's testimony and directly contradicted some of the prosecution's witnesses—including police officers and federal agents—who claimed to have seen Capone at the racetrack when he was supposedly bedridden. The nurses insisted that he had been ill for the entire period in question and that he could not possibly have left his home.

But the momentum turned in favor of the prosecution a little while later when the government began its cross-examination of Dr. Phillips, strongly suggesting that his memory might have been faulty and that the faultiness had something to do with the fact that Capone had paid well for his services.

"You testified you were called to Capone's house on the thirteenth of January. How often did you visit him after that?"

"Three times a day the first week, twice a day the second week, and after that he began to improve, so I didn't see him . . ."

Something wasn't adding up.

"Now, how long was he confined in bed? And by that I mean . . . not going to the horse races," attorney Grossman asked.

"Close on to three weeks or a little over," the doctor said.

The lawyer pushed. So how long was he really confined to the house?

"Under my instructions, three or four weeks after that."

And yet Dr. Phillips signed an affidavit on March 4—fully seven weeks after his initial examination—saying his client was too sick to travel to Chicago for a court date.

At that point, Judge Wilkerson, leaving nothing to chance, took over the interrogation for Grossman. (Years later, Wilkerson and Grossman would become partners in private practice.)

"You say he was in bed three weeks?" the judge asked.

"Yes, or a little longer."

Judge Wilkerson pointed out that the government had presented testimony from a pilot that Capone and his friends had flown to Bimini on February 2.

"How could he do that if he was in bed all the time?"

The doctor said it was possible Capone had flown to Bimini against medical advice.

"Are you sure that you did not exaggerate the seriousness of this man's condition?"

"Your honor, as sure as I am sitting here."

Which wasn't exactly answering the question.

Capone leaned forward in his chair, paying close attention. The muscles in his jaw tightened as he worked over a piece of gum. He seemed to chew harder whenever the prosecution scored a point. And with Wilkerson asking the questions, the prosecution was scoring a lot of points.

Later, Capone's lawyers tried to argue that their client wasn't guilty of contempt because he had been unaware of the doctor's false statements. Even the doctor claimed that he had not carefully read his signed statement on Capone's health. But Judge Wilkerson would have none of it. Capone's lawyers had spent most of the trial attempting to prove that the doctor's letter contained an accurate statement of the defendant's condition. There was no use trying to change the argument now that their defense was falling apart, the judge warned. Besides, Wilkerson complained, if Capone wanted to make such a claim, he should have taken the stand and testified. But Epstein, fearful of exposing his client to cross-examination, wouldn't allow it.

On the third and final day of the trial, the defense presented its closing arguments; Judge Wilkerson repeatedly interrupted, poking holes in the lawyer's arguments. When Grossman began presenting the prosecution's summation, Capone began chomping at his gum with vengeance, though his eyes remained placid. Everyone in the room, including Capone, could see where this was heading. It was clear the judge had made up his mind.

Finally, Judge Wilkerson announced his verdict: guilty.

He sentenced Capone to six months in Cook County Jail. But he agreed to let Capone remain free for thirty days while his lawyers filed their appeal.

The judge pushed back his chair to leave. The court clerk and bailiff rose. Capone froze for a moment, clenched his gum between his teeth, and smiled broadly. When the court adjourned, he chatted with his lawyers, put on his hat, and walked out of the courthouse, where reporters and photographers waited.

The reporters asked how he felt.

"If the judge thinks it's correct, he ought to know," said Capone. "You can't overrule the judge."

But you can appeal, and that was precisely what he would do.

George Johnson did not present evidence or make arguments in court during the trial, trusting attorneys from his office to handle the case. Since taking office, he had yet to argue a case himself. He preferred to maneuver behind the scenes and to let the results speak for themselves. Neither did he issue a statement upon completion of the case. But suddenly, with Capone dealt another heavy blow, the newspapermen began to recognize Johnson's strategy. The *Trib*, in an editorial, wrote that the sentence issued by the court had nothing to do with Capone's legendary career in crime, but it was nevertheless an important development. For more than a decade, the gangsters had consistently and routinely beaten the system, had made the law seem foolish and weak. Now that some of those gangsters were going to jail on tax and contempt charges, and others, such as Mops

Volpe, faced deportation for violations of immigration law, the situation had reversed. The law, like a severed vine, had found a way to cling and to grow strong again. "These are all new and, to the gangsters and politicians associated with them, startling developments of the last six months. If the law's approach has not been a direct attack upon the gravest crimes of the outlaws . . . it is nevertheless the first real breach which had been made in their protections."

The *Trib* was right, and Capone knew it, too.

DEATH AND TAXES

On a cold and rainy Wednesday morning, March 4, 1931, Capone was back in court—municipal, this time—with another one of his longtime attorneys, Michael Ahern. Ahern was a polished, fast-talking Irishman who had been representing Capone and other gangsters with terrific results for years. He was a tall and handsome man, broad-shouldered, with a smile that engendered trust. Before starting his career as a lawyer, he'd taught at a Catholic high school. In 1921, he successfully represented some of the Chicago White Sox players accused of throwing the 1919 World Series. And though he had spent the better part of his career defending wealthy gangsters, Ahern was still respected among courthouse colleagues as a straight shooter and worthy adversary.

Ahern and Capone appeared before Judge Frank M. Padden to make a modest proposal: Prior to the upcoming vagrancy trial, Capone and Ahern wanted all references to "Scarface" and "Scarface Al" stricken from the court record.

"Alphonse Capone is this man's right name," Ahern said.

The judge granted the request.

Later that same day, *Chicago Daily News* columnist Howard Vincent O'Brien waited in a drugstore on the South Side, at Eighteenth and Michigan, for an appointment with Jack Guzik. O'Brien and Guzik had been meeting privately for weeks. Guzik explained to the writer that Capone hadn't cared much for the way biographer Fred Pasley had told his story and he was thinking about doing the job himself. The big fellow wanted to interview O'Brien to see if he might make a suitable ghostwriter. Though Capone had said just a few weeks earlier that he had no interest in producing an autobiography, he'd given the matter more thought. By now he may have realized that his prime bootlegging days were behind him. The money wasn't flowing as it once did. He also may have realized that there was a better than fair chance he would soon be incarcerated for one crime or another. His family was going to need scratch, and a book could bring in some legitimate money. Everyone else, it seemed, was cashing in on the Al Capone story—especially Hollywood screenwriters.

A few months earlier, in November 1930, the movie *Doorway to Hell* became a hit. Lew Ayres played a gangster named Louis Ricarno, who quits Chicago for Miami but gets sucked back into the business. Two months later came *Little Caesar,* adapted from the W. R. Burnett novel and starring Edward G. Robinson as Rico Bandello, the snarling, tightly wound little monster who was seen as a Robin Hood–like hero to his neighbors. The first underworld movie of the talking-picture era, *Little Caesar* set the tone for future gangster films. In both the book and the movie, Bandello is portrayed as a leader, a businessman, a general manager of crime. He has an edge like a rusty razor, but he does his best to kill only when he feels he must. Robinson's portrayal was so straightforward, so tough, and so evocative that *Little Caesar* would, over time, have a profound influence on the nation's perception of Capone. Just as Gary Cooper became Lou Gehrig for millions of Americans who never saw Gehrig play and never heard him give his "luckiest man" speech at Yankee Stadium, the guttural, ham-fisted Robinson would become Capone.

The movie was a huge smash, and another was on the way. Producer Howard Hughes, a wealthy aviator and engineer trying to establish himself in Hollywood, had purchased the film rights to a book called *Scarface,* and hired the legendary Chicago journalist Ben Hecht to write a screenplay.

Howard Vincent O'Brien was no Ben Hecht, but he was one of the city's best-loved columnists. He passed his screening by Guzik, and the time came for him to meet Capone and get this new autobiography under way.

At first glance, O'Brien didn't seem like Capone's type. He was a slender, bald-headed man, with the long, taut fingers of a classical pianist. He wrote with a quizzical sense of humor and a warm touch, poking gentle fun at everyone, especially himself. There were plenty of other scribblers, including Walter Winchell and Damon Runyon, who already knew Capone, already drank with him, and already understood bootleg culture. They would have relished the chance to tell Capone's story, although they probably would have filled it with more bull than the Chicago stock-yards. O'Brien was a much humbler sort. His columns chronicled family vacations, the virtues of bald-headedness, and the frustrations of folding laundry. Like Will Rogers, he fancied himself a quip artist, a humorist, and a lowbrow philosopher. A typical sampling went like this: "Insurance statistics tend to show that if you carefully follow all the rules for healthful living you will live exactly an hour and twenty minutes longer than if you didn't." His selection suggests that Capone was looking for a writer who would capture his more human side.

When he had met Guzik for the first time, O'Brien had expected a vicious beast—a "Bengal tiger," to use his own term. Instead, he got a teddy bear, "scarcely over five feet, with a cherubic face and close-shaven blue jowls." The men adjourned to a speakeasy on Madison Street. Guzik claimed he had no stake in the place, nor in any other establishments in the Loop. Before getting down to business in that first session, Guzik had a few things he wanted to get off his chest, mostly regarding his recent conviction for tax evasion. He'd been sentenced to five years in jail but remained free while his lawyers prepared an appeal. The court, he said, had got it all wrong. They'd only looked at his gambling income and not his disbursements. The judge, he moaned, listened to only one side of the story. Guzik was particularly upset with George Johnson, whom he had tried—and failed—to bribe.

"That guy sent me up for five years," he said. "But he's a good, honest, sincere guy. I'd give a lot to bust that rap. It's tough on my family. I don't want my daughter's children thinking of their grandfather doing time in the pen. I've tried to get out of it. I'd pay a lot. . . . I've taken it pretty high, too—you'd be surprised how high. But you can't touch that guy Johnson. He's a square shooter."

O'Brien came to enjoy Guzik's company. The fat little gangster asked good questions, O'Brien wrote in his notes after the meeting, and later in his memoirs. He was impressed, too, with the mobster's focus on integrity. "Greasy Thumb," Guzik's nickname, came from the speed with which he peeled off bills for bribes. He admitted to O'Brien that he was fortunate that so many judges and prosecutors could be relied upon to accept his boodle. And yet Guzik said he found such dishonorable men morally repulsive. Then there were the "reformers," the goo-goos, who seemed to disgust Guzik so thoroughly that he couldn't find the words.

Some reformers, he said, had approached him to ask if they could arrange to have their own homes bombed—not too seriously, of course—so they might "play the martyr role and achieve useful publicity for themselves."

The writer also was impressed with the care Guzik showed in vetting him for the ghostwriting job. It showed not only excellent due diligence but also genuine concern for the boss's well-being. "It seemed to me," wrote O'Brien, "that these men, by the nature of their occupations, have learned to be quick judges of character, and to depend, even with their lives, upon necessarily snap judgments. Apparently, the final decision in my case was satisfactory. It was decided that I was not a snooper, and that though my ways might not be theirs, I could be depended upon for a square deal—that I was 'an honest sincere guy.'"

That conclusion finally reached, Guzik met O'Brien in the drugstore on the appointed wintry March afternoon, the sun already having ducked behind Michigan Avenue's long row of two- and-three-story car dealerships. The fat gangster stepped to the luncheon counter, ordered a Coke, downed it in a few quick gulps, then turned to O'Brien, as if he hadn't seen him sitting there until that moment, and said, "All right, let's go."

This was the moment O'Brien had been waiting for. While most of his newsroom peers saw Capone as good copy, nothing else, O'Brien recognized that the gangster was much more: that he was history, the ultimate symbol of the Roaring Twenties, a menacing and explosive product of Prohibition, a tragic hero whose name would resonate for generations to come. If Capone was ready to talk and to be honest, O'Brien believed the resulting book would be "the most significant contribution to current history that could possibly be written."

Guzik and O'Brien walked across the street to the Lexington Hotel. In the lobby, O'Brien noticed a toy-rifle range, like the sort found at carnivals, offering target practice for five cents a shot, perhaps set up for guests of a convention. Swarthy men in pearl gray spats and fawn-colored fedoras loitered about. Guzik led the way to the fourth floor, where he stopped in front of a door and rang the bell. A chain on the inside rattled and the door crept open an inch or two before swinging wider. The men went in.

"The heart of the great spiderweb of lawlessness was like the office of a bank president," O'Brien wrote. O'Brien and Guzik were talking about golf when Capone marched energetically into the room. He was big and bulky, and dressed in a double-breasted blue serge suit, with a dark tie and a soft collar. O'Brien was surprised to see how young Capone looked, how nimbly he moved across the room and into the seat behind his desk, and had to remind himself that this international celebrity was still only thirty-two years old.

"I suppose we might have a little something to drink," Capone said.

"Red ink?" Guzik suggested.

"Not at all," said Capone. "It'll be champagne."

A waiter appeared, as if from nowhere, with a bottle of 1915 Piper Heidsieck, followed by a sumptuous and bountiful meal: antipasto, spaghetti, and "such Parmesan cheese as one only reads about in this country." Capone seemed pleased that O'Brien seemed pleased. The evening was marred only by a brief outburst by Capone—one that petrified O'Brien. A waiter had been slow about something. O'Brien wasn't even sure what it had been. Capone roared like "a creature of the jungle." But the mood passed as quickly as it came. More food arrived. O'Brien tasted fennel for the first time, and again, Capone seemed pleased that his guest liked it. A slender man, O'Brien did his best to keep up with Capone and Guzik at the table, but when the squab arrived he finally gave up.

When they were finished, Capone picked up a piece of Lexington Hotel stationery and jotted a letter authorizing O'Brien to "act as my agent in the sale of the manuscript of my autobiography." Capone said he thought the book could net him "millions." O'Brien tried to adjust his new partner's expectations, but he wasn't sure his message was sinking in.

Soon after, the writer took the train to New York, where a friend in the publishing business told him Capone's story might be worth $1 million, but only if he told the down-and-dirty truth about his misdeeds. No one wanted to hear that he was good to his mother and helped feed the poor. So O'Brien returned to Chicago to see just how forthcoming the gang boss would be. Not very, as it turned out. Capone rattled on a lot about his hatred of publicity. He complained about newspaper reporters who never gave him a fair shake. He criticized Fred Pasley's biography. He griped about the way cops harassed even the most lawabiding members of his family. He swore that no one understood the difficult economics of the bootlegging business, which he called "a lousy racket for the retailer."

O'Brien tried to change the subject. He asked if Capone had ever ordered executions, but got no answer. More specifically, he asked if Capone had used a baseball bat to murder his friends Albert Anselmi and John Scalise at a banquet in Indiana.

"I can't tell you that," Capone replied. "It wouldn't be fair to my people."

In the end, O'Brien concluded that Guzik might have had more power than his so-called boss. Capone, he wrote, was "a symbol, and by no means the potentate he is supposed to be. He is the commander of an army, a proconsul, holding his position not so much from force as from a certain facility at the dramatic, a certain flair for the mysterious, and above all, from the affection, rather than the fear, of those he leads."

He also concluded, unfortunately, that there would be no book.

———

While Capone was busy wiping the name "Scarface" from the legal records and wining and dining his prospective ghostwriter, George Johnson had been compelling key members of Capone's gang to testify secretly before a grand jury. Johnson was hoping the grand jury would agree to issue two indictments: one charging Capone with tax evasion, the other charging him with violations of the Prohibition Act. Already, several of Capone's closest associates had agreed to talk.

One of them was Louis LaCava, who had started out as a floor sweeper and worked his way up to a position of power in Cicero's speakeasies and gambling clubs. He described working for a number of men, including Dean O'Banion, Frankie Pope, and Johnny Torrio, before Capone came to power. LaCava testified that, in the early days of Capone's rule, when the boss had been more of a hands-on supervisor, he and Capone had held the only keys to a strongbox containing records from some of Cicero's biggest gambling halls, including the Ship, the Subway, and Lauderbach's. The safe opened only when both keys were used simultaneously. Capone inspected the books almost daily, LaCava testified. Pope testified to the grand jury, too, although it's not clear whether he supplied any useful information.

Fred Ries told the grand jury that he had worked in some of the same Cicero establishments as LaCava from 1924 to 1927. He said he had the impression that Capone, his brother Ralph, Frank Nitti, and Jack Guzik were partners in the organization, but Ries took most of his orders from Guzik. He estimated that the mob's gambling shops in Cicero employed between thirty-five and forty men in those years and netted profits of between $25,000 and $30,000 a month.

Pete Penovich, who ran some of the outfit's gambling shops, confirmed that Guzik, not Capone, received most of the profits from the Cicero casinos, although he noted that the profit margins were not as great as many imagined and that Guzik and other proprietors gambled away much of what they earned. Penovich didn't have much to say about Capone, but the feds were optimistic they'd soon squeeze more out of him. Frank Wilson had arranged a wiretap at the home of Penovich's girlfriend, Marie Moran, who ran a high-priced call-girl operation. Once he had incriminating evidence against the girlfriend, Wilson intended to use it to put pressure on Penovich.

The feds were finally coming on strong. When the gangster Louis Alterie claimed he had nothing to do with the gang or with bootlegging, Johnson charged him with perjury. No more messing around. Early on the morning of March 12, federal agents raided the Cotton Club in Cicero, Ralph Capone's biggest money-making operation, where a minstrel show was under way at the time. The agents carted off booze; arrested a manager; and, in the hunt for business records, used an acetylene torch to pry open a safe. In another raid, the feds seized phone records from the Lexington Hotel. Meanwhile, Johnson continued indicting members of the Capone syndicate who were not cooperating with his investigation, including two of Capone's brewers, Bert Delaney and Steve Svoboda.

At about the same time—the spring of 1931—Eliot Ness finally got into the act.

Early in the morning on March 25, he led a team of ten Prohibition agents on a brewery raid in Cicero. After surrounding the building, Ness and his men used a truck as a battering ram to smash through two sets of reinforced doors, surprising the three brewers inside. There were no shots fired, no punches thrown, no dynamite blown. Ness and his men found twenty-three thousand gallons of beer in fourteen vats, and when they cracked them open with axes—as much for the cameramen on hand as for the disposing of the beer—a thick wave of foam several inches high spread across the floor, filling the building's every nook and cranny, and spilling out the garage door that Ness had come in through. In the newspaper photos—with Ness, there always were newspaper photos—it looked as though the agents were clomping through snow.

Over the weeks and months to come, Ness would blitz more breweries. The raids hurt Capone, robbing him of income as his legal bills mounted. Some customers complained that Chicago's beer baron, trying to boost his profits during these tough times, had begun filling his thirty-two-gallon barrels with a mere thirty gallons of beer. They may have been right, but even so, Eliot Ness was far from the sharpest thorn in the big fellow's side.

On March 13, 1931, George Johnson got what he'd been working toward for the past two years: an indictment of Al Capone for tax evasion.

For now, Capone was charged with only one felony count for 1924. The indictment stated that Capone had earned a net income of $123,101.89 in 1924 and failed to pay taxes on that amount—taxes that would have come to $32,489.24. The taxes had been due on March 15, 1925. Had Johnson waited two more days to file the charges, the statute of limitations would have run out. So he obtained the indictment, asked the grand jury to keep it under wraps for the time being, and went back to work. It wasn't perfect. It wasn't everything he'd hoped. But it was a start.

For Johnson, it was vitally important that no one learn of the initial indictment. He was still hoping to charge Capone with tax evasion from 1925 to 1929. He didn't have much confidence in his case, though. He felt that his witnesses were balky, unreliable, and could, perhaps, flee the city. He worried that a judge might decide that Capone's tax evasion was a misdemeanor crime, not a felony. He also worried that most of his evidence was circumstantial. Would it be enough in the eyes of the law to prove that Capone spent money, or would he need to show that Capone received income, too? The first was easy, the second damn near impossible.

But he could hem and haw no more. The time had come to push ahead.

Meanwhile, Frank Wilson and his fellow revenue men continued knocking on doors, tapping phones, and twisting gangsters' arms until they talked. The feds also were trying to protect men such as Fred Ries and Louis LaCava, who had already testified. "Any information that the defendant had been indicted would have caused witnesses to be even more reluctant than they were to testify against this defendant," Johnson wrote at the time in a letter to U.S. Attorney General William Mitchell.

Already, Johnson said, the government's witnesses were "fearful and reluctant." They would be more fearful, more reluctant, and more vulnerable to Capone's assassins if news leaked that a trial was imminent. It wouldn't matter if Capone was on his way to the Big House. He would leave behind plenty of men capable of carrying out his orders. There also was the chance that Capone might try to flee the country. So the officers of the court and members of the grand jury were sworn to secrecy.

The press never learned of the sealed indictment. Neither did Capone's attorneys.

But somehow, Capone did.

UNITED STATES AGAINST AL CAPONE

Spring settled across Chicago, melting the last piles of sooty snow that clung like plaque to the city's alleyways and curbs. Rain washed winter's accumulated grime down the sewers and out into Lake Michigan. Blades of grass sprouted from fields of mud. Children pumped their bicycle tires full of air and took to the streets. The warm western breezes brought a small measure of relief to the growing number of men, women, and children forced by the Depression to leave their homes and live in parks; under Wacker Drive; and in vacant, unheated buildings.

Normally, Capone would have returned to Miami and remained there until May or June, until Chicago warmed up just a little more and there was no chance of another cold snap. But his lawyers told him to stick around. He split his time between his family home on South Prairie Avenue and his suite of rooms at the Lexington Hotel.

On April 3, 1931, Capone got a piece of good news: The state's attorney's office announced that it had dropped its charge of vagrancy against him. Prosecutors said they had been unable to find a police officer willing to testify against the city's most notorious criminal. Capone had been in Chicago eleven years. For eleven years he'd been selling whiskey and beer in the age of Prohibition. For eleven years he'd been the leader of an organization that robbed, gambled, assaulted, and killed. And for eleven years the local cops hadn't touched him. It was a remarkable record.

But Chicago proved that spring that it was not completely beyond redemption: On April 7, voters at long last threw Big Bill Thompson out of office for good. Thompson had tried to question his opponent Anton J. Cermak's patriotism by using Polish slurs against him. Cermak's reply helped boost his popularity among immigrants: "It's true I didn't come over on the *Mayflower*," he said. "But I came as soon as I could." Cermak, a Democrat, thumped Big Bill by the largest margin in the history of mayoral elections in Chicago, winning by nearly two hundred thousand votes. It was the end, declared the *Trib,* of "the most puissant machine Illinois has known."

The city celebrated in a scene that looked like Mardi Gras, with ticker tape and shredded telephone directories dropped from office windows in the Loop; trumpets, trombones, and cowbells echoing in the streets; firecrackers exploding in midair; and, of course, with thousands of glasses of whiskey, beer, and wine raised in toasts to the new mayor. Within his first hour in office, Cermak fired three thousand of Thompson's appointees, including untold numbers of city workers as loyal to Capone as they were to Thompson. A genuine housecleaning was under way. "I'm going to give the people of Chicago the best administration they ever had," boasted the mayor-elect, and he set out to prove it.

Meanwhile, in Washington, Herbert Hoover attended the annual Gridiron Club dinner, in which politicians and journalists act out satirical skits, a tradition in Washington since 1885. With the Depression deepening, there wasn't much to laugh about in the nation's capital, but the dinner went on, sticking mostly to political rather than economic gags. In one skit, a ship named the *Eighteenth Amendment* was battered by wind and rocked by waves. Fiorello H. LaGuardia, a New York congressman and future beloved mayor, rushed up to the ship's captain and shouted, "The ship's sprung another leak!" "More water coming in?" asked the captain. "No," shot back LaGuardia, "more Scotch!" Cue the chorus, which sang (to the tune of "Sailing, Sailing over the Bounding Main"):

> *Pro-hi-bi-tion, sailing the stormy spray*
> *She's floating yet, but getting wet*
> *And wetter every day.*

When one of the ship's officers asked the sailors who would stick with the teetering ship, only a stowaway, "Al Capone," volunteered. The actor portraying Capone sang:

> *You made me what I am today,*
> *I hope you're satisfied.*

You built me up until
I stand here in my pride.
I make a billion every week,
I've done well from the start.
Don't dare to repeal,
Or you will feel
The curse of an aching heart.

The press coverage didn't indicate whether the president laughed.

———

For a little while, it seemed to George Johnson that all the pieces were coming together. Capone's top partners were still refusing to turn on the big fellow, but several of his lower-ranking soldiers were providing useful evidence. Eliot Ness was buzzing around like a fly, pestering the bootleggers. He wasn't gathering much useful evidence against Capone, but he was generating publicity, which didn't hurt the government's cause. And Frank Wilson had begun putting together a detailed financial blueprint of the Capone syndicate, including a thorough accounting of the kingpin's recent spending. If the feds couldn't determine exactly how much Capone had earned, the thinking went, maybe a future jury would be impressed to learn how much he had *spent*. Soon—perhaps in weeks—Johnson would be ready to bring more charges against Capone. Johnson was not the sort to rush, but he was under pressure from Washington. He told his bosses he thought he might be ready to go to trial before the end of the year.

Then he hit a bump in the road.

One day in late April or early May 1931 (Johnson couldn't precisely recall), one of Capone's attorneys paid a visit. Johnson didn't say which attorney, although it probably was Michael Ahern. The attorney said that Capone had heard from one of his sources that the grand jury had already issued a secret indictment for failure to pay income tax and that further indictments were on the way. Johnson didn't mind that Capone knew about the possibility of further charges, but he was thunderstruck to hear that Capone knew about the already-issued indictment. The defense counsel told Johnson that he would fight any attempt to have Capone tried in Chicago, arguing that it would be impossible for his client to get a fair hearing, given his renown.

Johnson offered no reply.

Clearly, Capone's attorney was looking for an edge, looking to start the negotiations on his own terms: If the government would agree to a "reasonable sentence," he said, Capone would consider pleading guilty. He didn't say what "reasonable" might mean, and Johnson didn't ask. He wasn't ready to negotiate, and he wasn't happy that he had lost the element of surprise in his carefully plotted strategy. Just when Johnson thought he was holding a strong hand, a new card had been dealt, and he was no longer so sure of his play. He told Capone's lawyer that he would let his superiors in Washington know that he'd been approached with the offer of a plea deal.

With that, the meeting ended.

———

With Capone keeping quiet and lawyers on both sides scrambling, the news hounds couldn't stand the silence.

One cracked.

The headline in *Real Detective Magazine* read "AL CAPONE IS DEAD." The story claimed that Capone, enmeshed in a nasty love triangle, was shot and killed in 1929 and replaced as mob chieftain by a look-alike who had undergone surgery to add the scars to his face. The story was accompanied by "before" and "after" photographs. A brave reporter from the United Press syndicate approached Capone—or maybe it was his impostor—and asked for comment on the incredible story.

"Who do I look like?" he asked with a laugh.

Then he paused and thought about it for a moment. Maybe it wasn't such a bad idea after all. "Let 'em think I'm dead," he said.

———

On the evening of May 7, George Johnson boarded an overnight train to Washington. He reached Union Station at 8:35 A.M., stepped outside into the warm morning air, and headed directly to the office of Assistant Attorney General G. A. Youngquist. His appointment was for nine thirty, but by arriving early Johnson hoped that Youngquist might spare him a few extra minutes.

Like Johnson, Youngquist was a Swede. The G. A. stood for Gustav Aaron. When Hoover had picked him to head the Justice Department's

Prohibition and Taxation Division, Youngquist had assured the newspapermen that he was dry "politically and personally," but, like the president, he was no fanatic. Letters between Youngquist and Johnson suggest that the men were courteous but hardly intimate. In some of the correspondence, Youngquist seems impatient with Johnson's tentative approach to the Capone case, although he never says so explicitly.

Now Johnson reviewed the details of his meeting with Capone's attorney and explained to Youngquist all the various ways he imagined he might lose if he took this, the biggest and most important case of his career, to trial. A more egotistical man would have relished the chance to challenge Capone in court. A bolder man might have embraced the once-in-a-lifetime chance to go toe-to-toe with Public Enemy Number One in a packed courthouse with newspapermen from across the world reporting his every utterance. A more ambitious man might have seen this moment as his launching pad to higher office or to the wealth and fame of a prestigious private practice.

Not Johnson. All he could focus on was the possibility that he might lose. He told Youngquist that he was inclined to accept a plea deal if Capone's lawyers would agree to a fair prison term for their client. Youngquist listened. He didn't rule out a deal, but neither did he encourage one. Go back to Chicago, the assistant attorney general said, and do your job. Build the strongest case you can. And don't make any deals without consulting us.

When Johnson returned home, Capone's lawyers came calling again. This is what good criminal defense lawyers did—they explored all the angles; they took the prosecution's temperature to see how hot they were for a trial; they assessed the opposing attorney's mood to get a sense for what kind of case they were up against.

Capone could have hired a tax specialist. He also could have hired Clarence Darrow, the nation's most famous defense attorney and a showman of spectacular pedigree, who likely would have turned the case against Capone into a morality play, casting the gangster as a scapegoat for the failure of Prohibition and a small fry compared to the sharks of American industry who profited from the run-up in stocks before the stock market crash of 1929. But Capone chose Ahern and Thomas D. Nash because they were expert dealmakers. He chose them because he knew and trusted them. He didn't necessarily expect his lawyers to keep him out of jail, but he figured they would make the best of a bad situation.

As an opening bid, Ahern and Nash told Johnson that Capone would plead guilty if the feds would agree to a prison sentence of eighteen months.

Johnson told them to forget it. Eighteen months wasn't enough. That much he was sure of.

Ahern and Nash made no counteroffer. They thanked Johnson for his time. But the process was under way, and in making the first offer, Capone's legal men had anchored the negotiations. They had indicated to Johnson that in seeking a plea deal they wouldn't be talking about five to ten years, they'd be talking two to five.

Johnson's next move was to meet with the judge who would be hearing the case, James H. Wilkerson—the same judge who had found Capone guilty of contempt just two months earlier—and to let him know that the lawyers were talking about a plea deal.

Wilkerson had a massive office on the sixth floor of the federal building. Yet despite its great size, the judge's chamber always seemed cluttered, just as his light brown hair, despite being neatly combed and completely his own, always looked like a cheap toupee. A carousel of law books stood near the door. More legal tomes lined the walls. Wilkerson's L-shaped desk was as big as a lunch counter. He sat in a big swivel chair, its arms and seat covered in distressed leather. When he wasn't flipping through law books he could often be seen playing with the dials on the massive radio that took up much of the surface of his desk. He was not a fat man, but he had a long, heavy face, all jowls, with the flesh from his neck hanging over his shirt collar and obscuring the top of his tie. Nothing in his appearance inspired fear, but he was like an old basset hound with a mean streak, and lawyers who knew him approached with caution.

Born in 1869 in northern Missouri, James Herbert Wilkerson was the son of a Union soldier, John W. Wilkerson, who had marched with General William Tecumseh Sherman on Atlanta during the Civil War, and, afterward, never stopped telling his twelve children all about it. James was a bookish boy, much too fond of the classroom to ever remain on the family farm. He left home at age sixteen and earned a bachelor's degree in philosophy at DePauw University, where he met his future wife, Mary E. Roth of South Bend, Indiana. From there he went to work as a schoolteacher and principal in Hastings, Nebraska. He moved to Chicago, passed the bar exam, and started his own law practice. Twenty years later, after working as a county prosecutor and as the U.S. attorney for the Northern District of Illinois, he was appointed to serve as a federal judge in the U.S. District Court for Northern Illinois, replacing Kenesaw Mountain Landis, who stepped down to become commissioner of baseball.

Wilkerson had been on the bench only two months when a case of huge national importance came before him. On July 1, 1922, four hundred thousand railroad shop workers walked off their jobs, crippling the nation's system of transportation. In many cities and towns, the strike turned violent. President Harding and his commerce secretary, Herbert Hoover, had tried to get the strike settled quickly but failed. The violence continued and ratcheted higher. In September, Attorney General Harry M. Daugherty, the man who had named Wilkerson to the federal bench, went to the new judge and asked him to order an end to the strike. Wilkerson complied. The judge ruled that the strikers were engaged in a widespread conspiracy to interrupt commerce and intimidate replacement workers. Going further, he restrained the strikers and union leaders from "hindering or obstructing" the railway companies, from loitering, picketing, or congregating in the vicinity of railroad operations, and even from writing letters or using telephones to promote a strike. Freedom of speech? Irrelevant! The right to peaceful assembly? Overruled! Even some within Harding's administration called Wilkerson's injunction a travesty of justice and a mockery of the Constitution. But the strike was smashed.

Time and again in the years that followed, Judge Wilkerson proved himself an iconoclast. Having once held the same office as George Johnson, Wilkerson sometimes showed frustration at the U.S. attorney's inability to build cases against bootleggers. It wasn't that Johnson was soft. And no one ever accused the prosecutor of being on the take. But the problem with Johnson, as Wilkerson saw it, was that he had failed to address some of his office's fundamental problems. Prohibition agents were out on the streets trying to make arrests, but they weren't coordinating with the U.S. attorney's office. So the agents would bust bootleggers at random, arresting whoever happened to be on hand at the time of their raids, and then present their cases to Johnson. But Johnson didn't have time to work on all those cases—and, not having been involved in the investigations, he had no way to know which ones were airtight and which were leaky. "Evidence is obtained and indictments are returned, then the witnesses disappear and the district attorney's office is left to try the case without any evidence," the judge complained. If the U.S. attorney wanted better results, Wilkerson said, he should take command of the entire process: choose his targets, assign investigators, supervise the field agents in the gathering of evidence, charge the criminals deemed most worthy of jail time, and then and only then bring the cases before a judge. "We have case after case in which the bartender is brought in, but the owner cannot be found," the judge complained. "It makes a farce out of Prohibition enforcement."

Johnson sat down across from Judge Wilkerson and laid out the situation. He began by shifting the blame to his superiors, saying that the bureaucrats in Washington were considering a plea bargain in the Capone case "by reason of the difficulties the government had encountered in the investigation and the hazardous nature of the government's case." Johnson said he was especially worried about his two key witnesses—Ries and Shumway—given that the case depended so heavily on their testimony. If one of them were killed, or if one of them recanted, he told the judge, he didn't know what he would do. But that wasn't all. Johnson had built his career on felony income tax cases. Typically, he charged criminals twice—first with the misdemeanor failure to pay income taxes, and at the same time with the felony of defrauding the federal government.

But one of the men recently convicted in that manner by Johnson—an Illinois state legislator named Lawrence C. O'Brien—had petitioned the U.S. Circuit Court of Appeals, claiming that the felony charge was bogus, that it amounted to the government charging him twice with the same crime. If the court of appeals overturned O'Brien's conviction, all of Johnson's tax convictions would come undone. Frank Nitti, Ralph Capone, and Jack Guzik would all go free or have their sentences sharply reduced. The case against Al Capone would collapse.

Those weren't Johnson's only worries. As he now explained to the judge, the government's best evidence against Capone dated to 1924 and 1925. Johnson had been racing the clock to beat the six-year statute of limitations on some of his charges. But he told Wilkerson that the law was unclear and would likely remain unclear until an appeals court made future rulings. For the felony charges, the statute of limitations might be just three years. A good defense lawyer would no doubt exploit this gray area in the law.

Finally, the government had calculated Capone's income based in part on a letter from one of Capone's lawyers, Lawrence Mattingly, but Johnson wasn't sure the letter would be admissible at trial. Capone's lawyer had written the letter as part of an attempt to negotiate a settlement. At the time, Mattingly had declared that the numbers were merely estimates produced in an attempt to help Capone satisfy the Bureau of Internal Revenue and that they should not be interpreted as an admission of guilt. But that's precisely how Johnson had used them.

For all these reasons and possibly more, Johnson fretted, Capone could beat the rap.

Had Johnson gone to the judge to give him a preview of the case or merely to express his insecurities? Was he hoping that Wilkerson would give him assurances? It might have been nice to know, for example, how the judge felt about the admissibility of the Mattingly letter, or how he would be inclined to rule on the statute of limitations. Or was Johnson being sincere? Was he genuinely interested in cutting a deal and checking to make sure the judge would approve one?

Wilkerson didn't tip his hand.

Johnson came out of the meeting in the same position he went in: inclined to deal.

Capone was still a free man. Free to run. Free to hide. Perhaps even free to kill.

Knowing that he'd been indicted, knowing that he might soon face a trial, and knowing that some of the men in his organization had already ratted and would soon be compelled to testify against him in court, he surely must have considered the possibility of eliminating a few of the government's key witnesses. In the rip-roaring 1920s, when Capone was at the peak of his powers, execution was an important part of down-and-dirty criminal defense work. If bribes to cops and lawyers didn't make a case go away, a bullet to the back of the skull of a prosecution witness often did the trick.

This was different, though. First of all, Capone was dealing with the feds, not the Chicago police. Bribery was out of the question. George

Johnson was truly untouchable. Killing Shumway and Ries might have
weakened the government's case, but they were well hidden, and it would
be difficult if not impossible to get to them. Others, such as Pete Penovich
and Louis Alterie, didn't know all that much, didn't say all that much,
and continued to profess their loyalty to Capone. There was no point in
killing those guys. So Capone put his faith in his attorneys, all but certain
he would wind up doing time, but hopeful that it wouldn't be too long a
stretch. He was only thirty-two. If he spent four or five years in jail, he'd
still come out a young man.

Even so, before the criminal proceedings could go any further, Chicago was hit with one more sensational gangland murder, one more big
story for the newspapermen who were already talking about how much
they would miss the big fellow when he went off to the joint, one more
hit—as if for old times' sake—that sounded like the work of Capone, even
if he couldn't be connected to it.

Mike "the Pike" Heitler was a heavyset, illiterate Jewish gangster who'd
been trolling the underworld since the days of Big Jim Colosimo. Heitler
had started out in prostitution. Despite his longevity, though, he was no
elder statesman in the gang world. Rather, he was a hanger-on, an annoy-
ance, a thick wad of gum on the sole of the shoe of a man such as Capone.
No one trusted Heitler. No one liked to do business with him. But despite
several prison terms and an enemy list as long as Lake Shore Drive, he
somehow stuck around. He was always showing up somewhere, always
looking for a little action. Until the night of April 29, 1931.

That evening, at the Legion Cigar Store just west of the Loop, Heitler
played poker with some of Capone's men, including Lawrence "Dago"
Mangano, Frankie Pope, and a couple of minor hoodlums identified only
as Hank and Fritz. After the game, they all had dinner at the Chicago and
Northwestern railroad station and left the restaurant in Heitler's car.

The next day, Heitler's car was found in a ditch near the town of
Itasca, twenty-five miles west of Chicago. Fifteen miles north of Itasca,
in the town of Barrington, a charred torso was found in the smoldering ruins of an icehouse. A false tooth, two gold crowns, and an un-
burned bit of underwear helped police identify the melted corpse as that
of Heitler.

The cops came looking for Capone, and they came in force. They
smashed in doors at the Lexington Hotel, scattered the customers at a

dance hall on West Madison, and in Cicero stormed the Western Hotel—formerly known as the Hawthorne Inn—which had somehow been completely vacated in anticipation of their arrival. Capone was nowhere. The cops settled for arresting nine of his associates.

But when it became clear that Capone couldn't be connected to the murder, the hunt for Heitler's killer trailed off quicker than a drunkard's conversation. It turned out that Mike the Pike was not one of the informants feeding the feds information about the mob's operations. His murder probably was related to a gambling debt or a personal insult. Heitler had racked up lots of both. Capone waited until the dust settled and then, as usual, granted interviews in which he dismissed the hullabaloo with a shrug.

By June 5, Johnson could wait no longer. He announced the indictment of Al Capone on charges of income tax evasion. Between 1924 and 1929, the government alleged, Capone had earned at least $1,038,654.84. The gang kingpin probably took in much more—perhaps several million dollars a year—but the feds were able to pin him down only for about an annual average of $173,000 ($2.3 million a year by today's standards), a figure that certainly didn't live up to the hype. The indictment didn't say how much of the income came from bootlegging, how much from gambling houses, how much from dog and horse racing, and how much from brothels. For now, it didn't matter. The bottom line, said Johnson, was that Capone owed taxes of $215,080.48, and the time had come to make him pay. The maximum penalty: thirty-two years in jail and $80,000 in fines, although the toughest sentence ever handed down in a tax-evasion case in any court to that point was Jack Guzik's, and he got only five years.

The *Tribune,* noting that Johnson had never lost a tax case against a gangster, cheered his diligence and determination. By taking out Ralph Capone, Frank Nitti, and Jack Guzik, the feds had knocked three legs out from under Capone's throne, and he was tumbling. "Capone's gang lieutenants have talked to save themselves," one agent told the *Trib.* "Capone has been pushed around so much his power has waned."

Johnson, though, didn't boast about the indictments. In fact, he stayed on the sidelines as his assistants posed for photos with members of the grand jury. Capone, too, sought to make as small a splash as possible. His bail was set at $50,000, which meant he would need to post a $5,000 bond to remain free pending his arraignment. Capone went to the court clerk's office the same day as Johnson's announcement, signed the necessary papers, and settled his tab. He said nothing to reporters who pushed forward and lobbed questions at him.

A week later, he was indicted again—this time on charges that he was the leader of a conspiracy to violate Prohibition laws, the indictment based in part on evidence collected by Ness. The Prohibition charges didn't offer a lot of detail about Capone's crimes. The indictment mentioned that Capone was referred to in wiretapped telephone conversations as Number One, or Snorky. It claimed that Capone's men bought trucks to move beer and equipment to make beer and transferred money from the sale of beer, but it never pinned anything firmly on Capone and never explained his precise role in the supply chain. The indictment claimed that Capone purchased a truck for bootlegging in 1925, but that was about as detailed as it got. That's why Johnson had decided to emphasize the tax case. The Prohibition charges were vague and carried smaller potential penalties. If convicted, Capone would get no more than two years in jail and $10,000 in fines.

Capone's lawyers grew more anxious. They asked for another meeting with Johnson. This time, Johnson and Ahern negotiated in earnest. After months of soul searching, Johnson remained torn. He could take Capone to trial and hope the judge and jury would put the gangster away for five to ten years, but he was concerned the process might drag on for months or even years. President Hoover wanted results fast. But if political expedience were the only issue, Johnson might have overcome his uncertainty and pushed for a trial. His bigger concern was the law.

Though he would admit it only in confidential letters to his most immediate supervisors in Washington, Johnson thought there was a good chance a jury would find Capone not guilty. The government's evidence was weak, and the law was unclear in several key areas. Tax laws were always changing, and appeals courts were still in the process of settling key issues. Most worrisome of all were the statutes of limitations. If the courts gave narrow definitions as to the statutes, much of Johnson's case would go up in smoke. On top of all that, there were psychological issues beyond all control. Most Americans hated paying taxes and hated the nation's ban on booze. What if jurors decided to take out their anger on the government by giving Capone a break?

His whole career as U.S. attorney had led him to this moment, and now it had come down to a gut check for Johnson: Should he risk everything or hedge his bets?

Anyone who knew George E. Q. Johnson knew he was no high roller. After consulting with his bosses in Washington, he made up his mind: He would agree to a prison term of two and a half years—two years on the tax charges and six months on the Prohibition charges—if Capone would agree not to file an appeal and if he would begin serving his sentence immediately. He wouldn't get the big headlines that a trial would no doubt bring, but he would get his man behind bars. That's what counted.

Ahern insisted on two conditions of his own. He wanted Johnson to get the approval of his bosses in Washington—and to get it in writing—so there would no chance of the deal coming undone; and he asked Johnson for a promise that Capone would face no questions prior to sentencing.

The deal was done.

"Case 23,852," shouted the court clerk Joseph O'Sullivan, "United States against Al Capone!"

Along with everyone else in the room, Capone stood. All eyes turned to his big, bulky frame, clad today in a banana yellow suit that one reporter called "bilious" and another called "shrieking." If this was to be his last public appearance for some time, he was going out in style.

Judge Wilkerson entered and settled behind the bench. Everyone sat again. It was 2:00 P.M. on Tuesday, June 16, 1931. Outside, skies were blue, the air breezy and warm. Sailboats skimmed along Lake Michigan. But the air inside the courtroom was thick and heavy, the mood somber.

"Alphonse Capone," said Dwight H. Green, an assistant U.S. attorney, "in indictment 22,852 you are charged with attempting to evade and defeat your income taxes for 1924. Do you plead guilty or not guilty?"

Capone pushed back his chair and rose again.

"Guilty," he said, his voice a whisper.

"In indictment 23,232," Green went on, "you are charged with attempting to defeat and evade your income taxes for the years 1925, 1926, 1927, 1928, and 1929, and with willful failure to file returns for the years 1928 and 1929. Do you plead guilty or not guilty?"

"Guilty," he mumbled.

Assistant U.S. Attorney Victor E. LaRue stood, faced Capone, and said, "Indictment 23,256 charges you with conspiracy to violate the National Prohibition Act. How do you plead: guilty or not guilty?"

"Guilty," said Capone.

And then it was over.

Wrote the *Chicago Herald and Examiner*, "In those quiet few minutes . . . Chicago was throwing off the shackles of a man and an organization that has represented lawlessness, viciousness and a flout to its self-respect for ten long years."

Judge Wilkerson ordered everyone to come back in two weeks, on June 30, for the sentencing. The clerk called another case. Capone and his bodyguard moved toward the elevator.

Outside the courthouse, police held back thousands of men and women. If Capone had looked up as he stepped outside, he would have seen office workers lined up like pigeons on every one of the federal building's eight balconies.

It was not an angry mob. There was no widespread public outrage over Capone's crimes. People were simply curious to see if the great Capone could really be caught. And if he was going away, they wanted to catch one more fleeting glimpse before he vanished.

———

Meanwhile, the government took a victory lap.

"Personally, I do not believe there could be any more distinct accomplishment that would tend to create public confidence in the proper enforcement of the National Prohibition Act," wrote Dwight E. Avis, a top-ranking Treasury Department official, in a confidential memo to George Johnson. "I congratulate you."

In Washington, Attorney General Mitchell told reporters that Capone's prosecution proved that gang leaders could be stopped "if you have honest men on the job and a real purpose." He said he hoped the job done in Chicago would encourage local officials across the country to more aggressively pursue their local bootleggers, and promised that the men who got Capone—including tough-guy accountant Frank Wilson—would soon be on their way to New York to take on that city's bootleggers.

President Hoover sent word to Chicago that he wished to congratulate Johnson in person. The president was in Springfield, Illinois, as part of a cross-country tour in support of his economic recovery plan. Though he was getting pounded daily in the press, Hoover continued to insist that the economy would soon be on its feet again. Meanwhile, factories closed and jobs vanished. Banks fell. Men and women lost their homes. Hoover knew what was happening, but Americans had the sense that he didn't quite *feel* it. In a national address a few days earlier in Indianapolis, he sounded more like a college professor, explaining the Depression, disassembling and assembling it for his audience, going over its causes and effects, and explaining what the United States would learn from the ordeal, as if it was a bunch of statistical aberrations and not a beast that was eating people alive. "We are suffering more today from frozen confidence than from frozen securities," he said, when, in fact, many people had lived through a winter of frozen fingers and toes. The people in the audience didn't boo; the Indianans were too polite to boo a president. But they didn't cheer, either.

The president's cold, clinical response gave the nation's down-and-out someone to gripe about. As shantytowns began springing up in public parks and along railroad tracks, the inhabitants started calling their tent-filled, campfire-warmed communities Hoovervilles. As men turned their pants pockets inside out to show they were broke, the protruding flaps of fabric became known as Hoover flags. Sleeping bags made from newspaper? Hoover blankets. Jackrabbits? Hoover hams. And at the old, abandoned criminal courts building in Chicago, at the corner of Dearborn Street and Austin Avenue, where dozens of homeless men took shelter every night, someone hung a crudely drawn sign that read "Hotel Hoover." Mayor Cermak ordered the sign removed.

In Springfield, Hoover spoke at the rededication of Abraham Lincoln's tomb, and returned to the theme of law enforcement, which had been the centerpiece of his inaugural speech two and a half years earlier, when his life had been ever so much simpler, his dreams ever so much more within reach. And while he didn't mention Capone by name, several reporters the next day wrote that the president's remarks seemed like a response to news of Capone's guilty plea. "There can be no man in our country who, either by his position or his influence, stands above the law," Hoover said. "That the republic cannot admit and still live. For ours is a government of law and a society of ordered liberty, safeguarded only by law." The *Chicago Herald and Examiner,* in its June 17 edition, became the first paper in the country to accurately describe Hoover's long-running obsession with Capone:

"The President for months has never started his exercise period with cabinet members without asking, 'Have you got Capone yet?' "

Added the news story: "They got Capone."

After placing a wreath at Lincoln's grave, Hoover motored to the governor's mansion, where he shook hands with Johnson and congratulated him on his work. After the meeting, Johnson would reveal none of the details of the conversation, merely saying, "The president was very kind in what he said to me." He tried to downplay what was undoubtedly the biggest case of his career: "There isn't any genius in myself or my staff," he said. "All I had was the imagination enough to see that the income tax law would serve to bring these big-shot hoodlums to justice. The rest was work and more work."

But finally he did admit satisfaction: "Everywhere I went—to New York, Washington, and other cities—they asked me, 'How is Al Capone?' It's going to give me a great kick now to be able to tell them, 'He is at Leavenworth.' "

THE SO-CALLED UNTOUCHABLES

Eliot Ness, too, cherished the moment of Capone's guilty plea.

There were two weeks to fill before Capone's sentencing, and newspaper reporters tried to hold their readers' attention over that stretch with inside stories of the investigation. The national press corps quickly discovered that Ness, a sensitive, mild-mannered, twenty-eight-year-old graduate of the University of Chicago, gave terrific interviews. His stories, unlike Johnson's, had guns and beer and the threat of violence in them. He even had a catchy nickname for his squad of gangbusters, and once the newsmen heard it, they practically fell all over themselves dashing for their typewriters. "The Untouchables," Ness called his men, explaining that they'd earned the name because they were fiercely resistant to bribes— although Ness, showing off a bit, said he was aware that the phrase was more often applied to India's lowest caste.

The young Prohibition officer told reporters stories of his big busts in Chicago Heights (which weren't so big) and his harassment of Capone (which wasn't so bothersome), and the newspaper guys ate it up. "We had to weigh our problems and find a vulnerable point," Ness told the *New York Times*. "We decided on the breweries because their product is bulky and because they have the toughest transport problem."

No one noticed or cared that his stories had no payoff, that they included no big-name arrests, that Chicago had not exactly gone dry, or that Capone himself never seemed aware of the existence of Ness and his Untouchables. It didn't matter. It was good ink, as the newsmen put it.

In letters to the editor and editorials nationwide, it was agreed almost unanimously that Johnson and the feds had done the right thing. While it might have been nice to nail Capone for murder, the American system of justice had functioned properly. The government had worked hard to build the best case possible. The case had been based on solid evidence. Capone, confronted with the facts, admitted his guilt. His reign of tyranny was likely done. The American way had prevailed.

But as the sentencing approached, skepticism began to sink in. Why should Capone get a deal? What if he served a short stint and got out, only to make more trouble? With most of the papers reporting that Capone would likely get no more than three or four years, and with the United Press syndicate reporting—with impressive accuracy—that the prison term agreed upon by Capone and Johnson was exactly two and a half years, a small but steady backlash began to build.

C. A. Mesh of Peoria wrote a letter to the editor of the *Trib* saying it didn't seem right that "a hoodlum dictator . . . can impose his will upon a federal court and determine for himself the sentence he will accept."

One *Tribune* scribe jotted a poem, which he called "The Greatest Crime!":

> *What is the greatest crime of all?*
>
> *What foul deed does most appall?*
> *What sin takes such horrid shape*
> *That he who does it finds no escape?*
> *Let us review the base deeds of all times*
> *And find which one is the crime of crimes.*
> *First, take old Cain that killed his brother;*
> *Well, he may have had cause, somehow or other.*
> *Nero fiddled while Rome burned, but—*
> *We excused him because he was just a nut.*
> *And Captain Kidd, the Scourge of the Seas,*
> *May have simply had some mind disease.*
> *Bluebeard gave all his wives the gate,*
> *But maybe they jawed him for coming in late.*
> *Benedict Arnold's deed was most black,*
> *But maybe the poor fish needed the jack.*

So while all of these guys just raised the deuce,
We'll find in each case some real good excuse.
But Capone's case shows with great positiveness
The one crime for which there is no forgiveness.
The whole Ten Commandments you can treat almighty lax,
But kind heaven help you if you dodge your income tax.

Frank Loesch, former president of the Chicago Crime Commission and creator of the Public Enemy list, wrote to President Hoover on June 29, telling him that news of Capone's plea bargain had created "a very distinct undertone of dissatisfaction." Chicagoans wanted to see Capone knocked out, not lightly slapped, he suggested. But Loesch assured the president that regardless of the outcome of the case against Capone, he hoped that he would be granted permission one day to tell the world "how much you had to do with it and how much of the impetus was personally given by you."

Hoover continued taking a terrible beating in the press. Friends of former president Calvin Coolidge were hinting that Coolidge might be persuaded to run again, in 1932, if the American people felt strongly enough that his help was needed in rebuilding the nation's battered economy. Hoover, meanwhile, fully intended to run for reelection and win. He remained confident that the economy would soon turn around. Two days after receiving Loesch's letter, Hoover wrote back. While he didn't address concerns about the wisdom of the plea bargain, he did write that he looked forward to taking credit for Capone's conviction. "Some time when the gentleman you mention is safely tucked away and engaged in very hard labor," wrote the president, "you can tell all about it."

Before the plea bargain had been sealed, the government's victory in the case was already beginning to feel to some like a loss, another example of Capone gaming the system. On June 26, four days before Capone's sentencing, Attorney General Mitchell wrote a scathing, six-page letter to Johnson, blaming him for letting his prey squirm off the hook.

"It was, no doubt, a tactical mistake to receive the plea of guilty and then allow two or three weeks to elapse before sentence is imposed," the attorney general wrote. "The effect of that is to start the public discussing what the penalty ought to be. . . . If Capone had pleaded not guilty in the first case and then withdrawn his plea and pleaded guilty on the day when the court was ready to impose sentence and send him to the penitentiary, and the first news of his plea of guilty had been accompanied by a sentence and immediate commitment to the penitentiary, we would have avoided the unfavorable reaction which might result from what appeared to be too moderate a sentence, and at least avoided getting the public excited about the severity of the punishment to be imposed."

Even though Mitchell, Youngquist, and others at the Department of Justice had approved the plea bargain with Capone—and signed off specifically on the two-and-a-half-year prison term—Mitchell was beginning to back away from it, leaving Johnson holding the bag in case something went wrong. If Capone found any room to maneuver, if he appealed part of the sentence, or somehow managed to reduce his jail time, Mitchell said Johnson would get no support from Washington. If it appeared that Capone had somehow outwitted the feds, wrote Mitchell, "the results would be disastrous and the reaction would be such that we would have been better off never to have commenced the effort to bring him to justice."

Mitchell went on to say that he'd read the statement Johnson had prepared for his announcement of the plea deal and thought Johnson had made the mistake of "minimizing" the strength of his own case. Rather than a statement asserting Capone's long and deadly list of crimes and the righteousness of his imprisonment, Johnson had written something more like an apology, eight pages long on legal-size sheets. In his written statement, which he had circulated among his superiors but not yet read to the court, Johnson repeatedly used the word "circumstantial" to describe the evidence against Capone. He reminded the judge that the witnesses he planned to call to testify were lowlifes and liars. He confessed that his legal arguments were wobbly and that his physical evidence was scant. But if he could negotiate a plea bargain, at least Capone would be gone and Chicago would be "free of the stigma attached to it."

In other words, he seemed to say: Let's get this over with.

On June 29, Capone's lawyers asked the judge to postpone the sentencing hearing. In return for the postponement, they agreed to drop the customary stay of execution, meaning that Capone would begin serving his prison term immediately upon sentencing. Wilkerson agreed.

As summer wore on, the gangster remained free. In July he submitted a letter to the Bureau of Internal Revenue in which he proposed a plan to help settle his tax debt. He said he planned to raise $150,000 in cash by selling his home in Miami, the furniture within, two yachts, and an automobile. But that proposal was never made public, and newspaper readers following the Capone case were beginning to suspect that the gang chief was somehow getting off easy. It didn't help that Capone gave one of his now famous pity-me interviews to the *New York Times* shortly before his sentencing hearing.

"I've been made an issue, I guess, and I'm not complaining," he said as he sat behind his desk at the Lexington, his hulking frame clad in black silk pajamas. "But why don't they go after all those bankers who took the savings of thousands of poor people and lost them in bank failures? How about that? Isn't it lots worse to take the last few dollars some small family has saved—perhaps to live on while the head of the family is out of a job—than to sell a little beer, a little alky? Believe me, I can't see where the fellow who sells it is any worse off than the fellow who buys it and drinks it."

Two days before the sentencing hearing, Johnson checked in with Judge Wilkerson to make certain that he would still go along with the plea deal. Wilkerson asked if Johnson had the attorney general's approval in writing, and Johnson said he did. Wilkerson raised no other concerns. The U.S. attorney took that to mean everyone was in agreement.

Shortly before 10:00 A.M. on July 30, 1931, a squad of police cars took Capone from the Lexington Hotel to the federal building, where thousands once again waited outside to see him. It was a hot day, thermometers pushing past seventy even before sunrise. The skies were bright blue with a few light clouds.

Capone entered the building from the Adams Street side and took the elevator to Judge Wilkerson's court, which was packed, mostly with men and women who worked in the building. The courtroom was warm and getting warmer. To help keep the crowds under control, credentials were required to get into the building—only reporters, lawyers, and office workers were granted entry.

The judge dispensed with a few routine cases before getting around to Capone, making the gangster wait.

Finally, Wilkerson began. He said he understood that the defendant had agreed to plead guilty and that U.S. Attorney Johnson had agreed to recommend a judgment, but the judge reminded the parties before him that Johnson could do no more than *recommend* an outcome. The final decision belonged to the judge, and Wilkerson said he intended to make his decision only after hearing from Capone.

Capone's lawyers had been assured their client would not be compelled to answer questions.

After some sharp back and forth with Michael Ahern, Wilkerson admitted he'd been angered by newspaper accounts that took for granted that a plea bargain had been prearranged and that his role was merely to sign off on it.

"It is time for somebody to impress upon this defendant that it is utterly impossible to bargain with a federal court," the judge said.

Capone and his lawyers were dumbfounded.

They complained that they'd been misled. Johnson was humiliated. He explained that he had given Capone's lawyers reason to believe that their negotiated prison sentence would be approved by the court. He said that when Attorney General Mitchell and Assistant Attorney General Youngquist had signed off on the plea deal, he had assumed that Wilkerson would do the same. He offered to show the judge the letter from Mitchell, written a few days earlier, in which Mitchell confirmed his satisfaction with a two-and-a-half-year sentence.

None of that mattered, Wilkerson said. Only the judge could hand down a sentence, and he was not going to do it in this case, not without hearing evidence first.

Ahern was furious. He sensed from Wilkerson's attitude that the judge was interested in giving Capone a much steeper sentence than two and a half years. He insisted that Capone be permitted to withdraw his guilty plea.

Johnson agreed that Capone ought to be permitted to withdraw the plea. It was only fair.

Fine, said Judge Wilkerson, and he ordered the men to return the next day to discuss a trial date. The next day the trial was set for October 5.

Capone had entered the court looking sharp, as usual: his shirt pressed, hair combed, expression cool as ice. But he was wilting. His collar had soaked through, his slicked-back hair turned to a thicket of curls at the back of his head, and the look on his face was one of total shock.

What happened?

Judge Wilkerson had changed his mind. It could have been the hubris of Capone's *Times* interview. It could have been the fact that so many newspapers blatantly reported the terms of the plea bargain, which should have been kept a secret.

Or it could have been—as one Chicago newspaper columnist would suggest years later—that Wilkerson had received a secret order from President Hoover, saying that he wanted Capone's case to go to trial.

George Murray, a columnist for the *Chicago American* who had great sources in the underworld, told the story in his column twenty-five years later. "Two days before Capone was to come to court, Wilkerson was visited by the confidential secretary of the man in Washington," Murray wrote, adding a guarantee that his unnamed source for the information was in a position to know the truth. "The Judge never revealed what was said, but he emerged from chambers visibly shaken. The wonder is that Wilkerson never told it to Johnson."

True? No one can say. But when Murray's column appeared on July 23, 1956, someone—perhaps Johnson's son—carefully clipped it from the newspaper, wrote the date at the top of the clipping, and retrieved from Johnson's personal files a twenty-five-year-old manila envelope marked "Court Records—July 30—10 A.M.–2 P.M." He slipped the Murray column into the envelope and closed it again.

"WHO WOULDN'T BE WORRIED?"

Beneath a scrim of gray clouds at two in the afternoon on October 3, 1931, with the start of his trial just three days away, Al Capone stepped out of his car and onto the golden brown campus of Northwestern University in Evanston, Illinois. Dressed in a bright purple suit to match the school's colors, Capone eased his way through a crowd of students to one of the western entrances at Dyche Stadium. He and some of his men, including Jack McGurn, had come to watch a football game: Northwestern versus Nebraska. It was a big game, but just a warm-up to a bigger contest scheduled for the following Saturday: Northwestern against Notre Dame. Capone was not letting his legal troubles get in the way of his sporting interests. Unfortunately, he and his pals had terrible seats: forty-five rows up from the field at about the five-yard line. But the weather was warm, the green grass of the football field was rimmed with faces, and all eyes were on the field, as opposed to Capone.

Five plays into the game, Northwestern broke through with a touchdown, and the fans sitting around Capone released hundreds of purple balloons skyward. When the home team scored two more touchdowns in the first quarter, good cheer spread through the grandstand, and the mood grew giddy. At some point, word spread that Capone was in attendance. Necks craned. A rumbling noise rose through the crowd. Some reporters thought they heard jeering, others cheering. Perhaps it was both.

A reporter found him and asked if he was bothered by the attention.

"I'm here to see the game," he said. "I'm going to stick it out."

But when the first half ended, he got up to leave. A stream of four hundred spectators followed, providing an unofficial, ominous escort to the gate. By then it was clear he was being taunted. Even a pack of Boy Scouts joined in the razzing.

––––––

Two days later Capone woke up at 7:45 A.M. at the Lexington Hotel, feeling like hell. He showered, shaved, and slid into a blue serge suit. He shoved a bunch of peppermint cough drops in his pocket.

Mae and Sonny were with him at the Lexington. They'd come up from Miami for the trial, but they would stay at the hotel when Capone left that morning for the courthouse. Though it might have evoked sympathy for the defendant, Mae was apparently too stubbornly shy to allow herself and her son to be put on display for a jury, not to mention for the newspaper reporters, photographers, and movie-reel cameramen.

In anticipation of Capone's arrival, thousands of Chicagoans once again stood shoulder-to-shoulder on the sidewalks around the federal courthouse. Most of the congestion was on Clark Street, in front of the building's side entrance. Photographers showed up before dawn to get good parking spaces, then climbed to the roofs of their cars, unfolded their tripods, and hoisted their big, boxy cameras into place. Robert J. Casey of the *Chicago Daily News* described the scene as "high carnival in all but confetti and strewing of roses." But the crowds were looking for a caravan of police cars, and Capone surprised them by pulling up in a single, unmarked car at the Dearborn entrance to the federal building.

"Are you worried?" a reporter shouted when Capone emerged, already working on his first cigar of the day.

"Who wouldn't be worried?" he replied as he hopped off the running board and toward the courthouse, accompanied by his bodyguard, Phil D'Andrea.

To another reporter he mentioned he was sorry to be missing the third game of the World Series, Cardinals versus Athletics. A photographer snapped a picture, his flash blowing a cloud of smoke in the air. Capone never stopped moving.

He walked inside and took an elevator to the sixth floor, where Judge Wilkerson and all the lawyers involved in the case waited. In the room next to Wilkerson's court, workers were stringing wires for a temporary telegraph office. Over the course of the trial, reporters from as far as England were expected to transmit between eighty thousand and a hundred thousand words of copy a day.

Though Capone probably didn't know it, several of his closest associates and former associates were gathered two floors up, in the office of George Johnson, waiting to see if they would be called as witnesses. Johnny Torrio, Fred Ries, and Louis LaCava, among others, sat there, under guard. In all, seventy-five witnesses had been subpoenaed. "It looks like the whole state of Florida is here," said Capone's former mentor, Torrio, now retired and supposedly living on his investments in the Sunshine State. Though he would not be called to testify, Torrio had already answered questions for the feds. He didn't say much.

The courtroom was a grand space, befitting the magnitude of the event at hand, with ornate columns rising to the lofty ceiling, bronze sconces holding small electric lightbulbs on the walls, and a massive arch over the door. Painted above the entrance to the court were quotations from the U.S. Constitution that had faded and become difficult to make out. The room was warm. Open windows failed to stir the air, and Capone quickly perspired through his collar. He sat only a chair's width from Johnson, who wore his usual gray woolen suit and gold-rimmed spectacles. Judge Wilkerson looked out at the crowded courtroom through horn-rimmed glasses. A green glass lampshade on his judge's bench cast the right side of his face in light and the left in shadow. He, too, wore a gray woolen suit, no robe. He ordered the newspapermen who had set up folding chairs all around the defense table to slide their chairs back and give Capone and his lawyers some room.

After calling the court to order, Judge Wilkerson made a move that most of the reporters in the courtroom didn't even notice. He took his list of prospective jurors and swapped it with another judge's.

Why?

A few days earlier, Frank Wilson of the Bureau of Internal Revenue had received a phone call from his best informant: racetrack owner and Capone partner Eddie O'Hare.

"The big fellow is going to outsmart you," O'Hare had said. He went on to explain that Capone or one of his men had bribed someone at the courthouse and obtained a list of prospective jurors. "They're passing out $1,000 bills. They're promising political jobs. They're using muscle, too." The goal, wrote Wilson in a 1933 memo, was "planting one or more friends" of Capone on the jury.

When Wilson got the tip, he told Wilkerson. After waiting until the last possible moment, Wilkerson made the switch, bringing in a jury he knew hadn't been threatened or bribed.

It was the first of many bad breaks for defendant Capone.

————

Michael Ahern, Capone's lead attorney, approached the bench.

All the prospective jurors were white and male. No surprise there. But Ahern was disturbed by other characteristics of the group seated before him. Almost all of the men were from small towns surrounding Chicago, almost all were Anglo-Saxon Protestants, and almost all were past the age of forty-five. Ahern found it difficult to believe that such a seemingly conservative group could have been selected randomly. Where were the men in their twenties and thirties? Where were the steelworkers who liked to knock back a few cold ones with lunch? Where were the sophisticated city-dwellers who might have enjoyed the occasional cocktail-fueled night on the town? Where were the Italians?

But that wasn't all that bothered Capone's lawyer. Almost all of the men in the jury pool had recently served on other juries. Some had served more than half a dozen times. Every trial is different, of course, but most lawyers operate on the assumption that experienced jurors are more prone to convict than newcomers to the process. The veterans come to feel like a part of the courthouse team. They bond with judges. They start to feel like important cogs in the crime-fighting machine. For the defense, they're dangerous and best avoided.

Ahern used all ten of his peremptory challenges to get rid of the most offensive candidates. They included four men who had served on the federal grand jury that heard tax charges against Ralph Capone and one who had served on the grand jury investigating Prohibition law violations by Al Capone. But Ahern couldn't toss out all the jurors. He was incredulous. In a region of more than 1 million eligible jurors, he asked the judge, was it so hard to find fresh faces? He might have asked more specifically: Was it so hard to find men who had not already served on Capone juries?

"It seems more than a coincidence that so many of these jurors are repeaters," Ahern said. "It is not a fair manner of selection." There was no way for Ahern to know how this jury pool was assembled—whether the names were selected at random or culled from a list of recent jurors.

Until the 1960s, most federal courts used the "key man" system to find jurors. Court clerks asked prominent citizens to nominate prospective jurors, and "key men" from these lists found themselves summoned again and again. Nothing in the law said a jury had to be randomly selected, only that it represent a fair cross section of the community. Judges liked key men because they already had knowledge of the criminal justice system. They made the process run more smoothly. And over the course of the 1920s, as judges also discovered that older and more conservative jurors were more likely to convict bootleggers than younger and more liberal ones, they honed their lists of key men accordingly.

In this instance, Ahern objected, as countless defense attorneys had done in countless cases before. He asked Wilkerson to throw out the entire pool of jurors and start again. Wilkerson, without comment, denied the request.

Some reporters had expected jury selection to take days. It took less than three hours.

In the end, eleven of the twelve jurors seated for the trial hailed from small towns in northern Illinois. Nine of twelve had recently served in other cases. One juror—an insurance salesman from Edisonville named Arthur O. Prochno—had served nine times. "Like other newspaper readers," wrote juror Prochno, in an article printed five years after the trial, "I had formed a pretty fair picture of Capone [prior to the trial]. I understood that he was a terrible man who did not hesitate to murder those who stood in his way. . . . To me . . . he epitomized all that was evil."

Though they tended to focus more on the jurors' rural backgrounds than their depth of experience, some of the reporters covering the trial agreed with Ahern's conclusion that the deck had been stacked against Capone as a result of the key man system. "Capone is to have no trial by his peers," reported the *Tribune*. "It is to be by the men who reflect the opinions of the countryside, whose minds are formed in the quiet of the fields or in the atmosphere of wayside villages."

Damon Runyon, who had come in from New York to cover the trial of his occasional drinking buddy for the Hearst syndicate, said he detected the "fragrant whiff of green fields and growing rutabagas and parsnips" in the courtroom. The jurors, he continued, were a bunch of hayseeds—"horny-handed tillers of the fruitful soil, small-town storekeepers, mechanics, and clerks."

In addition to his stories for Hearst, Runyon also agreed to write a column for the *Chicago Herald and Examiner* under the pseudonymous byline of "Otto Nertz," described by the paper as a former blacksmith turned apple vendor who would provide the view of the "man in the street." Nertz began his first column with this bit of vintage Runyon: "I ain't got nothing against Snorky Capone, except wishing he would turn on a better brand of tap beer in the Loop. On my last birthday I took a speedboat ride up the Chicago River, and a lungful of water I got at that time tasted very similar to Snorky's beer. As for his hard liquor, all I can say is—three drinks and you get a nosebleed." Nertz, not surprisingly, agreed with Runyon that Capone seemed to be facing a surprisingly bumpkinish jury. "All these gents is eager to get in the box. If they get in they'll be able to pass their old age sitting on the cracker barrel back home saying, 'Did I ever tell you that when I was a juror in Snorky Capone's case . . . ,' etc."

Before it ever began, Capone complained to his lawyers that Judge Wilkerson would never give him a fair trial. Given that Wilkerson had overseen the conviction of Ralph Capone and had already thrown out Al's plea bargain, the defendant had good reason for his apprehension. No one needed to remind him that he faced a maximum sentence of thirty-two years and fines of $80,000.

But Ahern ignored Capone's complaints. For reasons the lawyer never explained, he chose not to seek a change in venue. The only logical explanation is that Ahern, a Chicago operator to the core, felt comfortable and confident operating in the city limits. But if Ahern thought that the same old tricks that had worked in county court would work in federal court, he was in for a surprise.

The next day, prosecutor Dwight Green opened with a summary of the case against Capone.

The government would prove, he said, that Capone raked in huge profits from gambling houses, brothels, and speakeasies; that he lived a life of luxury, with a "palatial" home in Miami and extravagant shopping sprees in Chicago; that he had earned income of more than $1 million from 1924 to 1929; and that he had intentionally sought to hide that income to avoid paying income tax. In summary, he said, "The evidence will show that during all these times the defendant had plenty of money to pay a tax to the government, but that, instead of paying the taxes, he dissipated, concealed, and covered up those assets and money."

Ahern made no opening statement. He was joined at the defense table by Albert Fink, a fifty-seven-year-old lawyer with protruding ears, sagging jowls, and a mostly bald head. Early in his career, Fink had specialized in income tax law and interstate commerce but of late had been taking on more humdrum cases, representing angry spouses angling for divorce and public officials accused of corruption, among others. For Fink, the Capone case might have been personal. In 1925, while he was honeymooning on a yacht on Long Island Sound with his second wife, the former Lucille Roades of New York, the ship was intercepted by a Coast Guard cutter. Prohibition agents climbed on board and searched Fink's vessel. Fink and his wife were charged with possession of twenty-three bottles of intoxicating liquor and forced to pay a $500 fine.

It was Fink, at the start of the trial, who told Judge Wilkerson that he and Ahern intended to challenge the constitutionally of the tax evasion charge against Capone. The government was accusing Capone of failing to pay his income tax *and* engaging in a conspiracy to evade payment. Failure to pay was a misdemeanor; conspiring to evade payment was a felony. Ahern and Fink intended to argue that the two charges were essentially the same, asking Wilkerson to dismiss the felony charge. Jack Guzik had made the same contention, unsuccessfully, in his recent trial and an appeal was pending. Judge Wilkerson said he would reserve judgment on the matter until after the feds had presented evidence establishing Capone's income.

The government's first witness was Charles W. Arndt, chief of the income tax division for the Chicago office of the Bureau of Internal Revenue, who reported that the government had no record of any income tax having been paid under the name Alphonse Capone or any of his known aliases, including Scarface Capone, Snorky Capone, A. Costa, Al Brown, or Scarface Brown. Capone smiled. He leaned back in his chair. With hairy hands and "fat, powerful fingers," as Meyer Berger, a young reporter for the *New York Times,* put it, he drummed the table and flicked at the leather straps of his expensive briefcase.

Next came Leslie Shumway, dressed drably in brown, his bald head shining under the bright lights from the ceiling. He and Fred Ries, the gambler who had helped seal the conviction of Guzik, were considered the linchpins of this case, as well as the men most likely to be assassinated in an attempt by Capone to derail the trial. Now Shumway avoided making eye contact with Capone. He spoke so softly that spectators were forced to lean forward to hear what he said. He testified that he had kept the books at some of Capone's Cicero gambling dens, and that the shops moved from one location to another as they were shut down by cops. When Assistant U.S. Attorney Jacob Grossman showed Shumway a set of books, Shumway confirmed their authenticity. They showed that profits for one of Capone's dives had been $300,000 for 1924, $117,000 for 1925, and $170,000 for a four-month stretch of 1926. The ledgers ended at about the time of Assistant State's Attorney William McSwiggin's murder, when the cops cracked down on speakeasies and casinos in Cicero.

A few of the jurors were seen yawning during the bookkeeper's testimony, but they sat up in their chairs and paid close attention to the next witness, because he was so commandingly handsome. Capone, too, seemed transfixed.

This was Rev. Henry C. Hoover—no relation to the president or the FBI director—a tall, blond-haired, broad-shouldered man with a pompous air about him. He was only about thirty-five, but he wore pince-nez glasses perched on the bridge of his nose, an affectation that had seemingly gone out of style with Teddy Roosevelt. But on Reverend Hoover, a star witness from central casting if ever there were one, they looked dashing.

In 1925, Reverend Hoover had led a group of angry vigilantes on a series of raids against brothels and gambling dens in Cicero and neighboring Stickney. On May 16, 1925, the day of the Kentucky Derby, recalled Reverend Hoover, he and his men stormed one of Capone's Cicero gambling houses, at 4818 West Twenty-second Street. They overturned whiskey bottles and tossed roulette wheels and card tables to the street. It was here, Reverend Hoover said, that he had bumped into Capone. And it was here that the ledger used at Capone's tax trial had been seized. The gangster—at that time a top aide to Torrio—had been alerted to the raid and had rushed over from the Hawthorne Inn. He was wearing a pajama top and the pants from a suit. His face was unshaven. He was shoving cash in his pockets when the reverend interrupted him.

"He turned to me," Reverend Hoover testified, "and he said, 'This is the last raid you'll ever pull.' "

Capone then vanished. He returned thirty minutes later, clean-shaven, dressed, and apparently in a better mood.

"Reverend," he said, according to the witness's testimony, "why can't you and I get together? Give me time to get my money out of this place. If you'll let up on me here in Cicero, I will withdraw from Stickney."

For some reason, this caused a few chuckles in the courtroom. It may have been the reverend's shabby impersonation of Capone that amused the audience. Reverend Hoover blushed at the laughter and continued.

" 'Mr. Capone,' I said, 'as far as I am concerned, the only understanding you and I will ever have is this: You must observe the law or get out.' "

Capone tapped his foot on the courtroom floor, folded his arms, and stared unblinkingly.

When the prosecution finished questioning the reverend, Michael Ahern stretched his long legs and rose from the defense table. He removed his eyeglasses, wiped them with his handkerchief, returned them to his face, and began peppering the witness with questions: Did he and his raiders have a search warrant with Capone's name on it? The answer was no. Why wasn't Capone arrested? Reverend Hoover said he had tried to get the sheriff to arrest Capone but had failed. Was Hoover certain that the man he met was really Al Capone? Another member of the raiding party had testified that he wasn't sure if the man he saw that day was Ralph Capone or Al Capone. Could Reverend Hoover also have been confused? There were holes in the reverend's story, and Ahern did a good job of jabbing at them. But he failed to hit the witness with a knockout punch.

Had Capone's lawyer gone back and read old newspaper stories from the time of the raid, he might have noticed a glaring discrepancy in Reverend Hoover's testimony: At the time of the raid in 1925, the reverend had said that Capone had not been in the gambling joint when the raid began. At that time, Reverend Hoover had told reporters that another man—someone named Joseph Smith—revealed himself as the owner of the gambling joint, and that Capone had come along only later, when the raiding party was finishing up its work, and had tried to bribe the raiders to make them go away.

Reverend Hoover's testimony helped establish that Capone was the owner of the casino tied to Shumway's ledger. And the ledger was the only piece of physical evidence that showed income for Capone. Ahern could have damaged the reverend's credibility by pointing out the conflicts in his testimony, but he missed his chance.

In the biggest case of his career, Ahern was coming up short from the start. But there's no reason to suspect that he was giving it less than his full effort. It seems more likely that he was in over his head. As a defender of safecrackers, gamblers, and whores, he was as good a lawyer as Chicago had to offer for the common criminal. He knew that the best way to help a client to beat a rap was to make the cops look like the bigger criminals, which usually went over well with Chicago juries. But Ahern had little if any experience that would prepare him to go up against the massive forces of the federal government in an income tax case—much less an income tax case that was turning out to be a referendum on the sanctity of American law. One can only wonder what Clarence Darrow would have done had he been sitting at Capone's table. And at this point in the trial, Capone might have been asking himself that very question.

When court was adjourned for the day, Capone, his lawyers, and his bodyguard, Phil D'Andrea, posed for a few pictures in the courtroom. The boss seemed to be in fine spirits. The men left the building through the doors on Dearborn Street, where mounted police officers held back the crowd and extra traffic cops kept the streets clear. The man of the hour lingered awhile, waving to the crowds and chatting with strangers, until one of his men encouraged him with a gentle push to get into the backseat of a waiting taxi. Capone's fedora caught on the edge of the door as he entered the car. He grabbed his hat and shut the door. The taxi whirled away and the crowds disappeared.

BIG SPENDER

The second day of testimony brought another critical moment.

As soon as Judge Wilkerson gaveled the start of the session, the government called George G. Slentz, a Bureau of Internal Revenue lawyer, as its first witness. One of George Johnson's assistants, Samuel G. Clawson, asked Slentz to examine a letter written on September 30, 1930, by Lawrence Mattingly, Capone's tax lawyer at the time. It was the letter Mattingly had written in an attempt to settle Capone's tax debt. It was his "belief," Mattingly had written, that Capone's income for 1926, 1927, 1928, and 1929 did not exceed $26,000, $40,000, $100,000, and $100,000, respectively.

Ahern and Fink sprang to their feet simultaneously and rushed to the bench, asking Wilkerson to bar the evidence. The letter was an attempted compromise, not a confession, but the jury would surely perceive it as an admission of guilt, the two lawyers complained. There had been no threat of criminal charges at the time of the attempted settlement. Capone had merely been trying to do what the government demanded of him: pay his taxes, better late than never. "Congress doesn't want to send people to jail," Ahern complained. "Congress wants people to pay their taxes. It wants them to come in and settle with their government before criminal or civil action is started so it won't have to be started." And that's what Capone had been trying to do.

Ahern cited examples of cases in which admissions made in attempts at compromise had been ruled inadmissible in criminal proceedings, but Judge Wilkerson was not persuaded. "When a man makes such statements," the judge said, "he does so at his own peril. He cannot bind the government not to prosecute him." He would allow the jury to hear the evidence and see Mattingly's letter.

Once it appeared that he would lose his bid to throw out the letter, Ahern tried another tack: He argued that the letter should be viewed as evidence that Capone was not trying to evade paying his income taxes at all. In fact, said Ahern, it showed that Capone was attempting to settle his account. At the very least, Ahern believed, that should prove that Capone was not engaged in the felonious act of defrauding the government.

Only time would tell if that argument would impress the jury.

Over the next several days, prosecutors would try to establish that Capone was a lavish spender. If they couldn't prove he had income, they would prove he had money, which must have come from somewhere. Runyon explained the strategy nicely: "Your Uncle Sam argues that if a man spends a raft of money he must necessarily have a raft of money to spend, a theory that sounds logical enough unless your Uncle Sam is including horse players."

McLean Smith, a desk clerk at the Metropole Hotel, testified that Capone kept a suite of five rooms, rang up thousands of dollars in bills, and always paid in cash.

"Did you ever see Mr. Capone give any tips?"

Smith smiled, "reminiscently," as the *Daily News* put it, before saying yes, he'd been tipped well by Mr. Capone.

Capone's gofer in Miami, Parker Henderson Jr., was asked to examine $35,000 worth of Western Union money transfer orders and to say who had received the money. Capone, he said. Who paid for the Capone family's mansion in Palm Island? Henderson was asked. Capone, he said. Who paid for the installation of the swimming pool and concrete wall around the property? Capone. Later came more proof of Capone's extravagant spending habits: a weekly meat bill of $250; a telephone bill one winter that added up to $8,400; and an interior decorator's charge for $1,725. A baker testified that he delivered bread to Capone's home and charged him $3 or $4 a day. An ironworker said he built Capone a gate for $490. A jeweler said he sold Capone eight diamond belt buckles at $275 per. A department store clerk said she sold Capone linen and kitchenware for $800. Another offered details on Capone's underwear, made from the same silk as fine ladies' gloves, which cost an astonishing $12 a pair. A tailor said Capone ordered twenty-three suits, most of them double-breasted, in a two-year span. And a Marshall Field & Company salesman made it known that Capone liked the right-hand pockets of his overcoats made bigger and stronger than the left-hand pockets, presumably to accommodate his gun.

One witness said Capone liked to peel bills off a roll of cash "that would have choked an ox."

Upon cross-examination, Capone's lawyer asked, "Wouldn't the size of the roll depend on the size of the ox?"

Capone seemed as bored as the rest of the audience, except at one moment when the contractor who built the dock at his home in Miami complained that the gang chief still owed him $125. At that bit of testimony, Capone's jaw clenched so firmly, according to the *Daily News,* "that the scar on his cheek stood out like a cord." Capone then whispered to his attorneys that the contractor didn't get his money because he didn't finish the job and left his scow and tools behind. Call him a tax cheat, call him a killer, he seemed to say, but don't call him a man who doesn't pay his bills.

For the reporters in from London, Boston, and New York, some of the testimony must have been unfathomably dull. How could they justify their expense reports? At one point, the baker was asked if he delivered only bread or if he sometimes brought cake, too? At another point, the butcher was asked if Capone could have possibly consumed so much meat. "One man couldn't eat all that," the butcher dutifully reported. And so it went for days, dollar by dollar, receipt by receipt, gratuity by gratuity. The great gangster Capone was beginning to look like nothing more than the last of the big-time spenders. Forget about winning the beer wars; Capone seemed more interested in shopping for drapes and kitchenware. And while he may have struck fear into the hearts of his machine-gunning rivals, there was no denying that the store clerks loved to see him coming.

But if the trial was not living up to its hype, that's the way Johnson wanted it. He showed that Capone's casinos made money. He showed that the money from those casinos was deposited in bank accounts and that money from those bank accounts was wired to Miami, where Capone's associates picked it up for him. No doubt Johnson would have preferred to find an account or vault with Capone's name on it, but he was making do with what he had. He would stack one piece of evidence atop another, like bricks, until he built an inescapable set of walls.

―――――

Only one newsworthy incident interrupted the slow and steady proceedings. On October 10, after another long morning of testimony from store clerks and contractors, Wilkerson announced that court would break for lunch. Capone and his bodyguard, Phil D'Andrea, started toward the door. But Mike Malone, one of the Internal Revenue agents working with Frank Wilson, thought he spotted a bulge under D'Andrea's jacket, around his right hip. Malone whispered to Wilson, and the two agents quickly caught up with Capone and D'Andrea. The federal agents shoved D'Andrea into the corridor, threw open his jacket, and grabbed his gun.

D'Andrea, a pudgy man with gold-rimmed glasses, put up no struggle. He politely told Wilson and Malone that he was permitted to carry the weapon because he served as a deputy bailiff for the municipal court. He pulled out a badge to prove it. But a quick check revealed that D'Andrea's term as a deputy bailiff had expired months ago. He was taken into custody and would eventually serve six months in jail for contempt of court. The bodyguard's arrest would have no bearing on Capone's trial, but it was one more piece of bad luck for the gang boss, one more indication that the breaks were not going his way.

The Capone defense had thus far absorbed one body blow after another without raising a hand to strike back. If Ahern had a plan to reverse his client's fortunes, he would need to use it fast.

―――――

The next day, October 11, Ahern at last launched an attack. Capone, he said, was a victim of a conspiracy. The defendant had tried to settle his tax debt. He had tried to compromise. But the feds never truly cared about crime. They were only interested in punishment.

Ahern told reporters he would call agents from the Bureau of Internal Revenue as witnesses and ask them to explain why so many so-called legitimate citizens had been permitted to repay their back taxes without the threat of criminal charges. He said he also intended to remind jurors that the income tax was a tax on income. The government had to prove that Capone made money and failed to pay his taxes on those earnings. His spending habits made for sensational headlines and made his client look like a monarch, especially given the Depression gripping the nation. But for the purposes of this trial, said Ahern, spending and lifestyle were irrelevant.

October 13 brought another day of mundane testimony. Fred Ries appeared. Reporters in the room perked up as Ries glumly took the stand, hopeful that they might hear about something more tantalizing than Capone's taste for high-end housewares and haberdashery. But even Ries failed to excite. Though he had seen Capone often in Cicero's busiest gambling dens, and though he confirmed that three of those dives brought in hundreds of thousands of dollars a year in income, his testimony failed to prove that any of the gambling income went to Capone. The money always went to Guzik, he said. "Jack told me not to turn over money to anybody but him or someone he sent down, not even Al," Ries testified.

After that the government presented a few bank tellers and clerks who testified that Guzik and others had deposited money from gambling operations. But the only evidence linking Capone to the syndicate came from a handwriting analyst who identified the gangster's signature on the back of a check that had been deposited at one of the banks.

There was no telling how much longer the trial would last. The feds had not yet called Johnny Torrio to the stand. Neither had they called Pete Penovich, or any of the other gunmen and gamblers who ran with the Capone gang. They had made almost no attempt at all to link Capone to the city's vast network of speakeasies, breweries, or gambling halls. The government's entire case to that point was circumstantial.

Perhaps Ahern was waiting for the government to go for the knockout before he counterpunched.

Until that moment, George Johnson had been silent throughout the trial, letting his assistants question the witnesses. But at about two twenty in the afternoon, when his team finished the examination of the handwriting expert, Johnson slowly and quietly rose from his seat, looked up at Judge Wilkerson, and approached the bench. Silence settled over the room as the jurors and spectators watched the slightly built prosecutor make his way across the floor.

In his five years in office, the reticent Johnson had never interrogated a witness, never raised an objection, never spoken a word in court as far as anyone could recall. He'd always left the speaking parts to others.

Now came the moment he'd been waiting for.

"Your honor," he said, "the government now rests."

Ahern and Fink were staggered.

They had anticipated that the government would continue calling witnesses for at least one more day, and they were not entirely prepared to start calling their own. What was happening?

Fink shot from his chair to complain. The prosecution had intentionally kept the defense in the dark, he said. They had refused to provide a detailed list of their charges and claims, also known as a bill of particulars. As a result, Capone's team had no idea how many witnesses were to be called or how long the government might go on presenting evidence. Now they were trying to pull a fast one.

Fink said he and Ahern still intended to call witnesses from New York, Philadelphia, and possibly Washington to testify on Capone's behalf, but they would need a couple of days to bring them to Chicago. The witnesses, he said, would offer evidence of Capone's massive losses as a gambler—"the only business he ever has admitted being in." The prosecution had proved only one thing over the course of the trial: that Capone spent money. The defense wanted to strike back. They wanted to show that Capone not only spent enormous sums of money but that he also gambled enormous sums. One bookmaker would testify that Capone placed between twenty-five and thirty bets a week, gambling thousands at a time and losing about sixty grand a year. And that was just one bookie. They would attempt to prove that Capone assumed that gambling income was not taxable—an incorrect assumption, but nonetheless a plausible one. They also would try to show that Capone's massive gambling losses offset his gains. If they could convince the jury that Capone's failure to pay income tax had been an honest mistake, Ahern and Fink believed, they might at least beat the felony counts and help Capone avoid a lengthy term in federal prison. Finally, they intended to argue that the government's entire case was nothing but a politically motivated attempt to make Capone a scapegoat for the failure of Prohibition.

But they weren't ready.

Of course, Ahern and Fink could have put Capone on the stand to testify to his gambling losses and to his naïveté when it came to settling his tab with Uncle Sam, but they had no intention of doing that. They were afraid of subjecting him to cross-examination by the government. They also toyed with the notion of putting Johnny Torrio on the stand to discuss Capone's career and compensation. But again, they dropped the idea.

Fink went on complaining: The government had been preparing its case since 1928, he said. Capone's team hadn't done any work until July 30, 1931, when Judge Wilkerson threw out the proposed plea bargain. It wasn't fair to shut down the defense before it had time to answer all the charges. He asked for a two-day delay in the trial.

Wilkerson refused.

Fink tried Plan B. He asked the judge to allow the defense team ten hours in front of the jury to present its defense.

Wilkerson said they could have four.

The judge banged his gavel and court was adjourned until the following day.

THE VERDICT

With the jury out of the room, before starting his closing arguments, Ahern asked one more time if Wilkerson would consider correcting what he believed to be a series of errors made by the court over the course of the trial.

Would the judge consider throwing out the Mattingly letter that the government had construed as an admission of income for Capone? No, said the judge. Would he revisit the issue of the statute of limitations? No, said the judge. Then, with nothing to lose, Ahern threw the Hail Mary: Calling the case a corruption of the Constitution, he asked Wilkerson to toss out all the charges, issue a directed verdict of not guilty, dismiss the jury, and set Capone free. No doubt he knew the judge's reply before he heard it.

The jury reentered the courtroom, took their seats, and Ahern prowled before them like a lion in a cage, confinement making him angrier by the moment. He began his closing statement. The jurors could see he was furious, although they didn't know what, exactly, had set him off.

Commandingly, Ahern reminded the jurors that they had promised when they were appointed to this panel that they would acquit the defendant if the evidence failed to establish his guilt. They had vowed that they would not be ashamed to return to their friends, families, and business associates when the trial was over and to say that they had set free the great Capone. It was time, he said, to see if they were true to their words.

"You are the only barrier between this defendant and the encroachment of government," he said, staring down the jurors, beseeching them, searching for the words that would move and persuade them as he presented his argument. "The government has sought by inference and presumption to prove this man guilty. Its evidence can hardly be called even circumstantial. . . . Why do they seek conviction on this meager evidence? Because he is Alphonse Capone! Because he is the mythical Robin Hood you read so much about in all the newspapers! They have no evidence."

Ahern continued to stalk back and forth across the well-worn wooden floor in front of the jury box. At one point, as the slender lawyer began to warm up, he stopped and slapped his hand on the railing in front of the box. *Thwack!*

"Delenda est Capone!" Ahern exclaimed. "Do you know what that means?"

In the days of the Roman Empire, Ahern went on, Cato the Elder became obsessed with the destruction of Carthage. *"Delenda est Carthago!"* he would tell the Senate every time he rose to speak, even when the subject at hand had nothing to do with the Mediterranean state. "Carthage must be destroyed!" He made it his motto, his mission, his mania. And Carthage was destroyed, largely because of Cato's persistence. Today, Ahern said, government officials have taken up the role of Cato, putting their personal obsessions ahead of the Constitution, sending up the cry "Capone must be destroyed!"

The government had dedicated a huge number of man-hours and terrific sums of money in building its case, said Ahern. They were trying to make Capone the fall guy for a disastrous law—Prohibition—that had cost the nation countless millions and sent thousands of men to early deaths. But the jury could send the government a message, Ahern said. The jury could tell Washington that the problem was bigger than Capone. Ask yourselves this question, Ahern implored the jury: If this were a civil trial to determine Capone's tax debt, how much would you say he owed? How much income has the government firmly proved? If you can't answer, he asked the jurors, how can you send this man to prison?

Ahern was working himself into a lather. He slapped the railing of the jury box again and again. He paused for a drink from the water cooler and summoned one more burst of energy, one more big breath of air. He was working toward his climax, hoping to make jurors see the case as he did.

Moving quickly, he reviewed the evidence presented by the prosecution, reminding them again that every last bit of it was circumstantial. Even the Mattingly letter, which was so critical to the government's case, was a deeply flawed piece of evidence. He reminded the jurors that the Mattingly letter contained only theoretical estimates and the government had come up with no corroboration, no bank ledgers, no canceled checks, no nothing. Despite its obsession, despite its manpower, despite its budget, he said, the government of the United States had utterly failed to prove Capone's guilt.

Fink stepped in at times, giving his partner a break, to make the more technical, unemotional arguments. Capone had failed to pay his taxes, Fink said, but that was hardly the same as attempting to defraud the government. Judge Wilkerson interrupted him at one point: Isn't it possible to defraud by remaining silent when one has a responsibility to speak? the judge asked. Fink said no. An attempt, by definition, requires action. Wilkerson rose from his seat and paced as Fink went on telling the jury that Capone was not the kind of man to shirk his duties or debts. "A tin horn or a piker might," he said, "but no one has ever accused Capone of being a piker."

Then Ahern took over again, resuming his heated oratory.

It was getting late. Shadows rose along the walls. The corners of the courtroom grew dark. Capone hunched forward in his seat, big shoulders curved beneath a bright green suit. His jaw worked another mint. His eyes locked on his lawyer's every move.

Ahern reminded the jurors that Capone had been tricked into a confession. The confession was false and inadmissible, he said, even though the judge had admitted it. Capone never had a chance, he said.

"It was all a plot, gentlemen," thundered Ahern, "to get this defendant to make admissions that he had a tax liability! The cry had gone out: *'Delenda est Capone!'*"

He banged the railing again with the palm of his hand.

"Capone must be destroyed!"

The words rang out, and the courtroom fell silent. For a moment there was no motion, not a sound. Finally, a few feet shuffled and a couple of chairs creaked. The tension broke.

Capone allowed himself a smile.

That night, George Johnson sat at his desk with a pencil and a legal pad and began outlining his closing argument.

"Capone must be destroyed?" he scribbled, perhaps unnerved, perhaps amused by Ahern's attempt to make the federal government the bad guy in the trial of the nation's most notorious criminal. Then he jotted his re-

sponse: "This is an orderly, lawful prosecution by the duly constituted authorities." On he went across twenty-three pages, organizing his thoughts
and planning his attack, before condensing his strategy into ten typewritten
sheets that he would use in guiding the jury to its conclusion.

If Ahern had gotten under Johnson's skin, the placid prosecutor wasn't
showing it. The next morning in court, before the biggest crowd yet to
attend the trial, Johnson began in his usual, understated style. The only
thing unusual about it was that Johnson was addressing a jury.

"Gentlemen of the jury," he began, "as the United States attorney, the
responsibility for the closing argument rests with me, and I shall promise
you that the argument will be brief, and that I will devote myself to the
facts in the record."

He began by addressing Ahern's complaint that the feds were bent on
destroying Capone, facts be damned. It wasn't so, he said. Every morning,
Johnson explained, millions of American go to work, "and every one of
those workers must pay an income tax on every dollar they earn above
the sum of $1,500. The government has no more important function,
except in the emergency of war, than to enforce the revenue laws of this
government, and if the time ever comes in the United States when our
American people will pay taxes only when the government seeks to find
out what they owe, or when it begins an investigation of their affairs to
determine their tax, then government will fail, then the army and navy
will disband, and our institutions will disappear, our courts will be swept
aside, American civilization will fail, and organized society will revert to
the days of the jungle, where every man will be for himself."

Johnson, having handled these cases before, knew that the simplest
argument was best. Forget about bootlegging. Forget about gunplay. Stick
to the obvious. Calmly hewing to his notes, in even tones and run-on
sentences, he continued. There would be no pounding on the railings for
Johnson, no intemperate displays of emotion, no Latin quotations. He
looked into the jury box and saw men much like himself—plainspoken
family men, small-town strivers, men who took pride in following society's rules—and he knew just how to talk to them.

"I have been a little bewildered in this case at the manner in which the
defense has attempted to weave a halo of mystery and romance around
the head of this man," he said, gesturing toward Capone. "Who is he?
Who is this man who during the years that we have considered here has

so lavishly expended what he claims to be almost half a million dollars? Is he the little boy . . . who succeeded in finding the pot of gold at the end of the rainbow . . . or maybe, as his counsel says, is he Robin Hood?" But Robin Hood was supposed to take from the rich and give to the poor, Johnson reminded the jurors. "Was it Robin Hood in this case who bought $5,000 worth of diamond belt buckles, to give to the unemployed? Was it Robin Hood in this case who bought a meat bill of $6,500? Did that go to the unemployed? It went to the house on Palm Island, where one witness testified they came and went and where there was poker. Did he buy those twenty-seven-dollar shirts to protect the shivering men who sleep under Wacker Drive at night? No."

He went on to outline Al Capone's career, focusing on his affluence, his power, his acquisitions, but not at all on the violence that attended his business affairs. It might seem strange that Johnson would try to stigmatize Capone by saying he played poker at his home on Palm Island and not mention the St. Valentine's Day Massacre or the murder of William McSwiggin, but the prosecutor knew what he was doing. There was no point in reminding the jury that they were being asked to convict Capone on a mere tax charge when he was allegedly involved in much greater crimes. Like a boxer in control of a fight in the late rounds, he was being careful not to take unnecessary risks.

He reminded the jurors of Capone's interest in various gambling establishments, reminded them that Reverend Hoover had given testimony establishing Capone as the owner of at least one casino. He explained one more time how gambling profits were wired from a bank in Cicero to a Western Union office in Miami, where Capone's men picked up the cash for their boss. Capone was the mastermind of the operation, he said, operating from a perch so lofty that he never needed to get his hands dirty. His greatest crime, Johnson said, was not running brothels and casinos; his greatest crime was designing and operating an elaborate underground syndicate built with the express purpose of avoiding income tax.

Once again, Johnson's argument wasn't exactly true—Capone didn't build his syndicate to avoid taxes. The tax dodging was a consequence of the lifestyle and career he'd chosen. But it sounded good. From there, the prosecutor went on to shoot down his opponent's arguments one by one, in mind-numbing detail, explaining why prosecutors called some witnesses and not others, why they emphasized certain bits of evidence and neglected others. He compared Ahern to an artist who, with the addition of a line here and there, can cast a portrait in any light he likes, making his subject "look either like a sage or a fool." Ahern, he said, had taken isolated facts and contorted them to give the impression that federal prosecutors had a weak case and were motivated by personal animus for the defendant. Johnson took the higher ground. He urged the jurors to weigh all the evidence, including the evidence presented by Capone's lawyers. But ask yourselves, he beseeched the jury, whether you can trust those who speak on behalf of a man such as Al Capone.

"This, gentlemen of the jury," he said, building calmly toward his conclusion, "is not a case of a public clamor." In his five years as U.S. attorney, he said, he was "never more sincere, or more determined . . . than I am in this case." In those five years, he said, he had never prosecuted a case in which "the facts cry out louder as evidence of a violation of the law of the United States."

Though the case had been a difficult one, Johnson said, he had refused to compromise his ethics. He had refused to present witnesses who were less than reliable. Opposing counsel, he said, had told the jury that this case would be remembered for generations to come. But Johnson told the jurors to ignore that comment, "to treat this case as if the defendant were John Brown." He continued, "I am asking you to be fair and impartial to the defendant, and I am asking you to be fair and impartial to the government."

If future generations do remember the trial of Al Capone, he said, "they will remember it for an important reason. They will remember it for the reason that it will establish this: whether any man can be above the law, whether any man can so conduct his affairs that he can escape entirely the burdens of government. And that is the record, gentlemen of the jury, that your verdict will write in this case."

The jury needed eight hours and ten minutes to reach its decision.

At 10:50 P.M. on Saturday, October 17, Ahern got word that the panel had come to a verdict. He called Capone at the Lexington Hotel. Fifteen minutes later Capone was back in the courtroom. He took a seat, removed his hat, and mopped his sweaty forehead with a handkerchief.

The court was called to order. Members of the jury filed back in and took their seats in the jury box. Outside, the city streets were dark and quiet. About fifty spectators had somehow gotten word of the imminent verdict and hustled to the courthouse to witness the moment. Capone and his lawyers sat up straight and looked at the faces of the jurors, trying to read something in their various expressions. Judge Wilkerson strode to the bench, and everyone stood. The judge sat, faced the jury, and asked, "Gentlemen, have you reached a verdict?"

"Yes, sir," said the foreman, his voice barely audible.

"You may hand your verdict to the clerk," said the judge.

The clerk took the prepared form, cleared his throat, and began to read.

What happened next left everyone—including the judge—a little confused.

"We the jury find the defendant guilty on counts one, five, nine, thirteen, and eighteen in the second indictment," the clerk announced, "and not guilty on counts two, three, four, six, seven, eight, ten, eleven, twelve, fourteen, fifteen, sixteen, seventeen, nineteen, twenty, twenty-one, and twenty-two."

A long moment of silence followed, as if everyone in the room tried to figure out what all those numbers meant. To Capone, who had always been pretty good at calculations, it must have sounded positive: seventeen "not guilties" to five "guilties." He smiled nervously.

The judge looked at the piece of paper, handed it back to the clerk, and asked him to read it again so the attorneys could make sense of what they'd heard. The clerk ended up reading it twice. Lawyers on both sides began scratching at their ledgers. It took them several minutes to figure out what the verdict meant—and for Capone to be informed that he had nothing to smile about. He would face a maximum sentence of seventeen years—five years for each of the three felonies and one year for each of the two misdemeanors—and a maximum fine of $50,000. It could have been worse, but it certainly didn't qualify as a victory.

Sentencing would take place the following week, said Judge Wilkerson. He banged his gavel. Court was adjourned.

Capone hustled out the door and down the elevator.

———

One week later, Capone appeared in court again to hear Judge Wilkerson announce the sentence. The gangster smiled at some of the spectators in the courtroom and shook hands with his attorneys. None of his family joined him.

The crowd of about two hundred hushed when Judge Wilkerson entered the room. Capone edged forward on his swivel chair, cupped his right hand over his ear, and opened his bushy-browed eyes wide.

First, Wilkerson addressed a motion by Ahern to have the entire verdict dismissed.

The motion, he said, is denied.

Capone sat back in his chair.

Ahern asked the court to record his objection to the decision.

Then Judge Wilkerson asked the defendant to stand and approach the bench.

Capone rose, stepped solemnly toward the judge, and stood with his hands behind his back. The room was silent.

On the first felony count, said the judge, he sentenced the defendant to five years in prison and a $10,000 fine.

Capone grimaced.

On the second felony count, said the judge, he sentenced the defendant to five years and a $10,000 fine.

Capone bounced a little on his feet and nervously licked his lips.

On the third felony count, said the judge, he sentenced the defendant to five years and a $10,000 fine.

Capone's fingers locked and unlocked behind his back.

On each of the two misdemeanor counts, the judge continued, the defendant was sentenced to one year in jail and a $10,000 fine. A murmur rose from the room, but Wilkerson pretended not to hear it. He added that two of the three felony counts would run concurrently, and he gave Capone credit for some of the time he'd already served for contempt. "The result," he said, "is that the aggregate sentence of the defendant is eleven years in the penitentiary and fines aggregating $50,000."

It was, by far, the stiffest sentence ever handed down in a tax case.

Capone, one newspaper reporter wrote, looked like a man who had just been slapped in the face. His whole body trembled. After a few seconds, he appeared to compose himself.

He turned to his lawyers and shook their hands, but without his usual vigor. The light had gone out of his eyes.

"Well, so long," he said. "Good-bye."

EPILOGUE

Just like that, Capone was gone.

Never again would he terrorize, peddle booze, or live the life of a titan.

At the close of his trial, he entered Cook County Jail, where so many of his men had come and gone over the years, pausing briefly near the entrance to talk yet again with reporters.

"What do you say, Al?" one of the scribes asked.

"It was a blow to the belt," he answered, referring to the eleven-year sentence. "But what can you expect when the whole community is prejudiced against you? I've never heard of anyone getting more than five years for income-tax evasion."

That evening, Capone settled into a cell on D Block, in the hospital ward, where accommodations were a little nicer than in the rest of the prison. He shoved aside his tin plate of corned beef and cabbage, settling for coffee and a few bites of rice pudding. While the prisoner brooded, word of his incarceration spread across the nation by radio and in boldface banner headlines. Read a front-page headline in the *New York Times,* "CAPONE CONVICTED OF DODGING TAXES."

Most of the newspaper coverage carried a celebratory tone, as if a troublesome pest or virus had finally been wiped out. Ironically, though, some Americans felt sympathy for Capone, perhaps for the first time. Though no one doubted his criminality, it seemed perverse to some that the government had failed to charge him with more serious crimes. Few could relate to a cold-blooded killer, but everyone could relate to a tax cheat. Even some editorial writers expressed disappointment with the outcome of the case, saying it was a shame the government had found it

necessary to rely on legal trickery to put Capone away. "It is ludicrous,"
commented the *Boston Globe,* "that this underworld gang leader had been
led to the doors of the penitentiary at last only through prosecutions on
income tax and liquor conspiracy laws." And the *Washington Evening Star*
complained that while it was no doubt satisfying to see Capone behind
bars, "there will remain a sense that the law had failed."

Capone's lawyers also felt the law had failed, albeit for different reasons, and they went to work trying to get his sentence reversed. They
began by obtaining a stay that would keep their client from being shipped
off to federal prison until his appeals were heard. At least for the time
being, Capone would remain in Cook County Jail.

Before long, though, George Johnson received an anonymous telegram saying Capone was getting a little too comfortable at Cook County.
More specifically, claimed the informant, the gangster was using the jail
as the new headquarters for his criminal enterprise. Capone had paid off
the warden, according to the tip, and now he had the freedom to make
phone calls, send telegrams, and dispatch messengers around the city.
He even had secretarial help, the informant reported. Some of his fellow inmates who happened to be longtime associates, including William
White and Phil D'Andrea, were permitted to leave their cells to fraternize
with Capone. Prisoners were allowed a limited number of visitors, but
Capone was said to be circumventing the rule by having his gangster pals
pretend to visit the other inmates in his ward. Among his guests were
Jack Guzik, Frankie Rio, Red Barker, Murray Humphreys, Johnny Torrio, and a Capone girlfriend identified only as "Marion." When guests
arrived, Capone served them good whiskey. Women were brought in,
too, and paid to "put on an obscene performance for the entertainment
of Capone's guests."

A *Chicago Herald and Examiner* headline blared "CAPONE RUNS UNDER-
WORLD FROM CELL." No one suggested that the gang boss was using his
influence to order hits, although there were any number of witnesses and
informants from his trial whom he might have liked to see eliminated. The
allegations only stated that he was still calling the shots in his gambling
and booze business. Still, as the news spread across the country, the feds
were embarrassed. In an unusual move for a prosecutor, Johnson visited
the jail and investigated the situation personally. Already, rumors around
the federal building in Chicago said that Johnson might be rewarded with

a judgeship for his work on the Capone case. The newspapers also said that President Hoover was urging Judge Wilkerson to consider a campaign for governor. If Wilkerson didn't run, the papers said, the president probably would nominate the judge for a seat on a higher court.

Johnson could have charged Capone with contempt of court if he found the gangster had been breaking prison rules, but an investigation by a federal agent concluded that many of the allegations had been exaggerated. Still, Johnson insisted on a clampdown at the jail. From that time on, Capone was allowed to see only his relatives and lawyers. He would be permitted no more phone calls than any other prisoner.

Determined to show the press that he was no coddler of criminals, Warden David Moneypenny led reporters on a tour of the jail, showing them Capone's austere living accommodations. "I'm in jail," Capone griped to the reporters. "Aren't they satisfied?"

Soon after, though, another scandal erupted that seemed to confirm the public's suspicion that Capone was being coddled: Warden Moneypenny was caught borrowing one of Capone's cars, a sixteen-cylinder Cadillac, for a drive to Springfield, Illinois. He claimed he didn't know the car belonged to Capone. On Thanksgiving, the prisoner was permitted to skip the prison fare and sup from a huge hamper of food sent by his mother. Inside the hamper was a turkey with all the trimmings and a huge container of spaghetti. Capone shared the meal with his four cell mates, "one of whom is a Negro," noted the *Tribune*. After the meal, an ice-cream truck pulled up outside the jail and delivered a slice of layer cake and a scoop of ice cream to each prisoner in the facility, compliments of inmate Capone.

In filing their appeal of Capone's sentence, his lawyers decided to focus on a technicality: Capone's indictment had been written in vague language that had made it impossible to defend, the lawyers argued. But the appeals court wasn't buying it. In a ruling issued on February 27, 1932, the court declared that the indictment had included more than enough detail for Capone's lawyers to understand the charges and to plot their defense. Furthermore, said the court, if the lawyers had not been satisfied with the indictment when it had been issued, they should have said so at the time and asked the district attorney to furnish additional details.

After a long winter in jail and a long, dull process of appeals, it looked as if Capone were nearly out of options. His lawyers would make one more pitch, to the U.S. Supreme Court, and if that failed, Capone was bound for a federal penitentiary.

On the morning of March 10, 1932, Capone gave an interview to Arthur Brisbane, an editor in the Hearst newspaper chain, and once again thrust himself into national headlines. Nine days earlier, in Hopewell, New Jersey, someone had kidnapped the infant son of Charles and Anne Lindbergh. Lindbergh was still one of the nation's most beloved heroes, even five years after his legendary flight across the Atlantic. The kidnapping triggered national hysteria and a massive hunt for the missing child. Capone seemed to be greatly disturbed by the crime. If the feds would allow him to briefly leave his jail cell, he said in the interview with Brisbane, he would work with the government to find Lindbergh's baby. Capone implied that his underworld ties might help him unearth information that law enforcement officials could never get. He even offered collateral, saying his brother John would hold his place in jail.

Capone didn't reveal his plan for finding the baby, saying only, "I know I could help. . . . I know a lot of people." At first, Lindbergh expressed interest, but two of the men leading the investigation into the kidnapping—Frank Wilson and Elmer Irey of the Internal Revenue Bureau—knew Capone from their work on his tax case and felt strongly that the gangster had nothing to offer. They urged Lindbergh to ignore Capone's overture. When Lindbergh received a demand for ransom, it was the soft-spoken, iron-willed accountant Frank Wilson who suggested that the serial numbers on the gold certificates paid as ransom be recorded before they were delivered to the kidnapper. It was a novel approach, and it worked. Those serial numbers led investigators to Bruno Richard Hauptmann, who was eventually convicted and executed for the crime. Unfortunately, by that time, the Lindbergh baby had already been found dead.

In 1936, Frank Wilson was named chief of the Secret Service. He didn't generate many headlines—no surprise—but he made huge strides in reducing the production and distribution of counterfeit money, cutting the government's annual losses from $1.5 million to $50,000. He also instituted techniques for protecting the president that would remain standard procedure for decades to follow. He retired in 1947 and died in 1970 at age eighty-three.

On May 2, the U.S. Supreme Court declined to hear Capone's appeal. Though he expected to be sent to the penitentiary at Leavenworth, Kansas, where his brother Ralph and other members of his gang had been sent, Capone learned just prior to his departure that the feds were sending him to the penitentiary in Atlanta. It seemed they didn't want too many Chicago gangsters in one place. The next day, at Cook County Jail, he said good-bye to Mae, Sonny, Theresa, Mafalda, and his brother Matt.

Eliot Ness was among the federal agents assigned to escort Capone to the old Dearborn Station. Later, Ness would dramatize his account of the trip across town, giving the impression that he and Capone had exchanged terse words, even though newspaper accounts made it clear that the two men traveled in separate cars. In all likelihood, they never met: not on that day, not ever.

Capone's departure signaled the end of Ness's glory days.

He would spend most of the rest of his career as the public safety director in Cleveland. While he maintained his high ethical standards and helped erase corruption from Cleveland's police department, his reputation was tarnished over time by rumors of heavy drinking and marital infidelity. In 1942 he smashed his car after a night of drinking. Soon after, he resigned his post. His drinking grew heavier. His shoulders began to slump, and the lines in his face grew deeper and wider. He ran for mayor of Cleveland in 1947 but didn't seem to have his heart in it. Humiliated by the election loss, he drank more heavily than ever. After a couple of promising jobs in the private sector, he eventually wound up selling frozen hamburger patties to restaurants. He died from a heart attack in 1957.

On May 3, 1932, a damp and gray day, the *Dixie Flyer* rumbled out of Chicago, Atlanta-bound. Capone sat shackled to a car thief named Vito Morici, surrounded by federal agents. The big fellow smoked cigars, smiled for photographers, and chatted with reporters, perhaps aware that his window of opportunity for such impromptu press conferences was about to slam shut.

"What do I think about it all?" he asked in reply to a reporter's question. "Well, I'm on my way to do eleven years. I've got to do it, that's all. I'm not sore at anybody, but I hope Chicago will be better off and the clamor will be satisfied." He added that he thought it might be best if booze sales were legalized again. Otherwise, he said, "they'll find that sending me away won't help Chicago much."

Like Babe Ruth en route to spring training or Clark Gable on tour to promote a new movie, Capone electrified the crowds gathered at whistle-stops along the route. "They pressed alongside the Pullman cars and peered into the window," the *New York Times* reported. "Capone answered their waves with broad smiles and the gesture of a handshake." He continued his dialogue with reporters for much of the trip. He complained once again that he'd been misunderstood, that he'd only been giving people what they wanted. Anyway, he grumbled, bootlegging was a lousy business, hardly the gold mine everyone thought. He griped, too, about President Hoover. If it hadn't been for politics—politics and publicity—he would have been permitted to pay his back taxes and walk away. But taxes had never really been the issue. It was politics. Hoover wanted to make an example of him. Hoover needed a conviction so he could campaign for reelection as the man who locked up Capone.

"I don't think that's playing fair," he said, "but they've got me and I'll have to take the medicine."

———

The U.S. Penitentiary at Atlanta—opened in 1903—was big and imposing, heavily barred and bolted. It was designed to make inmates feel hopeless. Its perimeter wall—thirty-seven feet high, four feet thick, and enclosing twenty-three acres—was the world's largest concrete structure at the time of its completion in 1910. Among criminals, Atlanta was known as the toughest of the federal pens.

Upon arrival, Capone turned over the $231 in his pocket, as well as sixteen religious medals, a rosary, a nail clipper, a fountain pen, a wallet, and a single key. He received a pair of blue denim overalls with the number 40886 stitched on a trouser leg. In his medical examination he weighed in at 255 pounds, which suggested that Ma Capone had kept her son well fed during his six-month stay in Cook County Jail. He had 20/20 vision in his right eye and 20/40 in his left. His blood pressure was on the high side, at 130/100. Doctors also recorded that he was suffering from arthritis, a deviated septum (made worse by his surgery three years earlier performed by a prison doctor in Philadelphia), and a severely swollen prostate gland, which probably made it difficult for him to urinate or ejaculate.

He was thirty-three years old.

A psychological exam found him normal in every way. He displayed no psychotic behavior. His memory was good. His IQ measured at ninety-five, which was an average score. In a free-association exercise, he did just fine. For "table," he said "eat on." For "sweet," he replied "sugar." For "gun," he said "shoot."

But the most important result of Capone's medical workup came from a Wasserman blood test, which returned positive for "nervous system syphilis," also known as tertiary syphilis. In all likelihood, the news came as a shock to Capone. Asked when he thought he had contracted the sexually transmitted disease, Capone told doctors he had first noticed a lesion on his penis in 1921, when he was twenty-two years old. At the time he hadn't sought treatment. The medical report didn't indicate whether Capone told his wife about the infection, or whether he had passed the disease on to her. After the initial lesion on his penis, Capone had probably suffered a few other symptoms, including rashes on his hands and feet, muscle aches, and fatigue. But those, too, would have passed without treatment. Capone may have forgotten about them over time. For most untreated syphilis patients, the disease lies dormant and symptoms never return. But in about 15 percent of cases, after years or even decades of dormancy, the disease comes back and begins destroying the nervous system. It causes dementia, paralysis, and gradual blindness. The mind warps. In some cases the brain damage is severe enough to be fatal.

Prison doctors started Capone on one of the standard treatments for advanced syphilis—bismuth therapy (penicillin had not yet become available)—but they knew they were too late to alter the outcome. In the months and years ahead, Capone would confront a fate much worse than prison.

On his first night in the federal pen, Capone burned through half a dozen two-dollar cigars, according to one of his cell mates, Morris "Red" Rudensky, a burglar and safecracker who had known the crime boss slightly a few years earlier when Rudensky had worked in the Midwest as a freelance bootlegger. At night, said Rudensky, Capone would cry out in his sleep, "No, no, no!" Rudensky had the impression that Capone was being chased in his dreams. Overall, though, Rudensky was surprised to find that his bunkmate wasn't "hateful or vitriolic." He prattled on about his wife and son almost endlessly, wondering, "How in hell can a fat dago like me have a son that good-looking?" And when Rudensky teased Capone about famous characters from his past—Dean O'Banion and Bugs Moran, to name a couple—Capone would laugh and say the same thing he'd said back in the days of his peak power: It was a shame those guys had insisted on fighting over the booze business when there had been more than enough dough to go around.

"If we ever all hooked up," he said with a chuckle, "I could've been president."

He was upset with his attorneys. It still seemed absurd to him that he was doing time for taxes, of all things. But he seemed more wistful than angry. He longed to walk the sidewalks of Chicago again, or to lie in the shade at his Palm Island estate, or to "follow the ponies," as he put it, at any of his favorite racetracks. Once in a while Capone would suffer a "flare-up," as Rudensky put it, a brief outburst of fury or a seizure that resembled an epileptic fit, but such incidents were brief, coming and going "like firecrackers."

Capone got his exercise playing baseball (terribly) and tennis (not quite terribly, but not terribly well). In his youth, he had been somewhat graceful, but now he carried far too much weight around his gut to move with any nimbleness. For eight hours a day he cobbled shoes in the prison factory. When the warden introduced new rules limiting family visits to one a month, Capone wrote a respectful letter of protest, noting that the policy would be a tremendous hardship for families such as his that had to travel great distances to visit the prison. He went on to say he thought he was doing an excellent job running the stitching machine in the shoe shop and wondered if he might have a chance to try another job, "at the Baker Shop or at the Tennis court as a helper, as I am familiar with both details." If the warden would grant his request, he said, he would be happy to help out in the shoe shop in his spare time. "Sure hope you will consider me," he concluded, "and give me a chance to advance myself."

A newspaper report early in 1933 claimed yet again that Capone was being coddled: allowed to wear his $12-a-pair silk underwear, to sleep on a hospital bed instead of the cot in his cell, and to spend more than his allotted time on the tennis courts. There were rumors that Capone was having money smuggled into the prison and using it to buy protection from his fellow inmates and favors from his guards. Rudensky would claim years later in his autobiography that Capone hid his cash in the hollowed-out handle of his tennis racket. The Bureau of Investigation checked out the rumors but found nothing amiss, and the warden assured his bosses in Washington that the nation's most famous prisoner was receiving no special treatment.

By now, Capone had dumped his Chicago lawyers and hired a pair from Washington, D.C.: William E. Leahy and William J. Hughes. In the spring of 1933 they were pursuing an appeal that seemed promising. A year earlier, in *U.S. v. Scharton,* the Supreme Court had ruled that tax evasion did not constitute fraud. That meant the statute of limitations for tax evasion was only three years, not six. If the ruling could be applied to Capone, his felony charges would be reduced to misdemeanors and his prison sentence would be shortened.

But when the new lawyers appeared in federal court in New Orleans to have their appeal heard, Judge E. Marvin Underwood said there was an important difference between Scharton's case and Capone's. Scharton's lawyers had raised their concerns about the statute of limitations at the start of the trial and raised it again on their initial appeal. Capone's trial lawyers had made almost no mention of and no objection to the statute of limitations. Since Capone's complaint on the statute of limitations was never heard in the original district court or in the first court of appeals, Judge Underwood said, he had no right to intervene. On January 25, 1933, Capone received the following telegram from his lawyers: "DECISION AGAINST YOU ON GROUND POINTS SHOULD HAVE BEEN RAISED ON APPEAL DO NOT LOSE HEART."

They would try again, appealing to the U.S. Supreme Court, but to no avail.

Capone's Chicago lawyers, Ahern and Fink, had blown it. From the start of the trial in Chicago, they had chosen the wrong approach. First they had tried to prove that Capone had no income. Then they had admitted he had income but claimed that his losses had offset his earnings.

Those were the arguments they had thought would give them the best shot to win in Judge Wilkerson's court in Chicago.

In hindsight, though, they should have seen that they had no chance with Wilkerson—especially after he had tossed out Capone's plea agreement and insisted on taking the case to trial. And when Wilkerson said at the start of the trial that he did not intend to listen to arguments concerning the statute of limitations, they should have asked him again and again, creating a record of objections at the trial. They should have begun laying the groundwork for their appeal.

Now it was too late. Capone would have to do his time. The best he could hope for would be to have his sentence shaved by a couple of years for good behavior.

As he settled in, Capone learned of an opening in the book bindery shop and again requested a transfer. In making his pitch, he cited his experience at the Brooklyn paper company where he had worked as a teenager. He also requested permission to learn to play a musical instrument. His first choice, he said, was the bass. The records don't say whether his request for an instrument was granted.

He continued to receive visitors. Mae and Sonny were his most frequent guests, coming almost every month. Every so often, one of his old cronies somehow got in to see the old boss. On birthdays and holidays, he never failed to send telegrams to his friends and family. In 1933 he composed Mother's Day poems for his wife and mother. Mae's poem went like this:

> *We have set apart a Mother's day*
> *From all the days in the year*
> *And I want to bring my tribute to somebody precious and dear.*
> *I want to wish all gladness and happiness to the sweetest woman—my wife.*
> *For you are part of Mother's day*
> *And the greatest part of my life.*

After the poem, he added a note: "With passing years the realization of my debt of gratitude grows more profound, and my love ever deeper and stronger for you, and May God Bless you and love to all. Your dear husband, Al."

He penned a different poem for his mother and attached almost the identical note at the bottom of the page.

In the end, President Hoover's triumph in putting Capone behind bars wasn't enough to get him reelected. Not even close. Franklin Delano Roosevelt, the governor of New York, defeated Hoover in a landslide, carrying all but six states and tallying 57.4 percent of the popular vote.

Now came the hard part. Roosevelt inherited a national crisis as serious as any since the Civil War. The unemployment rate had risen to about 25 percent. The stock market was still in the tank. Americans had lost more than $2 billion in deposits as ten thousand banks had failed since 1929. Throughout his campaign for the presidency, Roosevelt had blasted Hoover for being too timid. The time had come for the new president to take control.

"We have nothing to fear but fear itself," Roosevelt said on March 4, 1933, in his inaugural address. In his first hundred days in office, Roosevelt moved with remarkable speed to kick-start the economy and get Americans working again. With the help of a cooperative Congress he delivered the Emergency Banking Relief Act, the Public Works Administration, the Civilian Conservation Corps, the Tennessee Valley Authority, the National Industrial Recovery Act, and the Federal Deposit Insurance Corporation. He also began dismantling Prohibition. By the end of 1933, booze flowed freely again. It may or may not have helped boost the economy, but it certainly made people feel better.

Hoover bounced back, eventually. Upon leaving the White House, he returned to Palo Alto, California, and became chairman of the board of the Boys' Clubs of America, holding the position for the next twenty-five years. When war erupted in Europe, Hoover, acting as a private citizen, started the Polish Relief Commission, which fed three hundred thousand Europeans and saved countless lives. In 1946, when famine threatened much of Europe, Hoover, now seventy-two, traveled thirty-five thousand miles in fifty-seven days and designed a massive relief organization that once more rescued untold thousands of people from hunger and starvation.

In 1947, Congress asked Hoover to offer recommendations for a complete reorganization of the executive branch of the federal government. Roughly 70 percent of his cost-cutting, efficiency-boosting recommendations were made law under President Harry Truman. By 1947, many Americans had begun to recognize Hoover's integrity and to realize that he could not have prevented the Depression. That year, Congress voted to rename the Boulder Dam in his honor. When the former president died in 1964, at age ninety, more than seventy-five thousand people attended his funeral service in Iowa.

"Being a politician is a poor profession," he wrote late in life in reply to a letter from an American school student, aptly summing up his career. "Being a public servant is a noble one."

The Roosevelt administration also worked fast on matters unconnected to the Depression. On August 1, 1933, Attorney General Homer S. Cummings wrote a memo suggesting that the government might be served well "having a special prison . . . in a remote place—on an island, or in Alaska, so that the persons incarcerated would not be in constant communication with friends outside." Cummings believed that the general prison population would be more easily rehabilitated and controlled if the most troublesome criminals were pulled out.

Capone wasn't violent, but he was certainly a nuisance to the feds, with the seemingly endless string of newspaper stories documenting his underwear selection, his ongoing contact with the underworld, and his repeated judicial appeals. A week after his initial memo, Cummings selected Alcatraz Island for the new, maximum-security prison. Alcatraz is a craggy, thumb-shaped rock that sits in the middle of San Francisco Bay like a scab on a gorgeous face. The Golden Gate Bridge, then under construction, rises just to the west, Berkeley and the Oakland Hills to the east, and the glittering hills of San Francisco to the south. The island already contained an old military prison, so it didn't take much time or money to get it ready for new inmates. Gun galleries, gates, and watchtowers were added. The result was one of the strangest prisons ever built. With dense fogs and chill winds blowing in from the Pacific, sailboats, fishing vessels, and ferries churning the water, and waves lapping at the island's shore, the place was stark yet beautiful, isolated yet surrounded with the bounties of life. If the gleaming lights of San Francisco tempted prisoners to escape, the icy, swirling waters usually would change their minds.

On August 19, 1934, Capone and forty-two other prisoners from Atlanta were loaded on a specially equipped train, shackled to their seats, and transported cross-country to San Francisco. They were joined at Alcatraz by more than one hundred inmates from other prisons around the country. The feds never explained why Capone was assigned to Alcatraz, but it seems fairly clear that it was a public relations move. Capone had not hurt anyone or threatened to hurt anyone during his time in prison. He had not attempted escape, nor did anyone believe he was considering an attempt. But the federal government wanted publicity for its new prison. It wanted everyone to know that Alcatraz was the toughest slammer in the land. It wanted criminals everywhere to fear being sentenced to time on the Rock, as Alcatraz quickly became known. And if the feds had learned one thing from their ongoing relationship with Capone, it was this: The man got headlines.

Capone—prisoner number eighty-five—was assigned to cell 181. Like all the other cells, his was nine feet long and five feet wide, with bars overlooking the cell block and little natural light. Prisoners were roused from bed at six thirty each morning. They had no radios. They were permitted to shave three times a week with razors that were passed through the bars and then immediately recovered by guards. Capone's first job was in the laundry. When he and the other inmates weren't working, they were allowed to smoke, talk, read books, and play musical instruments, but not to congregate. Mind-numbing isolation was intended to be a big part of the punishment on the Rock.

At Alcatraz, Capone seemed determined to improve himself. On June 1, 1935, his library card showed he had borrowed the following books: *Common Errors in English Corrected*; *Rudiments of Music*; *How to Enjoy Music*; *American Home Book of Building*; *Practical Flower Gardening*; *Sailing Alone Around the World*; and *Life Begins at Forty*. That same year, in his application for parole, he wrote, "I am 36 years old, and all of my life I have always tried to be a man, I have always keep [sic] my word, at no time did I ever steal or force anyone to give me anything by force, I have keep [sic] up all of my family all of the time, and the good Lord knows, I have, and intend to keep on doing so all my life, I have made mistakes, all of us have, but sure hope & pray for no more, and will prove it if given one more chance, as I sure owe to my dear Son, Wife, Mother and the rest of my family, for the grief I have caused them."

He wrote often to Mae, promising he would be different when he returned home. Part of being different, it seemed, included ditching a woman with whom he had had an affair. He never mentioned the woman's name. Nor did he say when and where the romance had occurred. In a letter dated March 3 (probably 1935), he gushed, "Now dearest, let us forget business and unpleasant happenings and let me tell you dear, that I love, and adore you more now than ever . . . when your dear dad gets lucky and comes home again into your wonderful arms it will be a new daddy, and yours alone, so please dear believe me, as I sure will prove it to you later. . . . I love you alone and forgotten all about the other party."

Though he regularly attended chapel, it was music, not religion, that seemed to offer Capone the greatest solace. When he wasn't reading books, he taught himself to play the mandola (an eight-stringed, teardrop-shaped instrument similar to a mandolin). In one letter to Sonny, he said that he had seen the movie *Rainbow on the River* in prison, ordered the sheet music for piano, and transposed it for mandola. "Son of mine," he bragged, "when I come home, I will play not only that song, but about 500 more, and all mostly Theme Songs from the best Shows. In other words Junior, there isn't a song written that I can't play."

At one point while at Alcatraz, Capone composed an original song, called "Madonna Mia." The lyrics went like this: "With your true love to guide me, let whatever betide me, I will never go wrong. There's only one moon above, one golden sun, there's only one that I love, you are the one." He gave the sheet music to Vincent Casey, a young Jesuit priest, who visited inmates at Alcatraz and counseled Capone every week for two years.

Prison may have brought out the artistic and religious side of Capone, but his time at Alcatraz was not entirely serene. As the syphilis continued to attack his central nervous system, he was increasingly prone to emotional outbursts. He lost his temper and yelled at inmates and guards, seemingly for no reason.

On the morning of June 23, 1936, Capone was at work in the prison basement, swabbing the floor between the laundry room and the shower. Nearby, in the barbershop, a Texas bank robber named James C. Lucas was waiting for his monthly haircut. Lucas was one of the joint's hardest prisoners. Once, he had supposedly asked Capone to finance a plot to smuggle machine guns into Alcatraz. Capone laughed and dismissed the scheme as absurd. Whether that encounter was the cause of the trouble or not, Lucas was ready to explode.

While Capone was mopping and the barber was distracted, Lucas grabbed a pair of scissors. He pried the two blades apart, kept one, dropped the other, and threw himself at Capone. The blade sliced into the lower left side of Capone's back. Capone wheeled around and clobbered Lucas with a fist to the face. Lucas flashed the blade again, catching Capone on his left thumb.

Somehow Capone got hold of his mandola, picked it up, and swung it like a club at his attacker. After that, a guard jumped in and tore the men apart. Despite the two gashes, Capone was not badly hurt. No organs had been punctured. The tip of the scissor blade was still embedded in his thumb, but it was easily removed by doctors. From time to time the press reported other attacks on Capone, but the warden usually denied their occurrence, and prison records show no other serious incidents. Most of the time he was a well-behaved inmate.

On Saturday, February 5, 1938, Capone showed up in the prison mess hall wearing his blue uniform, which was supposed to be worn only on Sundays and holidays. A guard told him to go back to his cell and put on his gray coveralls. He went back to his cell, changed, and then returned to the mess hall and drank a cup of coffee. When he finished, instead of returning directly to his cell, he wandered aimlessly, as if lost. When he finally made it back to his cell, he threw up and sat down on the toilet, where he began to mumble incoherently. When a guard came to see what was happening, Capone was writhing on the floor. He was taken to the prison hospital and restrained.

"Guess I'm a little wacky," he said when he finally came around. "What happened, Doc?"

Capone's syphilis was attacking his brain with greater force. "I am very much of the opinion that the case is one of general paresis," said his doctor, referring to the inflammation of the brain that leads to dementia and paralysis.

Within days, word leaked to the newspapers that Capone had lost his mind. His wife and brother frantically phoned the warden and sent him telegrams, searching for answers. The warden replied with a telegram on February 9 that said Capone was "QUIET, COMMUNICATIVE, COOPERATIVE, APPARENTLY COMPREHENDS HIS CONDITION."

A week later, Capone had made enough of a recovery to write to his son, who was enrolled at the University of Notre Dame, studying to be a lawyer but contemplating a switch to medicine. He assured Sonny that he was fine. When he returned home, he informed his son, "we three will be the happiest in all God's creation." Delicately, without the least bit of bossiness, he urged his son to stick with his plan to get a law degree—at least until Capone was out of prison and the whole family could discuss the decision. "Give your Mother a million kisses for me," he closed.

All through 1937 and 1938, his wife, mother, and brother Ralph sent frequent letters to the warden, trying to get a better sense of Capone's medical condition and his prognosis for recovery. The answers were vague and unsatisfying, and on at least one occasion Mae was urged by the warden to put off a scheduled visit. In the spring of 1938, with only about a year to go on his federal sentence, thanks to time off for good behavior, Capone wrote to his mother, pledging that his health was improving and that he would be fine by the time he came home the following year. "Mother dear please do not worry no more about your dear Son, as God has been good to us Mother," he wrote. "Tomorrow, I will go to Mass and that means prayers for you, and for the rest of our dear family."

But his personality was changing like the San Francisco weather, fog replacing clarity and clarity replacing fog unpredictably. At times he seemed irritable and childish. At other times he took a complete departure from reality. Even when he was fairly well grounded, though, he spoke in grandiose terms of his plans to build factories employing tens of thousands of men. He promised to alleviate the widespread poverty of Mexicans in America. He said habitual lawbreakers should be segregated from society to prevent the contagion of their criminality. For the prison doctors who impressed him as competent and kind, he promised to build hospitals and put them in charge.

"His mood is happy and he has no enemies," one of his doctors wrote. "He still has some disturbances of consciousness at times as his mind wanders and he hears God and the Angels verbally reply to his prayers etc. He however retains partial insight into these and says he probably imagines some of the things he hears."

One day in the summer of 1938, Capone picked up his bedpan and used it to pound the head of an inmate named Ryan, who had been mopping the bathroom and had asked Capone to empty his waste elsewhere. The blow to the head left Ryan with a small cut, nothing serious, but the attack was one more sign of Capone's seesawing emotional state.

By the autumn of 1938, his doctors were considering a more dramatic course of treatment. At the time, in advanced cases of syphilis, patients were injected with the malaria virus. The elevated body temperatures brought on by malaria were believed capable of destroying the syphilis organism. It was a risky treatment. The malaria had to be allowed to burn hot and long to kill the syphilis, but not so hot and long that it killed the patient or caused brain damage. Doctors would use quinine to fight off the malaria and reduce body temperatures after they felt the fever had done its job.

Though the doctors at Alcatraz had little experience treating syphilis with malaria, Capone signed a letter giving them permission to proceed. Ralph also signed off on the decision. But during one treatment, on September 16, 1938, something went wrong. Capone felt a deep chill followed by a huge spike in temperature, to 104 degrees. He became confused and tore apart one of his prayer books. When he began having severe convulsions, doctors quickly shot him full of quinine to bring down the fever, along with a dose of morphine to reduce the pain. One of his doctors, Romney M. Ritchey, wrote that the attack "strongly suggested an embolism"—or obstructed artery—"perhaps resulting from the Malarial chill." For days afterward, he remained disoriented, noisy, and restless. Twice he soiled his bed.

Undeterred, the doctors tried again less than a month later. This time they came even closer to killing him. His temperature soared to 105 degrees. "At the time of his last chill," wrote one doctor, "he had a violent seizure and it was felt that it might be the end of him. Morphine had no effect upon the convulsions but intravenous quinine was effective and the malaria was terminated. . . . Further attempts at malarial therapy would be ill advised."

Eventually, the prison psychiatrist noted that Capone appeared to recover from the malarial treatment and suffered no evident long-term damage. A layman, he reported, "would notice little about him to suggest abnormality." But weeks later, Capone was still not in good shape. His memory was patchy. His emotions were under control only sporadically. His thoughts, according to his psychiatrist, were "superficial and lacking in purposeful direction." When asked to subtract seven from ninety-three, Capone answered "fifty-six."

––––––––––

While Capone deteriorated, Ralph managed most of his brother's affairs, conferring with his attorneys, making sure that all his tax bills and attorneys' fees were paid, and arranging for his postprison medical care. Ralph was out of the booze business and out of prison but still doing work appropriate to his old nickname of Bottles: He toiled as a salesman for Waukesha Waters of Chicago, which billed itself as the purveyor of the "finest domestic and imported waters."

In all likelihood, he was still involved in running what remained of his brother's old criminal enterprise. But it wasn't much. The end of Prohibition took most of the cash out of Capone's mob. The tax convictions of Jack Guzik and Al and Ralph Capone had destroyed much of the outfit's business network. Some of the outfit's men remained active in gambling. Some ran nightclubs and restaurants. But there was nothing or no one left to hold together the scattered pieces of what had once been the Capone empire.

Jack McGurn got out of the machine-gunning business and played a lot of golf after Capone's imprisonment. He turned out to have a great gift for the game and might have made a career as a professional player. But early on the morning of February 15, 1936, he was gunned down by three men in a bowling alley northwest of the Loop. The crime went unsolved.

The portly Jack Guzik surprised his doctors and lived to age seventy before dying of a heart attack in 1956. A heart attack also took out John Torrio, who died in his barber's chair in 1957, at age seventy-five. Bugs Moran went to prison in Ohio in 1946 for the robbery of a Dayton tavern. After that, the feds put him in Leavenworth for another bank job. He died there of lung cancer in 1957.

Frank Nitti was one of the few Capone men who stepped up his crooked activity and took on more power in Capone's absence. He proved himself at least as competent as Capone in running the action. In 1932, four Chicago police officers stormed into Nitti's office without a warrant. Though Nitti put up his hands and made no attempt to resist the cops, he was shot anyway—in the back near the spinal cord, then in the neck and chest. Amazingly, he survived, and continued to oversee much of Chicago's organized crime operations for the next decade. In 1942 Nitti married Eddie O'Hare's former secretary, Annette Caravetta. On March 18, 1943, Nitti was indicted for extorting millions of dollars from movie executives and their union employees. The next day, he went for a walk along the railroad tracks near his home in suburban Riverside, Illinois. In front of several witnesses, he put a gun to his head, pulled the trigger, and fired three times before connecting with a fatal blow.

In 1932, less than a year after Capone's trial, Judge James H. Wilkerson was nominated by President Hoover to the federal Seventh Circuit Court of Appeals, based in Chicago. The announcement from the White House said the nomination was made "in recognition of his fine service in the war on gangsters and organized crime." But Wilkerson ran into stiff opposition during Senate confirmation hearings. Lobbyists for organized labor, still furious about the role the judge had played in 1922 in breaking up a nationwide railroad strike, fought hard to prevent his promotion. In the end, Senate Democrats blocked the nomination. When President Hoover offered to try again, Wilkerson declined. He remained a U.S. district court judge until 1941. In retirement, he set up a private practice with two of the lawyers who had worked with George Johnson on the case against Capone: Jacob Grossman and William J. Froelich. Wilkerson died in 1948 at age seventy-eight.

Johnson stayed on as U.S. attorney for the Northern District of Illinois for less than a year after securing Capone's conviction. Though no one knew it at the time, the end run he made in going after Capone—ignoring serious crimes and charging the suspect with a related crime that is easier to prove—would become standard procedure, especially in federal courts. Even now, when a suspected international terrorist is locked up for violating immigration law, or when O. J. Simpson was jailed for stealing sports memorabilia, newspapers refer to their convictions as "Capone-style cases." There's some inherent dishonesty involved in certain instances— when the punishment does not quite fit the crime—but there's no question that the strategy works and that George Johnson showed the way.

On December 7, 1932, President Hoover appointed Johnson to a newly created position as a judge in the same U.S. district court where Wilkerson served. Hoover made the appointment while the Senate was in recess, so no legislative confirmation was required. But the following year, the Senate allowed Johnson's appointment to expire. It was nothing personal, purely political. Johnson was a Hoover man, and Hoover's men were out of favor.

Some men with Johnson's credentials might have tried for higher office. In a city famed for corruption, he had emerged as a symbol of righteousness and integrity. When gangsters had owned Chicago and no one had known how to stop them, he had done the job and emerged with his reputation unsoiled. If he had decided to run for mayor or governor, he would have been tough to beat. But Johnson had never had much interest in politics. He had come through his war against the gangsters with little or no swelling of the ego. He went back to his private law practice. He spoke at Boy Scout banquets and Swedish-American society events, and attended his wife's community theater productions. He lived quietly and happily.

When his son George Johnson Jr. was preparing for combat in World War II, his father wrote to him; "You have proven your character and ability, and a man who has character and integrity with ability and energy will always get along and make good. I have never seen it to fail in a single instance." When George E. Q. Johnson died in 1949, the *Chicago Daily News* paid him a fitting tribute: "As long as organized crime and crooked politics challenge society," the newspaper said, "he will be remembered as the man who fought and defeated the most ruthless crime syndicate of our day."

––––––

In his last months on Alcatraz Island, Capone spent most of his time in the hospital. On January 4, 1939, his brother John bought a $35,000 cashier's check and gave it to Capone's new lawyer, Abraham Teitelbaum. Teitelbaum turned over the check plus about $3,000 in cash to the federal court clerk in Chicago, paying all of his client's fines and court costs. Two days later, his felony sentence complete, Capone was ferried to Oakland, escorted to a train, and transported to Los Angeles. At ten o'clock the following morning, he arrived at the Federal Correctional Institution at Terminal Island, south of downtown Los Angeles, where he would serve one more year for his misdemeanor convictions.

Capone's health grew worse. He had difficulty remembering his birthday. Asked to add two plus five plus two, he answered twelve. Asked to repeat "The ragged rascal ran around the rugged rock," he said, "The

little ragged muffin ran around the ragged road." He threw tantrums during which he would destroy everything he could get his hands on. Still,
his sentence was nearly up, and his family was preparing for his return to
the free world. The only question was whether Capone was still capable
of functioning in it. Doctors thought not. They urged the family to put
Capone in a hospital.

Before Capone went free, he had to pay an additional $20,000 in fines
connected to the misdemeanor counts. On November 3, 1939, his brother
John paid with checks. Where was all this money coming from? The government was still trying to get Capone to pay more than $300,000 in back
income taxes—and getting nowhere. They had searched for assets they
might seize and had taken a lien against his house on Palm Island—to no
avail. If Capone had money stashed somewhere, the feds couldn't find it.

On November 8, 1939, Eddie O'Hare left his office at Sportsman's Park
and got in his car. He set an automatic pistol on the seat beside him and
took off toward the Loop. On a busy stretch of Ogden Avenue near
Rockwell Street on the city's Southwest Side, another car drew alongside
O'Hare's. O'Hare gunned the engine and tried to get away. Two shotgun blasts flew from the approaching car. The driver's side window of
O'Hare's car shattered into tiny pebbles. His head and neck burst open,
and blood sprayed across the car's steering wheel and windshield. He died
instantly. The car flew across the street, careened a few seconds along a
trolley track, and smashed into a light pole.

Initially, police investigators thought O'Hare had probably been killed
in a dispute over racing receipts from Sportsman's Park. But in the days
ahead, cops and reporters speculated that O'Hare might have been killed
on orders from Capone as punishment for helping the feds in their investigation of his income taxes. After the hit, two former inmates from Alcatraz
told newspaper reporters that Capone had been angry at Fast Eddie and
wanted him dead. Capone's medical records show that he frequently expressed anger at his own attorneys for their poor performance at his trial;
at Judge Wilkerson for his apparent bias; and at the newspaper magnate
William Randolph Hearst for what Capone perceived to be years of unfair coverage. But if he ever mentioned O'Hare, the psychiatrists never
noted it.

Capone could have ordered the hit on O'Hare. Though his mind was turning to mush, he had moments of lucidity. Newspapermen at the time of the murder speculated that Capone initiated the attack to send a message that he was back in business: Chicago beware. That seems unlikely. Capone was neither capable of nor interested in picking up where he left off.

But he might have had another motive. The family needed cash— lots of it—to pay Capone's fines and to see that he got the best medical care possible upon his release. In rounding up money, the Capones might have gone to O'Hare. After all, Capone and O'Hare had been partners in the racing business. While Capone sat in prison, O'Hare had grown fantastically wealthy. He owned Sportsman's Park, the Chicago area's most popular horse-racing venue at the time; had a big stake in the Chicago Cardinals, one of the city's two professional football teams; and was in the process of working out a deal to start a roller derby league that would cover much of the southern United States. He owed much of his success to Capone, and Capone may have remained a silent partner in his organization. If the Capone family felt O'Hare was holding back on them in their time of financial need, or if they felt like he'd received more than his fair share, they might have made him pay with his life.

On the other hand, O'Hare had never stopped serving as an informant for the feds, which meant that any number of criminals might have wanted him dead. As if to remind the world that some things in Chicago hadn't changed, the O'Hare murder went unsolved despite a great wealth of clues and any number of motives.

After the assassination, Frank Wilson, formerly of the Bureau of Internal Revenue and now chief of the Secret Service, stated publicly for the first time that O'Hare had indeed played a key role in the investigation and conviction of Capone. He described O'Hare as the best informant he'd ever had.

But Eddie O'Hare's greatest legacy turned out to be his son, Edward Henry "Butch" O'Hare.

The elder O'Hare had always had high hopes for the boy. When Butch decided he wanted to attend the U.S. Naval Academy at Annapolis, Maryland, Eddie may have pulled strings on his son's behalf. He certainly had the connections, both in Missouri, where Butch went to high school, and in Illinois. Did Eddie offer information on Capone in exchange for a favor on his son's admission? No one knows. But Butch did attend Annapolis, and he did become a navy fighter pilot.

On February 20, 1942, a swarm of Japanese bombers roared over the Pacific, on their way to attack an American carrier, the USS *Lexington*. Six Grumman F-4 "Wildcats," one of them piloted by Butch O'Hare, took off to intercept the enemy planes. O'Hare and his wingman were the first to reach their targets. But when his wingman's guns jammed, O'Hare found himself alone in confronting nine Japanese bombers. He soared straight at them, attacking the planes one by one, darting and diving, until five went down and a sixth took damage. Just as O'Hare ran out of ammunition, support arrived to finish off the depleted Japanese attack force. The *Lexington* was saved. In awarding Butch O'Hare the Medal of Honor, President Roosevelt described the pilot's accomplishment as "one of the most daring, if not the single most daring action in the history of aviation." Less than two years later, he was shot down over the South Pacific and killed. In 1949 Chicago named its principal airport in his honor.

After seven years, six months, and two weeks of federal confinement, Capone was finally set free on November 16, 1939. To avoid detection by the press, he was taken by train to Pennsylvania and met by his family. From there, the Capones drove to Union Memorial Hospital in Baltimore, where Al would be treated by the eminent syphilis specialist Dr. Joseph Earl Moore, of Johns Hopkins University. At first the family thought Capone would remain in Baltimore for a few weeks. He wound up staying a few months. There are no details on the course of his treatment. But there was only so much the doctors could do. Even penicillin would not have saved him.

The remainder of his life was not all madness. He enjoyed long periods of lucidity and decent health. After his release from the hospital, he spent most of his time in the house at Palm Island, lying about in his pajamas, smoking cigars, casting a fishing line into Biscayne Bay, and playing cards. Sometimes a friend would pick him up and take him to a driving range, where he practiced his golf swing. After a few months he was well enough to go out occasionally to nightclubs and restaurants. Old friends dropped by, but Capone seldom spoke of his former bootlegging life. "He seems to have a blank memory about that phase of his life," his doctor told the Associated Press in August 1940. "He is more cheerful than before . . . but he isn't a well man by a long shot."

That same summer, a federal judge ruled that Capone still owed the United States $265,877 in back taxes. Summoned to testify about his ability to pay, Capone at first claimed he was too ill to appear in court. He produced a note to that effect from Dr. Kenneth Phillips, the same physician who had been accused of contempt of court in 1929 for helping Capone fake an illness. Finally, on February 17, 1941, Capone agreed to testify in a private meeting with federal officials in Miami. He looked fairly healthy: fat and balding, smiling broadly behind tinted glasses, puffing on a big cigar. He wore a striped suit, with a straw hat and a white bow tie. He claimed in the meeting that he had no income and very few assets.

Astoundingly, he never did pay his tax debt.

A few years later, in about 1945, the Capones received a surprise: Al's oldest brother, Vincenzo, resurfaced nearly four decades after leaving the family's Brooklyn home.

It turned out he'd joined the circus and traveled throughout the United States and Central America before settling in Homer, Nebraska, where he had changed his name to James Hart, married, and raised a family. After lying to local residents about his background and claiming to be a veteran of World War I, he was appointed a commander of the local American Legion post and served as Homer's town marshal. In the early 1920s, while his younger brother had been making a name in bootlegging, Hart had served as a special officer for the Indian Service, investigating liquor sales to Indian tribes. Twice he had been charged with murder and twice he had been acquitted. When he was caught stealing from shops in Homer— including his father-in-law's grocery—he was dismissed as town marshal. When the American Legion learned that he hadn't served in the war, he was relieved of his membership. Finally, he reconnected with the Capone family—and asked if he could borrow money.

Theresa was the only one who recognized him. When newspaper reporters got wind that another Capone brother had surfaced, they managed to overlook most of his sordid history. The irony, for the newspapermen, was too great to resist: Al Capone's brother had been a lawman.

In truth, the only Capone man who seemed capable of living cleanly was Al's boy, Sonny.

Sonny grew into a shy, quiet, and sullen young man. He never tried to get into his father's business and never tried to cash in on his famous name. Mostly, he wanted to be left alone.

In December 1941 he married Diana Ruth Casey, a Miami Beach native whose family owned a popular local bar called Casey's Oasis. They bought a house near the beach on Tenth Avenue in Miami and began raising a family. They had four girls. Sonny opened a flower shop. At the start of World War II, though partial deafness made him exempt from war service, he quit the flower shop and went to work as a mechanic's apprentice at the Miami Air Depot. After the war he sold used cars. Later he and his mother ran a restaurant called Ted's Grotto at 6970 Collins Avenue, which they owned along with Al's brother John. Mae operated the cash register and Sonny served as a maître d'.

In 1964, after his wife left him—taking the girls and moving to California—Sonny filed for divorce. The following year, on a shopping trip to the Kwik Chek, where Sonny was a regular customer, he filled his cart with groceries and paid for them. But he also stuffed two bottles of aspirin and some batteries in his pockets—retail value, $3.50—and tried to slip them out of the store. A detective stopped him at the door.

When a criminal court judge asked him why he'd stolen from the store, he answered, "Everyone has a little larceny in them, I guess."

The story of his arrest made headlines worldwide. Nine months later he legally changed his name to Albert Francis, dropping Capone. He was never heard from publicly again. He died in 2004, at age eighty-six.

Mae Capone never overcame her shyness. In fact, she emerged from her anonymity only once in all the years after her husband's release from prison, and even then it was only to take up the fight to protect her privacy.

In 1959, Desi Arnaz—the producer and costar of the popular TV comedy series *I Love Lucy*—launched a television series called *The Untouchables,* starring Robert Stack as the ax-swinging Eliot Ness, based loosely on the book by Ness and Oscar Fraley. In five episodes, actor Neville Brand portrayed Al Capone. The series infuriated Mae. It made Capone and the gangsters famous again—perhaps even more famous than they'd been in the 1920s, thanks to the multiplicative powers of television—and it cemented many of the stereotypes of the day. The feds were unemotional, efficient, and brave. The gangsters were wisecracking and dim-witted but most of all cold-blooded.

Sonny Capone tried to intervene. He'd gone to high school with Desi Arnaz in Miami. But when he called Arnaz and asked him to cancel *The Untouchables,* Arnaz refused. The show was a huge success, running for four seasons, making Eliot Ness a household name.

Finally, Mae sued. In her complaint, she said that she and her son were running a restaurant, not bothering anyone, and trying to avoid publicity, when Desilu (Arnaz's production company), CBS, and the show's sponsor, Westinghouse, forced them back into the spotlight. As a result of the unwanted attention, Mae claimed in the lawsuit, Sonny's children were mocked at school, and Sonny and Mae were forced to sell their restaurant and open at a new location.

A federal judge ruled that the television show had indeed "overstepped the bounds of decency" but that there was nothing the Capone family could do about it. Al Capone was part of history now, said the judge. His story was fair game.

With that, Mae resumed her private life. In 1986, at age eighty-nine, she died at the Hollywood Hills Nursing Home in Florida. Theresa Capone was long gone by then, having died of natural causes in 1953. Ralph lived to age eighty before a heart attack killed him 1974. Mafalda died in 1988 at age seventy-six.

Those who saw Al Capone in his final days were usually impressed by how healthy he appeared. He looked tanned and happy, sturdy and well fed. But anyone who spoke to him could see that his mind was melting away fast. "Nutty as a fruitcake," said his old partner Jack Guzik after a visit to Palm Island.

By 1942, a limited supply of penicillin had become available, and Capone became one of the first syphilis patients in the United States treated with the antibiotic. But by then it was too late for the medicine to do much good.

Capone continued to slide. He suffered seizures, threw fits, and became frequently disoriented. He required the constant attention of an aide. His speech grew more slurred. In carrying on a conversation he would wink a lot for no apparent reason and hop randomly from one subject to the next. He whistled, hummed, and sang, seemingly at random. In the summer of 1945 he was well enough to travel north for part of the summer, staying at a cabin owned by Ralph in Mercer, Wisconsin, and returning to his old home on South Prairie Avenue in Chicago.

At family gatherings, the Capones would reflect on all that had happened to Al. They wondered how much of his behavior in the 1920s might have been attributable to syphilis. Had his judgment been impaired? If he'd been thinking clearly would he have shunned the spotlight? Would he have escaped the ire of the federal government? The Capones agreed that Al had been unfairly made a scapegoat for the failures of Prohibition, but they also agreed that he had brought the troubles upon himself—and the family.

By 1946 Capone was too unstable to travel. Still, he continued to make news. When Winston Churchill visited Miami Beach in 1946, he was asked if knew he would be a neighbor of Al Capone's. "Oh," replied Churchill, "the former distinguished resident of Chicago!"

By then, though, Capone's mind was so wasted that he probably would not have recognized the former British prime minister. Capone was "nervous and excitable," according to his doctor, and largely unaware of the world around him. He was incapable of leaving home by himself and had little interest in going anywhere but to the drugstore for Sen-Sen breath mints and Dentyne gum, which he chewed with manic fervor. Like a child, he hoarded candy bars, hiding them in his bedroom.

The Associate Press reported that Capone "spent his days dawdling with a tennis racket, aimlessly batting a ball into a net with childlike happiness."

The nervous chewing of gum and the mindless swatting of tennis balls may have been Capone's way of staving off panic attacks. Memory and fear melted together like wires in a shorted-out machine. All it took was a loud pop or the crunch of car tires to set off one of his paranoid delusions. Suddenly he would imagine that it was all over, that the assassins had finally caught up with him.

He slept not in the master bedroom but in a smaller room at the front of the house, overlooking the front lawn, so he could see and hear the automobiles coming down the road. In Chicago, when he had been among the world's most fearsome men, he had seldom been seen carrying a gun. But he had had a calling card, a signature way of killing, and everyone had known it. A car would come out of nowhere, a window would roll down, and the nose of a Tommy gun would emerge, barely visible. Then, before anyone could duck for cover, a flash of orange would light the inside of the attack car, a sharp *Brruup! Brruup!* would echo through the night, and the death car's engine would roar as its driver made his escape.

That was the Capone way: quick and terrifying.

Now, though, he might have prayed for such a quick ending. Though he appeared to be in no pain, he was a lost soul.

On January 18, 1947, he marked his forty-eighth birthday. It was a quiet celebration, spent with family. At four in the morning on January 19, he collapsed with what appeared to be a stroke. A Catholic priest came to the house and administered the last rites.

For the next fourteen hours, Capone lay in a coma. The United Press reported him dead. Reporters camped out beyond the gates of his home, waiting for news. Ralph Capone brought them bottles of cold beer. Then, to everyone's surprise, he snapped out of it. He rallied briefly. But soon after he contracted pneumonia. Doctors and nurses and relatives cared for him around the clock for the next six days.

On January 25, America's most infamous criminal died. His wife, son, mother, sister, and two of his brothers were by his side. Capone was laid to rest in a new suit: double-breasted and dark blue, with a black tie, white shirt, and white shoes. His attorney told reporters that the gang chief left no will and no inheritance. The Palm Island home, according to the lawyer, was "mortgaged to the hilt."

The *Tribune* bade him farewell with an editorial that said, "Al Capone was a vile influence on Chicago from the day he came here until he was finally rendered harmless by an occupational disease of his original vocation of pandering."

His body was shipped to Chicago by car, with Ralph Capone along for the last ride. On February 4, a bitterly cold, gray day, late in the afternoon, his casket was lowered into the earth between those of his father and his brother Frank at Mount Olivet Cemetery, on Chicago's far South Side. The crowd on hand was small. Reporters appeared to outnumber mourners. There were no emotional tributes, no long eulogies, just a few perfunctory words from a priest who felt he owed it to Capone's devout mother to perform the ceremony.

A few years later, the family moved Capone's body to Mount Carmel Cemetery, in the western suburb of Hillside. More than sixty years later, visitors from around the world travel to see the final resting place of the man whose name and image remain synonymous with crime. They leave flowers, cigars, bottles of whiskey, cans of beer, toy guns, and St. Valentine's Day cards.

The marker reads:

ALPHONSE CAPONE
1899–1947
MY JESUS, MERCY

The phrase my "My Jesus, Mercy" comes from a Catholic prayer that reads, in part,

> *To the souls of those who strove*
> *for hardly anything but riches and pleasures;*
> *Jesus, Mary, Joseph! My Jesus, mercy.*
>
> *To the worldly-minded,*
> *who failed to use their wealth*
> *and talents in the service of God;*
> *Jesus, Mary, Joseph! My Jesus, mercy.*
>
> *To those who witnessed the death of others,*
> *but would not think of their own;*
> *Jesus, Mary, Joseph! My Jesus, mercy.*

It is a prayer for souls suffering in purgatory.

ACKNOWLEDGMENTS

I came to this book knowing almost nothing about organized crime in Chicago. But Jack Clarke, perhaps the city's greatest expert, generously agreed to tutor me. I sat for days at Jack's kitchen table on the South Side, drinking coffee and watching him smoke Kools. He was dying of lung cancer and knew it. But when he felt well enough, he took me around town and introduced me to characters I never would have met otherwise. He knew he wouldn't live to see this book, but he trusted me to get the story right. I hope he would approve.

I interviewed and gained valuable insights from several members of the Capone family, including Deirdre Marie Capone, Al's great-niece; Lorrayne Rayola, his former sister-in-law; Harry Hart, his nephew; Madeleine Capone Morichetti, another sister-in-law; and Regina Maritote, the granddaughter of Frank Maritote (aka Diamond). They were gracious with their time and helped me see that the Capones were a loving, close-knit family, burdened by Al's infamy but never broken by it. Chris Knight Capone believes himself to be the grandson of Al Capone. Regardless of what the DNA tests finally say, he proved to be a tireless researcher who tracked down valuable information and generously shared it with me.

Huge thanks go to Dennis Hoffman, professor of criminal justice at the University of Nebraska at Omaha, for sharing the collection of papers that once belonged to George E. Q. Johnson and for offering me his excellent advice. I'm also indebted to George Johnson Jr. and his wife, Mary Ann, for sharing the papers, photographs, and scrapbooks of George's father, and for making me feel like a part of their family in my visits to their Michigan home. Paul Daugherty taught me everything there is to know about Calvin Goddard and the science of ballistics. I wish I could have used more of it in the book. Daniel Okrent tutored me on the history of Prohibition. And Mark Haller of Temple University, one of the nation's preeminent scholars of crime, allowed me to dig through his files and gave me a crash course in the history of organized crime that I will never forget.

Thanks also to Father Matt Eyerman at St. Columbanus Church, Scott Forsythe at the National Archives, Patti Reid at the IRS, Matthew Schaefer at the Herbert Hoover Presidential Library and Museum, John Russick and Rob Medina at the Chicago History Museum, Leigh Bienen at Northwestern University, Laura Beil, Tim Anderson, Vikki Amrine, Charles Bidwill II, Joyce Archer, Vern Apke, Jim Cheevers, Carola Eisenberg, Gretchen Van Dam, Bob Fuesel, Sissy DeMaria, Ron Shuffield, Barbara Hagen, Lynn Novick, Andres Schcolnik, Ben Harris, Conrad Kirby, Craig Pfannkuche, Ann K. Sindelar, Scott Forsyth, Charlie Newton, Louis Glunz and the Glunz family, Kimberly Hagarty, Conrad Kirby, Edward M. Burke, Babe Ahern, Jackie Schaller, Barry Jubek, Gary Zimet, Don Steinitz, Joel Berg, Lori Azim, James D. Calder, Marc Cormier, Karen Blumenthal, Gus Russo, C. J. Box, Matt Fernandes, John Binder, Mario Gomes, Perri Strawn, Pat Byrnes, Lou Carlozo, Mark Caro, James Finn Garner, Jim Powers, Stu Shea, Richard Babcock, Suzy Takacs, Mitchell Kaplan, Leslie Silverman, and Robert Kazel. A special thanks to all my friends at the Les Turner ALS Foundation for their courage and inspiration.

I had help with microfilm from Cassie del Pilar, Elizabeth Murtaugh, Holly Fox, Solomon Lieberman, Jason Breslow, and Lizz Kannenberg. Lieberman and Adam Verwymeren worked with me to create my website, www.getcapone.com. I also was assisted by many dedicated librarians and archivists at the Chicago History Museum, National Archives, Library of Congress, Newberry Library, Western Reserve Historical Society, Herbert Hoover Presidential Library, Chicago Public Library, Skokie Public Library, New York City municipal archives, New York Public Library, Northwestern University archives, University of Chicago archives, U.S. Naval Academy archives, Michigan Historical Museum, Philadelphia municipal archives, Chicago Crime Commission, Kankakee County Museum, and New York City Police Museum.

Heidi Trilling is an independent editor of unmatched talent. She offered invaluable criticism, snappy design input, and brilliant line editing of this book—delivering all with her keen sense of humor. My work is vastly better thanks to her instincts for words and storytelling, and for that I'm deeply grateful.

Thanks to Jeff Thurston for help with fact-checking. And big, big thanks to my friends Ron Jackson, Richard Cahan, Joseph Epstein, Robert Kurson, and Bryan Gruley for their excellent advice and editing.

This is my third book for Bob Bender, my editor at Simon & Schuster. He has been with me every step of the way, with a steady hand, keen insight, and unwavering support. Words cannot express my appreciation. At Simon & Schuster, thanks also go to Johanna Li, Kelly Welsh, David Rosenthal, Katie Rizzo, and Victoria Meyer. I'm incredibly fortunate to call David Black my agent and friend. In 1931, before he went to jail, Al Capone contemplated writing a book. If he'd had an agent like David, he wouldn't have blown the deal, and his story might have had a much happier ending.

Huge thanks go to the members of the East Coast affiliates of the Eig Syndicate: Phyllis, David, Matt, Lew, Penny, Judy, Jake, Ben, and Hayden. Thanks, too, to my Florida outfit: Gail Tescher, Don Tescher, SuAnn Tescher, and Jonathan Tescher. And here in Chicago, of course, I would be nowhere at all without my own gang of juvenile delinquents: Lola "Baby Face" Eig, who showed impeccable timing by arriving just as this book was completed; Lillian "Lollipop" Eig, who makes me laugh and smile, and energizes me every day; and Jeffery "The Cool Way" Schams, who always has my back.

Finally, my never-ending gratitude and love to my wife, Jennifer Tescher, for her love, her wisdom, and her invincible spirit. My story begins and ends with her.

SOURCES

I live in the heart of Chicago, two blocks from the corner where Sammy "Nails" Morton bit the dust, three blocks from the spot where Al Capone's men bought their machine guns, and half a mile from the site of the St. Valentine's Day Massacre. Almost every day I see a big black bus with the words "Untouchable Tours" driving around town, filling tourists' heads with stories about the old gangsters who once roamed these streets. The stories are always entertaining, and sometimes they're true.

Years ago, when I was in the middle of writing my first book, I started kicking around the idea of telling Capone's story the right way, or "on the square," as the gangsters of his day would put it. I made phone calls, visited libraries, and read books. But it didn't quite click. I couldn't find the right angle.

Then one day at the library, I was reading an article about the prosecutor who led the government's case against Capone in 1931, George E. Q. Johnson. His son was quoted in the article saying that he had turned over all of his father's papers to a college professor at the University of Nebraska at Omaha in the hopes that the professor would write his father's story. This was in 1985. I tracked down both the college professor, Dennis Hoffman, and George E. Q. Johnson's son, Gene, who was ninety-five years old and living in Indiana, a ninety-minute drive from my home. Hoffman and Gene Johnson told me the same thing: The biography never got off the ground. The old man's papers had been collecting dust for twenty years.

A few days later I was on a plane for Omaha. When I reached Professor Hoffman's office, he started pulling down one big box after another until he covered the entire surface of a long conference table. The boxes were like treasure chests—filled with seventy-five-year-old yellowing paper. They were gold to me.

Here were transcripts of wiretaps typed by Eliot Ness; memos and telegrams from President Herbert Hoover and his cabinet members plotting to put Capone behind bars; and handwritten notes jotted by prosecutors expressing their innermost doubts and fears as they tried to build a case that would be the most important of their lives, a case they knew from the start was fundamentally flawed. Here was the real story of Al Capone.

The National Archives had none of these papers. Neither did the Library of Congress or the Chicago History Museum. No one but Professor Hoffman had seen this material since George E. Q. Johnson had packed up his boxes.

Just like that, I had found my story.

But it was only the beginning.

Soon I persuaded the IRS to turn over formerly secret files—raw intelligence files—that they had never before released. I found another college professor—Mark Haller of Temple University—who had been granted access twenty years earlier to even more of the IRS's secret files and who had carefully preserved his notes. Later I learned that the National Archives had agreed to release all of Capone's prison records, including hundreds of pages of his personal letters and his complete medical records. Finally, I tracked down several Capone family members and got them to talk.

I spent nearly three years investigating. Little by little, I got to know Capone the man, not the myth.

At one point, while digging through the files of the late Chicago journalist Howard O'Brien at the Newberry Library, I came across a handwritten letter from Capone in which he had authorized O'Brien to ghostwrite his autobiography. As I dug through the rest of the boxes at the Newberry, I had dreams of discovering Capone's unpublished manuscript. Alas, the book was never written. Still, O'Brien did leave behind more than a hundred pages of notes from his meetings with Capone, and they were immensely valuable in giving me a sense of the gangster's true character.

My theory about the St. Valentine's Day Massacre stems from the discovery of a single sheet of paper—a letter written by Frank T. Farrell in 1935—found within the FBI archives. The letter is available for all to see on the FBI's website.

I owe a great debt to the countless newspaper and magazine reporters who covered Capone in his lifetime. I also drew on the work of Capone's biographers Fred Pasley, John Kobler, Robert J. Schoenberg, and
Laurence Bergreen. These sources and more—in addition to hundreds of
interviews—form the core of this book. I've relied as much as possible
on primary materials: interviews, newspaper articles, government documents, and books from Capone's own time. Nothing in these pages is
invented or embellished.

NOTES

CHAPTER 1: THE GETTING OF IT

Page

3   *hands in his pockets:* Courtney Riley Cooper, *Ten Thousand Public Enemies* (Boston: Little, Brown, 1935), 17.

3   *"Got some nice-looking girls inside":* Ibid.

3   *lit by a bare bulb:* Irle Waller, *Chicago Uncensored* (New York: Exposition Press, 1965), 67.

4   *changeable greenish gray:* "Capone Interviewed at Lombardo's Bier," *Chicago Evening American,* September 11, 1928.

5   *thirty thousand hardy souls:* U.S. Census data.

5   *2,218 licenses for saloons:* Stephen Longstreet, *Chicago, 1860–1919* (New York: David McKay, 1973), 136.

5   *five thousand full-time prostitutes:* Vice Commission of Chicago, *The Social Evil in Chicago* (Chicago: Gunthorp-Warren, 1931), 34.

6   *"Having seen it":* Rudyard Kipling, *American Notes* (Boston: Little, Brown, 1899), 91.

7   *"I do not love the money":* Donald L. Miller, *City of the Century* (New York: Simon & Schuster, 1996), 213.

7   *Capone printed cards:* Fred Pasley, *Al Capone, The Biography of a Self-Made Man* (Binghamton, N.Y.: Ives Washburn, 1930), 19.

8   *"You were God's worst enemy":* John Kobler, *Ardent Spirits: The Rise and Fall of Prohibition* (New York: Da Capo Press, 1993), 12.

8   *"Like an overworked businessman":* Frederick Lewis Allen, *Only Yesterday: An Informal History of the 1920s* (New York: Perennial Classics, 2000), 67.

CHAPTER 2: GOOD-BYE, DIAMOND JIM

Page

10 *he would pour them out:* Walter Noble Burns, *The One-Way Ride* (Garden City, N.Y.: Doubleday, 1931), 6.

11 *spaghetti à la Colosimo:* William J. Helmer and Rick Mattix, *The Complete Public Enemy Almanac* (Nashville: Cumberland House), 40.

11 *As he walked into his office:* "Colosimo Slain," *Chicago Tribune,* May 12, 1920.

11 *blood oozing:* Ibid.

11 *$9-a-week cloth cutter:* Capone medical records, Alcatraz Federal Penitentiary, National Archives, San Bruno, California.

12 *Brooklyn's small-time icemen:* Oliver Pilat and Jo Ranson, *Sodom by the Sea: An Affectionate History of Coney Island* (Garden City, N.Y.: Doubleday, 1941), 273.

12 *police in New York caught up with Yale:* "Colosimo Slain by Black Hand for $150,000," *Chicago Tribune,* December 14, 1920.

13 *Chicago's biggest beer-making operations:* Bob Skilnik, *Beer: A History of Brewing in Chicago* (Fort Lee, N.J.: Barricade Books, 2006), 127.

13 *"Torrio is unhampered":* "Crime Kings Known," *Chicago Daily News,* November 17, 1924.

14 *profit of $250,000:* Elmer L. Irey and William J. Slocum, *The Tax Dodgers* (New York: Greenberg, 1948), 8.

14 *less than most dogcatchers:* *Chicago Daily News Almanac and Year-Book, 1923,* 341.

14 *salaries of $1,500 to $2,400 a year:* Irey and Slocum, *The Tax Dodgers,* 4.

14 *"There were no Civil Service":* Ibid.

14 *"He turned his back":* Ibid., 5.

15 *$10,000 on a single game of craps:* "Link Politics and Whisky to Cafe Slayings," *Chicago Tribune,* August 24, 1920.

15 *Torrio and Capone liked Morton:* "Capone Begs for Peace; Doesn't Want to Be Slain," *Chicago American,* October 13, 1926.

15 *once jumped a car:* "Autos Leap Four Foot Bridge Gap in Thief Chase," *Chicago Tribune,* September 1, 1922.

16 *on August 30, 1922, for instance:* "Caponi Waves Gun After Crash; Faces 3 Charges," *Chicago Tribune,* August 31, 1922.

16 *"I'll fix this thing so easy":* Ibid.

17 *he noticed a lesion:* Capone interview, Antiluetic Treatment Record for Beneficiaries of the United States Public Health Service, 1932, National Archives, San Bruno, California.

CHAPTER 3: A LITTLE HOUSE ON SOUTH PRAIRIE

Page

18 *"The business pays very well":* *Literary Digest,* October 30, 1926.

19 *"I've always liked Mike":* "Dundee's New Boss Manages Boxer's Affairs for Sport," *Davenport Democrat and Leader,* December 11, 1923.

19   *"They snatch guys":* John H. Lyle, *The Dry and Lawless Years* (Englewood Cliffs, N. J.: Prentice-Hall, 1960), 72.

20   *a small town called Angri:* Civil records, Comune di Angri; church records, Church of San Giovanni Battista, Angri, Italy.

20   *parents made and sold their own pasta:* Ibid.

20   *married a local girl:* Ibid.

20   *worked as a printer:* Ibid.

20   *became a barber:* 1900 U.S. Census.

21   *Gabriele's death:* John Kobler, *Capone* (New York: G. P. Putnam's Sons, 1971), 102.

21   *Sunday nights in summertime: Chicago Daily News Almanac and Year-Book, 1923,* 851.

22   *valued at about $15,000:* Cook County property tax records.

22   *6 percent interest:* Ibid.

22   *Sonny was Al's child but not Mae's:* Interview, Deirdre Marie Capone.

22   *a wonderful mother:* Interviews, Deirdre Marie Capone, Lorrayne Rayola, Francis Rolla, Madeleine Capone Morichetti.

22   *she stayed in her room:* Interview, Lorrayne Rayola.

23   *sexual indiscretions:* Interview, Madeleine Capone Morichetti.

23   *gifts that no ordinary girl:* Interview, Lorrayne Rayola.

CHAPTER 4: "I'M SURE IT WAS CAPONE"

Page

24   *punch him in the nose:* Emmett Dedmon, *Fabulous Chicago* (New York: Random House, 1953), 296.

25   *about fifty a year:* John Landesco, *Organized Crime in Chicago* (Chicago: University of Chicago Press, 1929), 97.

25   *chest ripped open with two blasts:* "Tony D'Andrea Shot; Dying," *Chicago Tribune,* May 11, 1921.

25   *the court system was a cesspool:* Landesco, *Organized Crime in Chicago,* vii.

26   *Dever . . . made a deal of his own:* John R. Schmidt, *The Mayor Who Cleaned Up Chicago* (De Kalb: Northern Illinois University Press, 1989), 78.

26   *step up their raids:* Ibid., 84.

26   *padlocked some four thousand:* James L. Merriner, *Grafters and Goo Goos* (Carbondale: Southern Illinois University Press, 2004), 111.

27   *Capone transferred his headquarters:* Walter Noble Burns, *The One-Way Ride* (Garden City, N.Y.: Doubleday, 1931), 37.

27   *roulette, faro, craps, blackjack:* Ibid., 39.

27   *"the United States of Volstead":* Fred D. Pasley, *Al Capone* (Binghamton, N.Y.: Ives Washburn, 1930), 39.

28   *"Free Kingdom of Torrio":* "The Free Kingdom of Torrio," *Chicago Tribune,* November 21, 1924.

28   *William K. Pflaum, received a visit:* "Bullets Fly in Cicero on Election Eve," *Chicago Tribune,* April 1, 1924.

29   *Frank Capone fell to the sidewalk:* "Gunman Slain in Vote Riots," *Chicago Tribune,* April 2, 1924.

29   *fifteen cars to carry the bouquets:* "Gangland Calls Truce while It Buries Capone," *Chicago Tribune,* April 6, 1924.

29   *the police officer who fired the fatal shots:* "Walk on Roses at Caponi's Bier," *Chicago Tribune,* April 5, 1924.

29   *Capone's take of the profits:* Government tax indictment of Al Capone, 1931.

30   *still lived above his mother's . . . fruit store:* "Gunman Killed by Gunman," *Chicago Tribune,* May 9, 1924.

30   *"I am sure it was Capone":* "Witnesses of Levee Slaying Mum on Killer," *Chicago Tribune,* May 10, 1924.

31   *Howard didn't just beat Guzik:* George Murray, *The Legacy of Al Capone* (New York: G. P. Putnam's Sons, 1975), 120.

31   *"curious to know what it was for":* "Caponi Hands Self to Police in Murder Case," *Chicago Tribune,* June 12, 1924.

CHAPTER 5: FUNNY NOTIONS

Page
32   *Theresa. . . . spoke only in Italian:* Interview, Lorrayne Rayola.

32   *shipped halfway around the world:* Ibid.

32   *To make her bracciola:* Interviews, Lorrayne Rayola and Deirdre Marie Capone.

33   *Dago Red:* Interview, Lorrayne Rayola.

33   sette-e-mezzo: Ibid.

33   *festivities wound down at about 3:* "Caponi Is Shot At," *Chicago Evening Post,* January 12, 1925.

33   *big Packard:* "Foes Gun for Capone; Shoot Driver in Car," *Chicago Daily News,* January 12, 1925.

33   *chicken dinners for five cents:* Chicago History Museum photograph.

33   *curtains over the rear windows:* "Foes Gun for Capone; Shoot Driver in Car," *Chicago Daily News,* January 12, 1925.

33   *overcoat, sport coat, and underwear:* "Vote Against More Police and Pay Raise," *Chicago Tribune,* January 13, 1925.

34   *"Well, we've got your Packard":* "Caponi Is Shot At," *Chicago Evening Post,* January 12, 1925.

34   *"some people have funny notions":* Ibid.

34   *staggered into his home:* "Torrio Shot Down by Gunmen," *Chicago Daily News,* January 24, 1925.

34   *Capone . . . sat down for a long interrogation:* "Grill Torrio Chief in Hunt for Clew," *Chicago Herald and Examiner,* January 26, 1925.

35   *"Well, Mr. Capone":* "Capone Is Missed," *Decatur Herald,* June 20, 1931.

36   *raid on a doctor's office:* "Raid Bares Vice and Rum Super-Trust," *Chicago Tribune,* April 7, 1925.

37   *Hayes ordered that the seized records be returned:* "Judge Returns Vice Records; U.S. Aroused," *Chicago Tribune,* April 11, 1925.

37   *steak dinners:* Ibid.

CHAPTER 6: A MAN OF DESTINY

Page

38   *$10 less than Capone's price:* "Get McSwiggin Death Clew," *Chicago Tribune,* April 29, 1926.

38   *big blue Lincoln:* "Resume Inquest into McSwiggin Slaying," *Chicago Evening American,* May 4, 1926.

38   *about five seconds:* "Get McSwiggin Death Clew," *Chicago Tribune,* April 29, 1926.

38   *Three fedoras and a set of horned-rim glasses:* Ibid.

39   *cabin at Round Lake:* "Capone Enjoyed Fireworks at Round Lake Hideaway," *Lansing State Journal,* June 9, 1987.

40   *a blond woman:* Laurence Bergreen, *Capone* (New York: Simon & Schuster, 1994), 184.

40   *phoned a couple of newspaper reporters:* "Al Caponi to Give Up Today, He Announces," *Chicago Tribune,* July 28, 1926.

41   *corner of Indianapolis Boulevard:* "Capone 'Mum' on M'Swiggin Case," *Chicago Daily News,* July 28, 1926.

41   *blue-serge suit:* Ibid.

41   *A. P. Madden met Capone:* Ibid.

41   *"Of course I didn't kill him":* "Caponi Taken Before Grand Jury," *Chicago Evening Post,* July 28, 1926.

42   *expected his court appearance to be brief:* "Caponi Gives Up, but Gets Jail Instead of Bail," *Chicago Tribune,* July 29, 1926.

42   *the 'great criminal':* "Escort Capone to Cicero," *Chicago American,* July 29, 1926.

42   *Rudolph Valentino:* "Valentino Is Here, Ready to Do Battle," *Chicago Daily News,* July 29, 1926.

42   *same suit:* Newspaper photos.

43   *"They pinned a medal on him":* "Caponi Freed of McSwiggin Death Charge," *Chicago Tribune,* July 30, 1926.

43   *Seven police officers on horseback:* "Capone Freed in M'Swiggin Case," *Chicago Evening Post,* July 29, 1926.

43   *His friend Louis Cowen:* Ibid.

43   *the only thing visible:* "Escort Capone to Cicero," *Chicago American,* July 29, 1926.

43   *"Who killed McSwiggin?":* Fred D. Pasley, *Al Capone* (Binghamton, N.Y.: Ives Washburn, 1930), 134.

43   *A cartoon in the* Chicago Tribune: "Scarface Al," *Chicago Tribune,* July 31, 1926.

44   *"If you think I did it":* Pasley, *Al Capone,* 134.

CHAPTER 7: HEAT WAVE

Page

45   *sleeping on flat roofs:* "Belated Heat Puts Strain on Free Ice Fund," *Chicago Tribune,* August 29, 1926.

45   *Dozens died from heat prostration:* "Heat Routed After 15 Die," *Chicago Tribune,* August 6, 1926.

46   *Sheldon . . . the most feared criminal:* "Capture Foley Pals Gunning for Rival Gang," *Chicago Tribune,* August 8, 1926.

46   *"I haven't an enemy in the world":* "Sheldon's Auto Bombed; Blame War over Beer," *Chicago Tribune,* February 6, 1926.

47   *Foley turned east:* "Identify Saltis, Two Gangsters as Foley Killers," *Chicago Tribune,* August 7, 1926.

47   *man with the shotgun closed in:* "Foley Slain by Gang; Saltis Is Named Killer," *Chicago Herald and Examiner,* August 7, 1926.

47   *"Jubilant":* Ibid.

48   *"I believe we have figured out a scheme":* "Police Planning New Attack to Break Up Gangs," *Chicago Tribune,* August 14, 1926.

48   *$500,000, by one account:* "Stege Solves Pistol Attack on 'Schemer,' " *Chicago Herald and Examiner,* January 21, 1927.

48   *Sbarbaro pointed out a greasy spoon:* "Gun Battle Thrills Michigan Av," *Chicago Herald and Examiner,* August 11, 1926.

49   *"Drive on quick!":* Ibid.

49   *"Skimmer," not "Schemer":* "Auto Leaps Four Foot Bridge Gap in Thief Chase," *Chicago Tribune,* September 1, 1922.

CHAPTER 8: "HE WILL KNOCK YOU FLAT JUST FOR FUN"

Page

50   *Capone was eating lunch:* "Machine-Gun Warfare Waged by Gangsters," *Los Angeles Times,* November 6, 1926.

51   *A twenty-five-to-one shot:* "Betting Coups Fail as Jockeys Vie for Glory," *Chicago Tribune,* September 20, 1926.

51   *Capone crawled under his table:* "Gang Fire on Capone Wounds 2," *Chicago Daily News,* September 20, 1926.

52   *"a veritable battalion of death":* "Machine Gun Army Raids Cicero!," *Chicago Herald and Examiner,* September 21, 1926.

53   *he doubted they were aiming for anyone:* "Cicero Machine Gun Wounds 3," *Chicago Evening American,* September 20, 1926.

53   *a meeting with his lawyers:* "Rivals Rain Bullets on Capone Nest," *Chicago Herald and Examiner,* September 21, 1926.

53   *the following suspects:* "Seize Gunmen after Bullets Riddle Cicero," *Chicago Tribune,* September 21, 1926.

54 *"a professional and amateur hobby"*: Elmer L. Irey and William J. Slocum, *The Tax Dodgers* (New York: Greenberg, 1948), 36.

54 *"Al is a fathead"*: Ibid.

55 *"beer operator"*: "Cicero Chiefs Indicted by U.S.," *Chicago American,* October 1, 1926.

55 *"This is just the beginning"*: "Cicero Chiefs Indicted by U.S.," *Chicago Evening American,* October 1, 1926.

55 *"The modern gangster"*: "Insect Powder," *Chicago Herald and Examiner,* October 4, 1926.

CHAPTER 9: THE PEACEMAKER

Page

57 *"Weiss will never kill me"*: Walter Noble Burns, *The One-Way Ride* (Garden City, N.Y.: Doubleday, 1931), 188.

57 *Hanging around with Greenberg*: George Murray, *The Legacy of Al Capone* (New York: G. P. Putnam's Sons, 1975), 29.

58 *"Weiss was a regular go-getter"*: "Weiss Soft Soaper of Racket; Insider Tells How He Worked," *Chicago Daily News,* October 15, 1926.

59 *Weiss introduced himself to a dancer*: "Story of Weiss' Love," *Chicago Evening American,* January 6, 1927.

59 *"Perhaps I suspected"*: "Weiss' Widow Tells of Honeymoon Days," *Chicago Evening American,* January 7, 1927.

61 *an estimated forty thousand members*: John Kobler, *Capone* (New York: G. P. Putnam's Sons, 1971), 34.

61 *"like a satanic specter"*: Bruce P. Zummo, *Little Sicily* (Chicago: Near North Publishing, 2001), 17.

61 *Capone sincerely wanted peace*: "Capone Begs for Peace; Doesn't Want to Be Slain," *Chicago Evening American,* October 13, 1926.

62 *a brothel called the Blue Goose*: " 'Cusicks,' Vice Dealers, Freed; Run New Dive," *Chicago Tribune,* March 4, 1924.

62 *"You buy a judge by weight"*: Murray, *Legacy of Al Capone,* 339.

62 *Nitti was born Francesco Nitto*: Mars Eghigian, *After Capone* (Nashville: Cumberland House, 2006), 3.

63 *"If I am convinced by anything"*: David Minter, *A Cultural History of the American Novel* (New York: Cambridge University Press, 1994), 86.

64 *saw his wife and son no more than four or five times a week*: "Gang Boundaries, Not Wards, Divide Chicago, Says 'Scarface Al,' " *Chicago Herald and Examiner,* March 9, 1927.

65 *"I tell them I want peace"*: "Capone Begs for Peace; Doesn't Want to Be Slain," *Chicago Evening American,* October 13, 1926.

CHAPTER 10: Q IS FOR QUINCY

Page

66 *Johnson was nineteen: Year Book, 1949: American Swedish Historical Foundation* (Philadelphia, 1949), 60.

66 *Thomas Edison's raspy phonograph:* Ibid.

66 *He stayed two weeks:* Ibid.

67 *"a forensic looking man":* Damon Runyon, *Trials and Tribulations* (Philadelphia: J. B. Lippincott, 1947), 228.

67 *Mathilda gave birth . . . without the help of a doctor: Year Book, 1949,* 58.

67 *rode drafty, horse-drawn buses: Lost Grove Township, 1869–1969* (no listed author or publisher).

67 *"I was taught":* "G. E. Q. Johnson Hits on Way to Rout Gangland," *Chicago Tribune,* December 21, 1930.

67 *thirty bushels before noon: Year Book, 1949,* 59.

67 *read by the light of homemade candles:* Ibid., 58.

68 *without a passionate edge to his voice:* "What Happened in the Case of Al Capone," *New York Daily News,* April 10, 1932.

68 *"looked like a poet":* "The Iowan Who Defeated Al Capone," *Iowan,* Summer 1993.

68 *He rented a desk: Year Book, 1949,* 62.

69 *honeymooned in Colorado:* "In the Society World," *Chicago Tribune,* September 11, 1906.

70 *Johnson's name appeared on a short list:* "Deneen, Here, to Discuss Senate Seat with Smith," *Chicago Tribune,* December 25, 1926.

70 *"I come of Swedish farmer stock":* "The Secret War on Gangdom," *Christian Science Monitor,* November 7, 1934.

71 *"PARTY MENTIONED":* Fred W. Sargent telegram, National Archives, College Park, Maryland.

71 *"It's all a surprise to me":* "Deneen Chooses Geo. E. Q. Johnson as U.S. Attorney, *Chicago Tribune,* January 30, 1927.

71 *"I come to this office":* "Johnson Takes Office as New U.S. Attorney," *Chicago Tribune,* February 15, 1927.

71 *He began keeping a scrapbook:* Personal papers of George E. Q. Johnson.

71 *he gained respect for Capone's skill:* Interview with Gene Johnson.

CHAPTER 11: SORRY ABOUT THAT, HYMIE

Page

73 *see the priests and parishioners:* "Bible Student Tells How Gangsters Killed Weiss," *Chicago Evening American,* October 15, 1926.

73 *A room opened up:* "Tall, Dark Stranger Rents Room for Ambush," *Chicago Evening American,* October 12, 1926.

73 *tarnished brass bed:* "Squalor Drapes Room Where Two Laid Deadly Ambush for Gangsters," *Chicago Daily News,* October 12, 1926.

73 *That same day, a beautiful blond-haired woman:* "Hunt Woman as 'Key' in Weiss Gang Slayings," *Chicago Evening American,* October 20, 1926.

74 *"something new, something novel":* "Saltis Trial on; State to Seek Death by Noose," *Chicago Tribune,* October 7, 1926.

74 *dressed for court like a banker:* Ibid.

75 *"of the utmost importance":* "Double Guards for Witnesses Against Saltis," *Chicago Tribune,* October 8, 1926.

75 *bombs exploded inside two businesses:* "Bombs, Scruples Hold Stage in Trial of Saltis," *Chicago Tribune,* October 10, 1926.

75 *"No such thing":* Ibid.

75 *offered his opposing counsel a bribe:* "O'Brien Faces an Inquiry," *Chicago Tribune,* November 30, 1911.

75 *O'Brien was shot in a saloon:* "Attorney O'Brien Wounded by Gunman in 1921," *Chicago Evening American,* October 11, 1926.

75 *someone crept along a window ledge:* "Saltis Plot is Seen in Raids on M'Donald Files," *Chicago Tribune,* October 11, 1926.

76 *At about three thirty:* "Bible Student Tells How Gangsters Killed Weiss," *Chicago Evening American,* October 15, 1926.

76 *trademark red tie:* "Bombs, Scruples Hold Stage in Trial of Saltis," *Chicago Tribune,* October 10, 1926.

76 *newsboy cap:* Crime scene photos, Chicago History Museum.

76 *he had $5,300:* "Charge Weiss' Friends Shot Him," *Chicago Evening American,* October 13, 1926.

77 *Blackish blood spewed:* Ibid.; crime scene photos, Chicago History Museum.

77 *Bullets pocked the street and sidewalk:* "Gang Dead Guns Blaze After Peace Parley," *Chicago Herald and Examiner,* October 12, 1926.

77 *piping hot Tommy:* "2 Die in Gang War," *Chicago American,* October 11, 1926.

77 *"I'm sorry Weiss was killed":* "Brown Says He's Sorry," *Chicago Tribune,* October 13, 1926.

77 *"I don't want to die":* "Capone Begs for Peace; Doesn't Want to Be Slain," *Chicago Evening American,* October 13, 1926.

78 *sixty gang killings so far for 1926:* "60 Lives Taken by Guns in Gang Feud," *Chicago Herald and Examiner,* October 12, 1926.

79 *"I'm a real estate man":* "Schemer Says He Never Heard of Rum Feud," *Chicago Herald and Examiner,* October 18, 1926.

79 *another peace summit:* "Capone Back Home After Gangs Sign Peace Pact," *Chicago Evening American,* October 22, 1926.

79 *leaders . . . held personally responsible:* "New Chicago Gang Killing," *Los Angeles Times,* October 22, 1926.

79 *"Gangland killings have come to an end":* "Capone Happy as Peace Reigns," *Chicago Herald and Examiner,* October 23, 1926.

CHAPTER 12: A SMILE AND A GUN

Page

81   *"We're big business without high hats"*: Kenneth Allsop, *The Bootleggers* (New Rochelle, N.Y.: Arlington House, 1961), 250.

81   *"tremendously aroused"*: Ibid., 247.

82   *"Nobody drove me out"*: "Capone Defies Hughes; Stays," *Chicago Herald and Examiner,* January 22, 1927.

83   *dressed in nothing but a pink apron:* "Pink-Aproned Capone Does Own Housework," *Chicago Herald and Examiner,* January 24, 1927.

83   *"More than fifty murderers"*: "Stege Exposes Chicago's Killers," *Chicago Herald and Examiner,* January 16, 1927.

84   *corpse turned to blood-caked ice:* "Find Clements Murdered as Brother Said," *Chicago Tribune,* December 31, 1926

84   *"Clements' death won't"*: "Gang Truce Unshaken, Says Alphonse Capone," *Chicago Herald and Examiner,* January 1, 1927.

84   *punching bags, horizontal bars:* Fred Pasley, *Al Capone* (Binghamton, N.Y.: Ives Washburn, 1930), 165.

CHAPTER 13: THE GRINDER

Page

85   *No important criminal cases:* "Federal Court Delays Big Cases Until Next Fall," *Chicago Tribune,* April 10, 1927.

85   *made him physically sick:* "G. E. Q. Johnson Hits on Way to Rout Gangland," *Chicago Tribune,* December 21, 1930.

85   *"The cause is slack thinking"*: Ibid.

86   *"Yes, George E. Q. is slower than the Second Coming"*: Ibid.

86   *annual budget of just $90,000:* "$30,000,000 Graft Charged by Olson in His Final Report," *Chicago Evening American,* December 29, 1926.

87   *Crowe was among the guests:* "Milano Owner Latest Victim of Guns," *Chicago Heights Star,* July 23, 1926.

87   *a peacock flickered in the window:* "Heights Bright Lights Dimmed by Milano Raid," *Chicago Heights Star,* April 23, 1925.

87   *looking like he just rolled out of bed:* Walter Noble Burns, *The One-Way Ride* (Garden City, N.Y.: Doubleday, 1931), 285.

88   *springs bent almost to the axles:* "Heights Bright Lights Dimmed by Milano Raid," *Chicago Heights Star,* April 23, 1925.

88   *he requested several continuances:* "Milano Owner Latest Victim of Guns," *Chicago Heights Star,* July 23, 1926.

88   *DeFrank was first to die:* "Arrest Wife and Alleged Suitor in Defrank Murder," *Chicago Heights Star,* May 11, 1926.

88 *followed by Jimmie Lamberta:* "Assassins Fail to Spare Women in Double Inn Killing," *Chicago Heights Star,* June 4, 1926.

89 *followed by Joe Salvo:* "Joe Salvo, Lamberta Kin, Is Murdered," *Chicago Heights Star,* August 3, 1926.

89 *followed by Joe Catando:* "Party's Ended as Shots Fell Two of Guests," *Chicago Heights Star,* August 10, 1926.

89 *followed by Tony "The Cavalier" Spano:* "Murdered Man Proves to Be Tony Spano-'Cavaliero,' " *Chicago Heights Star,* August 24, 1926.

89 *followed by Antonio DeStefano Pelledrino:* "Beer Killers Torture Their Latest Victim," *Chicago Heights Star,* September 3, 1926.

89 *"We're down":* "Three Killed in War of Bootleggers," *Chicago Tribune,* March 12, 1927.

90 *long black Cadillac:* "Saltis Predicts Vengeance for Killing of Koncil," *Chicago Tribune,* March 13, 1927.

90 *Koncil was at the wheel:* "Koncil and Hayes Slain by Own Pals, Police Assert," *Chicago Herald and Examiner,* March 13, 1927.

90 *six bullets in Koncil's back:* "Three Killed in War of Bootleggers," *Chicago Tribune,* March 12, 1927.

90 *Capone was vacationing in Hot Springs:* "Capone Broke; Lady Luck Gets His $1,500,000," *Chicago Herald and Examiner,* April 19, 1927.

CHAPTER 14: THE BETTER ELEMENT

Page

92 *it was probably thanks to Capone:* "Machine Guns Murder Novelty Last Year," *Chicago Tribune,* January 1, 1927.

92 *Dever loved the job's ceremony:* John R. Schmidt, *The Mayor Who Cleaned Up Chicago* (De Kalb: Northern Illinois University Press, 1989), 142.

92 *the job felt like a burden:* Ibid.

93 *"You have redeemed the city":* "Group of Civic Leaders Asks Dever to Run," *Chicago Tribune,* December 18, 1926.

93 *debated a pair of caged rats:* Lloyd Wendt and Herman Kogan, *Big Bill of Chicago* (New York: Bobbs-Merrill, 1953), 216.

94 *Dever banned the . . . newsreel films:* "Durkin's $2,295 Seized; Movies Bar His Pictures," *Chicago Tribune,* January 24, 1926.

94 *"crossing the threshold":* Wendt and Kogan, *Big Bill of Chicago,* 243.

95 *kick in at least $250:* Ibid., 250.

95 *"Thompson is a buffoon":* "Dever and Thompson," *Chicago Tribune,* February 23, 1927.

95 *"not all supporters of Thompson":* "Brennan and Big Bill War," *Chicago Tribune,* March 1, 1927.

95 *"the illiterate portion":* "Contest for Mayor Boils in Chicago," *New York Times,* April 4, 1927.

95   *"Hooray for Big Bill!":* Wendt and Kogan, *Big Bill of Chicago,* 263.

95   *"I'm for Big Bill":* Ibid., 269.

96   *Drucci kept a framed picture:* "The Late Mr. Drucci's and Some Other Arsenals," *Chicago Tribune,* April 6, 1927.

96   *"You take your gun off":* "Kill Drucci in Drive on Ballot Thugs," *Chicago Tribune,* April 5, 1927.

96   *Only the intervention of another officer:* "Police Kill Vincent Drucci in Election Round-Up," *Chicago Herald and Examiner,* April 5, 1927.

96   *police assigned 250 officers:* "Contest for Mayor Boils in Chicago," *New York Times,* April 4, 1927.

97   *"They was trying to beat Bill":* Wendt and Kogan, *Big Bill of Chicago,* 274.

97   *"Officially we have arrived!":* Ibid., 275.

CHAPTER 15: "THERE'S WORSE FELLOWS IN THE WORLD THAN ME"

Page
102   *"confederation of utterly conscienceless dictators":* Robert Hardy Andrews, *A Corner of Chicago* (Boston: Little, Brown, 1963), 104.

102   *net income of $300,000:* Internal Revenue Service archives.

102   *prostitutes there brought in more than $1,200:* Ibid.

103   *Capone grabbed 52 percent:* Ibid.

104   *hadn't even paid off the $4,400 mortgage:* Cook County property tax records.

104   *big, tough, and loudmouthed:* Interview with Charles Bidwill II.

105   *"I violate the Prohibition law—sure":* "Gang Boundaries, Not Wards, Divide Chicago, Says 'Scarface Al,' " *Chicago Herald and Examiner,* March 9, 1927.

107   *Morris Becker was approached by a racket:* "Gunmen Taken into Business for Trade War," *Chicago Tribune,* May 27, 1928.

107   *$1.75 to clean men's suits:* Ibid.

107   *"I now have no need of the state's attorney":* Ibid.

108   *a strike among elevator operators:* John H. Lyle, *The Dry and Lawless Years* (Englewood Cliffs, N.J.: Prentice-Hall, 1960), 189.

108   *"You know, you are famous":* William H. Stuart, *The 20 Incredible Years* (Chicago: M. A. Donohue, 1935), 464.

109   *"Capone's University of Gutbucket Arts":* Milton "Mezz" Mezzrow and Bernard Wolfe, *Really the Blues* (New York: Random House, 1946), 62.

109   *"Al always showed up":* Ibid., 63.

110   *Fats Waller . . . claimed:* Maurice Waller and Anthony Calabrese, *Fats Waller* (New York: Schirmer Books, 1977), 62.

110   *Milton Berle claimed:* Milton Berle and Haskel Frankel, *Milton Berle* (New York: Delacorte Press, 1974), 168.

110   *George Jessel . . . claimed:* John Kobler, *Al Capone* (New York: G. P. Putnam's Sons, 1971), 312.

110 *Joe E. Lewis got in trouble:* "Cabaret Man's Fears Told as Stabbing Clew," *Chicago Tribune,* November 9, 1927.

111 *it seemed as if Mae had cocooned herself:* Interview with Madeleine Capone Morichett.

111 *"There isn't a song written":* Capone letter, Alcatraz Penitentiary, National Archives, San Bruno, California.

111 *"Yes, sir," said a farmer:* "Hoover Now Hero of Flooded South," *New York Times,* July 31, 1927.

112 *need another three thousand officers:* "Soft Jobs End; Crime Is Cut," *Chicago Herald and Examiner,* August 19, 1927.

112 *"psychopathic examinations":* "Exile or Madhouse–Name It! Hughes Warns Gunmen," *Chicago Herald and Examiner,* August 19, 1927.

112 *first man tested was . . . McGurn:* "Police Win and Lose in First Psychopathic Test of City's Gunmen," *Chicago Herald and Examiner,* August 18, 1927.

112 *"I may have been all right":* Ibid.

112 *scores of bootleggers had applied:* "Bootleggers Watch Agents Take 'Exams,' " *Chicago Herald and Examiner,* June 5, 1927.

113 *"Give me a break":* "Chief to Probe U.S. Bar Link to Police," *Chicago American,* August 6, 1927.

113 *charges against the big fellow never came:* "Nip Beer Flow to Loop from Huge Brewery," *Chicago Tribune,* August 6, 1927.

113 *"Capone wasn't my kind of person":* Roger Touhy, *The Stolen Years* (Cleveland: Pennington Press, 1959), 69.

113 *"You owe me for eight hundred":* Ibid., 70.

114 *"Bootleggers must file income tax returns":* "Tax Return by Bootlegger Is Held Obligatory," *Chicago Tribune,* May 17, 1927.

CHAPTER 16: UNEASY LIES THE HEAD

Page

115 *federal government dropped all the charges:* "Gigantic Rum Lot Charge Is Dismissed," *Chicago Herald and Examiner,* November 2, 1927.

115 *Capone went shopping:* Internal Revenue Service archives and 1931 trial testimony.

115 *made the selections himself:* Ibid.

115 *paid cash:* Ibid.

115 *paid $1,200 to $1,500:* Ibid.

116 *charges for food and drink totaled $3,000:* Ibid.

116 *rarely did the hotel's manager . . . remind him:* Ibid.

117 *Lombardo was one of the friendliest bootleggers:* Walter Noble Burns, *The One-Way Ride* (Garden City, N.Y.: Doubleday, 1931), 229.

118 *Aiello put out word that he would pay $50,000:* "Police Order: 'Kill Killers,' " *Chicago Tribune,* November 22, 1927.

118   *drops of prussic acid:* Ibid.

118   *"It has come to pass, men":* Ibid.

119   *sent some of his men downtown to the police station:* Ibid.

120   *Marcus leaped to his feet:* "Nip New Gang War as Trio Seized Outside Bureau," *Chicago American,* November 21, 1927.

120   *O'Connor ran toward the gunman:* "Capone Guard Attempts to Kill Detective Chief," *Chicago Evening Post,* November 21, 1927.

120   *"Can't we settle this?":* "Blast Wrecks Den of Gang," *Chicago Tribune,* November 23, 1927.

120   *Capone was released:* "Police Surround Gang Stronghold," *Chicago Herald and Examiner,* November 23, 1927.

120   *"We haven't enough policemen":* Ibid.

120   *An officer was assigned:* Ibid.

121   *an Evanston woman called the police:* "House Bombed, Woman Cries; It's Only Cider," *Chicago Evening Post,* November 29, 1927.

121   *"We have this gang situation in hand":* "50 Gangsters Captured; New Truce Rumor," *Chicago Tribune,* November 24, 1927.

121   *"Mr. Capone was here":* "Chief Hughes Defies Underworld to Finish Fight for City Rule," *Chicago Herald and Examiner,* November 22, 1927.

121   *seven bodyguards:* "Capone, Ringed by Guards, Appears in Court and Is Freed," *Chicago Herald and Examiner,* November 23, 1927; "Caponi in Court; Photographers his Chief Fear," *Chicago Evening Post,* November 22, 1927.

122   *"Have all your friends been denatured?":* Ibid.

122   *heading to Wisconsin for some duck hunting:* "Al Capone and 20 Aides Flee City for Lives," *Chicago Herald and Examiner,* November 29, 1927.

122   *"I'm leaving for St. Petersburg":* "Caponi Puts Dry Curse on City in Farewell Bleat," *Chicago Evening Post,* December 6, 1927.

122   *"Let the worthy citizens of Chicago get their liquor":* Ibid.

123   *$100,000 a year in bonuses:* "Hotter Here Than in Florida for Caponi–Hughes," *Chicago Evening Post,* December 7, 1927.

123   *"My wife and my mother hear so much":* " 'You Can All Go Thirsty' Is Al Capone's Adieu," *Chicago Tribune,* December 6, 1927.

124   *visited a movie studio:* "Scarface Al–Came to Play, Now Look–He's Gone Away!" *Los Angeles Times,* December 14, 1927.

124   *Mary Pickford's old digs:* "Capone Comes Home," *Chicago Tribune,* December 17, 1927.

124   *took Mae to Tijuana:* "Caponi Jailed by Joliet Police," *Chicago Evening Post,* December 16, 1927; " 'Scarface' Capone Visits Races at Tia Juana Track," *Los Angeles Evening Herald,* December 10, 1927.

124   *"I am just a peaceful tourist":* " 'Scarface' Capone Here Because He's 'Tired' of Chicago," *Los Angeles Evening Herald,* December 13, 1927.

124   *"They're picking on me":* "Al Capone to Take 'Rest' in Chicago," *Los Angeles Evening Herald,* December 14, 1927.

125   *decided to get off in Joliet:* "Caponi Jailed by Joliet Police," *Chicago Evening Post,* December 16, 1926.

125 *pistol and two magazines of cartridges:* Ibid.

125 *purchased thirty diamond-studded belt buckles:* Affidavit of Samuel J. Steinberg, Internal Revenue Service archives.

CHAPTER 17: DEEPEST IN DIRT

Page

127 *Hughes opened the meeting:* "City 'Winning Crime War,'" *Chicago Tribune,* January 19, 1928; "Civic Leaders Hope City Crime on Wane," *Chicago American,* January 19, 1928.

127 *"All over the world":* "Civic Leaders Hope City Crime on Wane," *Chicago American,* January 19, 1928.

127 *48 percent of all felony charges were dropped:* John Landesco, *Illinois Crime Survey, 1929* (Chicago: University of Chicago Press, 1929), 35.

127 *In Milwaukee during the same period:* Ibid., 102.

129 *"We will not get far with the courts":* "City 'Winning Crime War,'" *Chicago Tribune,* January 19, 1928.

129 *"The public is at last aroused":* Charles G. Dawes, *Notes as Vice President, 1928–29* (Boston: Little, Brown, 1935), 78.

CHAPTER 18: PINEAPPLES AND COCONUTS

Page

130 *3605 Indian Creek Drive:* Internal Revenue Service archives.

130 *paid for six months of rent up front:* Ibid.

130 *under the name Albert Costa:* Ibid.

130 *stayed in touch with his associates:* FBI documents, National Archives, College Park, Maryland.

131 *504 pages to print them all:* Frederick Lewis Allen, *Only Yesterday* (New York: Perennial Classics, 2000), 241.

131 *he and eight friends had visited a nightclub:* "Capone Is Here and May Remain if He Behaves," *Miami Daily News,* January 9, 1928.

131 *"Miami's climate is more healthful":* "Capone Is Here as Sun Hunter, He Tells Quigg," *Miami Daily News,* January 10, 1928.

132 *"Mr. Capone was one of the fairest men":* "Asks Capone to Leave," *New York Times,* January 22, 1928.

132 *Capone would give Henderson . . . Western Union money orders:* Internal Revenue Service archives.

133 *He delivered more than $30,000:* Ibid.

133 *Lummus . . . offered to broker the deal:* "Miami Beach Seeks to Drive Out Capone," *New York Times,* June 28, 1928.

133 *four annual installments:* Lummus testimony, Internal Revenue Service archives.

133 *a $2,000 binder and an additional $8,000:* Ibid.

133 *Henderson deeded the property to Mae:* Ibid.

133 *started making improvements:* Internal Revenue Service archives.

134 *improvements cost $50,000 to $75,000:* Internal Revenue Service archives and 1931 trial testimony.

134 *precisely the same mugs:* FBI documents, National Archives, College Park, Maryland.

134 *"If I were guilty":* "Quiz Capone in N.Y. Killing," *Chicago Herald and Examiner,* July 10, 1928.

135 *exploding at a rate of about a dozen a month:* "Bomb Campaign Rouses U.S.," *Chicago Tribune,* March 28, 1928.

136 *"Dimey," as friends called him:* "Diamond Joe's Career One of Colorful Rise to Political Power by Poor Immigrant Youth," *Chicago Tribune,* March 22, 1928.

136 *he distributed baskets of food:* "Young, Old, and Unfortunate to Get Yule Cheer," *Chicago Tribune,* December 24, 1925.

136 *"If Dimey wants it":* "Diamond Joe's Career One of Colorful Rise to Political Power by Poor Immigrant Youth," *Chicago Tribune,* March 22, 1928.

137 *"Get out of the ward":* "Slay Diamond Joe Esposito," *Chicago Tribune,* March 22, 1928.

137 *blue Dodge:* "Esposito Death Car Is Identified," *Chicago Herald and Examiner,* March 24, 1928.

137 *"Oh, my God!":* "Five Seized in Esposito Killing," *Chicago Herald and Examiner,* March 23, 1928.

137 *Police found on his body:* "Diamond Joe's Career One of Colorful Rise to Political Power by Poor Immigrant Youth," *Chicago Tribune,* March 22, 1928.

137 *shot three times in the back of his head:* "Esposito Witness Is Slain," *Chicago Tribune,* March 23, 1928.

139 *The first came at 11:20 P.M.:* "Deneen's Home Is Bombed," *Chicago Tribune,* March 27, 1928.

139 *Johnson had recently been assigned a full-time . . . agent:* FBI memo dated April 7, 1928, National Archives, College Park, Maryland.

139 *called the police to arrange for additional protection:* Ibid.

140 *"There is no doubt who did this":* "Homes of Deneen and Judge Bombed," *New York Times,* March 27, 1928.

140 *"They are resorting to desperate means":* Ibid.

140 *a federal marshal . . . asked for troops:* "Illinois Free State," *New York Times,* March 30, 1928.

141 *connected back to the murder of . . . Esposito:* "Deneen Foes Lay Bombs to Senator's Followers," *Chicago Herald and Examiner,* March 28, 1928.

141 *"I ate regular":* Lloyd Wendt and Herman Kogan, *Big Bill of Chicago* (New York: Bobbs-Merrill, 1953), 308.

141 *sat slumped in a chair:* Ibid.

142 *"gabbled hysterically and spoke irrationally":* Ibid., 312.

CHAPTER 19: THE GRADUATION OF FRANKIE YALE

Page

143 *His former mentor . . . made weekly visits:* Undated Internal Revenue Service memo, Mark Haller collection, Temple University.

143 *Most of the guests were Chicago gangsters:* Ibid.

143 *he might pack salami sandwiches:* John Kobler, *Capone* (New York: G. P. Putnam's Sons, 1971), 222.

143 *organize an outing to a swank nightclub:* Internal Revenue Service archives.

144 *Lelia Russell . . . sent a letter:* Justice Department memo, National Archives, College Park, Maryland.

144 *started her career as a schoolteacher:* Justice Department personnel records.

145 *the guns were gone:* "Gun in Yale Matter Is Linked to Capone," *New York Times,* August 1, 1928.

145 *Much of the booze . . . flowed in from Europe:* Edward Behr, *Prohibition* (New York: Arcade, 1996), 130.

145 *walls constructed largely of champagne and whiskey crates:* Interview, Marc Cormier, Office of Tourism, St. Pierre and Miquelon.

146 *McCoy spent $100,000 on each trip:* Behr, *Prohibition,* 136.

146 *net profits estimated at $200,000 a month:* Ibid., 139.

147 *"I couldn't look upon the gangs":* Kenneth Allsop, *The Bootleggers* (New Rochelle, N.Y., 1961), 250.

147 *"Capone was relatively innocent":* Ibid.

147 *"Corruption begins at the top":* Ibid., 242.

148 *changing the labels . . . to read "Old Log Cabin":* Larry Engelmann, *Intemperance* (New York: Free Press, 1979), 143.

148 *huge increase in demand for motorboat licenses:* Ibid., 72.

148 *more than fifty thousand pint bottles of beer a day:* "Great Beer Fleet Keeps Detroit 'WET,' " *New York Times,* June 10, 1923.

149 *Yale was thirty-five:* World War I draft registration card.

149 *moving slowly through a busy residential neighborhood:* "Slay Importer of Killers for Chicago Gangs," *Chicago Tribune,* July 2, 1928.

150 *came to rest on the stone stairs:* Newspaper photos.

150 *no idea where Capone could be found:* "Gun in Yale Matter Is Linked to Capone," *New York Times,* August 1, 1928.

150 *excessively bright streetlamp:* "Quiz Capone in Miami about Yale Slaying," *Chicago Tribune,* July 10, 1928.

151 *"The year 1928":* Untitled speech, reprinted in *Credit Craft* magazine, unknown date and page number, contained in personal papers of George E. Q. Johnson.

152 *"more wisdom than sophistry or bunk":* "From the Notebook of Carl Sandburg," undated newspaper clipping contained in personal papers of George E. Q. Johnson.

CHAPTER 20: HOOVERIZATION

Page

153   *seventy thousand people filled Stanford University's football stadium:* "Hoover Formally Notified, Voices Issues; Opposes Dry Law Repeal or Nullification; Favors Hundreds of Millions for Farm Aid," *New York Times,* August 12, 1928.

154   *"I do not favor the repeal":* Ibid.

154   *She expected silence from her three children:* Eugene Lyons, *Herbert Hoover: A Biography* (Garden City, N.Y.: Doubleday, 1964), 7.

154   *sledding:* Ibid., 14.

155   *"Thee is going to Oregon":* Ibid., 17.

155   *"the best miner of them all":* Ibid., 168.

156   *He set hog prices so high:* William E. Leuchtenburg, *The Perils of Prosperity, 1914–32* (Chicago: University of Chicago Press, 1958), 41.

156   *One cartoonist's Valentine:* Joan Hoff Wilson, *Herbert Hoover: Forgotten Progressive* (Boston: Little, Brown, 1975), 60.

157   *"This is not an occasion":* "Hoover Greeted by Chicago Throng, Is Guest of Dawes," *New York Times,* July 16, 1928.

158   *"I will get into the background":* Ibid.

158   *the national income of the United States:* Leuchtenburg, *Perils of Prosperity,* 108.

159   *"Big business in America is producing":* Ibid., 202.

CHAPTER 21: "I DO NOT STAY UP LATE"

Page

160   *"Miss Parsons?":* Louella O. Parsons, *The Gay Illiterate* (Garden City, N.Y.: Garden City Publishing, 1944), 108.

161   *"Come early":* Ibid.

161   *"Al Capone doesn't live here":* Ibid.

161   *"The gangster chief was a dark, squat man":* Ibid., 109.

162   *"That paper that runs your column":* Ibid., 110.

162   *"Los Angeles":* Ibid.

162   *"What burned me up":* Ibid., 111.

CHAPTER 22: THE ENFORCER

Page

163   *"Oh! Look at the airplane":* "Aid of Lombardo Held at Inquest," *Chicago Daily News,* September 8, 1928.

163   *hoisting a real airplane:* "Crowds See Boston Store Prepare Plane Display," *Chicago Evening American,* September 7, 1928.

164 *help save a ten-year-old Italian boy:* "Kidnap Child; Ask $60,000," *Chicago Tribune,* July 11, 1928.

164 *tried to confine his public activities to the Loop:* "Lombardo's Rise to Power Speedy and Successful," *Chicago Evening American,* September 8, 1928.

164 *clothes reeking of cigarette smoke:* "Seize Capone! Slaying Order," *Chicago Evening American,* September 8, 1928.

164 *brown suit, hatless, and seemingly alone:* "Man Slain in Car; Lombardo Clew," *Chicago Daily News,* September 13, 1928.

164 *reached in his pocket for his own revolver:* "Capone's Pal Shot Dead in Loop," *Chicago Daily News,* September 7, 1928.

165 *Streetcars screeched to a stop:* "Lombardo, Capone Aid, Slain at Crowded Loop Corner," *Chicago Herald and Examiner,* September 8, 1928.

165 *ducked into a Regal Shoes store:* "Hunt 2 as Lombardo Slayers," *Chicago Evening Post,* September 8, 1928.

165 *blood pouring . . . from two small holes:* "Gang War—in the Thronged Loop," *Chicago Evening American,* September 8, 1928.

165 *Dumdum bullets:* "Aid of Lombardo Held at Inquest," *Chicago Daily News,* September 8, 1928.

165 *murders and assaults increased 37 percent:* David E. Kyvig, *Daily Life in the United States, 1920–1940* (Chicago: Ivan R. Dee, 2004), 178.

166 *"The hoodlum of 1920":* Fred Pasley, *Al Capone* (Binghamton, N.Y.: Ives Washburn, 1930), 336.

166 *three rooms connected to form a single suite:* Testimony of Walter Housen, Capone tax trial, 1931.

167 *housewives, old women with shawls:* "Capone Guard at Lombardo Rites," *Chicago Daily News,* September 11, 1928.

167 *One wreath spanned the entire width:* *Chicago Daily News* photo, September 11, 1928, contained in the archives of the Chicago History Museum.

167 *A clock built of pink gladiolas:* "Capone Interviewed at Lombardo's Bier," *Chicago Evening American,* September 11, 1928.

167 *Capone sent . . . a heart made of red roses:* "Bury Lombardo Today; Capone Sent Flowers," *Chicago Tribune,* September 11, 1928.

168 *He wore a black suit of fine wool:* "Capone interviewed at Lombardo's Bier," *Chicago Evening American,* September 11, 1928.

168 *Capone and his men tugged on cigars:* "Capone Guard at Lombardo Rites," *Chicago Daily News,* September 11, 1928.

168 *"Honest, . . . it's all a puzzle":* Ibid.

168 *He couldn't imagine why either of them had been killed:* "Gunmen Bury Lombardo with Kingly Pomp," *Chicago Tribune,* September 12, 1928.

168 *"There'll be no trouble":* Ibid.

168 *"I've tried to treat Tony Lombardo":* "Capone Interviewed at Lombardo's Bier," *Chicago Evening American,* September 11, 1928.

169 *$3,000 bronze coffin:* "Bury Lombardo with Gangland Pomp," *Chicago Herald and Examiner,* September 12, 1928.

169 *"How many men have you on your police force?"*: "Annihilate Mafia–Judge," *Chicago Tribune,* September 21, 1928.

170 *Frank J. Loesch . . . paid a visit to Capone:* "Loesch Tells of a Secret Call on Capone," *Chicago Tribune,* March 25, 1931.

170 *"I had only two dollars"*: "For Seventy Years He's Fought for His City," undated article, unnamed publication, Northwestern University archives.

170 *Capone's guards ushered Loesch:* "Loesch Tells of a Secret Call on Capone," *Chicago Tribune,* March 25, 1931; Loesch testimony before U.S. Senate Judiciary Committee, 1932.

171 *"When they talk about Al Capone being rich"*: "Loesch Wants Crooks Driven From City Hall," *Chicago Daily News,* April 26, 1929.

171 *"If you doubt the political sway of this man"*: Fred Pasley, *Muscling In* (New York: Ives Washburn, 1931), 41.

172 *"Today will stand out"*: "Chicago Does Its Voting in Record Peace and Quiet," *Chicago Tribune,* November 7, 1928.

172 *"Herbert Hoover and the promise"*: "Stock Trading Wave Sweeps to New Peaks of 5,745,000 Shares," *New York Times,* November 12, 1928.

CHAPTER 23: THE FORMIDABLE ALPHONSE

Page

174 *"Occasionally, he would succeed"*: Elmer L. Irey and William J. Slocum, *The Tax Dodgers* (New York: Greenberg, 1948), 28.

174 *From the newspapers, of course:* Ibid., xii.

174 *liens for $11,000:* "Brother of Al Capone Involved in U.S. Tax Suit," *Chicago Tribune,* October 23, 1928.

176 *beat the butcher with a crowbar:* "Two Indicted as Sluggers in Alleged Price Fixing," *Chicago Tribune,* October 8, 1927.

176 *"What police have attempted unsuccessfully"*: "Capone Wars on Racketeers," *Chicago Daily Journal,* May 28, 1928.

177 *The North Siders no longer had their headquarters:* "Court Demands Checker Taxi Books for Quiz," *Chicago Tribune,* October 27, 1928.

178 *Gusenberg stuck up a couple of well-dressed women:* "Identify Two as Men Who Took $14,000 in Jewelry," *Chicago Tribune,* November 3, 1928.

178 *Their proposed victim . . . looked like an easy mark:* "Broker Shoots Gunman in Auto on Loop Street," *Chicago Tribune,* November 6, 1928.

178 *William Davern Jr. was shot in the stomach:* "Sgt. Duvern's Son Wounded," *Chicago Daily Journal,* November 14, 1928.

179 *"A man who has been shot in the leg can't dance!"*: "Caponi Denies He Was Shot; Dances a Jig," *Chicago Evening Post,* September 21, 1928.

179 *The bullet . . . put a hole in his scrotum:* Clinical record, Atlanta Federal Penitentiary, September 12, 1932, National Archives, San Bruno, California.

CHAPTER 24: LITTLE CAESAR

Page

180 *He asked experts . . . to submit proposals:* Gene Smith, *The Shattered Dream* (New York: William Morrow, 1970), 9.

180 *he . . . watched the dark skies unleash their torrents:* Eugene Lyons, *Herbert Hoover: A Biography* (Garden City, N.Y.: Doubleday, 1964), 182.

180 *keep it plain, simple, and cheap:* "Hoover Silent on His Plans," *New York Times,* January 7, 1929.

181 *The Penney mansion was simple yet elegant:* J. C. Penney archives at Southern Methodist University.

181 *"a cloud over all our problems":* Herbert Hoover, *The Memoirs of Herbert Hoover: The Cabinet and the Presidency, 1920–1933* (New York: Macmillan, 1952), 275.

181 *"I should have been glad to have":* Ibid.

181 *"In that manner":* William E. Leuchtenburg, *The Perils of Prosperity, 1914:32* (Chicago: University of Chicago Press, 1958), 215.

182 *Bootleggers roamed the halls of Congress:* Edward Behr, *Prohibition* (New York: Arcade Publishing, 1996), 164.

184 *in his flat over a harness shop:* "Lolordo Shot in Home," *Chicago Herald and Examiner,* January 9, 1929.

184 *raised four wineglasses:* Ibid.

184 *"amazingly friendly murder":* Walter Noble Burns, *The One-Way Ride* (Garden City, N.Y.: Doubleday, 1931), 239.

185 *Samuel D. Light was called to the house:* FBI report, National Archives, College Park, Maryland.

185 *slide a ten-dollar bill into the palm:* Testimony at Capone's income tax trial, 1931.

185 *Capone . . . chartered a seaplane:* FBI report, National Archives, College Park, Maryland.

185 *sailed for Nassau:* Ibid.

186 *"We don't know a millionth of 1 percent":* "Edison Forecasts 'Hoover Prosperity,' " *New York Times,* February 12, 1929.

186 *Capone returned . . . February 12:* FBI report, National Archives, College Park, Maryland.

CHAPTER 25: ST. VALENTINE'S DAY

Page

187 *Children put the finishing touches:* "Will You Be My Valentine? City Hears Old Query," *Chicago Tribune,* February 15, 1929.

187 *guards prepared for the midnight execution:* "3 Killers Die in Chair Tonight; Stay Refused," *Chicago Tribune,* February 14, 1929.

187 *stockbrokers . . . nervously watched:* "Wall Street Drives Many Stocks Higher," *Chicago Tribune,* February 14, 1929.

188 *Elmer Lewis steered his Nelson-LeMoon:* Elmer Lewis interview with Chicago police officers, undated, Chicago Police Department records.

189 *past a drugstore, a barbershop, and boardinghouses:* Notes from Chicago police officers, February 15, 1929.

189 *a hot plate, a coffeepot, and a couple of boxes:* Crime scene photos.

190 *He saw smoke and smelled gunpowder:* Clair McAllister statement to police, February 14, 1929.

190 *"Who is it?":* Ibid.

191 *"Do you know me, Frank?":* Tom Loftus statement to police, February 14, 1929.

191 *"Cops did it":* Contained in some accounts of Tom Loftus's statement to police, February 14, 1929.

191 *"Do you remember when you first met":* Accounts of the Capone interview were contained in several newspapers, each one slightly different. "Lavish Capone Life and $5 Tips Bared," *New York Times,* October 10, 1931; "Expose Capone's Gold Flow," *Chicago Tribune,* October 10, 1931.

194 *That afternoon he did some fishing:* Herbert Hoover's daily calendar, Herbert Hoover Presidential Library, West Branch, Iowa.

CHAPTER 26: "AN UNSOLVED CRIME"

Page

197 *"I am sick and tired":* "Out of Racket, Capone Vows; Buys on Gulf," *Chicago Herald and Examiner,* February 23, 1929.

198 *recently lost $27,500:* International News Service wire story, February 22, 1929.

198 *"One leaves the dark-complexioned":* Ibid.

198 *"the most amazing crime":* "U.S. Attorney Blames Mob Killings on Easy Money Lure," *Chicago Herald and Examiner,* February 15, 1929.

199 *a phone call was received at the garage:* "Firing Squad Kills Seven in Big Gangland Massacre," *Chicago Herald and Examiner,* February 15, 1929.

199 *the work of the Purple Gang:* "Gunmen Slay Seven Rivals," *Chicago Evening Post,* February 14, 1929.

199 *woman who ran a boardinghouse:* "Latest Clue Pins Gang Massacre on Detroit Gunmen," *Chicago Evening Post,* February 16, 1929.

200 *searched for Sam Giancana:* "Giancanna Is Now Sought in Massacre," *Chicago American,* March 1, 1929.

200 *"police squad automobile beyond any doubt":* "Sensational New Clue Obtained in Gang Massacre," *Chicago Evening Post,* February 20, 1929.

200 *"It seems funny to me":* " 'Double Crossing' Is Seen Cause of Gang Massacre," *Chicago Evening Post,* February 21, 1929.

200 *"I can name fifty motives":* "Seize 9 Suspects in Gang Massacre," *Chicago Evening Post,* February 25, 1929.

200 *"Me, mixed up in that gang killing?":* "Me in Gang Killing? Don't Make Me Laugh, Says McGurn," *Chicago Evening Post,* February 28, 1929.

201 *room 1919A:* "Giancanna Is Now Sought in Massacre," *Chicago American,* March 1, 1929.

201 *"I didn't even know":* "Me in Gang Killing? Don't Make Me Laugh, Says McGurn," *Chicago Evening Post,* February 28, 1929.

CHAPTER 27: "THE MOST SORE NECESSITY OF OUR TIMES"

Page

203 *"Scarface Capone may have retired":* "Your Broadway and Mine," *Mason City Globe-Gazette,* February 28, 1929.

203 *"one of the authentic big men":* "Who Shot at Jack Dempsey," *Chicago Tribune,* February 26, 1929.

203 *R. B. Burdine . . . visited Capone:* "Al Capone Free with Champagne, Visitor Admits," *Chicago Evening Post,* June 13, 1930.

204 *"He had a colored man":* Ibid.

204 *Later . . . the money was returned:* Associated Press, June 13, 1930.

204 *" 'Scarface Al' Capone may be the next boss":* "Miami Destined to Be Ruled by King Scarface," *Chicago Tribune,* February 28, 1929.

204 *Agents examined Capone's phone records:* Internal Revenue Service files, Mark Haller collection, Temple University.

204 *the work of at least two real cops:* "Blames Police in Killings," *Chicago Herald and Examiner,* February 16, 1929.

205 *"An unwavering drive against booze":* "Police to Mop Up City," *Chicago Evening Post,* February 26, 1929.

205 *"It's a war to the finish":* "Murder in Chicago, Politics, the Police, the Courts," *Chicago Herald and Examiner,* February 16, 1929.

206 *"So let's give Soltis":* "A Grateful Customer," *Chicago Tribune,* March 14, 1929.

206 *"The world is not to be blamed":* "Shatter Gangland's Foundation—Booze! Citizens Cry," *Chicago Herald and Examiner,* February 19, 1929.

206 *Similar measures were proposed:* "Wet Drive Spreads in the Middle West," *New York Times,* March 29, 1929.

206 *He sat beside Jack Dempsey:* Fred Pasley, *Al Capone* (Binghamton, N.Y.: Ives Washburn, 1930), 84.

207 *He would get around to it:* "Capone's Bodyguard Jailed," *Chicago Herald and Examiner,* March 1, 1929.

207 *"I wasn't mixed up in it":* Associated Press, March 1, 1929.

207 *nineteen-page typewritten speech:* Herbert Hoover Presidential Library, West Branch, Iowa.

207 *"My countrymen":* Ibid.

208 *He arrived at the White House soaked:* Gene Smith, *The Shattered Dream* (New York: William Morrow, 1970), 10.

208 *"For me to go north":* "Capone Fears 'Winds' of Chicago, Seeks Delay," *Chicago American,* March 6, 1929.

208 *there was no point:* "Capone Will Be Here, U.S. Replies to Defy," *Chicago American,* March 5, 1929.

208 *Johnson made his plea to Mabel Willebrandt:* Johnson letter, National Archives, College Park, Maryland.

209 *They filled their notebooks:* FBI memos, National Archives, College Park, Maryland.

209 *Capone's lawyers began negotiating:* "Capone Returning to Demand Immunity," *Chicago American,* March 18, 1929.

209 *"They gave me chapter and verse":* Herbert Hoover, *The Memoirs of Herbert Hoover* (New York: Macmillan, 1952), 277.

210 *"Probably no private citizen":* "Scarface Al Capone Has Never Run Away," *New York Times,* May 26, 1929.

210 *the Treasury Department would soon assign additional agents:* "Washington Speeding Up," *New York Times,* March 18, 1929.

CHAPTER 28: THE BRIGHTEST DAYS

Page

211 *where a man could drink a highball:* "Squire Alphonse Capone Gets Two Big Loads Off His Chest," *Chicago Tribune,* March 6, 1929.

211 *"the brightest days are still ahead":* "Mr. Capone Gathers Roses," *Chicago Tribune,* March 7, 1929.

211 *"the raw spring climate":* "Squire Alphonse Capone Gets Two Big Loads off His Chest," *Chicago Tribune,* March 6, 1929.

212 *"Capone will be handled like the hoodlum":* "Capone Ready to Say Nothing at Quiz Today," *Chicago Tribune,* March 20, 1929.

212 *Wearing his trademark pearl gray fedora:* "Throng Trails Al Capone," *Chicago Daily News,* March 20, 1929.

212 *left his brother and a few pals:* Associated Press story, March 20, 1929.

212 *asked for . . . an autograph:* "Jury Grills Capone Two Hours," *Chicago Herald and Examiner,* March 21, 1929.

213 *"I ought to go into vaudeville":* Ibid.

213 *"So long, boys!":* "U.S. Jury Quizzes Capone," *Chicago American,* March 20, 1929.

213 *kosher corned beef sandwich:* Ibid.

213 *granted immunity:* Ibid.

213 *mostly "I don't know":* Ibid.

215 *signed on with Charles Waite:* "In Memory of Calvin Hooker Goddard, M.D., Col., U.S. Army," *Association of Firearm and Toolmark Examiners Journal,* October 1991.

215 *"[O]n the subject of bullets":* "Proceedings of the Thirteenth Annual Convention of the International Association for Identification," August 31, 1927.

216 *he received a call from Bert A. Massee:* "The Valentine's Day Massacre: A Study in Ammunition-Tracing," *American Journal of Police Science* 1, no. 1 (January–February 1930): 60–78.

216 *Seventy empty shells:* Ibid.

216 *Figuring out the make was easy:* Ibid.

216 *buckshot and smokeless powder:* Ibid.

217 *rounded up as many Tommy guns as he could:* Ibid.

217 *"the end of a blind alley":* Ibid.

218 *went back to his room at the Lexington:* "U.S. Arrests Capone," *Chicago American,* March 27, 1929.

CHAPTER 29: "HAVE YOU GOT CAPONE YET?"

Page

219 *the court was sixty-six feet long:* Hoover-Ball rules, Herbert Hoover Presidential Library, West Branch, Iowa.

219 *"Have you got Capone yet?":* "Capone Enters Guilty Plea; Faces 5 Years in Prison," *Chicago Herald and Examiner,* June 17, 1931.

220 *"I couldn't help wondering":* Elmer L. Irey and William J. Slocum, *The Tax Dodgers* (New York: Greenberg, 1948), 26.

220 *Under Coolidge, alcohol had been served:* "Dry Capital, Hoover's Aim," *Chicago Tribune,* March 2, 1929.

220 *"the dominant issue":* "Hoover Demands Respect for Law; Calls It 'Dominant Issue' in Speech before Publishers Here," *New York Times,* April 23, 1929.

221 *Johnson met with the city's social club directors:* "Clubs Ban Locker Liquor after Conferences," *Chicago American,* May 7, 1929.

222 *Managers at the Stevens Hotel announced:* "Stevens Hotel Bans Setups for Drinking," *Chicago American,* May 16, 1929.

222 *"the chief" was looking for a way out:* "Capone Is Broke and Wants to Retire," *Chicago American,* April 17, 1929.

223 *dead for no more than three hours:* "Scalise, Anselmi Slain in Revenge," *Chicago American,* March 8, 1929.

224 *"Imagine a little diner":* Walter Noble Burns, *The One-Way Ride* (Garden City, N.Y.: Doubleday, 1931), 256.

224 *"No, Al, please":* George Murray, *The Legacy of Al Capone* (New York: G. P. Putnam's Sons, 1975), 115.

CHAPTER 30: LOCKED UP

Page

226 *attended prizefights:* "Atlantic City Calls Capone 'Undesirable,' " *New York Times,* May 16, 1929.

227 *Moran had refused to go along:* "Capone Enters Jail to Serve One Year," *New York Times,* May 18, 1929.

227 *Scheduled departure was 9:05:* "Capone Begins Year's Jail Sentence," *Chicago Herald and Examiner,* May 18, 1929.

227 *It was Malone who spotted . . . Capone:* "Al Capone Gets One Year after His Arrest Here," *Philadelphia Evening Bulletin,* May 17, 1929.

228 *grabbed Capone by the hand:* Ibid.

228 *Capone lit a cigarette:* Ibid.

228 *"Phew":* Ibid.

228 *"I went into the racket":* "Caponi in Prison for Year; Chicago Gang War Ended, He Says," *Chicago Evening Post,* May 17, 1929.

229 *"What's the weight of that ring?":* "Al Capone Gets One Year after His Arrest Here," *Philadelphia Evening Bulletin,* May 17, 1929.

229 *Ten big Philly cops:* Ibid.

229 *Capone's face reddened:* Ibid.

229 *He pulled the diamond ring from his finger:* "Quaker Justice in Jig Time Jails Capone for Year," *Chicago Tribune,* May 18, 1929.

229 *"It's the breaks, kid":* "Al Capone Finds Prison Life Dull," *Philadelphia Evening Bulletin,* May 20, 1929.

230 *"a desperate measure":* "Declare Capone Sought Jail Term to Escape Death," *Philadelphia Evening Bulletin,* May 18, 1929.

230 *"He never gets in jail":* "Sister Tells How Good Al Is to His Folks," *Chicago Tribune,* May 18, 1929.

230 *"What would he want to go to jail for?":* " 'Al Didn't Seek Jail,' Says Wife," *Philadelphia Evening Bulletin,* May 18, 1929.

230 *"I'm here because I'm here":* "Capone Jailed for Year Here; Feels Secure," *Philadelphia Public Ledger,* May 18, 1929.

230 *One sly writer:* "A Line o' Type or Two," *Chicago Tribune,* May 18, 1929.

231 *arresting waiters who served ginger ale:* "Clubs Ban Locker Liquor after Conferences," *Chicago Evening American,* May 7, 1929.

231 *"I've arrested Capone":* "Declare Capone Sought Jail Term to Escape Death," *Philadelphia Evening Bulletin,* May 18, 1929.

231 *handcuffed to a guard:* "Aides Organize for Legal Fight to Free Capone," *Philadelphia Public Ledger,* May 19, 1929.

231 *"known throughout crookdom":* " 'Toughest Jail' Closes Door on Capone," *Chicago Tribune,* May 19, 1929.

231 *prison-issued black trousers:* "Capone Dons Garb of County Convict," *Philadelphia Public Ledger,* May 20, 1929.

231 *one of seventeen hundred:* "Capone Sealed in Prison Gloom; Predict Release," *Chicago Tribune,* May 20, 1929.

231 *fetid creek:* Ibid.

231 *set their bedding afire:* Ibid.

232 *"Not much like home here":* " 'Toughest Jail' Closes Door on Capone," *Chicago Tribune,* May 19, 1929.

232 *"You see, I want to get out of here":* "Capone Wants out; Denies He Broke in Jail," *Chicago Tribune,* June 5, 1929.

233 *"Yes, very comfortable":* "Capone Lolls in Luxuriously Furnished Cell," *Chicago Tribune,* August 20, 1929.

233 *"I have been quoted so much":* "Aides Organize for Legal Fight to Free Capone," *Philadelphia Public Ledger,* May 19, 1929.

233 *"Within the next few months":* Ibid.

CHAPTER 31: ELEGANT MESS

Page

234 *The arrest speaks for itself:* "Willy-Nilly, Prison Is Best Place for Al, Officials Say," *Chicago Tribune,* May 18, 1929.

234 *Word came from Miami:* Letter from J. Edgar Hoover to George E. Q. Johnson, July 18, 1929, National Archives, College Park, Maryland.

235 *He fired off a letter:* Letter from George E. Q. Johnson to attorney general, July 24, 1929, National Archives, College Park, Maryland.

236 *Eliot Ness was feeling restless:* Eliot Ness and Oscar Fraley, *The Untouchables* (New York: Pocket Books, 1987), 18.

236 *"almost felt like chucking the whole business":* Ibid.

237 *never got paddled, spanked:* Paul W. Heimel, *Eliot Ness: The Real Story* (Coudersport, Pa.: Knox Books, 1997), 16.

237 *"Elegant Mess":* Ibid., 17.

237 *Cs and C-minuses:* College transcript, University of Chicago archive.

237 *He had $410:* Ness and Fraley, *The Untouchables,* 22.

237 *Jamie . . . had a much sweeter deal:* Dennis Hoffman, *Scarface Al and the Crime Crusaders* (Carbondale: Southern Illinois University Press, 1993), 148.

238 *twenty-one pages on onionskin:* Eliot Ness collection, Western Reserve Historical Society, Cleveland.

239 *Late in September, Johnson went to Washington:* "Chicago Dry Cleanup Planned in Harmony, U.S. Attorney Says," *Chicago Tribune,* September 21, 1929.

239 *"A greater effort will be made":* Ibid.

240 *he didn't have the eyesight:* Frank Spiering, *The Man Who Got Capone* (Indianapolis: Bobbs-Merrill, 1976), 51.

240 *assigned to check out . . . one of the bureau's own agents:* Ibid., 47.

240 *"Wilson fears nothing":* Elmer L. Irey and William J. Slocum, *The Tax Dodgers* (New York: Greenberg, 1948), 36.

240 *"I could hardly scratch my head":* "How We Caught Al Capone," *Chicago Tribune,* June 14, 1959.

240 *One of them began hanging around the lobby:* Spiering, *Man Who Got Capone,* 87.

241 *"The courts had to see income":* "How We Caught Al Capone," *Chicago Tribune,* June 14, 1959.

241 *At twenty-six-to-one:* "Ralph Capone's Azov Wins by 2 Lengths at 26–1," *Chicago Tribune,* October 11, 1929.

243 *"Al Capone is a piker":* "Bear Hunt," *Time,* May 2, 1932.

243 *"Those stock market guys are crooked":* "Stock Market 'Too Crooked' for Al Capone," *Chicago Tribune,* November 3, 1929.

243   *"The little judgment I had":* Groucho Marx, *Groucho and Me* (New York: Da Capo Press, 1995), 103.

243   Oh hush thee: "The Little Fellow in Wall Street," *Saturday Evening Post,* January 4, 1930.

244   *"The jig is up!":* Marx, *Groucho and Me,* 197.

245   *"Tell them . . . I deny absolutely":* Philadelphia Evening Ledger, November 25, 1929.

CHAPTER 32: THE NAPOLEON OF CHICAGO

Page

248   *deviated septum:* Clinical record, Terminal Island, U.S. Bureau of Prisons, National Archive, San Bruno, California.

248   *tonsils:* "Capone's Tonsils Removed," *New York Times,* September 8, 1929.

248   *"In my seven years' ":* "Capone Jail Attack Feared," *Chicago Herald and Examiner,* March 16, 1930.

248   *Burke . . . had the misfortune of smashing his car:* "Find Killer's $319,850 Loot," *Chicago Tribune,* December 16, 1929.

249   *They also found twenty gallons of wine:* Ibid.

249   *Goddard . . . announced with great flourish:* "Prove Two Burke Gins Killed 7 of Moran Gang," *Chicago Tribune,* December 24, 1929.

249   *Police said . . . Burke had been the leader of the attack:* "Reveal Killer's Home a Fortress of Desperadoes," *Chicago Tribune,* December 17, 1929.

249   *at a bar in Calumet City:* William J. Helmer and Arthur J. Bilek, *The St. Valentine's Day Massacre* (Nashville: Cumberland House, 2004), 299.

250   *Frank T. Farrell composed a letter:* FBI archives.

251   *driven to the corner of Rush Street and Austin Avenue:* "Police Sergeant's Son Mysteriously Shot; Won't Talk," *Chicago Evening Post,* November 14, 1928.

251   *botched safecracking job:* George Murray, *The Legacy of Al Capone* (New York: G. P. Putnam's Sons, 1975), 88.

252   *They'd worked together in 1926:* "Police Hope to Seize Harvester Robbers Today," *Chicago Tribune,* March 8, 1926.

252   *disguised themselves as police:* "Slay Gang Betrayer in Bed," *Chicago Tribune,* March 25, 1926.

253   *"Just about the time I arrived":* "Find New Massacre Witness," *Chicago Herald and Examiner,* February 25, 1929.

253   *White worked as a federal informant:* FBI Headquarters File 62–20753, obtained under Freedom of Information Act.

253   *Federal agents were seen visiting:* Ibid.

253   *the director replied that the gangland killings:* J. Edgar Hoover letter, FBI archives.

CHAPTER 33: THE BIG FELLOW CHILLS

Page

254 *In Cleveland, thousands of unemployed:* "Jobless," *Time,* February 24, 1930.

255 *"No one will look with satisfaction":* Herbert Hoover, *State of the Union Addresses* (Whitefish, Mont.: Kessinger, 2004), 28.

256 *the sign on the door read Acme Sales Company:* "Raid Moran Den in Loop," *Chicago Tribune,* December 29, 1929.

256 *"Scotch? Scotch?":* "Moran's Liquor Vanishes; Detectives Laugh Off Raid," *Chicago Herald and Examiner,* December 31, 1929.

256 *Ness and his men were tapping phone lines:* Wiretap transcripts from the personal papers of George E. Q. Johnson.

256 *"My secretary made a call":* Eliot Ness manuscript, Western Reserve Historical Society, Cleveland.

257 *"Is Mike there?":* Wiretap transcripts from the personal papers of George E. Q. Johnson.

258 *"I'm in a swell spot now":* Ibid.

258 *"Did you get any today?":* Ibid.

CHAPTER 34: SILENT PARTNER

Page

261 *lanky and charming:* "Reporter Rogers," *Time,* March 15, 1937.

261 *It was Rogers whose investigation:* Ibid.

262 *indicted along with George Remus:* "Indicts Politicians in Big Liquor Plot," *New York Times,* November 3, 1925.

262 *monkeys on the dogs' backs:* "Here's an Idea! Monkeys as Jockeys in Dog Races," *Chicago Tribune,* December 20, 1927.

263 *"Financed and Operated by Home People":* Advertisement, *Edwardsville Intelligencer,* April 14, 1927.

263 *51 percent interest:* Frank Wilson memo, Internal Revenue Service archives, Mark Haller collection, Temple University.

263 *more than $100,000 in annual profits:* Ibid.

263 *He argued that there was no gambling:* "Dog Track Head Tells Costs of Running Plant," *Chicago Tribune,* July 3, 1929.

263 *"Yes. Something like that":* "You Don't Bet on Hounds—You Buy Them," *Chicago Tribune,* May 25, 1929.

264 *chew each bite of food twenty-five times:* Interview with Charles "Stormy" Bidwill.

264 *an average student:* Edward H. O'Hare personnel file, Department of the Navy, U.S. Naval Academy.

264 *"Does he realize":* Frank J. Wilson and Beth Day, *Special Agent* (New York: Holt, Rinehart, & Winston, 1965), 32.

265 *"one of the best undercover men":* "How We Trapped Capone," *Collier's,* April 26, 1947.

265   *Wilson also hoped to make a close examination:* Frank Wilson letter, April 8, 1929, Internal Revenue Service archives, Mark Haller collection, Temple University.

CHAPTER 35: "LADY, *NOBODY'S* ON THE LEGIT"

Page

266   *"Of course I'm going back":* "Al Tells His Plans," *Chicago Tribune,* March 16, 1930.

266   *thousands of people:* "Capone out Tonight," *Chicago American,* March 17, 1930.

267   *"Try and find out":* "Capone Speeds for Chicago," *Chicago Tribune,* March 18, 1930.

267   *two eighteen-pound turkeys:* "Prepare Feast for Capone's Return," *Chicago Tribune,* March 16, 1930.

269   *"No desperado":* "Coming Out Party," *Time,* March 24, 1930.

269   *Hope . . . on orders from Hoover:* James D. Calder, *The Origins and Development of Federal Crime Control Policy* (Westport, Conn.: Praeger, 1993), 133.

269   *Youngquist phoned the commissioner:* Ibid., 134.

269   *"not a matter of seriousness or importance":* Ibid.

270   *"prepared himself for almost every contingency":* Ibid., 135.

270   *Youngquist phoned the president:* Ibid., 136.

270   *"The most important areas for the enforcement":* Ibid., 132–33.

271   *"Do you want Capone?":* "Warned from Chicago," *Chicago Tribune,* March 22, 1930.

271   *"Just a minute, boys":* "Capone Gives Up to Stege; Quizzed on Disappearance," *Chicago Evening Post,* March 21, 1930.

271   *"Well, fellows, what do you want to know?":* Ibid.

272   *"The sun's shining once more, boys":* "Al Bids Good-bye after Annoying Calls," *Chicago American,* March 21, 1930.

272   *Capone was free to return:* "U.S. Writ (Fla.) Pops Up to Aid Citizen Capone," *Chicago Tribune,* March 23, 1930.

272   *"I never had a number":* "Capone's Story: By Himself," *Chicago Tribune,* March 22, 1930.

272   *French telephone:* Ibid.

273   *"I'm not telling anybody how to run the country":* "Al Capone Relates His Own Story of 'Racket' in Chicago," *Chicago American,* March 22, 1930.

274   *Adolphe Menjou . . . made a brief stop in Chicago:* "Movie Stars Back from France," *Chicago Tribune,* March 22, 1930.

274   *president of the Rapid City Chamber of Commerce sent word:* "Capone Spurns Bid to Great Open Spaces," *Chicago Tribune,* March 29, 1930.

274   *In Monticello, Iowa:* "Monticello, Ia., Is in Print, Thanks to Chicago's Al Capone," *Chicago Tribune,* April 2, 1930.

274   *Will Rogers sent a letter to the editor:* "Will Rogers Hears of a Drive That Imperils a Great Sport," *New York Times,* April 21, 1930.

274 *poor spinal alignment:* "Capone's Crime Complex Traced to His Vertebrae," *Chicago Herald and Examiner,* March 24, 1930.

275 *"we have our bandits":* "Chinese Papers Headline Doings of Local Gangs," *Chicago Evening Post,* June 4, 1930.

275 *In Java and Burma:* "Fame of Al Capone Extends to Indo-China, Says Foreman," *Chicago Evening Post,* May 16, 1930.

275 *"to do my level best to give Al Capone":* "Capone Fights Back, Charging Conspiracy," *New York Times,* May 25, 1930.

275 *"Now, Mr. Capone":* Transcript of interview, April 17, 1930, Internal Revenue Service archives.

277 *"He must have had plenty of room on his person":* Damon Runyon syndicated column, October 8, 1931.

CHAPTER 36: PUBLIC ENEMY NUMBER ONE

Page

278 *couldn't keep a lid on his bigotry:* "Asserts Gangsters Rule Great Cities," *New York Times,* March 23, 1930.

279 *"The Capones and Morans are not within the law":* "Law Enforcement by Stigma," *New York Times,* April 25, 1930.

279 *"Poverty wasn't a Public Enemy":* Robert Hardy Andrews, *A Corner of Chicago* (Boston: Little, Brown, 1963), 179.

279 *"The following article tells names and places":* "Gangsters Defy Cry of 'Drive 'Em Out'; Here's Who They Are," *Chicago Daily News,* February 7, 1930.

280 *"I am here for a rest":* "Al Capone Reaches Palm Island Home for 2 Weeks' Rest," *Miami Herald,* April 21, 1930.

280 *he took his son and his nephew for a ride:* Ibid.

281 *Capone and seven other men . . . flew to Cuba:* "American Gives Facts about Read's Visit at Al Capone's," *Chicago Evening Post,* July 12, 1930.

281 *Florida governor Doyle E. Carlton . . . petitioned a judge:* "Capone Guard Fined in Miami; Padlock Asked," *Chicago Daily News,* April 23, 1930.

281 *"He will not establish headquarters in Florida":* "Florida No Spot for Al Capone," *Chicago Evening Post,* March 24, 1930.

281 *stopped by detectives as they motored along Biscayne Boulevard:* "Capone Jailed in Miami; Police Defy U.S. Writ," *Chicago Herald and Examiner,* May 9, 1930.

281 *spent seventeen hours in jail:* "Capone and 3 Friends Spend Night in Jail," *Miami Herald,* May 14, 1930.

281 *smoked a cigar and chatted:* "Capone Gives $100 Bond on Third Arrest," *Miami Herald,* May 2, 1930.

282 *request that the gate . . . be padlocked:* "Capone Home Guard Suggested by Fisher," *Miami Herald,* May 17, 1930.

282 *"I can't understand this at all":* "Three Years for Ralph Capone," *Chicago Evening Post,* June 16, 1930.

282 *the feds raided more than two dozen . . . stills:* "Dry Agents Raid 24 Capone Stills in Cicero District," *Chicago Evening Post,* June 21, 1930.

283 *"We are being criticized very severely":* James D. Calder, *The Origins and Development of Federal Crime Control Policy* (Westport, Conn.: Praeger, 1993), 140.

283 *The new ordinance defined as a vagrant:* "Miami Makes Al a Bum," *Chicago Tribune,* May 24, 1930.

283 *Al and Mae hosted a party:* "Al Capone Host to Schoolmates of His Son, 11," *Chicago Tribune,* May 19, 1930.

283 *the list of invitees was not announced:* "Al Capone Host at a Musical; Guests Unnamed," *Chicago Tribune,* May 30, 1930.

284 *Capone had had a falling out with . . . Lingle:* Frank Wilson memo, December 12, 1933, Mark Haller collection, Temple University.

284 *"blistering tongue":* John Boettiger, *Jake Lingle, or Chicago on the Spot* (New York: E. P. Dutton, 1931), 27.

284 *"For [expletive] sake":* Ibid., 33.

285 *it was Lingle who had brought him dinner:* "Aiello Haunt Raided in Hunt for Lingle Killer," *Chicago Herald and Examiner,* June 10, 1930.

285 *$65-dollar-a-week salary:* "Lingle's Money Deals Bared," *Chicago Tribune,* June 29, 1930.

285 *At noon, he left his room:* Boettiger, *Jake Lingle, or Chicago on the Spot,* 15.

286 *stopped by* Tribune *Tower:* Ibid.

286 *one-thirty train to Homewood:* Ibid., 16.

286 *stopped at a newsstand:* "Gunman Slays Alfred Lingle in I.C. Subway," *Chicago Tribune,* June 10, 1930.

286 *Hy Schneider:* Ibid.

286 *The cigar hit the floor first:* "Reporter Killed by Gunman: Capone Gangster Accused," *Chicago Herald and Examiner,* June 10, 1930.

286 *A woman screamed:* "Eyewitnesses Tell How Killer Shot and Fled," *Chicago Herald and Examiner,* June 10, 1930.

286 *crimson puddle:* Boettiger, *Jake Lingle, or Chicago on the Spot,* 20.

286 *The killer stood briefly:* Ibid., 18.

286 *first through a busy intersection:* "Eyewitnesses Tell How Killer Shot and Fled," *Chicago Herald and Examiner,* June 10, 1930.

286 *the killer looked like Sam Hunt:* "Reporter Killed by Gunman: Capone Gangster Accused," *Chicago Herald and Examiner,* June 10, 1930.

287 *"The commanders of the squads":* "Gangs Raided; Chiefs Flee," *Chicago Tribune,* June 12, 1930.

287 *"I was fonder":* Ibid.

288 *he had shared a bank account:* "Lingle's Money Deals Bared," *Chicago Tribune,* June 29, 1930.

288 *invested more than $20,000:* Ibid.

288 *"Alfred Lingle now takes a different character":* "The Lingle Murder," *Chicago Tribune,* June 30, 1930.

288 *His price: $15,000, paid up front:* "Trap 15 in Lingle Raids," *Chicago Tribune,* July 1, 1930.

289 *It was ten at night:* "Brundidge Sees Capone about Lingle Killing," *Chicago Tribune,* July 19, 1930.

289 *"Come on in":* Ibid.

290 *A month later . . . Capone returned:* "Capone Back in Chicago," *Chicago Tribune,* August 2, 1930.

290 *A few couples out on the dance floor:* "Gang Kills at Hotel Dance," *Chicago Tribune,* August 20, 1930.

290 *"Here's what I want to tell you":* Boettiger, *Jake Lingle, or Chicago on the Spot,* 179.

291 *Thirty-five steel-tipped bullets:* "Joe Aiello Slain in Ambush," *Chicago Tribune,* October 23, 1930.

291 *Even the most law-abiding of the Capone brothers:* "Police Seize Capone's Brother," *Chicago Evening Post,* September 18, 1930.

291 *violet eyes, and a sunny personality:* Interviews with Regina Maritote and Francis Rolla (né Maritote).

292 *his lawyer . . . submitted a letter:* Mattingly letter, Internal Revenue Service archives, September 20, 1930.

292 *14,700 Americans reported incomes greater than $100,000:* "$7,000,000,000 Drop in Incomes in 1930, Tax Returns Show," *New York Times,* November 30, 1931.

292 *Thomas John Watson . . . made $60,000:* "Salaries," *Time,* March 12, 1934.

292 *Irving Thalberg earned a straight salary of $200,000:* Ibid.

CHAPTER 37: "THERE IS NO FRIENDSHIP AMONG HOODLUMS"

Page

294 *"Some of the boys say":* "How We Trapped Capone," *Collier's,* April 26, 1947.

294 *Johnson took it as a slap in the face:* Letter to Mitchell, personal papers of George E. Q. Johnson.

295 *long after his colleagues had gone home:* "How We Trapped Capone," *Collier's,* April 26, 1947.

295 *He found an open file cabinet:* Ibid.

295 Bird cage, 21, Craps: Ibid.

296 *Ries was bald, middle-aged:* "Monthly Take of $30,000 Told at Guzik Trial," *Chicago Tribune,* January 15, 1930.

296 *Wilson threw him in a jail:* Frank Spiering, *The Man Who Got Capone* (Indianapolis: Bobbs-Merrill, 1976), 141.

296 *Pete Penovich, Frank Nitti:* Frank Wilson memo, December 21, 1933, Internal Revenue Service archives.

296 *Knockout Brown:* Undated Wilson memo, Internal Revenue Service archives, Mark Haller collection, Temple University.

297 *trip to South America, paid for by a group of Chicago businessmen:* Ibid.

297   *"I'm investigating the income tax liability"*: Spiering, *Man Who Got Capone*, 128.

298   *Guzik had warned him never to pay . . . Capone:* Undated Wilson memo, Internal Revenue Service archives, Mark Haller collection, Temple University.

298   *Harry Curtis . . . visited the commissioner:* Burnet letter to Walter E. Hope, Herbert Hoover Presidential Library, December 18, 1930.

298   *"There have been other slight intimations"*: Ibid.

299   *Revenue from income taxes in 1930:* "The Price of Prohibition," *Arizona Law Review*, vol. 36, no. 1 (1994), pp. 1–10.

299   *"Ralph Capone and Jack Guzik"*: "G. E. Q. Johnson Hits on Way to Rout Gangland," *Chicago Tribune*, December 21, 1930.

300   *Calling himself Michael Lepito:* Spiering, *Man Who Got Capone*, 87.

300   *Malone heard rumblings:* Ibid., 135.

301   *industrial production steadily slid:* Frederick Lewis Allen, *Only Yesterday* (New York: Perennial Classics, 2000), 299.

301   *"What's that—a bread line or a bank?"*: Ibid., 300.

301   *business leaders met . . . to plan a relief campaign:* "14 Leaders Help Raise 5 Million for Unemployed," *Chicago Tribune*, November 15, 1930.

302   *The kitchen, neat as a pin:* "Capone Finances Mysterious Soup House for Jobless," *Chicago Evening Post*, November 14, 1930.

302   *"Nobody else was doing it"*: Ibid.

302   *"We like to see him take an interest"*: "Dug out by Root," *Albuquerque Journal*, November 15, 1930.

CHAPTER 38: CONTEMPT

Page

303   *"neat but not gaudy"*: "Capone Sister Wed; Seize 5 Armed Guards," *Chicago Tribune*, December 15, 1930.

303   *chorus of "oohs" and "ahs"*: Ibid.

303   *seashell pink taffeta:* Ibid.

304   *several high-ranking members of the Capone outfit:* "White on Trial Today; Al Capone Due in Court," *Chicago Tribune*, December 15, 1930.

305   *"We will send Capone to the chair"*: "Electric Chair for Capone Is Plea of Lyle," *Chicago Tribune*, December 19, 1930.

305   *"Dear Public"*: "A Night Letter from Ring Lardner," *Chicago Tribune*, February 3, 1931.

305   *He entered on the Clark Street side:* "Capone Arrested and Taken Before Detective Chief," *Chicago Evening Post*, February 25, 1931.

305   *conservatively and elegantly dressed:* Ibid.

305   *Epstein, a graduate of Northwestern:* "Benj. Epstein, Circuit Court Judge, Is Dead," *Chicago Tribune*, March 14, 1952.

306   *"But I am not going into the literary business"*: "Capone Arrested as 'Enemy,' " *Chicago Herald and Examiner*, February 26, 1931.

307   *"cat's eye"*: *Chicago Evening Post,* January 26, 1931.

308   *Wilkerson and Grossman would become partners:* "Jas. Wilkerson, Judge in Capone Trial, Is Dead," *Chicago Tribune,* October 1, 1948.

308   *"Your honor, as sure as I am sitting here":* "Judge Holds Capone's Fate," *Chicago Tribune,* February 27, 1931.

308   *The muscles in his jaw tightened:* "Capone Gets Six Months," *Chicago Herald and Examiner,* February 28, 1931.

308   *had not carefully read his signed statement:* "Capone, Sentenced, Faces More Woe," *Chicago Tribune,* February 28, 1931.

309   *The judge pushed back his chair:* "Capone Gets Six Months," *Chicago Herald and Examiner,* February 28, 1931.

309   *"If the judge thinks it's correct":* "Capone, Sentenced, Faces More Woe," *Chicago Tribune,* February 28, 1931.

310   *"These are all new":* "Capone to Jail," *Chicago Tribune,* March 2, 1931.

CHAPTER 39: DEATH AND TAXES

Page

311   *taught at a Catholic high school:* "Michael Ahern, Noted Lawyer, Dies," *Chicago Tribune,* September 23, 1943.

311   *"Alphonse Capone is this man's right name":* "Capone Brothers Both Win Delay of Their Trials," *Chicago Tribune,* March 21, 1931.

311   *Howard Vincent O'Brien waited in a drugstore:* Howard Vincent O'Brien personal papers, Newberry Library, Chicago.

313   *"Insurance statistics tend to show":* Howard Vincent O'Brien, *All Things Considered* (Indianapolis: Bobbs-Merrill, 1948), xiii.

313   *"Bengal tiger":* Howard Vincent O'Brien personal papers, Newberry Library, Chicago.

313   *"That guy sent me up for five years":* Ibid.

314   *"It seemed to me":* Ibid.

314   *"the most significant contribution to current history":* Ibid.

314   *toy-rifle range:* Ibid.

315   *1915 Piper Heidsieck:* Ibid.

315   *"act as my agent in the sale":* Ibid.

316   *"I can't tell you that":* Ibid.

316   *One of them was Louis LaCava:* "Missing Capone Tax Witness Found by U.S.," *Chicago Tribune,* March 6, 1931.

316   *Pope testified to the grand jury, too:* Ibid.

316   *Fred Ries told the grand jury:* Frank Wilson memo, Internal Revenue Service archives, Mark Haller collection, Temple University.

317   *Frank Wilson had arranged a wiretap:* Ibid.

317   *Louis Alterie claimed he had nothing to do with the gang:* "Louis Alterie Jailed by U.S. in Capone Quiz," *Chicago Tribune,* March 5, 1931.

317 *agents raided the Cotton Club:* "Raid Capone's Cotton Club; Burn into Safe,"
     Chicago Tribune, March 12, 1931.

317 *Bert Delaney and Steve Svoboda:* "U.S. Indicts 23 Capone Men; Federal Jury
     Strikes New Cleanup Blow," *Chicago Tribune,* May 2, 1931.

317 *Ness and his men found twenty-three thousand gallons of beer:* "Capone Brewery
     Raided by Drys; Three Arrested," *Chicago Daily News,* March 25, 1931.

317 *a thick wave of foam:* "Capone Brewery, Huge Beer Supply Raided in Cicero,"
     Chicago Tribune, March 26, 1931.

318 *filling his thirty-two-gallon barrels:* "Al Capone's Beer Measure Is Short, Dealers
     Complain," *Chicago Tribune,* May 15, 1931.

318 *net income of $123,101.89:* Federal indictment, personal papers of George E. Q.
     Johnson.

318 *He felt that his witnesses were balky:* Johnson memos to Justice Department of-
     ficials, personal papers of George E. Q. Johnson.

319 *But somehow, Capone did:* Ibid.

CHAPTER 40: UNITED STATES AGAINST AL CAPONE

Page

320 *state's attorney's office . . . dropped its charge of vagrancy:* "Capone Vagrant Case
     Dropped; Lack of Evidence," *Chicago Tribune,* April 4, 1931.

321 *"It's true I didn't come over on the* Mayflower*":* Douglas Bukowski, *Big Bill Thomp-
     son, Chicago, and the Politics of Image* (Champaign: University of Illinois Press,
     1998), 232.

321 *"the most puissant machine":* "Rise and Fall of Thompson's Machine Told," *Chi-
     cago Tribune,* April 9, 1931.

321 *Cermak fired three thousand:* "Mayor Cermak in; 3,000 Out," *Chicago Tribune,*
     April 10, 1931.

321 *"The ship's sprung another leak!":* "Gridiron Fete Depicts Fight to Rescue Leaking
     Dry Ship," *Washington Post,* April 28, 1931.

322 *One day in late April or early May:* Undated memo to Justice Department, per-
     sonal papers of George E. Q. Johnson.

323 *he was no longer so sure of his play:* Ibid.

323 *"Let 'em think I'm dead":* United Press syndicated story, May 1, 1931.

323 *Johnson boarded an overnight train:* Johnson letter to Youngquist, May 6, 1931,
     personal papers of George E. Q. Johnson.

324 *he was inclined to accept a plea deal:* Personal papers of George E. Q. Johnson.

324 *don't make any deals without consulting us:* Ibid.

325 *Capone would plead guilty:* Ibid.

325 *Johnson told them to forget it:* Ibid.

325 *Johnson's next move was to meet with the judge:* Ibid.

325 *A carousel of law books stood near the door:* *Chicago Daily News* photos, Chicago
     History Museum.

326 *The judge ruled that the strikers were engaged:* "Daugherty Obtains Order," *New York Times,* September 1, 1922.

326 *the problem with Johnson, as Wilkerson saw it:* "Judge Rebukes Drys as Their Witnesses Fail," *Chicago Tribune,* October 25, 1928.

327 *"Evidence is obtained and indictments are returned":* Ibid.

327 *shifting the blame to his superiors:* Undated memo from Johnson to Justice Department officials, personal papers of George E. Q. Johnson.

327 *especially worried about his two key witnesses:* Ibid.

329 *Heitler played poker with some of Capone's men:* "Hunt for Capone, Hold Nine Aids in Torch Mystery," *Chicago Tribune,* May 3, 1931.

329 *The cops came looking for Capone:* Ibid.

330 *Johnson could wait no longer:* "Capone Indicted by U.S.; Surrenders," *Chicago Tribune,* June 6, 1931.

331 *They asked for another meeting with Johnson:* Memos to Justice Department, personal papers of George E. Q. Johnson.

332 *Ahern insisted on two conditions of his own:* Ibid.

332 *"Case 23,852":* "Cell to End Capone Power," *Chicago Tribune,* June 17, 1931.

332 *his voice a whisper:* Ibid.

333 *"Guilty," he mumbled:* Ibid.

333 *office workers lined up like pigeons:* "Capone Enters Guilty Plea: Faces 5 Years in U.S. Prison," *Chicago Herald and Examiner,* June 17, 1931.

333 *"Personally, I do not believe":* Avis letter, personal papers of George E. Q. Johnson.

333 *"if you have honest men on the job":* "Capone's Fall Work of Honest Men on Job, Mitchell Says," *Chicago Tribune,* June 19, 1931.

334 *the audience didn't boo:* "Confidence Our Need: Hoover," *Chicago Tribune,* June 16, 1931.

334 *"Hotel Hoover":* "Mayor Orders Hoover Sign off Haven for the Needy," *Chicago Tribune,* September 2, 1931.

335 *"Have you got Capone yet?":* "Capone Enters Guilty Plea; Faces 5 Years in U.S. Prison," *Chicago Herald and Examiner,* June 17, 1931.

335 *"The president was very kind":* "President at Tomb of Lincoln Demands Obedience to Law," *New York Times,* June 18, 1931.

335 *"Everywhere I went":* "Johnson Hero at Capital for Capone Defeat," *Chicago Herald and Examiner,* June 18, 1931.

CHAPTER 41: THE SO-CALLED UNTOUCHABLES

Page

336 *aware that the phrase was . . . applied to India's lowest caste:* "Faced Many Perils in Capone Roundup," *New York Times,* June 18, 1931.

336 *"We had to weigh our problems":* Ibid.

338 *Frank Loesch . . . wrote to President Hoover:* Loesch letter, Herbert Hoover Presidential Library, West Branch, Iowa.

338 *Coolidge might be persuaded to run again:* "Coolidge Hinted 1932 Candidate," *Chicago Evening Post,* July 31, 1931.

338 *"Some time when the gentleman you mention":* Herbert Hoover letter to Frank Loesch, Herbert Hoover Presidential Library, West Branch, Iowa.

338 *a scathing, six-page letter:* Mitchell letter, personal papers of George E. Q. Johnson.

340 *he proposed a plan to help settle his tax debt:* Internal Revenue Service archives, Mark Haller collection, Temple University.

340 *"I've been made an issue":* "Capone Moralizes on Eve of Sentence," *New York Times,* June 30, 1931.

340 *Johnson checked in with Judge Wilkerson:* Johnson memos to Justice Department, George E. Q. Johnson personal papers.

341 *Wilkerson admitted he'd been angered:* "Capone 'Deal' Ruling Today," *Chicago Tribune,* July 31, 1931.

341 *"It is time for somebody to impress upon this defendant":* Ibid.

341 *entered the court looking sharp:* Ibid.

341 *collar had soaked through:* Ibid.

342 *"Two days before Capone was to come to court":* Chicago American, July 23, 1956.

CHAPTER 42: "WHO WOULDN'T BE WORRIED?"

Page

343 *he and his pals had terrible seats:* "Al Capone Watches Football Game in Evanston," *Chicago Tribune,* October 4, 1931.

343 *"I'm here to see the game":* "Crowd Jeers Capone from Football Stand," *New York Times,* October 4, 1931.

344 *Capone woke up . . . feeling like hell:* "Capone Rises at 7 for Trial," *Chicago Herald and Examiner,* October 8, 1931; "Sidelights on Trial," *Chicago Daily News,* October 6, 1931.

344 *peppermint cough drops:* "Mint-Drops Mirror Al from Fresh Viewpoint," *Chicago Herald and Examiner,* October 7, 1931.

344 *"high carnival in all but confetti":* "Swear in Jury to Try Al Capone," *Chicago Daily News,* October 6, 1931.

344 *single, unmarked car:* "Capone Worries as Jury Is Made Up in Tax Trial," *Chicago Evening Post,* October 6, 1931.

344 *already working on his first cigar:* Photo, *Chicago Herald and Examiner,* October 7, 1931.

344 *temporary telegraph office:* "Eve of Capone's Trial Finds U.S. Eager for Clash," *Chicago Herald and Examiner,* October 4, 1931.

345 *associates and former associates were gathered:* "U.S. Starts Trial of Capone Today," *Chicago Tribune,* October 6, 1931.

345 *Frank Wilson . . . had received a phone call from . . . O'Hare:* Wilson memo, December 21, 1933, Internal Revenue Service archives.

346   *Ahern used all ten of his . . . challenges:* "Swear in Jury to Try Al Capone," *Chicago Daily News,* October 6, 1931.

346   *"It seems more than a coincidence":* "U.S. to Begin Its Capone Evidence Today," *Chicago Tribune,* October 7, 1931.

347   *"Like other newspaper readers":* "I Was a Capone Juror," *Chicago Tribune,* May 10, 1936.

348   *"I ain't got nothing against Snorky":* "Mint-Drops Mirror Al from Fresh Viewpoint," *Chicago Herald and Examiner,* October 7, 1931.

348   *Capone complained to his lawyers:* "New Booze Quiz Ordered," *Chicago Tribune,* August 1, 1931.

348   *Dwight Green opened with a summary:* "U.S. Outlines Case," *Chicago Herald and Examiner,* October 8, 1931.

348   *"The evidence will show":* Ibid.

349   *In 1925, while he was honeymooning:* "Dry Navy Breaks Up Honeymoon, Seizing Yacht with Liquor," *New York Times,* August 11, 1925.

349   *Ahern and Fink intended to argue that the two charges were . . . the same:* "Capone Defense Attacks Law in Federal Court," *Chicago Evening Post,* October 7, 1931.

349   *Wilkerson said he would reserve judgment:* Ibid.

349   *"fat, powerful fingers":* "Parson Depicts Tilt with Capone in Raid," *New York Times,* October 8, 1931.

350   *Shumway confirmed their authenticity:* "Capone Halts Witness," *Chicago Herald and Examiner,* October 8, 1931.

350   *A few of the jurors were seen yawning:* "Parson Depicts Tilt with Capone in Raid," *New York Times,* October 8, 1931.

350   *with a pompous air about him:* Ibid.

351   *Capone tapped his foot:* Ibid.

351   *He removed his eyeglasses, wiped them:* Ibid.

351   *Capone had not been in the gambling joint:* "Seek Capone Following Raid on Gaming House," *Chicago Evening Post,* May 18, 1925; "Hunts for 'Scarface' Capone," *Chicago Daily News,* May 17, 1925.

352   *a gentle push to get into the backseat:* "Parson Depicts Tilt with Capone in Raid," *New York Times,* October 8, 1931.

CHAPTER 43: BIG SPENDER

Page

353   *income . . . did not exceed $26,000:* "Capone Loses Fight to Bar Confession," *New York Times,* October 9, 1931.

353   *Ahern and Fink sprang to their feet:* "Capone's Own Story of 'Take' Told to Jurors," *Chicago Daily News,* October 8, 1931.

353   *"Congress doesn't want to send people to jail":* "Capone Confession Bared!," *Chicago Herald and Examiner,* October 9, 1931.

353   *"When a man makes such statements":* Ibid.

355 *"Wouldn't the size of the roll":* "Capone Pal Seized with Gun at U.S. Trial," *Chicago Daily News,* October 10, 1931.

355 *"the scar on his cheek stood out like a cord":* Ibid.

355 *"One man couldn't eat all that":* Ibid.

356 *Malone . . . spotted a bulge under D'Andrea's jacket:* "Judge Jails Capone's Guard," *Chicago Tribune,* October 11, 1931.

356 *pulled out a badge:* Ibid.

356 *Ahern told reporters he would call agents:* "Capone Trial to Bare Tax Bargaining," *Chicago Herald and Examiner,* October 12, 1931.

357 *Ries glumly took the stand:* "Guzik Got Gambling Profits, Says Ries, U.S. 'Star' Witness," *Chicago Herald and Examiner,* October 14, 1931.

357 *"Jack told me not to":* Ibid.

358 *"the government now rests":* "Close Case Against Capone," *Chicago Herald and Examiner,* October 14, 1931.

358 *Ahern and Fink were staggered:* Ibid.; "Prosecution Rests in Capone Trial," *New York Times,* October 14, 1931.

358 *One bookmaker would testify:* "Bookmakers Tell of Thousands Bet on Word by Phone," *Chicago Herald and Examiner,* October 15, 1931.

359 *toyed with the notion of putting Johnny Torrio on the stand:* "U.S. Sums Up Capone Case; 'Guilty' Seen," *Chicago Daily News,* October 15, 1931.

359 *asked the judge to allow the defense team ten hours:* "Prosecution Rests in Capone Trial," *New York Times,* October 14, 1931.

CHAPTER 44: THE VERDICT

Page

360 *Ahern prowled:* "Capone as 'No Piker' Extolled in Pleas," *New York Times,* October 17, 1931.

361 *"Why do they seek":* Ibid.

361 "Delenda est Capone!: Ibid.

362 *Shadows rose along the walls:* Ibid.

362 *sat at his desk with a pencil and a legal pad:* Draft of closing arguments, personal papers of George E. Q. Johnson.

363 *"This is an orderly, lawful":* Ibid.

363 *condensing his strategy into ten typewritten sheets:* Ibid.

363 *"Gentlemen of the jury":* Transcript of closing arguments, personal papers of George E. Q. Johnson.

365 *At 10:50 P.M.:* "Capone Convicted of Dodging Taxes; May Get 17 Years," *New York Times,* October 18, 1931.

365 *He took a seat, removed his hat:* Ibid.

366 *left everyone . . . a little confused:* Ibid.

366 *He smiled nervously:* Ibid.

366 *Capone hustled out the door:* Ibid.

367 *cupped his right hand over his ear:* "Capone Sentenced to an 11-Year Term; Jailed Till Appeal," *New York Times,* October 25, 1931.

367 *Capone rose:* Ibid.

367 *Capone grimaced:* Ibid.

367 *nervously licked his lips:* Ibid.

367 *fingers locked and unlocked:* Ibid.

367 *"The result":* "Capone in Jail; Prison Next," *Chicago Tribune,* October 25, 1931.

367 *slapped in the face:* "Capone Sentenced to an 11-Year Term; Jailed Till Appeal," *New York Times,* October 25, 1931.

367 *"Well, so long":* Ibid.

EPILOGUE

Page

369 *"It was a blow to the belt":* "Wilkerson Gives Capone 11 Years and $50,000 Fine," *Chicago Evening Post,* October 24, 1931.

370 *Johnson received an anonymous telegram:* Telegram, personal papers of George E. Q. Johnson.

370 *"put on an obscene performance":* FBI memo, December 17, 1931, personal papers of George E. Q. Johnson.

371 *"I'm in jail":* "Capone Denies Jail Favors," *Chicago Tribune,* December 18, 1931.

371 *Moneypenny was caught borrowing one of Capone's cars:* "Jail Warden's Trip in Capone Auto Revealed," *Chicago Tribune,* December 22, 1931.

371 *After the meal, an ice-cream truck pulled up:* "Chicagoans Eat Tons of Turkey on Thanksgiving," *Chicago Tribune,* November 27, 1931.

372 *"I know I could help":* "Demand More Baby Ransom," *Chicago Tribune,* March 11, 1932.

373 *Eliot Ness was among the federal agents assigned to escort Capone:* "Capone Speeds to Atlanta," *Chicago Tribune,* May 4, 1932.

373 *the two men traveled in separate cars:* Ibid.

373 *selling frozen hamburger patties:* Paul W. Heimel, *Eliot Ness* (Coudersport, Pa.: Knox Books, 1997), 193.

373 *"What do I think about it all?":* "Capone Speeds to Atlanta," *Chicago Tribune,* May 4, 1932.

374 *$231 in his pocket . . . In a free association exercise:* Atlanta Federal Penitentiary records, National Archives, San Bruno, California.

375 *first noticed a lesion on his penis in 1921:* "An Analuetic Treatment Record," Atlanta Federal Penitentiary records, National Archives, San Bruno, California.

375 *half a dozen two-dollar cigars:* Morris "Red" Rudensky and Don Riley, *The Gonif* (Blue Earth, Minn.: Piper, 1970), 56.

376 *Capone would cry out in his sleep:* Ibid., 57.

376 *"If we ever all hooked up":* Ibid., 58.

376   *Capone wrote a respectful letter:* Capone letter, June 14, 1934, Atlanta Federal
       Penitentiary records, National Archives, San Bruno, California.

376   *A newspaper report early in 1933:* "Capone Coddled in Atlanta Prison," *Philadel-
       phia Evening Bulletin,* January 23, 1933.

377   *The Bureau of Investigation checked out the rumors:* Atlanta Federal Penitentiary
       records, National Archives, San Bruno, California.

377   *"DECISION AGAINST YOU":* Telegram, Atlanta Federal Penitentiary records, Na-
       tional Archives, San Bruno, California.

378   *His first choice . . . was the bass:* Capone letter, June 22, 1933, Atlanta Federal
       Penitentiary records, National Archives, San Bruno, California.

378   *Mae and Sonny were his most frequent guests:* Visitors' log, Atlanta Federal Peniten-
       tiary records, National Archives, San Bruno, California.

378   *Mae's poem:* Atlanta Federal Penitentiary records, National Archives, San
       Bruno, California.

380   *"Being a politician is a poor profession":* Timothy Walch, ed., *Herbert Hoover on
       Growing Up: Letters from and to American Children* (New York: William Morrow,
       1990), 34.

380   *Capone and forty-two other prisoners from Atlanta:* "Al Capone Is on Way to New
       'Devil's Island,' " *Chicago Tribune,* August 20, 1934.

381   *On June 1, 1935, his library card:* Alcatraz records, National Archives, San
       Bruno, California.

382   *"Now dearest, let us forget business":* Ibid.

382   *"Son of mine":* Ibid.

382   *He gave the sheet music to Vincent Casey:* "Capone May Have Had One Last Hit,"
       Associated Press, April 16, 2009.

382   *Capone was at work in the prison basement:* Alcatraz records, National Archives,
       San Bruno, California.

383   *The tip of the scissor blade was still embedded:* Ibid.

383   *"Guess I'm a little wacky":* Clinical record, February 5, 1938, Alcatraz records,
       National Archives, San Bruno, California.

384   *spoke in grandiose terms of his plans:* Psychiatric report, June 23, 1938, Alcatraz
       records, National Archives, San Bruno, California.

385   *doctors at Alcatraz had little experience treating syphilis:* Memorandum for the at-
       torney general, February 14, 1938, Alcatraz records, National Archives, San
       Bruno, California.

385   *deep chill followed by a huge spike in temperature:* Memo of Dr. Romney M. Ritchey,
       September 17, 1938, Alcatraz records, National Archives, San Bruno, Califor-
       nia.

385   *"At the time of his last chill":* Memo of Dr. Edward Twitchell, October 6, 1938,
       Alcatraz records, National Archives, San Bruno, California.

386   *When asked to subtract seven from ninety-three:* Memo of Dr. Twitchell, November 17,
       1938, Alcatraz records, National Archives, San Bruno, California.

387   *"in recognition of his fine service in the war on gangsters":* "Hoover Talks Governor-
       ship to Wilkerson," *Chicago Tribune,* December 15, 1931.

388   *"You have proven your character":* Letter of June 15, 1943, personal papers of George E. Q. Johnson.

388   *Asked to add two plus five plus two:* Medical report, April 4, 1939, Terminal Island Prison, National Archives, San Bruno, California.

389   *Eddie O'Hare left his office:* "Slay E. J. O'Hare, Race Track Head," *Chicago Tribune,* November 9, 1939.

390   *a deal to start a roller derby league:* "Expose O'Hare Gang Links," *Chicago Tribune,* November 11, 1939.

391   *he was taken by train to Pennsylvania and met by his family:* Bureau of Prison records, National Archives, San Bruno, California.

392   *Al's oldest brother . . . resurfaced:* "Capone Tax Quiz Turns Up Long Lost Brother," *Chicago Tribune,* September 20, 1951.

392   *Theresa was the only one who recognized him:* Ibid.

393   *Ted's Grotto:* Robert J. Schoenberg, *Mr. Capone* (New York: Perennial, 1992), 362.

393   *"Everyone has a little larceny in them":* Associated Press report, August 8, 1965.

394   *"Nutty as a fruitcake":* "Al Capone Dies in Florida Villa," *Chicago Tribune,* January 26, 1947.

395   *At family gatherings, the Capones would reflect:* Interview with Madeleine Capone Morichetti.

395   *"Oh," replied Churchill:* International News Service report, January 15, 1946.

395   *"nervous and excitable":* Associated Press report, June 28, 1946.

395   *Sen-Sen breath mints:* Ibid.

395   *he hoarded candy bars:* Interview with Madeleine Capone Morichetti.

396   *he collapsed with . . . a stroke:* "Capone Rallies After Stroke in Florida Home," *Chicago Tribune,* January 22, 1947.

396   *A Catholic priest . . . administered the last rites:* Ibid.

396   *His wife, son, mother, sister, and two of his brothers were by his side:* "Al Capone Dies in Florida Villa," *Chicago Tribune,* January 26, 1947.

396   *"mortgaged to the hilt":* "Died Broke, No Will," *Chicago Tribune,* January 27, 1947.

396   *His body was shipped to Chicago by car:* "Capone's Body on Way to City; Starts by Auto," *Chicago Tribune,* January 31, 1947.

397   *perfunctory words from a priest:* "Grave Receives Orchid-Decked Capone Casket," *Chicago Tribune,* February 5, 1947.

INDEX